Show Me
Macromedia®
Flash MX 2004

Que Publishing
800 East 96th Street
Indianapolis, IN 46240 USA

Show Me Macromedia® Flash MX 2004

International Standard Book Number: 0-7897-3068-5

Library of Congress Catalog Card Number: 2003095430

Printed in the United States of America

First Printing: January 2004

06 05 04   4 3 2

Que Publishing offers excellent discounts on this book when ordered in quantity for bulk purchases or special sales. For information, please contact:

U.S. Corporate and Government Sales

1-800-382-3419

corpsales@pearsontechgroup.com

For sales outside the U.S., please contact:

International Sales

1-317-428-3341

International@pearsontechgroup.com

Trademarks

Warning and Disclaimer

Publisher
Paul Boger

Associate Publisher
Greg Wiegand

Managing Editor
Steve Johnson

Authors
Andy Anderson
Mark Del Lima
Steve Johnson

Project Editor
Holly Johnson

Technical Editor
Matt West

Production Editor
Holly Johnson

Page Layout
Joe Kalsbeek
Kate Lyerla
Blaine Lyerla
Matt West

Interior Designers
Steve Johnson
Marian Hartsough

Indexer
Katherine Stimson

Proofreader
Beth Teyler

Team Coordinator
Sharry Lee Gregory

Acknowledgements

a

Perspection, Inc.

Show Me Macromedia Flash MX 2004 has been created by the professional trainers and writers at Perspection, Inc. to the standards you've come to expect from Que publishing. Together, we are pleased to present this training book.

Perspection, Inc. is a software training company committed to providing information and training to help people use software more effectively in order to communicate, make decisions, and solve problems. Perspection writes and produces software training books, and develops multimedia and Web-based training. Since 1991, we have written more than 70 computer books, with several bestsellers to our credit, and sold over 4.5 million books.

This book incorporates Perspection's training expertise to ensure that you'll receive the maximum return on your time. You'll focus on the tasks and skills that increase productivity while working at your own pace and convenience.

We invite you to visit the Perspection Web site at:

www.perspection.com

Acknowledgements

The task of creating any book requires the talents of many hard-working people pulling together to meet impossible deadlines and untold stresses. We'd like to thank the outstanding team responsible for making this book possible: the writers, Andy Anderson, Mark Del Lima, and Steve Johnson; the project editor, Holly Johnson; the technical editor, Matt West; the production team, Joe Kalsbeek, Kate Lyerla, Blaine Lyerla, and Matt West; the proofreader, Beth Teyler; and the indexer, Katherine Stimson.

At Que publishing, we'd like to thank Greg Wiegand for the opportunity to undertake this project, Sharry Gregory for administrative support, and Sandra Schroeder for your production expertise and support.

Perspection

About The Authors

Andy Anderson is a graphics designer and illustrator who has worked with Flash since it was released. A university professor, Andy is a sought-after lecturer in the U.S., Canada, and Europe. The remainder of his time is split between writing graphics and fiction books, and developing graphics, animations, and resource materials for various corporations and seminar companies. His clients include designers and trainers from the U.S. Government, Boeing, Disneyland, and other Fortune 500 companies.

Mark Del Lima is a visual and user interface designer. He has produced games and animation for a variety of clients including Apple Computer, Macromedia, LucasArts, and Goodby Silverstein & Partners. His award-winning work has been featured on Macromedia's SOTD and the Flash-Forward Film Festival. He is lead Flash designer at Orange Design, Inc. and co-founder of ersatzdesign, an art and design collective. He lives and works in San Francisco.

Steve Johnson has written more than twenty-five books on a variety of computer software, including Microsoft Office 2003 and XP, Microsoft Windows XP, Macromedia Director MX, Macromedia Fireworks, and Web publishing. In 1991, after working for Apple Computer and Microsoft, Steve founded Perspection, Inc., which writes and produces software training. When he is not staying up late writing, he enjoys playing golf, gardening, and spending time with his wife, Holly, and three children, JP, Brett, and Hannah. When time permits, he likes to travel to such places as New Hampshire in October, and Hawaii. Steve and his family live in Pleasanton, California, but can also be found visiting family all over the western United States.

We Want To Hear From You!

As the reader of this book, *you* are our most important critic and commentator. We value your opinion and want to know what we're doing right, what we could do better, what areas you'd like to see us publish in, and any other words of wisdom you're willing to pass our way.

As an associate publisher for Que, I welcome your comments. You can email or write me directly to let me know what you did or didn't like about this book—as well as what we can do to make our books better.

Please note that I cannot help you with technical problems related to the topic of this book. We do have a User Services group, however, where I will forward specific technical questions related to the book.

When you write, please be sure to include this book's title and author as well as your name, email address, and phone number. I will carefully review your comments and share them with the author and editors who worked on the book.

Email: feedback@quepublishing.com

Mail: Greg Wiegand
         Que Publishing
         800 East 96th Street
         Indianapolis, IN 46240 USA

For more information about this book or another Que title, visit our Web site at *www.quepublishing.com*. Type the ISBN (excluding hyphens) or the title of a book in the Search field to find the page you're looking for.

Contents

C

Introduction

Welcome to *Show Me Macromedia Flash MX 2004*, a visual quick reference book that shows you how to work efficiently with Macromedia Flash MX 2004. This book provides complete coverage of basic and intermediate Flash MX 2004 skills.

How This Book Works

You don't have to read this book in any particular order. We've designed the book so that you can jump in, get the information you need, and jump out. However, the book does follow a logical progression from simple tasks to more complex ones. Each task is presented on no more than two facing pages, which lets you focus on a single task without having to turn the page. To find the information that you need, just look up the task in the table of contents, index, or troubleshooting guide, and turn to the page listed. Read the task introduction, follow the step-by-step instructions in the left column along with screen illustrations in the right column, and you're done.

What's New

If you're searching for what's new in Flash MX 2004, just look for the icon: New!. The new icon appears in the table of contents so you can quickly and easily identify a new or improved feature in Flash MX 2004. A complete description of each new feature appears in the New Features guide in the back of this book.

Keyboard Shortcuts

Most menu commands have a keyboard equivalent, such as Ctrl+P (Win) or ⌘+P (Mac), as a quicker alternative to using the mouse. A complete list of keyboard shortcuts appears in the Keyboard Shortcuts guide in the back of this book.

Step-by-Step Instructions

This book provides concise step-by-step instructions that show you "how" to accomplish a task. Each set of instructions include illustrations that directly correspond to the easy-to-read steps. Also included in the text are time-savers, tables, and sidebars to help you work more efficiently or to teach you more in-depth information. A "Did You Know?" provides tips and techniques to help you work smarter, while a "See Also" leads you to other parts of the book containing related information about the task.

Real World Examples

This book uses real world examples to help convey "why" you would want to perform a task. The examples give you a context in which to use the task. The Flash example files that you need for each task are also available online at *www.perspection.com* or *www.quepublishing.com/showme*.

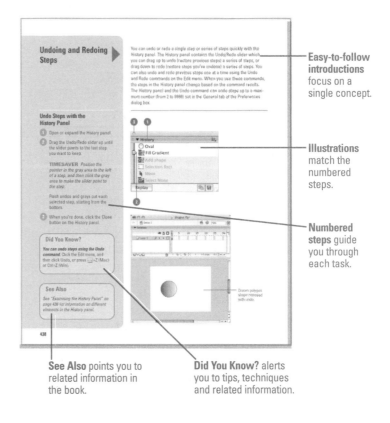

Easy-to-follow introductions focus on a single concept.

Illustrations match the numbered steps.

Numbered steps guide you through each task.

See Also points you to related information in the book.

Did You Know? alerts you to tips, techniques and related information.

Real world examples help you apply what you've learned to other tasks.

Troubleshooting Guide

This book offers quick and easy ways to diagnose and solve common Flash MX 2004 problems that you might encounter. The troubleshooting guide helps you determine and fix a problem using the task information you find. The problems are posed in question form and are grouped into categories that are presented alphabetically.

Troubleshooting points you to information in the book to help you fix your problems.

Flash for Windows and Macintosh

This book is written for the Windows and Macintosh version of Macromedia Flash MX 2004. Both versions of the software are virtually the same, but there are a few platform differences between the two versions. When there are differences between the two versions, steps written specifically for the Windows version end with the notation (Win) and steps for the Macintosh version end with the notation (Mac). In some instances, tasks are split between the two operating systems.

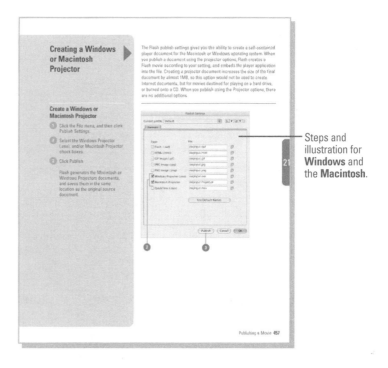

Steps and illustration for **Windows** and the **Macintosh**.

Getting Started with Flash MX 2004

Introduction

Flash is an application for developing rich content, user inter-faces, and Web applications. Macromedia Flash MX 2004 allows designers and developers to integrate video, text, audio, and graphics into rich experiences that deliver superior results for interactive marketing and presentations, e-learning, and applica-tion user interfaces. Most major commercial Web sites have implemented Flash content because of its cross-platform consis-tency, rich graphics capabilities, and small file sizes. After you create and fine-tune multimedia content in Flash, you can deliver it on the Web within a browser using the Flash Player. Flash Player is a software product developed by Macromedia for browsers on the Macintosh and Windows. Flash is the world's most pervasive software platform, used by over one million pro-fessionals and reaching more than 97% of Web-enabled desk-tops worldwide, as well as a wide range of consumer electronic devices, such as PDAs and mobile phones.

Macromedia Flash MX 2004 comes in two editions: Flash MX 2004 and Flash MX Professional 2004. Flash MX 2004 is a sub-set of the Professional edition. Flash MX Professional 2004 edi-tion has all the same features included in the standard edition. However, the Professional edition also contains additional fea-tures that are geared towards creating more sophisticated inter-active content, rich Internet applications, professional quality video, and easy deployment to devices. A complete description of Flash MX 2004 new features for both versions appears in the New Features guide in the back of this book.

Flash MX 2004 operates virtually the same on both Macintosh and Windows versions, except for a few keyboard commands that have equivalent functions. You use the [Ctrl] and [Alt] keys in Windows, and the ⌘ and [Option] keys on a Macintosh computer. Also, the term *popup* on the Macintosh and *list arrow* in Windows refer to the same type of option.

Preparing to Install Flash MX 2004

System Requirements

Before you can install Flash MX 2004 and development content, you need to make sure your computer meets the minimum system requirements. You can create Flash content on Windows and Macintosh computers. As a Flash developer, you also need to be aware of the system requirements for viewers of your Flash movies in a browser using the Macromedia Flash Player. Web users need to download and install the player in order to view and interact with Flash content. The Flash Player is free and widely distributed over the Web at *www.macromedia.com*.

Some Flash MX 2004 features require QuickTime 6.3 or QuickTime Pro 6.3. During the installation, use the *Recommended* installation type to install the required components. You can obtain the latest version of QuickTime at *www.quicktime.com*.

For Windows Computers

You need to have a computer with the following minimum configuration:

- 600-megahertz (MH) Intel Pentium III processor or equivalent.
- 128 megabytes (MB) of RAM, 256 MB or above recommended.
- 275 MB available disk space.
- 16-bit (thousands of colors), 1024-by-768 resolution.
- Microsoft Windows 98 SE, Windows 2000, Windows XP or later.

Flash MX 2004 must be activated over the Internet or phone prior to use. Windows 98 SE users must have Microsoft Internet Explorer 5.1 or later in order to activate over the Internet.

For Macintosh Computers

You need to have a computer with the following minimum configuration:

- 500 MHz PowerPC G3 processor or later.
- 128 megabytes (MB) of RAM, 256 MB or above recommended.
- 215 MB available disk space.
- 16-bit (thousands of colors), 1024-by-768 resolution.
- Mac OS X 10.2.6 or later, 10.3.

For Viewers in a Browser

Your visitors need to have a computer with the Flash Player and the following minimum configuration:

- **For Windows 98 and Me.** Microsoft Internet Explorer 5.x (98) or 5.5 (Me), Netscape 4.7, Netscape 7.x, Mozilla 1.x, AOL 8, or Opera 7.11.
- **For Windows 2000.** Microsoft Internet Explorer 5.x, Netscape 4.7, Netscape 7.x, Mozilla 1.x, CompuServe 7, AOL 8, or Opera 7.11.
- **For Windows XP.** Microsoft Internet Explorer 6.0, Netscape 7.x, Mozilla 1.x, CompuServe 7, AOL 8, or Opera 7.11.
- **For Macintosh OS 9.x.** Microsoft Internet Explorer 5.1, Netscape 4.8, Netscape 7.x, Mozilla 1.x, AOL 8, or Opera 7.11.
- **For Macintosh OS X 10.1.x or Mac X 10.2.x.** Microsoft Internet Explorer 5.2, Netscape 7.x, Mozilla 1.x, AOL 7, or Opera 6, and Safari 1.0 (Mac OS X 10.2.x only).

Installing Flash MX 2004

To perform a standard application install, insert the Macromedia Flash MX 2004 CD into the CD or DVD player on your computer, and then follow the on-screen instructions. Because the setup process is different for Macintosh OS X and Windows platforms, general steps are provided to help you get started, and the on-screen instructions will guide you through the rest. Make sure to have your serial number handy because you'll be asked to enter it during the installation process. If you're updating from a previous version of Flash, you'll be required to verify the older version with your serial number for the previous version. The Flash installation includes all the components you need, including the Flash Player 7, to develop Flash content.

Install Flash MX 2004

1. Insert the Macromedia Flash MX 2004 CD into your CD-ROM drive.

2. If necessary, double-click the CD icon, and then double-click the installer icon.

   The installer window opens, displaying the opening screen of the Flash MX 2004 installer software.

3. Click Install, and then follow the on-screen instructions to install the product; the installer asks you to read and accept a licensing agreement, indicate where you want to store the software, and enter a serial number.

   IMPORTANT *Macromedia, in an attempt to thwart software piracy, now requires online or phone activation of the program. The activation occurs during the installation process, but you can postpone it for 30 days of product installation. If activation is not achieved within 30 days, Flash will cease to function. You can click the Help menu, and then click Activate Macromedia Flash to complete the process.*

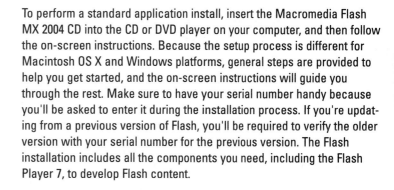

Launching Flash MX 2004

You can start Flash in several ways, depending on the platform you are using. When you start Flash, the computer displays a splash screen and then the Flash window. When you start a new Flash session or close all documents, a Start Page appears in the Document window, providing easy access links to open, open recent, create new, create from template, and tutorial actions to help you get started. You can also use the Extend link to access the Macromedia Flash Exchange Web site, where you can download additional applications and information.

Launch Flash in Windows

1 Click the Start button on the taskbar.

2 Point to All Programs, and then point to Macromedia.

3 Click Macromedia Flash MX 2004.

4 If an alert appears, asking you to update the help files, click Yes.

Did You Know?

You can hide the Start Page. On the Start Page, select the Don't Show Again check box.

You can show the Start Page. Click the Flash (Professional) (Mac) or Edit (Win) menu, click Preferences, click the Show Start Page option on the General tab, and then click OK.

You can set launch preferences to customize how Flash starts. Click the Flash (Professional) (Mac) or Edit (Win) menu, click Preferences, click the General tab, select an option in the On Launch section, and then click OK.

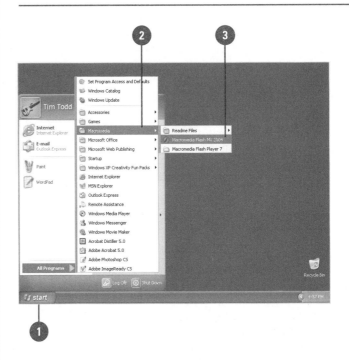

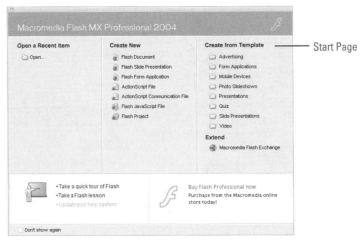

Start Page

Launch Flash in Macintosh

① Open the Applications folder (located on the main hard drive).

② Open the Macromedia Flash MX 2004 folder.

③ Double-click the Flash MX 2004 application icon.

④ If an alert appears, asking you to update the help files, click Yes.

Did You Know?

You can create a shortcut on the Macintosh. Drag and drop the Flash application to the bottom of the monitor screen, and then add it to the shortcuts panel.

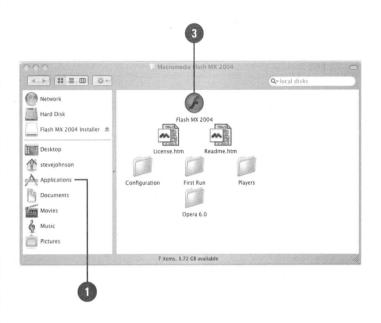

Shortcut for
Flash MX 2004

Viewing the Flash Window

Start Page
Provides easy access links to create and open Flash documents.

Toolbar or Tools Panel
Contains drawing and other related tools to create and manipulate graphics.

Panel Windows
Gives you access to authoring tools and attribute settings for elements.

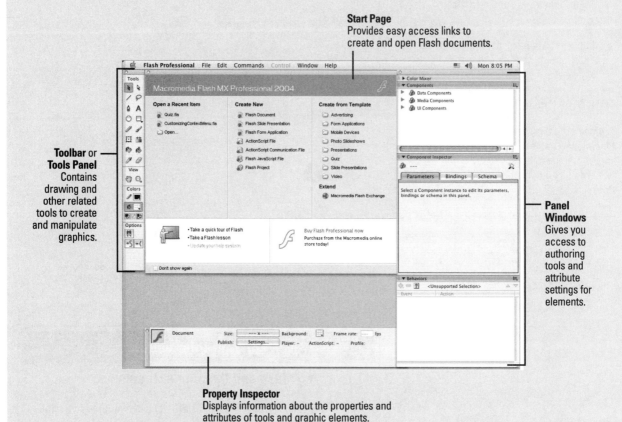

Property Inspector
Displays information about the properties and attributes of tools and graphic elements.

Document Window
Displays open Flash
documents, which includes a
Edit bar, Timeline and Stage.

Edit Bar
Displays what editing mode you
are working in and allows you to
switch scenes.

Timeline
Gives you a
visual
represent-
ation of
every frame,
layer and
scene in the
document.

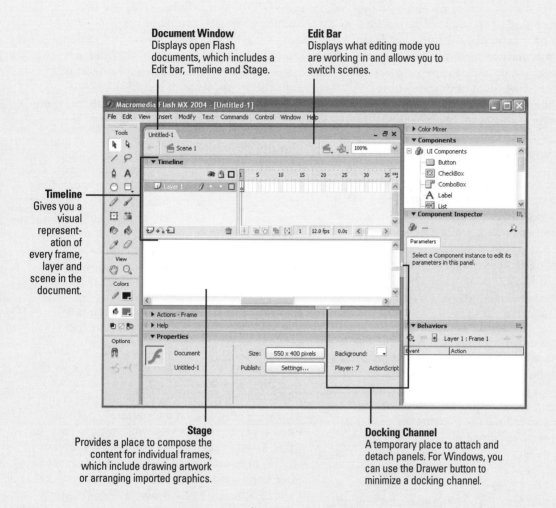

Stage
Provides a place to compose the
content for individual frames,
which include drawing artwork
or arranging imported graphics.

Docking Channel
A temporary place to attach and
detach panels. For Windows, you
can use the Drawer button to
minimize a docking channel.

Creating a Project Plan

Before you begin to create a movie in Flash, it's important to develop a project plan first. The project plan provides a road map for you to follow as you build your project in Flash. Without a project plan, you'll inevitably hit road blocks, which will cause you to waste time redesigning all of or portions of the movie. Planning a movie project involves determining its purpose, identifying the audience, logically developing the content, organizing the structure of the content, developing the layout and design, and identifying the delivery computer system. As part of the project plan, it's also important to include details about the look and feel of your production, its length and size, how it will interact with the viewer, and how and for whom it will be distributed. With a project plan in place, you'll be ready to create a movie in Flash.

Plan a Movie

Creating a movie can take a long time; it's worth the effort to plan carefully. The tendency for most first-time Flash developers is to start creating a movie without carefully planning the project. Before you begin, you need to develop and follow a plan. Otherwise, you might end up spending a lot of time fixing or completely changing parts of the movie, which you could have avoided from the beginning. You need to figure out the goal of the project, the look and feel of your production, its length and size, how it will interact with the viewer, and how and for whom it will be distributed. When planning a movie, it's important to accomplish the following:

Determine the purpose

Is it for training? Promotion? Sales? Marketing? Entertainment? Informing? The answer will determine the types of features you may want to include or exclude in the movie. If the purpose is to create a self-paced training product, you might want to include simple navigation, easy-to-use instructional material, and a help system. On the other hand, if the purpose is to create a sales promotion, you might want to include eye-catching graphics, videos, and audio to get users' attention and draw them into the presentation.

Identify the audience

How you create your movie will depend on how you classify the intended audience. If the intended audience consists of novice computer users, you will have to concentrate on making the navigational controls and layout as simple to use as possible. If the users are experienced computer users, you can include more advanced features and interactions.

Develop the content and organize the structure

The most beneficial planning tools for the multimedia developer are the script and schematic flowchart. The script tells the story of your movie production in text form. Just like in the movies, a script is used to describe each section, to list audio or video, and to provide a basis for the text that will appear onscreen or will be read by a voice-over talent. Schematic flowcharts are the best way to sketch the navigational structure of a movie and make sure that each of the sections is properly connected. After you have the script and schematic flowchart mapped out on paper, you will quickly see the correlation between what you have developed and what you will begin to set up in Flash.

Develop the layout and design of the movie

The storyboard tells the story of your movie in visual form. It helps you design the layout of each screen in your movie. The storyboard follows the script and develops visual frames of the movie's main transitional points, which help you develop the Flash media elements that you will use to create your movie. A storyboard can take a long time to develop, but the media elements you assemble and create in the process will shorten the overall development time.

Identify the delivery computer system and browser to be used for play back

Some computers are more up-to-date than others. You need to determine the minimum computer hardware and software requirements in which your movie will be delivered. The

hardware and software requirements will determine what types of media you can use and how the movie will play back. Some hardware requirements you need to consider for the delivery computer system are the CPU (central processing unit), which determines the speed with which your computer can compute data; RAM (system memory), which determines how fast files load and how smoothly they run; sound cards, which determine if you can use sound files; video cards, which determine the quality and speed of the graphic and video display; and monitor resolution, which determines the color display, size, and overall look of your movie. Some software requirements you need to consider are the operating system version and supported browser type and version. See "Preparing to Install Flash MX 2004" on page 2 for specific details about these requirements.

Sample script

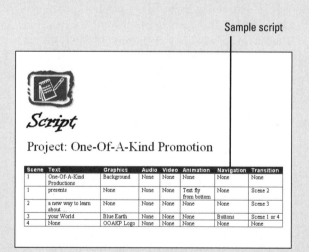

Sample flowchart

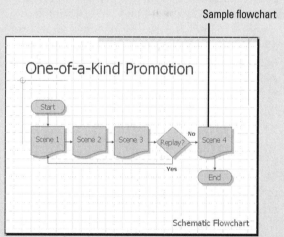

Building a Flash Project

After you develop a project plan, you can use Flash to create a movie according to the plan. Creating a movie involves six main steps: setting up movie properties, assembling media elements, positioning the media elements on the Stage and sequencing them in the Timeline, adding custom functionality and interactive elements, previewing and testing the movie, and finally publishing or exporting the movie for distribution.

Build a Movie with Flash

Before you start creating a movie using Flash based on your project plan, it's important to understand the process of developing Flash software. The basic steps for developing interactive multimedia software with Flash are listed below.

Step 1: Set up document properties

Before you start a Flash project, you need to create a new document and set up initial document properties for how your movie looks and operates. It is important to specify document property settings that affect the entire movie at the beginning of the project, such as how colors are defined, and the size and location of the Stage, so you don't have to redesign the movie later.

Step 2: Create or import media elements

Media elements include graphics, images, buttons, digital videos, sounds, and text. You can create new media elements in Flash or import ones that have already been developed. Flash provides several tools for creating media elements, including shape and paint tools, and text creation tools. You can also add media elements from the Library, a media storage area.

Step 3: Position the media elements on the Stage and sequence them in the Timeline

The Stage is the viewing area you use to display where media elements appear in a movie, and the Timeline is the area you use to organize what you want to occur at the time and duration you specify. You add media You use the Stage to create the look and feel for your production; you use the Stage and Timeline together to arrange the media elements in space and time. The Stage represents the media elements' position in space (where) and the Timeline represents the media elements' position in time (when).

Step 4: Add navigational components, interactive behaviors, and motion effects

Scripting allows you to add custom functionality to your movie, such as moving objects on the Stage, formatting text, storing and managing information, performing mathematical operations, and controlling the movie in response to specific conditions and events, such as a mouse click. In Flash, scripts are written in ActionScript, a Flash-specific programming language. To help you get started scripting and save you some time, Flash comes with built-in components, and scripts called **behaviors**. **Components** are elements you can use to quickly create a user interface. For example, components can include buttons, arrows, or other navigation elements that move the viewer to different parts of a movie or to different locations on the Web. After you add a component, you can use behaviors to add functionality to the component to make it do what you want. For example, you can use behaviors to control video and sound files. In addition to behaviors, you can use built-in Timeline effects to add motion to elements.

Step 5: Preview and test the movie

After you create your project, you use the Test Movie command to preview and test the movie to make sure it runs the way you want it to. It's important to test the functionality of your movie early and often during the development process to catch problems while they are still minor. As needed, you can make refinements and adjustments on the Stage and in the Timeline.

Step 6: Publish the document as a movie file for use over the Internet

When the movie runs the way you want it to, you can publish your production as a Flash movie that viewers can play on a Web page, using a browser. Flash publishes the movie file (.swf) and creates an HTML file with information to display the movie file. Viewers can't change the movies in the .swf format; they can only play them.

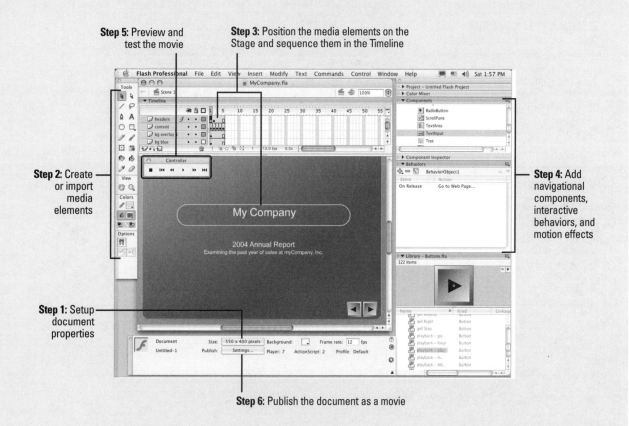

Step 5: Preview and test the movie

Step 3: Position the media elements on the Stage and sequence them in the Timeline

Step 2: Create or import media elements

Step 4: Add navigational components, interactive behaviors, and motion effects

Step 1: Setup document properties

Step 6: Publish the document as a movie

Creating a New Document

A file in Flash is called a **document**. Flash documents, which have the .fla filename extension, contain all the information required to develop, design, and test interactive content. Flash documents are not the same as the movies you play with the Flash Player. Instead, you publish your Flash documents as Flash movies, which have the .swf filename extension and contain only the information needed to display the movie. When you open a new Flash document, it's blank, ready for you to create or insert text, graphics, and other media content. By default, the first Flash document is titled Untitled1. You can create new documents in several ways: using the New command on the File menu, and by the New Document task pane. Flash numbers new documents consecutively. You can open and work on as many new documents as you'd like.

Create a New Blank Document

1. Click the File menu, and then click New.

   TIMESAVER *Click Flash Document on the Start Page to create a new blank document.*

2. Click the General tab.

3. Click Flash Document.

4. Click OK.

Did You Know?

You can open a new window with a copy of the current document. Create or open the Flash document you want to open in a new window, click the Window menu, and then click New Window.

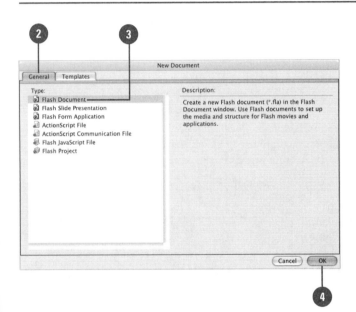

Creating a New Document from a Template

Flash makes it easy to create many common documents based on a template. A **template** opens a Flash document (such as an animation or set of menus) with predefined formatting and placeholder text, graphics, and actionscripts. Flash comes with a set of templates, which includes the following categories: Advertising, Form Applications (Pro), Mobile Devices, Photo Slideshows, Presentations, Quiz, Slide Presentations (Pro), and Video (Pro). If you can't find the template you want, you can check the Macromedia Flash Support Center Online Web site for more.

Create a New Document from a Template

1. Click the File menu, and then click New.

   TIMESAVER *Click a template category on the Start Page to open the New From Template dialog box, where you can select a template.*

2. Click the Templates tab.

3. Click a template category.

4. Click the template you want to use.

5. View the templates in the Preview box and read the description.

6. Click OK.

See Also

See "Saving a Document in Different Formats" on page 22 for information on saving a document as a template.

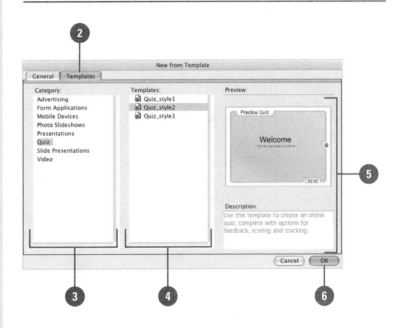

Opening an Existing Document

You can open an existing document file and the Flash program at one time, or you can open the file from within Flash. In Windows Explorer (Win) or Finder (Mac), you can double-click a Flash document to open the Flash program and the document. In Flash, you can use the Open section on the Start Page or the Open commands on the File menu to open a Flash document. You can open flash documents and movies in several formats, including .fla (Flash Document), .spa (FutureSplash Document), .ssk (SmartSketch Drawing), and .swf (Flash Movie).

Open a Flash Document

1. Click the File menu, and then click Open.

    TIMESAVER *Click Open or a recently opened Flash document name on the Start Page to open a document.*

2. Navigate to the drive or folder where the file is located.

3. Click the document file you want to open.

4. Click Open.

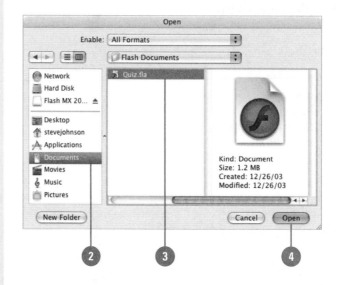

Did You Know?

You can open a recent file quickly. Click the File menu, point to Open Recent, and then click the appropriate file name.

You can open a recent file quickly from the Start menu (Win). Click the Start button, point to My Recent Documents, and then click the file name you want to open.

Flash Open Formats	
Format	**Description**
Flash Document (.fla)	A flash document you create and save in Flash authoring environment.
FutureSplash Document (.spa)	The Flash version 1 format for a Flash document (.fla).
SmartSketch Drawing (.ssk)	The Flash version 1 format for a ShockWave file (.swf).
Flash Movie (.swf)	A movie or ShockWave file you export or publish in the Flash authoring environment. When you open a movie, you cannot modify it.

Opening Sample Documents

The best way to learn about Flash is to view sample documents. When you installed Flash, you also installed some Flash sample files. These samples can give you ideas on how you can create rich media content with Flash. Some of the samples are complete applications, while others are independent sections. You can open the Flash document with the .fla extension to examine the project functionality, or you can open the Flash movie with the .swf extension to view the finished product.

Open a Sample Document

1. Click the File menu, and then click Open.

2. Navigate to the following location on your hard drive:

   Macintosh. <Macintosh HD>\Applications\Macromedia\ Flash MX 2004\First Run\ Samples\<samples folder>.

   Windows XP/2000. <boot drive>\ Documents and Settings\ <user name>\Local Settings\ Application Data\ Macromedia\ Flash MX 2004\ <language>\Configuration\Sample s\<samples folder>.

   TROUBLE? *If you don't see folders in Windows, change Folder Options to show hidden files and folders.*

3. Click the sample file you want to open.

4. Click Open.

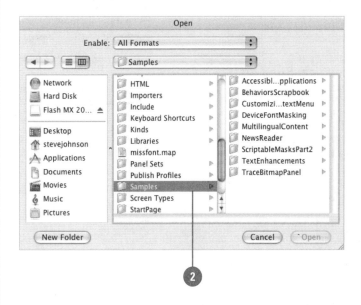

Did You Know?

You can get more information about the samples. Click the Help menu, and then click Samples.

You can get more samples online. Visit *www.macromedia.com/go/flashmx_ samples* on the Web.

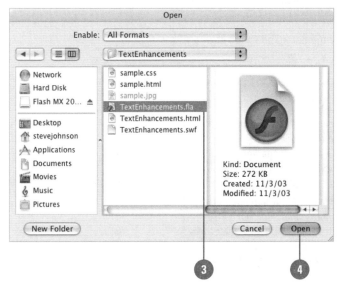

Changing Document Properties

When you create a new Flash document or open an existing one, you need to set up or change the document properties. You set document properties at the beginning of the project to make basic decisions about how your movie looks and operates. You use the Document Properties dialog box or the Property Inspector to specify document property settings that affect the entire movie, such as the background color, the size and location of the Stage, the **frame rate**—the number of frames per second the computer plays an animation, and the unit of measure for rulers. These settings apply only to the current document unless you set Flash defaults to apply to every document. You can use the Properties command on the Window menu to display the Property Inspector.

View Document Properties

1. Click the Selection tool in the Toolbar.

2. Click the Window menu, and then click Properties.

   TIMESAVER *Press ⌘+F3 (Mac) or Ctrl+F3 (Win).*

3. View the document properties at the top of the Property Inspector:

   ◆ **Stage Size.** The current size appears in the button label.

   ◆ **Background Color.** The color of the Stage background.

   ◆ **Frame Rate.** The speed at which the movie runs.

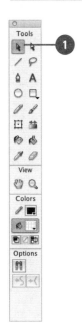

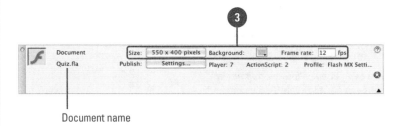

Document name

Did You Know?

You can change the background color quickly in the Property Inspector.
Open the Property Inspector, click the Background color box, and then select a color from the palette.

You can change the frame rate quickly in the Property Inspector. Open the Property Inspector, and then enter the number of animation frames to be displayed every second in the Frame Rate box.

Change Document Properties

1. Create or open a document.

2. Click the Modify menu, and then click Document.

   TIMESAVER *Click the Size button in the Property Inspector or double-click the frame-rate box in the Status bar on the Timeline.*

3. To set the Stage dimensions, do one of the following:

   ◆ **Specify size in pixels.** Enter values in the Width and Height boxes. The default size is 550 x 400 pixels.

   ◆ **Set size to an equal space around content.** Click Contents.

   ◆ **Set size to the maximum print area.** Click Printer.

   ◆ **Set size to default setting.** Click Default.

4. Click the Background Color box, and then select a color.

5. Enter a frame rate. For most computers playing from the Web, 8 fps (frames per second) to 12 fps is adequate. The default is 12 fps.

6. To specify the unit of measure for rulers, click the Ruler Units popup, and then select an option.

7. To set properties for all new documents, click Make Default.

8. Click OK.

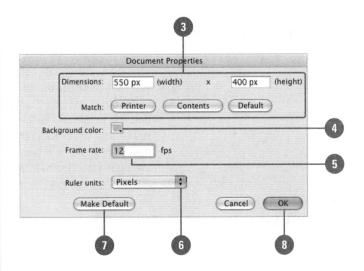

See Also

See "Displaying Rulers" on page 89 for information on using rulers.

Working with Document Windows

When you open multiple documents, you can use the Window menu or tabs at the top of the Document window (Windows only) to switch between them. Tabs are available only when documents are maximized in the Document window. You can click a tab name to switch and activate the document. By default, tabs are displayed in the order in which you open or create documents. When documents are not maximized, you can resize a Document window using the mouse. Each window has one or more buttons on the title bar that allow you to close or change a window's size. When you want to move or copy information between documents, it's easier to arrange several Document windows on the screen at the same time. However, you must make the window active to work in it.

Switch Between Multiple Documents in Windows

1. Click the Maximize button on the Document window.

2. Open more than one document.

3. Click a tab name to switch to the document.

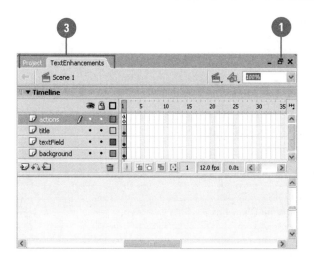

Arrange Multiple Document Windows

1. Click the Window menu.

2. Click a window command:

   ◆ **Cascade.** Fits the windows on the screen one on top of the other, showing the window title.

   ◆ **Tile.** Fits the windows on the screen side by side.

   ◆ **Document name.** Activates the Document window (brings it to the front).

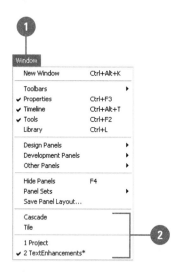

Resize and Move a Document Window

All windows contain the same sizing buttons:

◆ **Maximize (Win) or Zoom (Mac) button.** Click to make a window fill the entire screen.

◆ **Restore Down button.** Click to reduce a maximized window to a reduced size.

◆ **Minimize button.** Click to shrink a window to a taskbar button. To restore the window to its previous size, click the appropriate taskbar button.

◆ **Close button.** Click to shut a window.

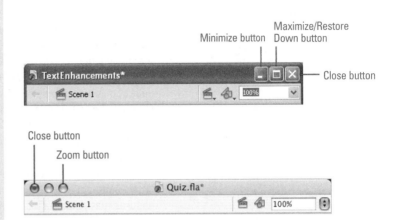

Use the Mouse to Resize a Window

1 If the window is maximized, click the Restore Down button.

2 Move the mouse over one of the borders of the window (Win) or bottom right-corner (Mac) until the mouse pointer changes into a two-headed arrow (Win) or black arrow.

The directions of the arrowheads (Win) show you the directions in which you can resize the window.

3 Drag the window border until the window is the size you want.

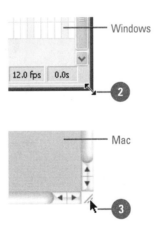

Saving a Document

When you save Flash MX 2004, a document within the authoring environment, the document is saved in the .fla format. If you want to display a document in the Macromedia Flash Player, you need to publish or export the document in the .swf format. When you save a new document, you give it a name and specify the location in which to save the file. Name your documents clearly so you can easily locate them later. Also, creating folders and subfolders with meaningful names helps to locate files easily and saves a lot of time. When you save an existing file, the file retains its original name and folder location unless you specify a change. To retain older versions of a document as you update it, use the Save As command and give each new version a new number with the old name, such as project1, project2 and so forth. Saving your files frequently ensures that you don't lose work during an unexpected power loss or computer problem.

Save a Document

1 Click the File menu, and then click Save As.

2 Type the new file name.

3 Navigate to the drive or folder location where you want to save the document.

4 Click Save.

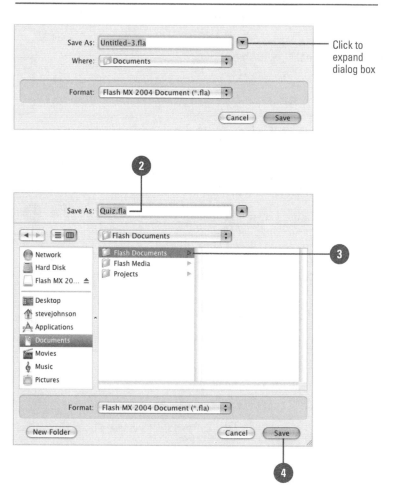

Click to expand dialog box

Did You Know?

You can revert to the last saved version of a document. Click the File menu, and then click Revert.

You can save more than one document at a time. Click the File menu, and then click Save All.

You can save and compact an existing document to reduce the file size. Click the File menu, and then click Save And Compact.

Save a Document with a Different Name or Location

1. Click the File menu, and then click Save As.

2. Type the new file name.

3. Navigate to the drive or folder location where you want to save the document.

4. Click the New Folder button (Mac) or the Create New Folder (Win).

5. Type the new folder name, and then press Enter (Win) or click Create (Mac).

6. Click Save.

Did You Know?

You can rename a folder in the Save As and Open dialog boxes (Win). Right-click the folder you want to rename, click Rename, type a new name, and then press Enter.

You can move or copy a file quickly in a dialog box (Win). In the Open or Save As dialog box, right-click the file you want to move or copy, click Cut or Copy, open the folder where you want to paste the file, right-click a blank area, and then click Paste.

There is a difference between Save and Save As. When you save an existing document using the Save command, Flash performs a quick save, which appends new content to the existing file. When you save a new document using the Save As command, Flash performs a complete save, which saves and compacts the content into a small file.

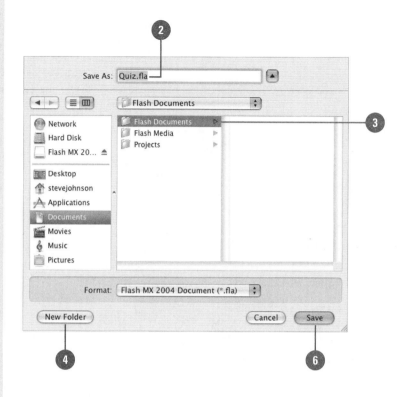

Saving a Document in Different Formats

A file type specifies the document format (for example, a template) as well as the program and version in which the file was created (for example, Flash MX 2004). You might want to change the type if you're creating a custom template or sharing files with someone who has an earlier version of Flash, such as Flash MX. You use the Save As dialog box to change the file type for a document. The Format popup (Mac) or Save As Type list arrow (Win) displays a list of the available formats for Flash.

Save a Document in the Flash MX Format

1 Click the File menu, and then click Save As.

2 Click the Format popup (Mac) or Save As Type list arrow (Win), and then click Flash MX Document.

3 Type the new file name.

4 Navigate to the drive or folder location where you want to save the document.

5 Click Save.

6 Click Save As Flash MX to complete the save or click Cancel to not perform the operation.

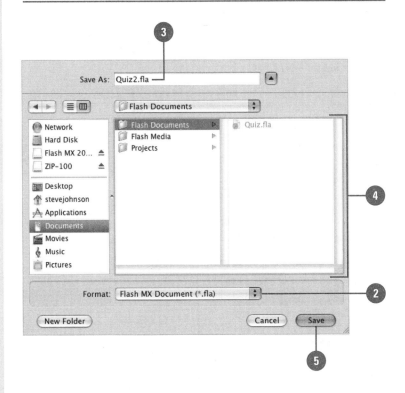

> #### Did You Know?
>
> **You can delete a file in a dialog box (Win).** In the Open or Save As dialog box, click the file you want to delete, click the Tools list arrow, and then click Delete.

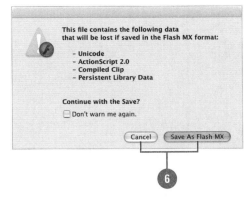

Save a Document as a Template

1. Click the File menu, and then click Save As Template.

2. Type a name for the new template.

3. Click the Category popup, and then click a category template.

4. Type a description for the new template.

5. Click Save.

See Also

See "Creating a New Document from a Template" on page 13 for information on creating a new document from a Flash template.

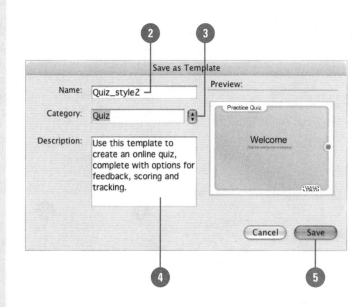

Getting Help While You Work

At some time, everyone has a question or two about the program they are using. The Flash Help system provides the answers you need. You can search a catalog of Help topics using keywords or phrases or using a table of contents to locate specific information. When you perform a search using keywords or phrases, a list of possible answers is shown to you in the Help panel, with the most likely answer to your question at the top of the list. If you need more instructional help, you can view a series of lessons on the How Do I tab on the Help panel. The How Do I lessons provide an introduction to using Flash: Quick Tasks, Basic Flash, and Basic ActionScript.

Get Help Information

1. Click the Help menu, and then click Help or How Do I.

2. Click the Table Of Contents button on the Help panel.

3. Double-click Help categories (book icons) until you display the topic you want.

4. Click the topic you want.

   The topic you want appears in the right pane.

5. Read the topic, and if necessary, click any hyperlinks to get information on related topics or definitions.

6. When you're done, click the Close button to close the panel, or click the Help title to collapse the panel.

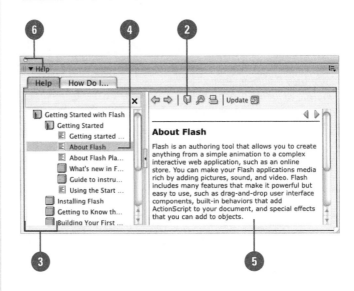

> ### Did You Know?
>
> **You can move backward and forward between help topics.** Click the History Back or History Forward button on the Help panel.

Search for Help Information

1. Click the Help menu, and then click Help or How Do I.

2. Click the Search button on the Help panel.

3. Type one or more keywords in the Search box.

4. Click Search.

5. Click the topic you want.

   The topic you want appears in the right pane.

6. Read the topic, and then if you want, click any hyperlinks to get information on related topics or definitions.

7. When you're done, click the Close button or click the Help title to close the panel.

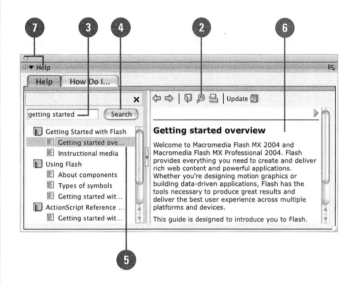

Did You Know?

You can find out what's new in Flash. Click the Help menu, and then click What's New.

You can download the latest help content from the Web. Click the Help menu, click Help, and then click the Download Help Content button on the Help panel.

You can print out the selected Help topic. Open the Help panel, select the Help topic you want to print, click the Print button on the Help panel, specify print options, and then click Print (Win) or OK (Mac).

Getting Online Support

If you need more detailed information about a Flash task or feature, you can find out the latest information on the Web from the Macromedia Flash Support Center and Flash Exchange Web sites. The Macromedia Flash Support Center provides technical notes, documentation updates, and links to additional resources in the Flash community, while the Macromedia Flash Exchange allows you to download additional applications and commands that other Flash users have developed and posted to extend the functionality of Flash. Some of the posted items are free while other charge a fee. You can access the Flash Support Center and the Flash Exchange from within Flash using commands on the Help menu.

Get Online Support Information

1. Click the Help menu, and then click Flash Support Center.

   Your Web browser opens, displaying the Macromedia support Web site.

2. Search on the Web site for the help information you need.

3. When you're done, close your Web browser.

Did You Know?

You can register to receive notices about upgrades and new products. If you haven't already registered during installation, click the Help menu, click Online Registration, and then follow the online instructions.

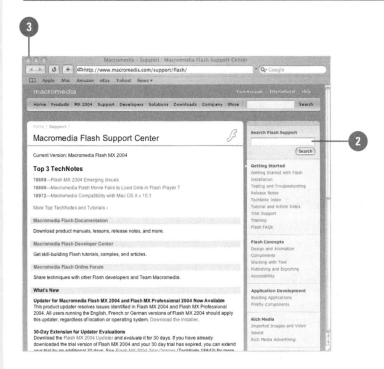

Get Resources from the Flash Exchange

1. Click the Help menu, and then click Flash Exchange.

   Your Web browser opens, displaying the Macromedia support Web site.

2. Click the Categories popup, and then select a category to display the resource types you need.

3. Scroll through the list, and then follow the on-screen instructions to download and purchase (if necessary) the resources you want.

4. When you're done, close your Web browser.

Did You Know?

You can access more commands on the Web from the Flash Exchange. Click the Commands menu, and then click Get More Commands.

Closing a Document and Quitting Flash

After you work on a document, you can close the document by closing the document, or by exiting Flash. You should save the document before closing it. Exiting Flash closes the current document and the Flash program, and returns you to the desktop. You can use the Exit command on the File menu (Win) or Quit Flash command on the Flash (Professional) menu (Mac) to close a document and exit Flash, or you can use the Close button on the Flash Document window title bar. If you try to close a document without saving your final changes, a dialog box opens, asking if you want to do so.

Close a Document

1. Click the Close button on the Document window, or click the File menu, and then click Close.

   TIMESAVER Press ⌘+W (Mac) or Ctrl+W (Win) to close a document. Click the File menu, and then click Close All to close all open documents.

2. If necessary, click Yes to save any changes you made to your open documents before the program quits.

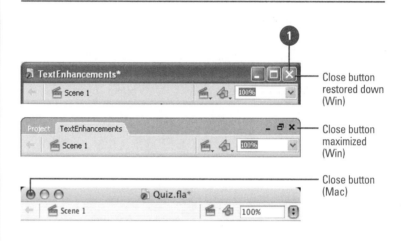

Close button restored down (Win)

Close button maximized (Win)

Close button (Mac)

Quit Flash

1. Choose one of the following:

   ◆ Click the Flash (Professional) menu, and then click Quit Flash (Mac).

   ◆ Click the Close button, or click the File menu, and then click Exit (Win).

2. If necessary, click Yes to save any changes you made to your open documents before the program quits.

Exit (Win)

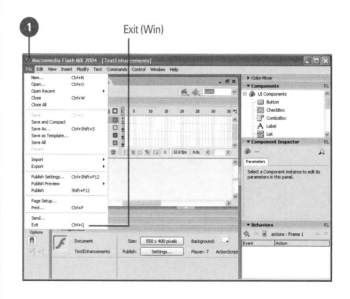

Working Within the Flash Environment

Introduction

Getting to know the Flash authoring environment makes you more effective and efficient as you create movies. You'll get to know the parts of the Flash window, which include the Toolbar, Timeline, Stage, panels, and Property Inspector.

The Toolbar, also known as the Tools panel, contains tools that you can use to draw, paint, select, and modify artwork. The Timeline represents the overall structure of a Flash document and controls the content. The Timeline consists of layers, frames, and scenes that make up a Flash document. Layers are like transparent sheets stacked on top of one another. Each layer can contain different images that appear on the Stage. A frame displays content at a specific moment on the Stage. The order in which frames appear in the Timeline determines the order in which they appear in the document. As you play a document, the playhead moves through the Timeline displaying the current frame with each layer on the Stage. If a project requires many animation sequences with hundreds of frames, you can organize the animations into scenes to make them easier to work with and manage. Below the Timeline is the Stage, which provides a place to compose the content for individual frames. Panels are windows that allow you to view, organize, and change elements and related options in a document. The Property Inspector is a specialize panel that allows you to change object specific attributes and options.

Flash uses built-in keyboard shortcuts designed specifically for Flash. The built-in keyboard shortcuts are organized into sets, which you can duplicate and customize to create your own personalized set. Flash allows to set preferences to customize the way you work in the program. As you design and develop a movie, you can print frames to review your work.

What You'll Do

Examine the Flash Window

Use the Timeline

Work with Layers

View and Organize Layers

Change Layer Properties

Use Guide Layers

Work with Frames

Work with Scenes

Use the Toolbar and the Edit Bar

Use the Main Toolbar

Use the Docking Channel

Work with Panels

Dock and Undock Panels

Group and Ungroup Panels

Create Panel Sets

Create Keyboard Shortcuts

Set Flash Preferences

Work with Page Setup

Print a Document

Examining the Flash Window

When you start Flash, the program window displays several windows of varying sizes you can use to create a movie. These windows include the Timeline/Stage, various panels, and the Property Inspector. Depending on your installation and previous program usage, not all of these windows may appear, or additional ones may be visible. You'll do the bulk of your work in Flash with these windows.

In Flash, windows appear in the workspace with a title bar, such as the Timeline window, or in a panel. A **panel** is a window you can collapse, expand, and group with other panels, known as a panel group, to improve accessibility and workflow. A panel appears with a shaded header bar, which includes the window title and additional options. A panel group consists of either individual panels stacked one on

Document Window
Displays open Flash documents, which includes a Timeline, Edit bar, and Stage.

Timeline
Gives you a visual representation of every frame, layer and scene in the document.

Main Toolbar
Contains buttons for commonly used commands. Point to a button to display a Tooltip.

Toolbar or **Tools Panel**
Contains drawing and other related tools to create and manipulate graphics.

Panel Windows
Gives you access to authoring tools and attribute settings for elements.

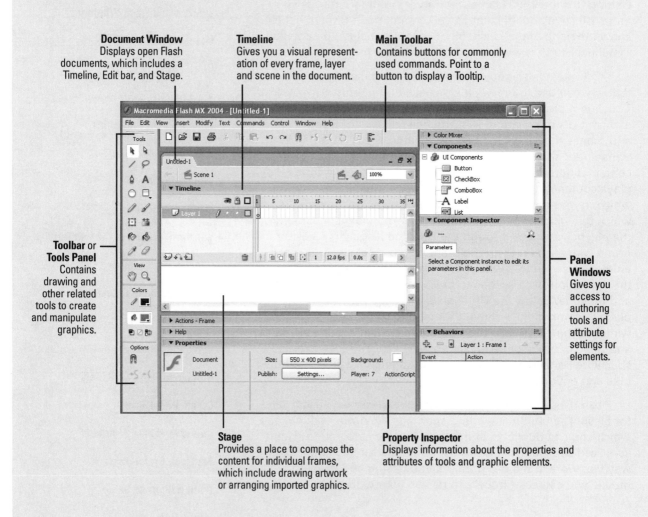

Stage
Provides a place to compose the content for individual frames, which include drawing artwork or arranging imported graphics.

Property Inspector
Displays information about the properties and attributes of tools and graphic elements.

top of the other or related panels organized together with tabs, such as the Components panel, to navigate from one panel to another.

The Flash window Title bar displays the filename of the open file, and the program name Macromedia Flash MX 2004. The Title bar also contains a Close button and resizing buttons.

A **menu** is a list of commands that you use to accomplish specific tasks. A **command** is a directive that accesses a feature of a program. Flash has its own set of menus, which are located on the menu bar along the top of the Flash window. On a menu, a check mark identifies a feature that is currently selected (that is, the feature is enabled or on). To disable (turn off) the feature, you click the command again to remove the check mark. A menu can contain several check marked features. A bullet (Win) or diamond (Mac) also indicates that an option is enabled, but a menu can contain only one bullet-or diamond-marked feature per menu section. To disable a command with a bullet or diamond next to it, you must select a different option in the section on the menu.

When you perform a command frequently, it's faster, and sometimes more convenient, to use a shortcut key, which is a keyboard alternative to using the mouse. When a shortcut key is available, it is listed beside the command on the menu, such as ⌘+F3 (Mac) or Ctrl+F3 (Win) for the Properties command on the Window menu.

Flash MX 2004 (for Windows) also includes a Main toolbar. The **Main toolbar** contains buttons for the most frequently used commands. Clicking a button on a toolbar is often faster than clicking a menu and then clicking a command. When you position the pointer over a button, a tooltip appears, displaying the button name.

The **Toolbar**, also known as the Tools panel, contains a set of tools you can use to create shapes, such as lines, rectangles, rounded rectangles, and ellipses. You can fill shapes with a color, pattern, or custom tile. The shapes and buttons you create in Flash are saved as media elements in the layers.

The **Document window** displays open Flash documents, which include a Timeline, Edit bar, and Stage. Flash MX 2004 (for Windows) also includes tabs to make it easier to switch back and forth between documents. At the top of the Document window is the Edit bar. The Edit bar displays what editing mode you are working in, and allows you to switch scenes.

The **Timeline** organizes and controls media elements over a linear Timeline in rows called channels and in columns called frames. The Timeline displays a movie's Timeline and monitors the playback frame-by-frame. A frame represents a single point in a movie. The Timeline includes layers that control different parts of the movie.

The **Stage** is the visible portion of a movie, on which you determine where your media elements appear. The Stage is the rectangle area below the Timeline where you place graphic content, including vector art, text boxes, buttons, imported bitmap graphics, or audio and video clips. You can define the properties of your Stage, such as its size and color.

The **Property Inspector** provides a convenient way to view and change attributes of any selected object or multiple objects, such as graphics and shapes, on the Stage in your movie. After you select an object, relevant commands and associated fields for it appear in the Property Inspector.

Using the Timeline

The Timeline represents the overall structure of a Flash document and controls the content. The Timeline consists of layers, frames, and scenes that make up a Flash document. Layers appear on the left side of the Timeline and frames contained in each layer appear in a row to the right of the layer. The Timeline header above the frames displays the frame numbers. At the bottom of the Timeline, a Status bar appears, displaying the current frame indicator, the current rate indicator, and the elapsed time indicator. Sometimes it is hard to work with frames in a small view in the Timeline. You can change the size of frames and display frames with tinted cells. In addition, you can display thumbnail previews of frame content, which is useful for viewing animations.

Change the Timeline Display

◆ To lengthen or shorten layer name fields, drag the bar separating the layer names and the frames in the Timeline.

◆ To lengthen or shorten the Timeline, drag the bar separating the Timeline and the Stage.

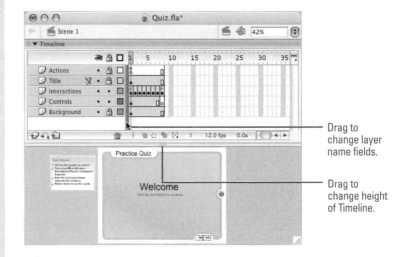

Drag to change layer name fields.

Drag to change height of Timeline.

Resize the Timeline Display

1 Do one of the following:

◆ If the Timeline is docked to the program window, drag the bar separating the Timeline from the program window.

◆ If the Timeline is not docked to the program window, drag the size box in the lower right corner (Mac) or the lower right corner (Win).

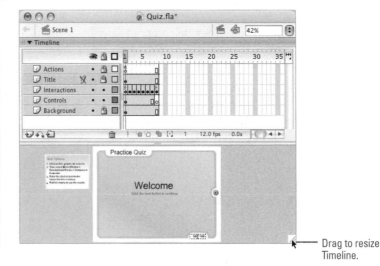

Drag to resize Timeline.

Change the Display of Frames in the Timeline

1. Click the Frame View button in the Timeline.

2. Select one of the following options from the list:

   ◆ To change the width of frame cells, select Tiny, Small, Normal, Medium, or Large.

   ◆ To decrease the height of frame cell rows, select Short.

   ◆ To turn frame sequence tinting on and off, select Tinted Frames.

   ◆ To display thumbnails of the content of each frame scaled to fit the Timeline frames, select Preview.

   ◆ To display thumbnails of each full frame, select Preview In Context.

     This is useful for viewing animation movement within their frames.

See Also

See "Working with Panels" on page 52 for information on using the Timeline panel.

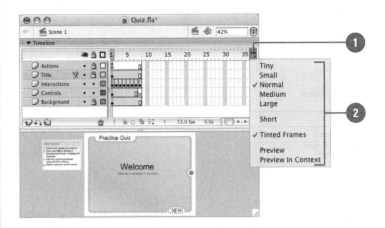

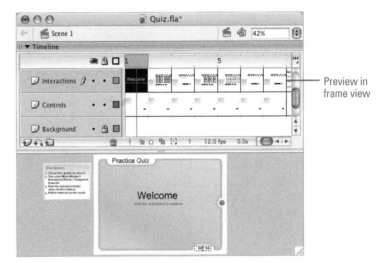

Preview in frame view

2

Working with Layers

Layers are like transparent sheets stacked on top of one another. Each layer can contain different images that appear on the Stage. You can draw and edit objects on one layer without affecting objects on another layer. Layers in a document are listed in the left column of the Timeline. Before you can work with a layer, you need to select it, or make it active. A pencil icon next to a layer or layer folder indicates it is active. Only one layer can be active at a time, even though you can select more than one layer. A new document comes with one layer, but you can add more to organize content on the Stage. As you create multiple layers of related content, you can create layer folders to make it easier to manage the layers.

Create a New Layer

1. Click the layer or folder in which you want to insert a layer above it.

2. Click the Insert Layer button at the bottom of the Timeline.

   The new layer appears above the selected layer.

Did You Know?

Flash names layers in order based on the highest number. If you add Layers 2 and 3, and then delete Layer 2. The next time you add a layer, Flash names it Layer 4.

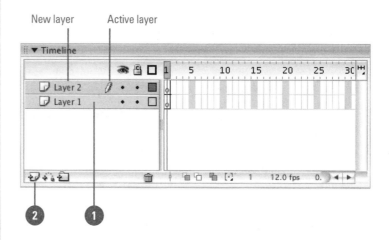

New layer   Active layer

Create a New Layer Folder

1. Click the layer or folder in which you want to insert a layer folder above it.

2. Click the Insert Layer Folder button at the bottom of the Timeline.

   The new layer folder appears above the selected layer.

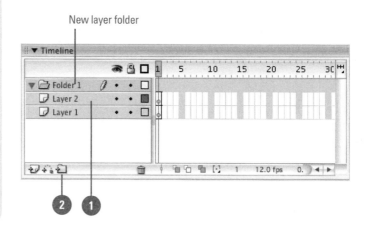

New layer folder

Rename a Layer or Folder

① Double-click the name of a layer or folder.

② Type a name.

③ Press Return (Mac) or Enter (Win).

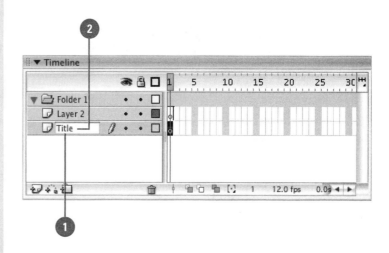

Delete a Layer or Folder

① Select the layer or folder you want to delete.

② Click the Delete Layer button at the bottom of the Timeline.

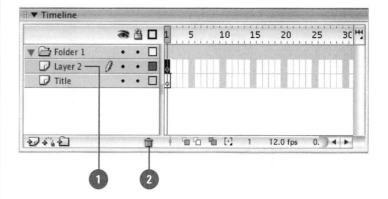

Did You Know?

There are several ways to select a layer. You can click the name of a layer or folder in the Timeline, click a frame in the Timeline of the layer you want to select, or select an object on the Stage that is located on the layer you want to select.

You can select multiple layers. To select contiguous layers or folders, click the first layer or folder, and then Shift+click the last layer or folder. To select discontiguous layers or folders, ⌘+click (Mac) or Ctrl+click (Win) the layers or folders you want to select.

Viewing Layers

Flash includes controls (Eye, Lock, and Outline icons) in the layers section of the Timeline that allow you to quickly hide, show, lock, or unlock layers and layer folders, and display objects on a layer as colored outlines. Using colored outlines makes it easier to distinguish which layer an object appears. When you hide a layer or folder with the Eye icon, a red X appears next to the name. When you lock a layer or folder with the Lock icon, a padlock appears next to the name. When you display layers as colored outlines with the Outline icon, a frame appears next to the name. When you change a folder, the controls affect all layers within a folder.

Show or Hide a Layer or Folder

1 Do one of the following:

◆ Click the Eye column to the right of the layer or folder to show or hide it.

◆ Click the Eye icon to show or hide all layers or folders.

◆ Option+click (Mac) or Alt+click (Win) in the Eye column to the right of a layer or folder to show or hide all other layers or folders.

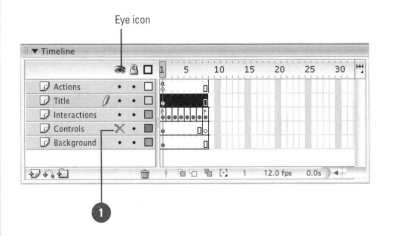

Eye icon

Lock or Unlock Layers or Folders

1 Do one of the following:

◆ Click in the Lock column to the right of the layer or folder to lock or unlock it.

◆ Click the Lock icon to lock or unlock all layers or folders.

◆ Option+click (Mac) or Alt+click (Win) in the Lock column to the right of a layer or folder to lock or unlock all other layers or folders.

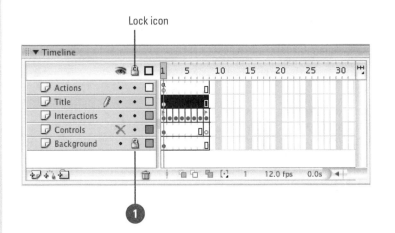

Lock icon

View the Contents of a Layer as Outlines

1️⃣ Do one of the following:

◆ Click the Outline column to the right of the layer's name to display all objects as outlines.

◆ Click the Outline icon to display objects on all layers as outlines.

◆ Option+click (Mac) or Alt+click (Win) in the Outline column to the right of a layer to display objects on all other layers as outlines.

See Also

See "Changing Layer Properties" on page 40 for information on changing the outline color.

Did You Know?

Hidden layers are visible when you publish a document. When you publish a Flash document as a .swf movie, hidden layers are visible in the Flash movie file.

Outline icon

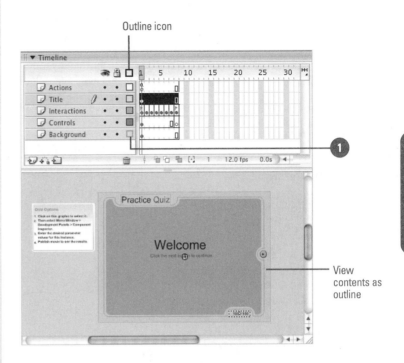

1️⃣

View contents as outline

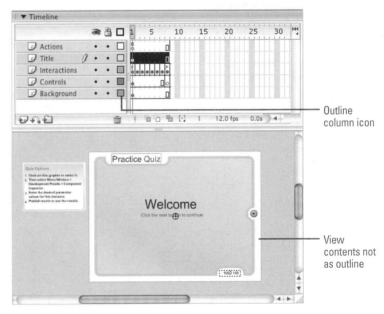

Outline column icon

View contents not as outline

Organizing Layers

In much the same way you organize files on your computer, you can use similar concepts to organize layers and layer folders in a document. You can expand or collapse a layer folder to show or hide it contents. You can also move a layer or folder into a layer folder or to another place in the layers list. Layer folders can contain layers and other layer folders. In addition, you can copy a layer or copy the contents of a layer folder.

Expand or Collapse a Layer Folder

 Do one of the following:

◆ Click the triangle to the left of the folder name to expand or collapse the folder.

◆ Control+click (Mac) or right-click (Win) any layer, and then click Expand All Folders or Collapse All Folders.

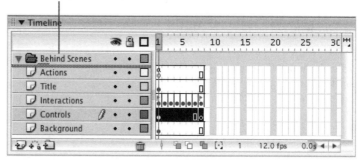

Expanded layer folder

Move a Layer or Layer Folder

◆ To move a layer or folder into a layer folder, drag the layer or folder to the destination layer folder name in the Timeline.

◆ To move a layer or folder to another location, drag the layer or folder to a new position in the Timeline.

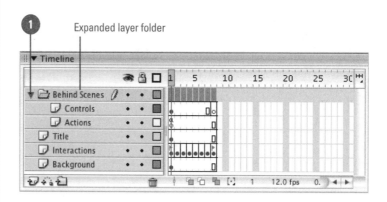

Drag Controls layer to the Behind Scenes folder

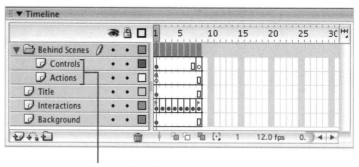

Layers in the folder

Copy a Layer

1. Click the layer you want to select.

2. Click the Edit menu, point to Timeline, and then click Copy Frames.

3. Click the Insert Layer button.

4. Click the new layer to select it.

5. Click the Edit menu, point to Timeline, and then click Paste Frames.

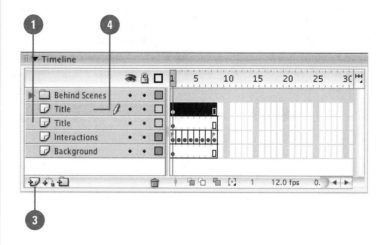

Copy the Contents of a Layer Folder

1. If necessary, click the triangle to the left of the folder name to collapse it.

2. Click the folder layer to select the entire folder.

3. Click the Edit menu, point to Timeline, and then click Copy Frames.

4. Select the layer below where you want to copy the layer folder.

5. Click the Insert Folder Layer button.

6. Click the new layer folder to select it.

7. Click the Edit menu, point to Timeline, and then click Paste Frames.

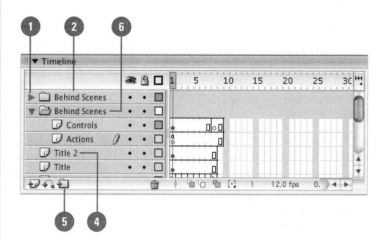

Changing Layer Properties

The Layer Properties dialog box makes it easy to changes several layer options at once. You can change a layer name, show or lock a layer, change a layer type or outline color, and modify the layer height to show more information in the Timeline. Setting layer properties of a folder automatically sets the properties for all the layers within that folder.

Change Layer Properties

1. Select the layer in the Timeline.

2. Click the Modify menu, point to Timeline, and then click Layer Properties.

3. Select from the following options:

   ◆ **Name.** Enter a new name.

   ◆ **Show.** Select this check box to show the layer.

   ◆ **Lock.** Select this check box to lock the layer or clear it to unlock the layer.

   ◆ **Type.** Select a layer option: Normal, Guide, Guided, Mask, Masked, or Folder.

   ◆ **Outline Color.** Click the Color box, and then select a color.

   ◆ **View Layer As Outlines.** Select this check box to view the layer as outlines.

   ◆ **Layer Height.** Click the popup, and then select a percentage to display more information in the Timeline.

4. Click OK.

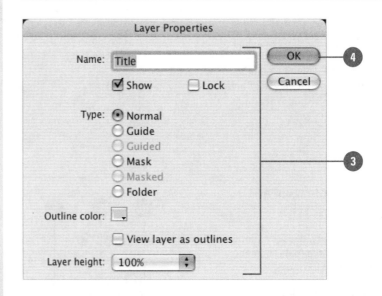

Layer Types

Layer	Description
Normal	The default layer type.
Guide	There are two types of guide layers: guides and motion guides. Guides help you place and align objects on the Stage, motion guides designate a path that an animated object follows.
Guided	Guided layers contain objects that follow an animation path. You need to link the guided layer to the motion guide.
Mask	Mask layers hide and reveal portions of linked layers that lie directly beneath the mask layer.
Masked	Mask layers contain elements that can be hidden or revealed by a mask layer.
Folder	Folder layers allow you to organize layers.

Using Guide Layers

Guide layers help you draw and align objects on layers that appear on the Stage. After you create a guide layer, you can align objects on other layers to objects you create on the guide layer. You can make any layer a guide layer. You can also create a motion guide layer to control the movement of objects in a motion tweened animation.

Create a Guide Layer

1. Click the layer you want to convert to a guide layer.

2. Control+click (Mac) or right-click (Win) the selected layer, and then click Guide.

Did You Know?

You can change a guide layer back to a normal layer. Control (Mac) or right-click (Win) the selected layer, and then click Guide.

You can convert a guide layer to a motion guide layer. Drag a normal layer onto a guide layer.

See Also

See "Using Snap Align" on page 94 for information on snapping items you draw or drag to snap to line or shapes.

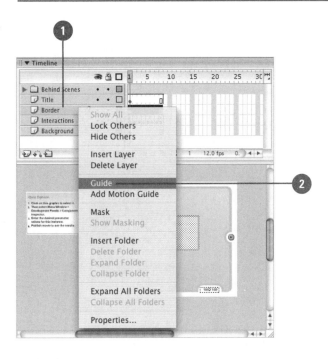

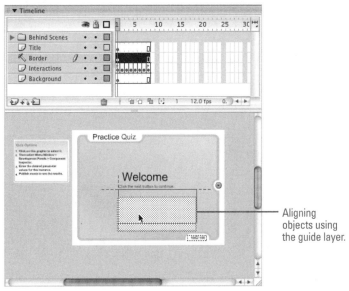

Aligning objects using the guide layer.

Working with Frames

A **frame** displays content at a specific moment on the Stage. The order in which frames appear in the Timeline determines the order in which they appear in the document. The Timeline displays each frame in sequential order from 1 to the end of the document. As you play a document, the **playhead** moves through the Timeline displaying the current frame with each layer on the Stage. When you work with frames, you can select, insert, delete, and move frames in the Timeline. When you move frames in the Timeline, you can place them on the same layer or a different layer. If you want to display a specific frame in a document, you can move the playhead to the frame in the Timeline to display the frame content on the Stage. Another type of frame is called a keyframe. A keyframe defines a change in an animation or uses actions to modify a document.

Select One or More Frames

◆ To select one frame, click on the frame.

   IMPORTANT *If the Span Based Selection preference is turned on, clicking a frame selects the entire frame sequence between two keyframes.*

◆ To select multiple contiguous frames, click the first frame in the sequence, hold down Shift, and then click the last frame in the sequence.

◆ To select multiple discontiguous frames, ⌘+click (Mac) or Ctrl+click (Win) the frames you want to select.

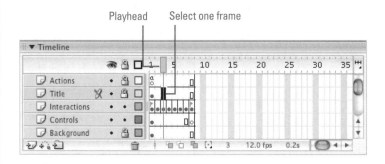
Playhead   Select one frame

Did You Know?

You can center the Timeline on the current frame. Click the Center Frame button at the bottom of the Timeline.

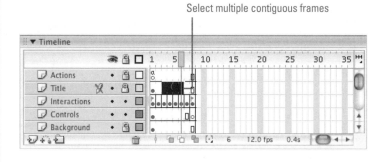
Select multiple contiguous frames

See Also

See "Using the Timeline" on page 32 for information on changing the view size of frames in the Timeline.

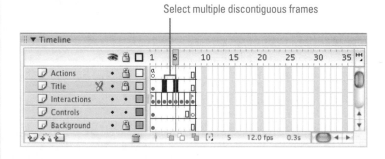
Select multiple discontiguous frames

Insert a Frame

1. Click the frame's location in the Timeline header, or drag the playhead to the frame where you want to insert a frame.

2. Click the Insert menu, point to Timeline, and then click Frame.

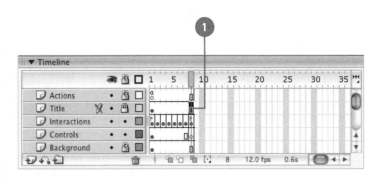

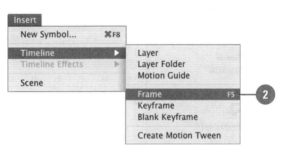

Delete Frames

1. Select the frame, keyframe, or sequence you want to delete.

2. Click the Edit menu, point to Timeline, and then click Remove Frame.

Did You Know?

You can move a frame sequence or keyframe. Drag the frame sequence or keyframe to another location in the Timeline.

You can copy a frame sequence or keyframe. Option+drag (Mac) or Alt+drag (Win) the frame sequence or keyframe to another location in the Timeline.

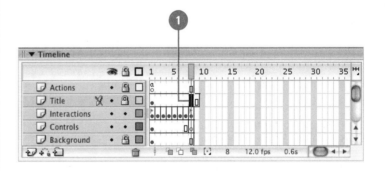

Working with Scenes ▶

If a project requires a lot of animations with hundreds of frames, you can organize the animations into scenes to make them easier to work with and manage. The Scene panel makes it easy to display the number of scenes in the document, select current scenes for editing, create new scenes, duplicate scenes, delete scenes, and reorder them. You can also use the Edit bar to select a scene to edit. When you select a scene, Flash displays it on the Stage. When you publish a document as a movie, the scenes play in order unless you add interactivity to play them differently. Be aware that scenes are treated like self contained movies, so transitions between scenes with interactivity may not be seamless.

Display the Scene Panel and Select a Scene

1 Click the Window menu, point to Design Panels, and then click Scene.

A list of scenes appears in order in the panel. In a new document, the Scene panel displays only the default Scene 1.

2 Click the scene you want to display.

Add a Scene

1 If necessary, open the Scene panel.

2 Click the Add Scene button in the Scene panel.

> ### Did You Know?
>
> ***Flash names scenes in order based on the highest number.*** If you add Scenes 2 and 3, and then delete Scene 2. The next time you add a scene, Flash names it Scene 4.

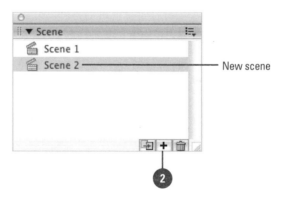

New scene

Rename a Scene

1. If necessary, open the Scene panel.

2. Double-click the scene you want to rename.

3. Type a new name.

4. Press Return (Mac) or Enter (Win).

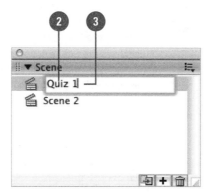

Delete a Scene

1. If necessary, open the Scene panel.

2. Click the scene you want to delete.

3. Click the Delete Scene button in the Scene panel.

4. Click OK to confirm the deletion.

TIMESAVER *If you don't want to display the Confirmation dialog box, press ⌘+click (Mac) or Ctrl+click (Win) the Delete Scene button.*

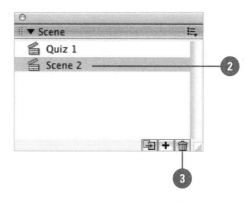

Did You Know?

You can undo the deletion of a scene. If you mistakenly delete a scene, you can undo; press ⌘+Z (Mac) or Ctrl+Z (Win).

You can reorder scenes in the Scene panel. In the Scene panel, drag a selected scene up or down in the list.

Using the Edit Bar

The Edit bar contains controls and information for editing scenes and symbols, and for changing the view size of the Stage. The Edit bar lets you know what editing mode you are working in and allows you to switch scenes. The Scene button allows you to edit a scene in document-editing mode, while the Symbol button allows you to edit symbols in the symbol-editing mode. The Back button on the Edit bar returns you to document-editing mode.

Show and Hide the Edit Bar

◆ To display the Edit bar, click the Window menu, point to Toolbars, and then click Edit bar to select the check mark.

◆ To hide the Edit bar, click the Window menu, point to Toolbars, and then click Edit bar to deselect the check mark.

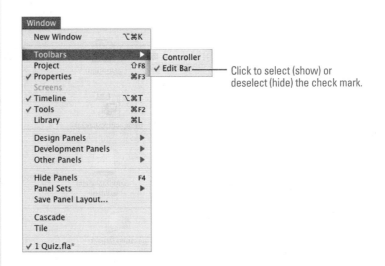

Click to select (show) or deselect (hide) the check mark.

Back button   Current scene or symbol being edited

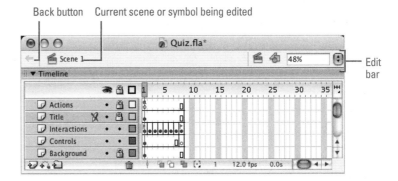

Edit bar

Change View Size of the Stage

1. Click the View Size popup in the Edit bar, and then select a view size percentage or an option:

   ◆ Fit To Window

   ◆ Show Frame

   ◆ Show All

> **Did You Know?**
>
> ***You can use the Hand tool to move the Stage to change the view.*** Click the Hand tool in the Toolbar, and then drag the Stage to change the view.

Select and type a view percentage

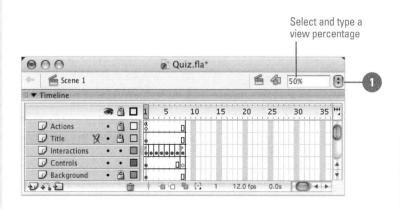

Select a Scene or Symbol to Edit

◆ To select a scene, click the Edit Scene button in the Edit bar, and then select a scene from the list.

◆ To select a symbol, click the Edit Symbol button in the Edit bar, and then select a symbol from the list.

Edit Scene button   Edit Symbol button

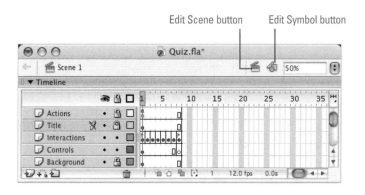

2

Using the Toolbar

The **Toolbar**, also known as the **Tools panel**, contains tools that you can use to draw, paint, select, and modify artwork. The Tools panel is divided into 4 main areas: (1) the tools area contains drawing, painting, and selection tools; (2) the view area contains tools for zooming and panning in the program window; (3) the colors area contains specific tool options for stroke and fill colors; and (4) the options area contains additional tool options for a selected tool. You can show or hide the Tools panel as necessary and customize the Tools panel to display the tools you use most often. When you customize the Tools panel, you can display more than one tool in a location. The top tool in the group appears with an arrow in the lower right corner of its icon. When you click and hold the pointer on the top tool, the other tools in the group appear in a pop-up menu. When you select a tool from the group, it appears in the Tools panel as the top tool.

Show and Hide the Tools Panel

◆ To display the Tools panel, click the Window menu, and then click Tools to select the check mark.

◆ To hide the Tools panel, click the Window menu, and then click Tools to deselect the check mark.

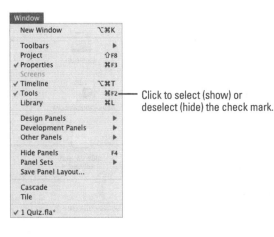

Click to select (show) or deselect (hide) the check mark.

Tools panel

Did You Know?

You can move the Tools panel. Drag the title bar or textured area at the top of the Tools panel to the desired location.

Customize the Tools Panel

1. Click the Flash (Professional) (Mac) or Edit menu (Win), and then click Customize Tools Panel.

2. Click a tool in the Tools panel graphic.

3. To add a tool, select the tool in the Available Tools list, and then click Add.

   TIMESAVER *You can add more than one tool to a location.*

4. To remove a tool, select the tool in the Current Selection list, and then click Remove.

5. Click OK.

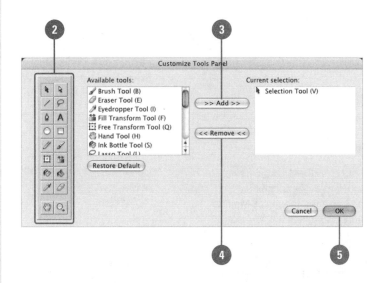

Did You Know?

You can restore the Tools panel to the default layout. Click the Flash (Professional) (Mac) or Edit menu (Win), click Customize Tools Panel, click Restore Defaults, and then click OK.

You can identify keyboard shortcuts for the Tools panel. In the Customize Tools Panel dialog box, the letter in parenthesis indicates the keyboard shortcut.

For Your Information

Creating Tools

Flash lets you design your own Tools, using the JSFL language. In addition you can download tools created by other authors at the Flash Exchange at http://www.macromedia.com/cfusion/exchange/index.cfm. Although Macromedia has yet to properly document the JSFL language, point your browser to *http://www.dynamicflash.co.uk/jsfl/* for a look at how JSFL is implemented in the Flash environment.

Using the Main Toolbar

If you use Windows, you can display and use the Main toolbar above the Document menu window to quickly access common document and object related commands, such as New, Open, Save, Print, Cut, Copy, Paste, Redo, Undo, Snap To Objects, Smooth, Straighten, Rotate And Skew, Scale, and Align. When you're finished working with the Main toolbar, you can hide it to create more workspace.

Show and Hide the Main Toolbar in Windows

◆ To display the Main toolbar, click the Window menu, point to Toolbars, and then click Main to select the check mark.

◆ To hide the Main toolbar, click the Window menu, point to Toolbars, and then click Main to deselect the check mark.

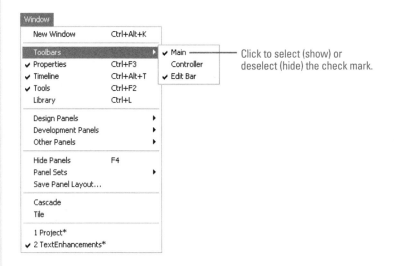

Click to select (show) or deselect (hide) the check mark.

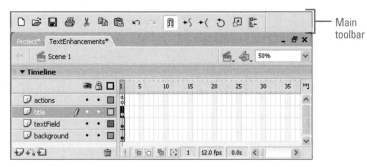

Main toolbar

> ### Did You Know?
>
> **You can use Undo and Redo commands on the menu bar.** The Undo and Redo commands on the Edit menu undo (returns you to a previous point) and redo (re-performs commands you undid) actions you've taken in a document. The names of the Undo and Redo commands change to reflect the current action.
>
> **Flash supports 100 undo and redo levels.** To change the number of undo levels, click the Edit (Win) or Flash (Professional) (Mac) menu, click the General tab, specify a number in the Undo Levels box, and then click OK. The lower the number of levels, the less amount of memory the program needs to run.

Using the Docking Channel

If you use Windows and need more workspace, you can use the Drawer button on the channel separator bar (a thin line along the edge of a docking channel) to quickly minimize a docking channel. When you click the Drawer button, the docking channel collapses to increase the size of the workspace. When you click the Drawer button again, the docking channel reopens. If you need to increase or decrease the size of a docking channel, you can drag the channel separator bar to resize the docking channel as you would any window.

Minimize and Maximize a Docking Channel in Windows

1. To minimize or maximize a docking channel, click the Drawer button on the channel separator bar.

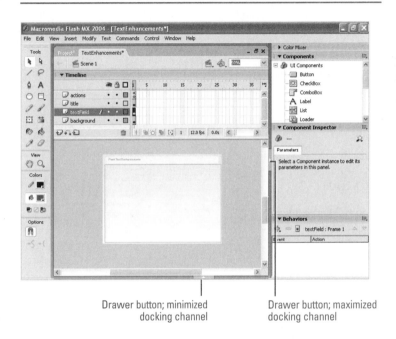

Drawer button; minimized docking channel

Drawer button; maximized docking channel

Working with Panels

Panels are windows that allow you to view, organize, and change elements and related options in a document. In Flash you work with several panel windows at one time. Instead of continually moving, resizing, or opening and closing windows, you can collapse or expand individual panels within a window with a single click to save space. A panel appears with a header bar, which includes the window title and three accessibility options: the panel gripper, the expander arrow, and an Options menu. You use the panel gripper to group or ungroup and dock or undock panel windows. You use the expander arrow to collapse or expand panels. The Options menu provides you with commands to group, rename, maximize, and close a panel, and use the Help system. The commands available on the Options menu vary depending on the panel.

Open and Close a Panel

1. Click the Window menu.

2. Do one of the following:

   - Click a panel name, such as Properties, Timeline, Tools, and Library.

   - Point to a panel category, such as Design Panels, Development Panels, and Other Panels, and then click a panel name.

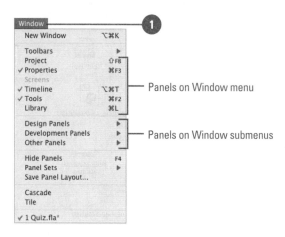

Panels on Window menu

Panels on Window submenus

Collapse and Expand a Panel

1. To collapse or expand an open panel, click the triangle or window title on the header bar of the panel.

   TIMESAVER To hide and show all panels, click the Window menu, and then click Hide Panels.

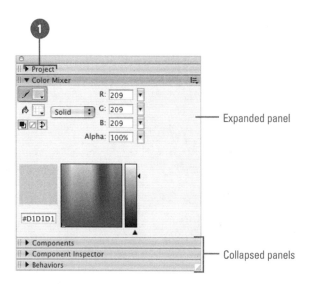

Expanded panel

Collapsed panels

Collapse and Expand the Information Area in a Panel

1. Open or expand a panel.

   IMPORTANT *Not all panels contain an information area.*

2. Click the triangle in the bottom right-corner of the panel.

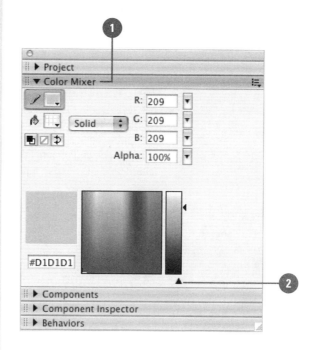

Use the Panel Options Menu

1. Open or expand a panel.

2. Click the Options button on the right side of the panel header bar.

3. Click a command from the list (commands vary). Common commands include:

   ◆ Help

   ◆ Maximize Panel

   ◆ Close Panel

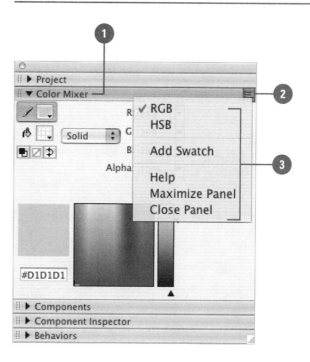

Docking and Undocking Panels

You can dock and undock, or temporarily attach and detach, panels or panel groups in docking channels. A docking channel is a region located on the left and right side of the Flash window to which you can temporarily attach and detach panels. You can only dock tool panels in a docking channel. Document panels and the Stage cannot be docked to a docking channel. When you drag a panel over a dockable area, an outline around the target dock appears. When you release the mouse button, the panel snaps to the dockable area and stays there until you move it. If you attempt to dock a panel over an undockable area, no outline appears. When a docking channel doesn't have any panels, the channel disappears until it is needed again.

Dock a Panel

1 Position the pointer on the panel gripper (the textured area left of the tile in the header bar).

2 Drag the window away from the panel to a docking channel.

Undock a Panel

1 Position the pointer on the panel gripper (the textured area left of the tile in the header bar).

2 Drag the window away from the panel to an empty area of the Flash window.

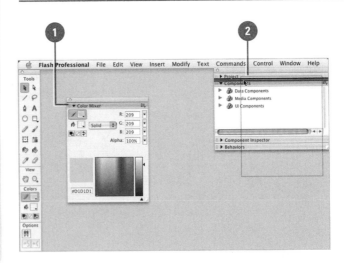

Grouping and Ungrouping Panels

You can group panels together to improve organization and workflow. When you group panels together, you can stack one on top of the other, or group related panels together as a tabbed panel group, such as the Component Inspector panel. You can add a panel to an existing panel group or you can create a new panel group. If you no longer need panels grouped together, you can ungroup them. You can use the panel gripper to group or ungroup as well as dock or undock panel windows.

Group Panels Together

1. Position the pointer on the panel gripper (the textured area the left of the tile in the header bar).

2. Drag the window away from the panel to another panel window.

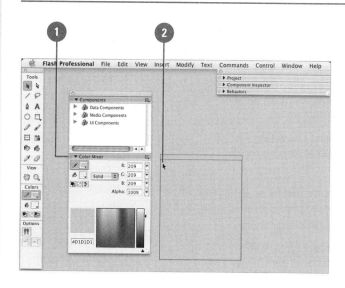

Ungroup Panels

1. Position the pointer on the panel gripper (the textured area the left of the tile in the header bar).

2. Drag the window away from the panel to an empty area of the Flash window or a docking channel.

Creating a Panel Set

As you work with Flash, you'll open, close, and move around windows and panels to meet your individual needs. After you customize the Flash workspace, you can save the location of windows and panels as a custom panel layout set, which you can display using the Panel Sets command on the Window menu. You can create custom panel sets, or use the default panel set provided by Flash. If you no longer use a custom panel set, you can remove it at any time.

Create a Panel Set

1. Open and position the panels you want to include in a panel set.

2. Click the Window menu, and then click Save Panel Layout.

   The Save Panel Layout dialog box opens.

3. Type a name in the Name box.

4. Click OK.

   The panel set is now saved.

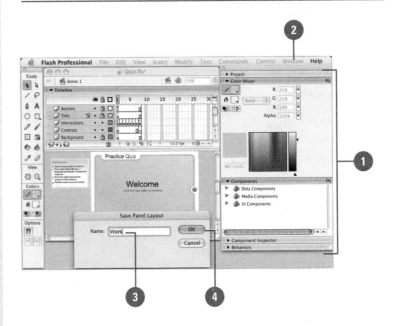

Display a Panel Set

1. Click the Window menu, point to Panel Sets, and then select a panel option:

   ◆ **Default Layout.** Displays the default Macromedia panel layout.

   ◆ **Custom panel name.** Displays a custom panel layout in which you created.

   ◆ **Training Layout.** Displays a panel layout with the Help panel easy to read.

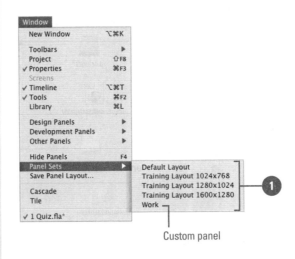

Custom panel

Delete a Panel Set

1 Using Finder (Mac) or Windows Explorer (Win), navigate to the following folder location for Panel Sets documents on your hard drive:

Macintosh. <Macintosh HD>\Applications\Macromedia\ Flash MX 2004\First Run\ Panel Sets.

Windows XP/2000. <boot drive>\ Documents and Settings\ <user name>\Local Settings\ Application Data\ Macromedia\ Flash MX 2004\ <language>\ Configuration\Panel Sets.

2 Select the text file for the custom panel set you want to delete.

3 Delete the file using the file management program.

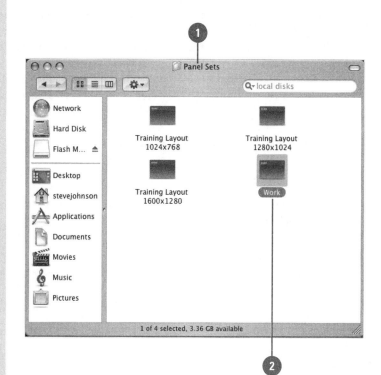

Did You Know?

You can hide all panels. Click the Window menu, and then click Hide Panels to select the check mark.

Creating Keyboard Shortcuts

Flash uses built-in keyboard shortcuts designed specifically for Flash. A complete list of the keyboard shortcuts is available in the back of this book. The built-in keyboard shortcuts are organized into sets, which you can duplicate and customize to create your own personalized set. If you use other programs, such as Macromedia Fireworks, Macromedia Freehand, Adobe Illustrator or Adobe Photoshop, and you are more comfortable using their keyboard shortcuts for common commands, you can select a built-in keyboard shortcut set from any of the graphics programs to use in Flash.

Create a Keyboard Shortcut Set

1. Click the Flash (Professional) (Mac) or Edit (Win) menu, and then click Keyboard Shortcuts.

2. Click the Current Set popup, and then select a set.

3. Click the Duplicate Set button.

4. Type a name for the new shortcut set.

5. Click OK.

Did You Know?

You can delete a custom keyboard shortcut set. Click the Flash (Professional) (Mac) or Edit (Win) menu, click Keyboard Shortcuts, select a shortcut set from the Current Set popup, and then click the Delete button. You cannot delete a built-in keyboard shortcut set that comes with Flash.

You can rename a custom keyboard shortcut set. Click the Flash (Professional) (Mac) or Edit (Win) menu, click Keyboard Shortcuts, select a shortcut set from the Current Set popup, click the Rename Set button, enter a new name, and then click OK. You cannot rename a built-in keyboard shortcut set that comes with Flash.

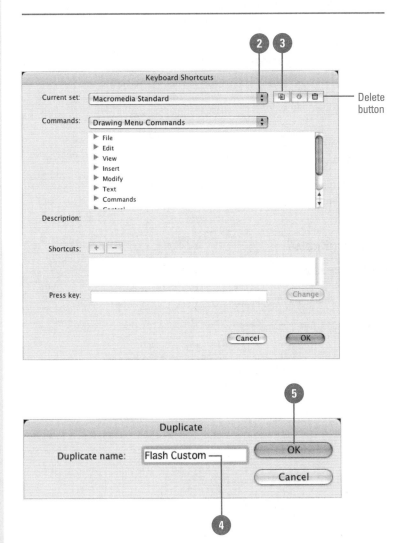

Add or Remove a Keyboard Shortcut

1. Click the Flash (Professional) (Mac) or Edit (Win) menu, and then click Keyboard Shortcuts.

2. Click the Current Set popup, and then select the set in which you want to change.

3. Click the Commands popup, and then select a shortcut category, such as Drawing Menu Commands, Drawing Tools, Test Movie Menu Commands, and Workplace Accessibility Commands.

4. Select the command for which you want to add or remove a shortcut in the Commands list.

5. Do the following:

   ◆ To add a shortcut, click the Add Shortcut (+) button, and then press the key combination to enter the new shortcut key in the Press Key box.

   ◆ To remove a shortcut, click the Remove Shortcut (-) button.

6. Click Change.

7. To add or remove additional shortcuts, repeat Steps 2-6.

8. Click OK.

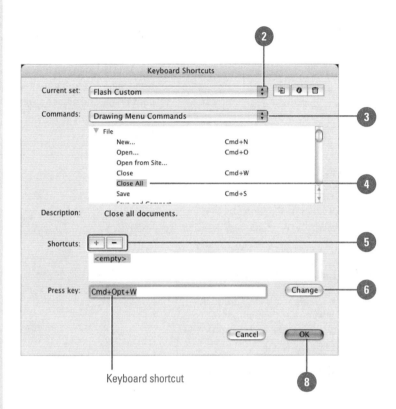

Keyboard shortcut

Setting General Preferences

Flash allows to set general preferences to customize the way you work in the program. Some of the preferences allow you to specify the number of undo levels, enable multiple selection, show tooltips, disable Timeline window docking, enable span-based selection in the Timeline, make the first frame of each scene in a document a named anchor, select a highlight color, and select a font to use when substituting missing fonts. You can also specify what you want to display or open when you launch Flash.

Set General Preferences

1. Click the Flash (Professional) (Mac) or Edit (Win) menu, and then click Preferences.

2. Click the General tab.

3. Select from the following options:

    ◆ **Undo Levels.** Enter a value from 2 to 9999 to set the number of undo/redo levels. The default level is 100.

    ◆ **Printing Options (Win).** Select the Disable Postscript check box if you have problems printing to a postscript printer.

    ◆ **Shift Select.** Select or clear this check box to control the selection of multiple elements.

    ◆ **Disable Panel Docking (Win).** Select this check box to disable or enable panel docking.

    ◆ **Show Tooltips.** Select this check box to display tooltips when the pointer points to a button or control.

    ◆ **Disable Timeline Docking.** Select this check box to keep the Timeline from attaching to the program window.

    ◆ **Span Based Selection.** Select this check box to use span-based selection instead of frame-based selection.

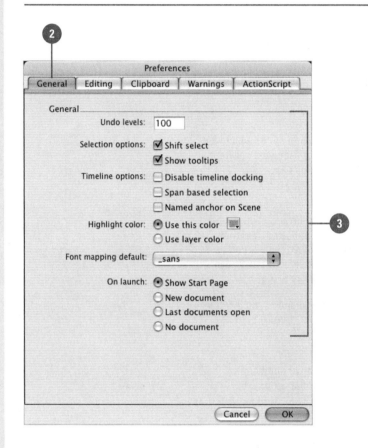

- ◆ **Named Anchor On Scene.**
  Select this check box to make
  the first frame of each scene in
  a document a named anchor.

- ◆ **Highlight Color.** Select the Use
  This Color option, and then
  select a color, or select the Use
  Layer Color option to use the
  current layer's outline color.

- ◆ **Font Mapping Default.** Click the
  popup, and then select a font to
  use when substituting missing
  fonts.

- ◆ **On Launch.** Select an option to
  specify which document Flash
  opens when you start the
  program.

  - ◆ **Show Start Page.** Displays
    the Start Page.

  - ◆ **New Document.** Displays a
    new blank document.

  - ◆ **Last Documents Open.**
    Opens the documents that
    were open when you quit
    Flash.

  - ◆ **No Document.** Displays no
    document.

4 Click OK.

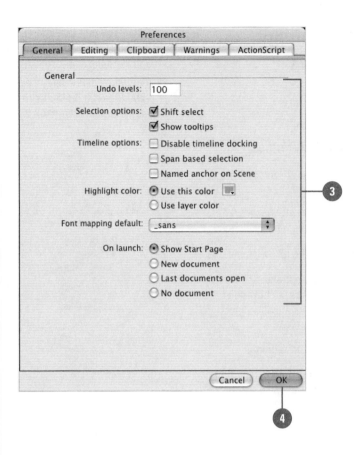

Setting Editing Preferences

When you edit text and graphics in a Flash document, you can customize the way you use Pen tools, draw connecting lines and smooth curves, and recognize line and shapes. You can also select text orientation options, which is useful when using English (horizontal) or Asian (vertical) language fonts. If you are using Flash MX Professional 2004, you can set Project preferences for closing and saving project files.

Set Editing Preferences

1 Click the Flash (Professional) (Mac) or Edit (Win) menu, and then click Preferences.

2 Click the Editing tab.

3 Select from the following options:

◆ **Pen Tools options.** Select check boxes to show pen preview, solid points, and precise cursors.

◆ **Vertical Text options.**

◆ **Default Text Orientation.** Select to make default orientation vertical, which is useful for Asian fonts.

◆ **Right To Left Text Flow.** Select to reverse the default text display direction.

◆ **No Kerning.** Select to turn off kerning for vertical text.

◆ **Drawing Settings.** Select options for Connect Lines, Smooth Curves, Recognize Lines, Recognize Shapes, Click Accuracy.

◆ **Project Settings (Pro).** Select check boxes to Close Open Files On Project Close, and Save Project Files On Test Project Or Publish Project.

4 Click OK.

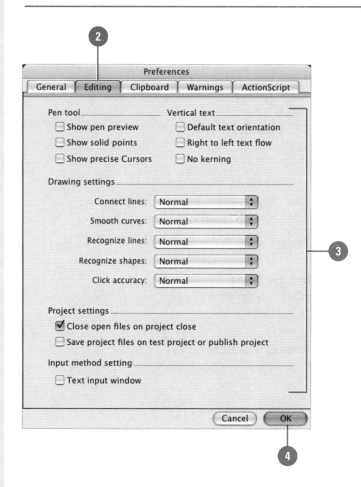

Setting Clipboard Preferences

When you copy or cut graphics to the Clipboard, you can set preferences to determine how you want to paste the graphic into a Flash document. The preference options give you control over the size and quality of the graphics you insert in a document. If you are using Windows, the Clipboard preferences include options for bitmaps and gradients in the Windows Metafile format. If you are using a Macintosh, the Clipboard preferences include options for the PICT format.

Set Clipboard Preferences

1. Click the Flash (Professional) (Mac) or Edit (Win) menu, and then click Preferences.

2. Click the Clipboard tab.

3. Select from the following options:

  ◆ **Bitmaps (Win).** Select options for Color Depth and Resolution to specify these parameters for bitmaps copied to the Clipboard. Select Smooth to apply anti-aliasing. Enter a value in the Size Limit box to specify the amount of RAM that is used when placing a bitmap on the Clipboard.

  ◆ **Gradients (Win).** Select an option to specify the quality of gradient fills placed in the Windows Metafile.

  ◆ **PICT Settings (Mac).** Select Objects to preserve data copied to the Clipboard as a vector graphic, or select one of the bitmap formats to covert the image. Enter a value for Resolution. Select the Include Postscript check box to include Postscript data. For gradients, select an option to specify quality in the PICT.

  ◆ **FreeHand Text.** Select the Maintain Text As Blocks check box to keep text editable in a pasted FreeHand file.

4. Click OK.

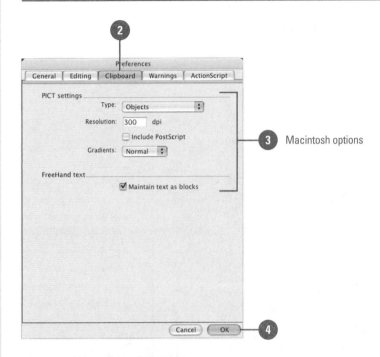

Macintosh options

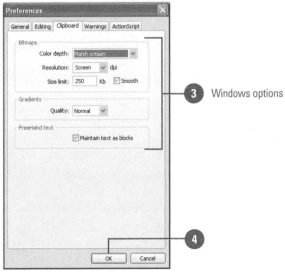

Windows options

Setting Warning Preferences

Flash provides warning messages when you perform actions that might create problems for your document or lose important data. The warnings help you avoid compatibility problems with Flash MX and character corruption from encoding, which makes your document readable, such as Western Europe (Windows), and let you know about missing fonts, URL changes, and symbol conversion. Additional warnings let you know when importing audio and video content inserts frames and when exporting a document to Flash version 6 r65 takes place.

Set Warning Preferences

1. Click the Flash (Professional) (Mac) or Edit (Win) menu, and then click Preferences.

2. Click the Warnings tab.

3. Select from the following check boxes:

   ◆ **Warn On Save For Macromedia Flash MX Compatibility.** When you try to save documents with content specific to Flash MX 2004 (Pro).

   ◆ **Warn On Missing Fonts.** When you open a Flash document that uses fonts that are not installed on your computer.

   ◆ **Warn On URL Changes In Launch And Edit.** If the URL for a document has changed since the last time you opened or edited it.

   ◆ **Warn On Reading Generator Content.** Displays a red X over any Generator objects to indicate the objects are not supported by Flash MX 2004.

   ◆ **Warn On Inserting Frames When Importing Content.** When Flash inserts frames in a document while you import audio or video files.

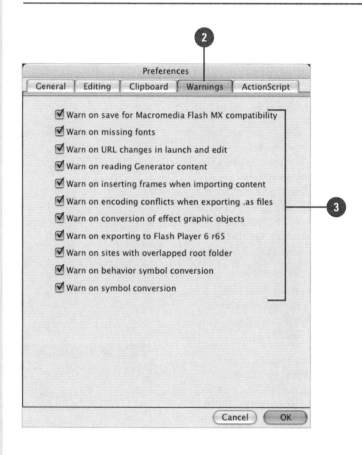

- **Warn On Encoding Conflicts When Exporting.** When selecting Default Encoding creates data lost or corruption. When you create a document with different language characters and select Default Encoding on a specific system corrupts the other languages.

- **Warn On Conversion Of Effect Graphic Objects.** When you attempt to edit a symbol with Timeline effects applied to it.

- **Warn On Exporting To Flash Player 6 r65.** When you export a document to this earlier version of the Flash Player.

- **Warn On Sites With Overlapped Root Folder.** When you create a site in which the local root folder overlaps with another site.

- **Warn On Behavior Symbol Conversion.** When you covert a symbol with a behavior attached to a symbol of a different type.

- **Warn On Symbol Conversion.** When you convert a symbol to a symbol of a different type.

4 Click OK.

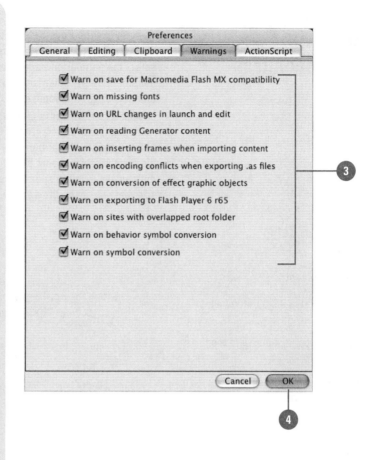

Working with Page Setup in Macintosh

You can use the Page Setup dialog box in Macintosh to select the size and location in the printer of the paper you want to use. You can also select the page orientation (portrait or landscape) that best fits the entire document or any selection. **Portrait** orients the page vertically (taller than it is wide) and **landscape** orients the page horizontally (wider than it is tall). When you shift between the two, the margin settings automatically change. **Margins** are the blank space between the edge of a page and the image. The printer only prints within these margins. You can use the Print Margins dialog box to change margins and layout. The layout options allow you to specify the frames you want to print, and the frame size and display on the page.

Work with Page Setup in Macintosh

1. Open a document.

2. Click the File menu, and then click Page Setup.

3. Click the Settings popup, and then click Page Attributes.

4. Select from the various Page Attributes options:

   ◆ **Format For.** Click the Format For popup, and then select a printer from the available options. If your printer is not accessible from the list, click the Edit Printer List, and then add your printer (you may need the printer CD, or access to the Internet, to load the latest drivers).

   ◆ **Paper Size.** Click the Paper Size popup, and then select from the available options. The default printer will determine the available paper sizes.

   ◆ **Orientation.** Click the Portrait, Landscape Left, or Landscape Right button.

   ◆ **Scale.** Enter a percentage value to increase (over 100) or decrease (under 100) the size of the printed document.

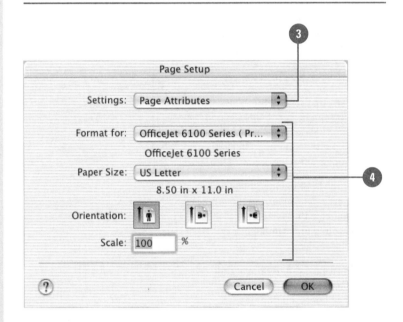

5 To create a custom page size, click the Settings popup, click Custom Paper Size, and then select from the various Custom Paper Size options.

6 Click the Settings popup, and then select Summary to view a text summary of your page setup options.

7 Click OK.

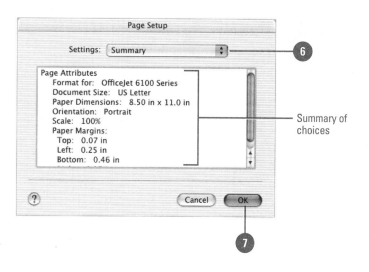

Summary of choices

Change Print Margins and Layout in Macintosh

1 Open a document.

2 Click the File menu, and then click Print Margins.

3 Enter Left, Right, Top, and Bottom page margins, and then select the Center check boxes to center material on the page.

4 Select from the Layout options:

◆ **Frames.** Click the Frames popup, and then click First Frame Only or All Frames.

◆ **Layout.** Click the Layout popup, and then select a layout option: Actual Size, Fit On One Page, or one of the Storyboard options.

◆ **Scale.** Enter a scale percentage value.

5 Click OK.

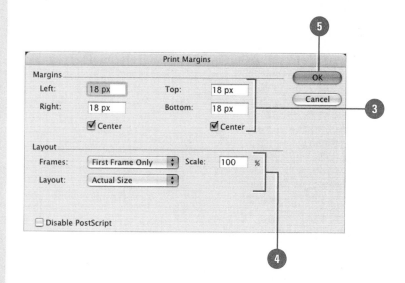

Working with Page Setup in Windows

You can use the Page Setup dialog box in Windows to select the size and location in the printer of the paper you want to use. You can also select the page orientation (portrait or landscape) that best fits the entire document or any selection. When you shift between the two, the margin settings automatically change. Margins are the blank space between the edge of a page and the image. You can also change page layout options, which allow you to specify the frames you want to print, and the frame size and display on the page. The printer only prints within these margins. Different printer models support different options and features; the available options depend on your printer and print drivers.

Work with Page Setup in Windows

1 Open a document.

2 Click the File menu, and then click Page Setup.

3 Select from the various Page Setup options:

   ◆ **Margins.** Enter Left, Right, Top, and Bottom page margins, and then select the check boxes to center material on the page.

   ◆ **Size.** Click the Size list arrow, and then select from the available options.

   ◆ **Source.** Click the Source list arrow, and then select from the available options.

   ◆ **Orientation.** Click the Portrait or Landscape option.

4 Select from the Layout options:

   ◆ **Frames.** Click the Frames list arrow, and then click First Frame Only or All Frames.

   ◆ **Layout.** Click the Layout list arrow, and then select a layout option.

   ◆ **Scale.** Enter a scale percentage value.

5 Click OK.

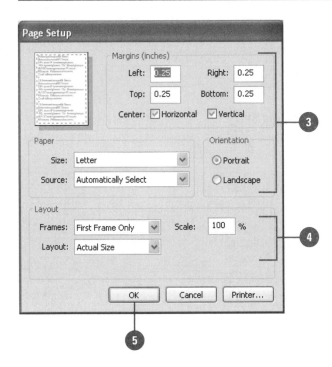

Set Printer Properties in Page Setup

1. Open a document.

2. Click the File menu, and then click Page Setup.

3. Click Printer.

4. Click the Name list arrow, and then select the printer you want to use.

5. Click Properties.

6. Select the printer options you want; each printer displays different options.

7. Click OK to close the Properties dialog box.

8. Click OK to close the Printer dialog box.

9. Click OK to close the Page Setup dialog box.

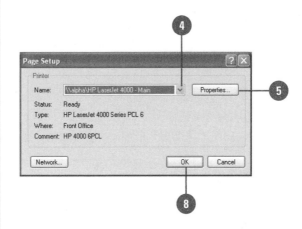

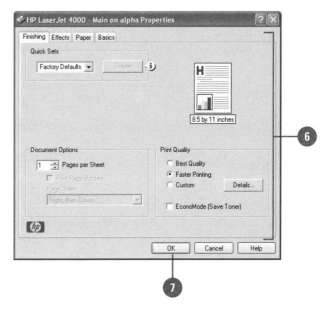

2

Printing a Document in Macintosh ▶

The Print command is probably the most used of all Flash's print options. In addition to normal printing functions, such as Copies and Pages, the Print command gives you other menus that let you control specific printing functions, such as output ink and color management. Understand that the options available for the Print command will be partially determined by the default printer. For example, if your default printer uses more than one paper tray, you will see options for selecting a specific tray for the current print job. In spite of the differences, there are some universal options to all print jobs, and these are covered here.

Print a Document in Macintosh

1 Open a document.

2 Click the File menu, and then click Print.

3 Click the Printer popup, and then select from the available printer descriptions.

> **IMPORTANT** *Changes made here, override any changes made in the Page Setup dialog box.*

4 Click the Presets popup, and then select from the available preset options.

5 Click the Print Options popup, click Copies & Pages, and then select the various options: Number Of Copies, Collated, Print All or Range Of Pages.

6 Click the Print Options popup, click Layout, and then select the various options: Pages Per Sheet, Layout Direction, and if you want a Border.

7 Click the Print Options popup, click Output Options, and then select the various options: Save As File, and what Format you want the file.

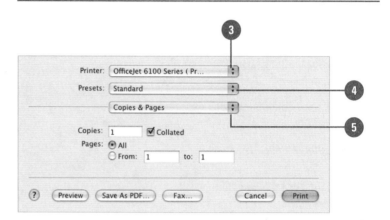

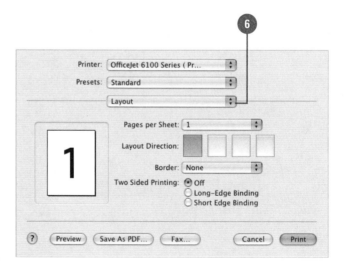

8. Click the Print Options popup, click Printer Features, and then select your options.

9. Click the Print Options popup, click Summary, and then view the summary of settings.

10. Click the following options to finalize your print:

   ◆ Preview

   ◆ Save As PDF

   ◆ Cancel

   ◆ Print

   ◆ Fax

11. If you need additional help along the way, click the Help button.

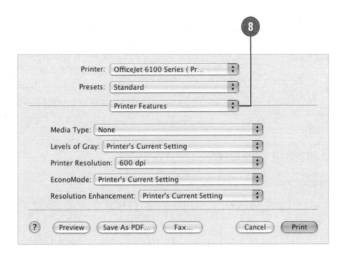

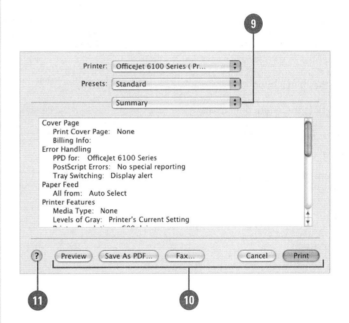

2

Printing a Document in Windows

Printing a paper copy is the most common way to preview and share your documents. You can use the Print dialog box to set how many copies to print, specify a range of pages to print, and print your document. Understand that the options available for the Print command will be determined by the default printer, and operating system. Different printers will display different options, there are some options that are fairly universal, and these options are covered here.

Print a Document in Windows

1. Open a document.

2. Click the File menu, and then click Print.

3. If necessary, click the Name list arrow, and then click the printer you want.

4. Type the number of copies you want to print.

5. Specify the pages to print:

   ◆ **All.** Prints the entire document.

   ◆ **Pages.** Prints the specified pages.

   ◆ **Selection.** Prints the selected item.

6. Click OK.

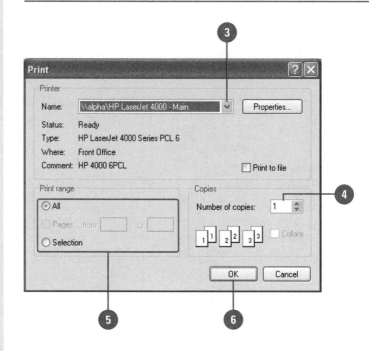

Creating Graphics

3

Introduction

Flash MX 2004 offers a full suite of tools for creating and editing graphics. When you draw in Flash, you create vector art. **Vectors** are mathematical descriptions of lines and points that, when connected, form shapes and objects. Vector-defined art is not limited by resolution like bitmaps are so they can be scaled to any size without a loss in quality or increase in file size. This is the basis of Flash; the main reason Flash files are so small and why they can be deployed on so many platforms. Vector graphics are also fully editable after they are created so you can continue to adjust their properties. Included in Flash are many of the drawing tools and procedures familiar to the seasoned user of vector drawing programs. It is also a good place for the beginner to learn. Sketch naturally with the Pencil and Brush tools or use vector-based objects such as the Rectangle or Oval tools or the new Polystar tool. Use the Pen tool to create lines and shapes with Bézier curves. Whatever is drawn can be edited and modified with a variety of tools and palettes. When you select an object or graphic on the Stage, the Property Inspector displays the attributes of that object that are modifiable such as fill and stroke color, position, and scale.

Changing Drawing Settings

The Editing tab on the Preferences dialog box contains a number of drawing settings that control the sensitivity and behavior of Flash's drawing tools. Make changes to the tolerance levels for smoothing or straightening, set the sensitivity for line and shape recognition, or fine-tune snapping. In each case, you can exercise greater control over your drawing or allow Flash to perform corrections and adjustments as you draw.

Change the Drawing Settings

1. Click the Flash (Professional) (Mac) or Edit (Win) menu, and then click Preferences.

2. Click the Editing tab.

3. Click any of the Drawing Settings to adjust options:

   ◆ **Connect Lines.** Determines how close the ends of any two lines need to be before Flash connects them. It also controls how straight a line has to be before it's converted into perfectly straight lines.

   ◆ **Smooth Curves.** Determines the amount of smoothing applied to a drawn line when Smooth or Straighten modes are used. The lower the smoothing applied, the closer the line appears to what you have drawn.

   ◆ **Recognize Lines.** Defines how a straight line drawn with the Pencil tool must be before it's converted into a perfectly straight line.

   ◆ **Recognize Shapes.** Sets how precise simple geometric shapes must be drawn before they are detected as shapes.

   ◆ **Click Accuracy.** Determines how near to a shape the pointer must be before Flash recognizes it.

4. Click OK.

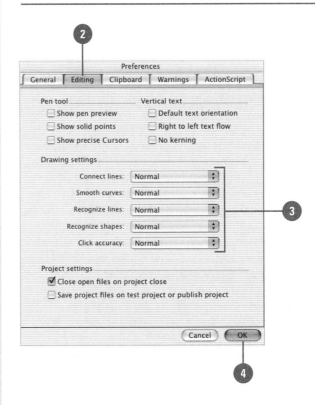

Drawing with the Line Tool

The Line tool draws perfectly straight lines in any direction you drag your mouse. In Flash, a line is called a **stroke** and there is a variety of thickness, styles, and colors that can be applied to it. You can also create your own line style for specific types of dashed, dotted or artistic lines. Create simple shapes, design elements, or use it as a starting point for a drawing. You can constrain the path a line draws to 45-degree angles or create closed shapes by intersecting the lines you draw. When a line overlaps another line on the same layer, it essentially 'cuts' it into two pieces that can be edited as separate objects.

Use the Line Tool

1 Click the Line tool in the Toolbar.

The pointer becomes a crosshair that you can drag anywhere on the Stage.

TIMESAVER *Press N to select the Line tool.*

2 Click and drag on the Stage, and then release the mouse when the line is the length you need.

A preview of the line appears as you drag. A circle beneath the crosshair indicates the line's endpoint.

Did You Know?

You can use the Shift key to create a 45 degree line. Click the Line tool, hold down the Shift key, and then drag to draw a 45 degree line.

See Also

See "Changing Stroke and Fill Colors" on page 90 for information on using color.

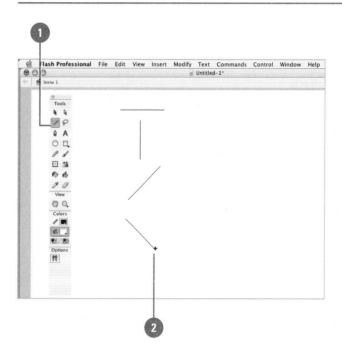

3

Drawing with the Pencil Tool

Use the Pencil tool for freeform drawing. When you draw with the Pencil tool you are creating strokes. It works the same way as a real pencil with options for smoothing and straightening. Depending upon which mode you choose, Flash makes corrections to the drawn line. Smooth mode softens the curve of the line you draw while Straighten mode transforms the line into a series of straight-line segments and standard curves. Additionally, Flash performs shape recognition to the lines you draw so that if it detects something approximating a simple geometric shape such as a rectangle, oval, or triangle, it converts your drawing into whichever shape it detects. To bypass these modifications, select Ink mode. This mode allows for the most freeform drawing with minimal correction by Flash.

Use the Pencil Tool in Straighten Mode

1 Click the Pencil tool in the Toolbar.

The pointer becomes a pencil. The Pencil tool options appear at the bottom of the Toolbar. The default mode is Straighten.

TIMESAVER *Press Y to select the Pencil tool.*

2 Draw on the Stage with the Pencil, and then release the mouse.

A rough preview of the line appears as you draw. In Straighten mode, Flash transforms the line into a series of straight-line segments and standard curves.

Did You Know?

Flash converts rough shapes into clean, geometric shapes. If you draw a rough rectangle in Straighten mode, Flash converts your shape into a clean rectangle with straight sides. It does the same for other shapes, such as ovals and triangles. Set the tolerance level of shape recognition in the Editing preferences.

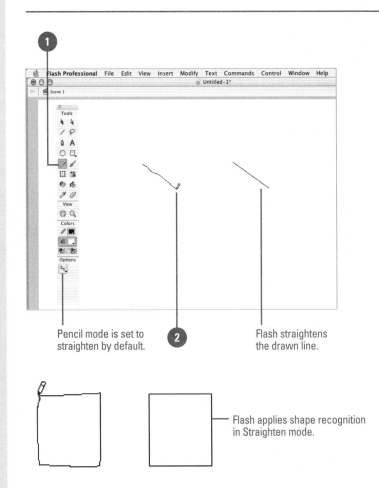

Pencil mode is set to straighten by default.

Flash straightens the drawn line.

Flash applies shape recognition in Straighten mode.

Use the Pencil Tool in Smooth Mode

1. Click the Pencil tool in the Toolbar.

   The pointer becomes a pencil. The Pencil tool options appear at the bottom of the Toolbar.

2. Click the Pencil mode popup in the Options area of the Toolbar, and then click Smooth.

3. Draw on the Stage with the Pencil, and then release the mouse.

   A rough preview of the line appears as you draw. In Smooth mode, Flash smoothes the line you draw into curved line segments.

Did You Know?

You can disable straightening and smoothing. Click the Pencil mode popup in the Options area of the Toolbar, and then click Ink mode to yield a line closest to the line you've drawn with minimal corrections performed by Flash.

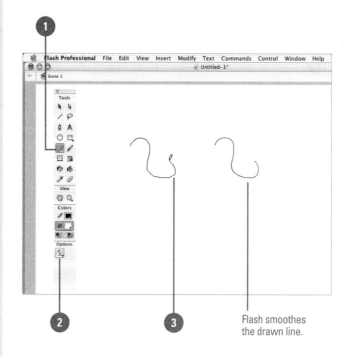

Flash smoothes the drawn line.

Use Ink mode for more freeform drawing.

Drawing Shapes with the Rectangle and Oval Tools ▶

The Flash Toolbar includes several tools for quickly creating simple geometric vector shapes. They are easy to use; you just click and drag on the Stage to create the shapes. The Rectangle tool creates rectangles with square or rounded sides. The Oval tool creates circular shapes such as ovals and circles. Both can be constrained to certain aspect ratios by holding the Shift key or drawn freeform without the key modifier. These shapes can be comprised of Strokes, which are lines that surround and define the shape, Fills, which are a color or texture inside the shape, or both. Because they are comprised of vectors, they are editable after they are created with any of Flash's editing tools.

Draw with the Oval Tool

1. Click the Oval tool in the Toolbar.

   TIMESAVER *Press O to select the Oval tool.*

2. Select a Stroke and Fill Color from the Colors area of the Toolbar.

3. Click and drag on the Stage, and then release the mouse.

   A preview of the oval appears as you drag.

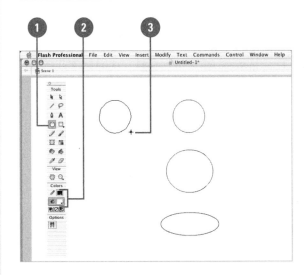

Draw with the Rectangle Tool

1. Click the Rectangle tool in the Toolbar.

   TIMESAVER *Press R to select the Rectangle tool.*

2. Select a Stroke and Fill color from the Colors area of the Toolbar.

3. Click and drag on the Stage, and then release the mouse.

   A preview of the rectangle appears as you drag.

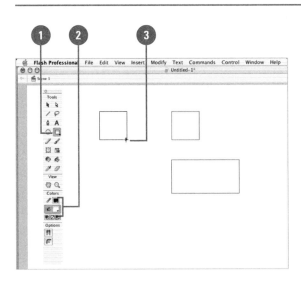

Draw a Rounded Rectangle

1. Click the Rectangle tool in the Toolbar.

2. Click the Round Rectangle Radius button in the Options area of the Toolbar to open the Rectangle Settings dialog box.

3. Enter a value for the corner radius.

4. Click OK.

5. Click and drag on the Stage, and then release the mouse.

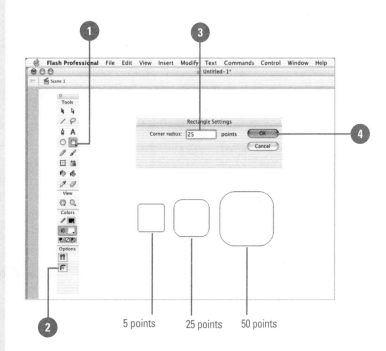

5 points   25 points   50 points

Did You Know?

You can enter values ranging from 0 to 999 points in the Rectangle Settings dialog box . A value of zero gives you a straight-sided-square. Higher numbers produce squares with more rounded sides.

You can hold down the Shift key while dragging to produce a perfect square with equal sides or a perfect circle. If you want to draw an oval or a rectangle without a stroke or fill, you can set either of these options to No Fill in the Colors area of the Toolbar or in the Color Mixer.

You can draw shapes withour a stroke or a fill. Set either of these properties to No Fill in the Colors section of the Toolbar or in the Color Mixer.

See Also

See "Changing Stroke and Fill Colors" on page 98 for information on changing shapes.

3

Using the Polystar Tool

Working in much the same way as the Oval and Rectangle tools, the new Polystar tool allows you to easily create complex vector shapes. You can use this tool to create polygons and stars with up to 32 sides. Choose between creating a polygon or a star. Both styles have characteristics that can be adjusted in the Property Inspector before you draw the shape. Both the polygon and star style can have up to 32 sides, with the star style having an additional star point size that can be set. Experiment with several options to get the kind of shape you want.

Draw a Polygon or Star Shape

1. Click and hold the Rectangle tool in the Toolbar, and then point to Polystar Tool.

   The pointer becomes a crosshair that you can drag anywhere on the Stage.

2. Click Options in the Property Inspector.

   TIMESAVER *Press ⌘+F3 (Mac) or Ctrl+3 (Win) to open the Property Inspector.*

3. Click the Style popup, and then select Polygon or Star.

4. Enter a value for the number of sides. You can create an object with up to 32 sides.

5. For the Star style, you can specify an additional option for your point size. You can enter a value ranging from .10 to 1.0 points.

6. Click OK.

See Also

See "Editing Strokes with the Ink Bottle" on page 102 for information on editing an object.

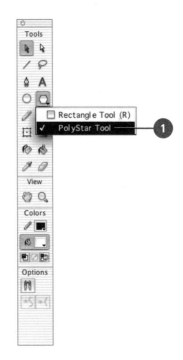

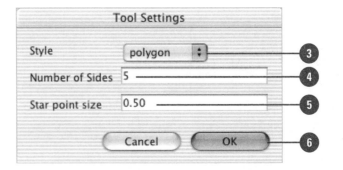

Understanding Selections

When you create vector graphics in Flash, they are comprised of distinct elements that can be selected separately or as a whole with a variety of selection tools. The type of editing you need to perform determines which tool you use. For example, a simple rectangle drawn is comprised of four line segments that surround the contour of the shape and one fill in the center. Each of these five parts can be selected in tandem or individually with the Arrow Selection tool. Likewise, any stroke that intersects another stroke or fill splits them into distinct elements that can be selected separately.

In Normal selection mode, holding down the Shift key adds to the selection any additional elements you click on. You can change this option in the General tab of the Preferences window so that it isn't necessary to use the Shift key to perform this function. Double-click any stroke to select other strokes connected to it or double-click a fill to select it and any strokes that touch or intersect it. To select an entire shape (strokes and fills) or just a portion of it, you can drag a selection rectangle with the Arrow tool or draw a freeform selection area with the Lasso tool. These methods work best for very complex shapes with many intersecting strokes and fills, or if there is only a portion of the shape you need to edit.

The Sub-Selection and Pen tools allow you to select the entire shape (strokes and fills) simultaneously, making its anchor points and Bézier handles visible for editing. Use this method when you need to edit the contours of the shape with precision.

3

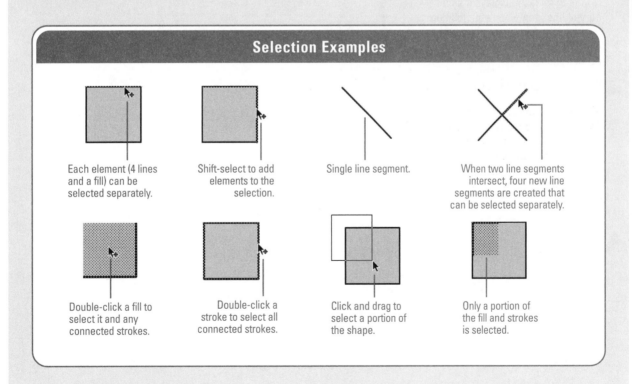

Selection Examples

Each element (4 lines and a fill) can be selected separately.

Shift-select to add elements to the selection.

Single line segment.

When two line segments intersect, four new line segments are created that can be selected separately.

Double-click a fill to select it and any connected strokes.

Double-click a stroke to select all connected strokes.

Click and drag to select a portion of the shape.

Only a portion of the fill and strokes is selected.

Selecting Strokes with the Arrow Tool

There are a variety of ways to select objects in Flash. You can select an object's stroke or fill or both. You can use the Arrow tool to select parts of the object or drag over a portion of it to create a selection rectangle. The Property Inspector displays the properties of what is selected including Stroke line weight and style, Fill color, pixel dimensions, and X and Y coordinates. When a stroke or fill is selected, a dotted pattern appears over it indicating it has been selected. This makes editing and modifying graphics simple and illustrates the versatility of the vector-based graphics model used in Flash.

Select a Stroke with the Arrow Selection Tool

1. Click the Arrow tool in the Toolbar.

   The pointer becomes an arrow.

   TIMESAVER *Press V to select the Arrow tool.*

2. Position the arrow on the edge of the shape.

   Notice that Flash displays a small curved line icon when you position the arrow over a Curve point and a corner line icon when over a Corner point.

3. Click on any part of the stroke.

   Flash only selects a portion of it. This is because what appears to be one whole shape is actually a series of lines connected by points and each can be selected separately.

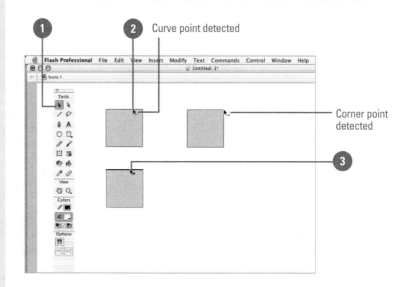

Curve point detected

Corner point detected

Select Multiple Stroke Segments

1 Click the Arrow tool in the Toolbar.

The pointer becomes an arrow.

TIMESAVER *Press V to select the Arrow tool. You can temporarily switch to the Arrow tool from any other tool by pressing ⌘ (Mac) or Ctrl (Win).*

2 Click on any part of the stroke to select one segment.

3 Hold down the Shift key, and then click other strokes to add them to the selection.

Did You Know?

You can turn off the Shift-select feature in the General tab of the Preferences dialog box. When this feature is disabled, you can add to the selected segments by clicking them without the need to hold down the Shift key. In this mode, holding the Shift key and clicking a selected stroke segment deselects that segment.

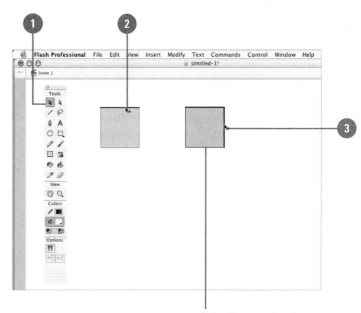

Shift-select to add stroke segments to the selection.

Select Connected Stroke Segments

1 Click the Arrow tool in the Toolbar.

The pointer becomes an arrow.

2 Double-click any part of the segment or stroke to select all connected strokes.

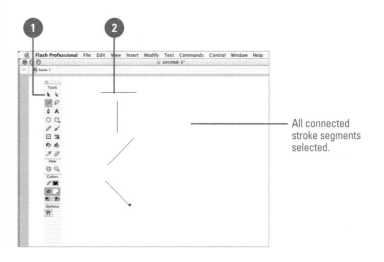

All connected stroke segments selected.

Creating Graphics **83**

Selecting Strokes and Fills with the Arrow Tool

The Arrow tool provides the most simple and versatile procedures for selecting objects in Flash. The Arrow tool selects anything you click on (provided it isn't on a locked layer). Double-clicking shapes with the Arrow tool selects all fills and strokes that are connected. Shift-selecting allows you to add to the selection only what you need. Alternately, dragging a selection rectangle on the Stage with the Arrow tool creates a bounding box that selects anything you drag it over. This bounding box method is the most reliable technique for selecting very complex objects with many intersecting strokes and fills.

Select Fills with the Arrow Selection Tool

1. Click the Arrow tool in the Toolbar.

   The pointer becomes an arrow.

2. Position the arrow in the Fill area or the center of the shape and click.

   The fill becomes highlighted with a dotted pattern to indicate it has been selected. Hold down the Shift key to add other strokes and fills to the selection.

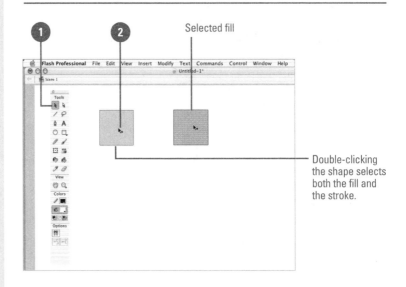

Selected fill

Double-clicking the shape selects both the fill and the stroke.

Select with a Selection Rectangle

1. Click the Arrow tool in the Toolbar.

   The pointer becomes an arrow.

2. Click on the Stage above and to the left of the shape you want to select and drag to create a Selection Rectangle, and then release the mouse when the bounding box fully encloses the shape.

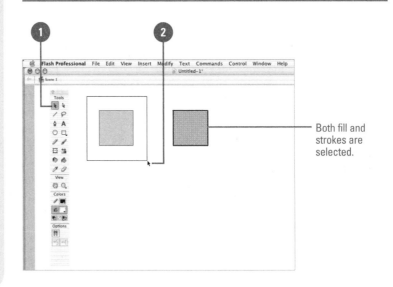

Both fill and strokes are selected.

Making Selections with the Lasso Tool

Use the Lasso tool when you want to select shapes that are too close to shapes you don't want to select. This tool allows you to draw around the shape , selecting everything contained in the shape you draw. In the default mode, you can draw a freeform lasso around the object you want to select. You can also choose the Polygon mode for defining the selected area with a series of straight-line segments.

Select with the Lasso Tool

① Click the Lasso tool in the Toolbar.

TIMESAVER *Press L to select the Lasso tool.*

② Draw around the shapes you want to select.

Flash draws a preview of the selection lasso as you draw.

③ To complete the selection, return to the point where you started.

Did You Know?

You can combine several ways to select single or multiple objects. Holding the Shift key adds line segments and fills to the selection. Shift-selecting items that have already been selected deselects them.

Select with the Lasso Tool in Polygon Mode

① Click the Lasso tool in the Toolbar.

② Click the Polygon Mode button in the Options area of the Toolbar.

③ Click near the area you want to select. Move the pointer and click again. Keep clicking until the object or portion you want to select is surrounded.

④ Double-click to complete the selection.

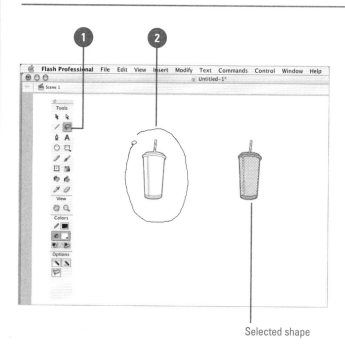

Selected shape

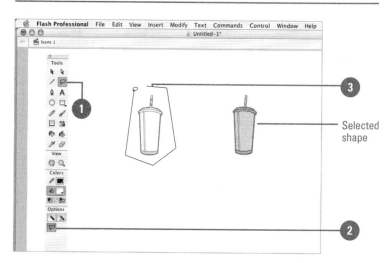

Selected shape

Zooming In and Out with the Magnifying Glass

Because the Stage and Work Area in Flash share the same space with a variety of panels, palettes and windows, it is often necessary to change the magnification level. You can use the Magnifying Glass to zoom out and see the entire piece or zoom in to do more detailed work on a small portion. The tool is made up of two modifiers: a plus (+) symbol in the circle indicates enlargement of the Stage and a minus (-) indicates reduction. Flash allows magnification levels from 8 percent to 2000 percent.

Zoom In

1. Click the Zoom tool in the Toolbar.

2. Click the Enlarge button in the Options area of the Toolbar.

   The pointer becomes a magnifying glass with a plus (+) symbol in it.

3. Click on the area of the Stage you want to zoom into.

   TIMESAVER *Press Z to select the Zoom tool. To temporarily toggle between the Enlarge and Reduce Modifiers buttons in the Options area of the Toolbar, press Option (Mac) or Alt (Win).*

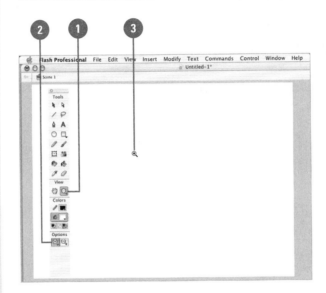

Zoom Out

1. Click the Zoom tool in the Toolbar.

2. Click the Reduce button in the Options area of the Toolbar.

   The pointer becomes a magnifying glass with a minus (-) symbol in it.

3. Click on the area of the Stage you want to zoom out from.

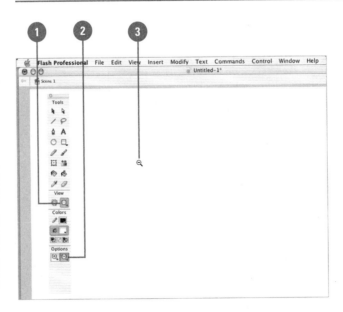

Zoom Into a Specific Area by Dragging on the Stage

① Click the Zoom tool in the Toolbar.

② Click the Reduce or Enlarge button in the Options area of the Toolbar.

③ Click on the area of the Stage you want to magnify and drag the pointer.

Did You Know?

You can change the magnification level in several places. The Zoom Control field in the top right hand corner of the Stage allows you to enter a value or access a popup with various magnification levels. You can also change the magnification submenu in the View menu or use the keyboard shortcuts ⌘+ - (Mac) or Ctrl+ - (Win) to zoom out, and ⌘+ + (Mac) or Ctrl+ + (Win) to zoom in. Quickly switch to 100 percent magnification by pressing ⌘+1 (Mac) or Ctrl+1 (Win).

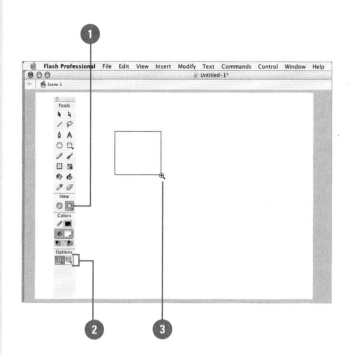

Moving Around with the Hand Tool

At certain magnifications, parts of the Stage may not be viewable. Use the Hand tool to quickly move to different parts of the Stage without having to change the magnification level. The Stage is the active area of your movie, the only area that will be visible in the exported Flash movie. The gray area around the Stage is the Work Area. The Hand tool allows you to easily access artwork or other objects contained in this space if you are doing detailed work at high levels of magnification.

Move the Stage View

1. Click the Hand tool in the Toolbar.

   The pointer becomes a small hand that moves the entire Stage revealing other parts of the Stage as you drag.

   TIMESAVER *Pressing the space bar temporarily changes the active tool to the Hand tool. Continue holding as you drag.*

2. Click and drag the Stage to move the view.

Did You Know?

You can turn off the visibility of the Work Area (the gray space around the Stage) and quickly change the View scale to 100 percent. Toggle the Work Area option in the View menu or use the keyboard shortcut ⌘+Shift+W (Mac) or Ctrl+Shift+W (Win). This is a great way to temporarily see what is viewable in the exported Flash file (.swf) when you are working with large images that extend past the Stage boundaries.

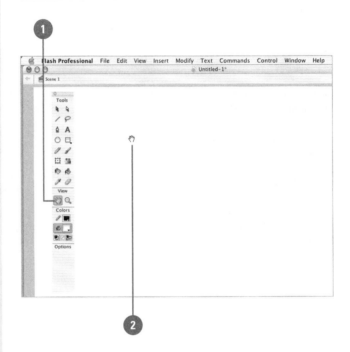

For Your Information

Using the Work Area

It is important to remember that even though only the objects and artwork on the Stage are visible in the exported movie, Flash still includes objects that are located in the Work Area. They might not be visible, but they contribute to the overall file size. It is a good idea to clean up your files before exporting the final movie. You can clean up by removing any artwork outside the boundaries of the Stage or by putting them on a guide layer.

Displaying Rulers

Ruler bars are located on the top and left sides of the Stage and serve several purposes. They let you measure the width and height of Flash elements and they let you place guides on the screen to control placement of objects on the Stage. In all, Rulers serve a very important role. When you display rulers, you can use guides to help you correctly align objects with other objects. By using guides, you have access to precise alignment systems. To use the guides, the ruler bars must first be visible. When you no longer need the rulers, you can hide the rulers to free up more workspace.

Show and Hide Rulers

1. Click the View menu, and then click Rulers.

   A check mark next to the option means its visibility is enabled.

2. To hide rulers, click the View menu, and then click Rulers to remove the check mark and hide the rulers.

   TIMESAVER *Press*
   ⌘+Option+Shift+R (Mac) or Ctrl+Alt+Shift+R (Win) to turn the ruler on and off.

Did You Know?

You can change the unit of measure displayed on the Rulers. Click the Modify menu, click Document, click the Ruler Units popup, select a unit of measure, and then click OK.

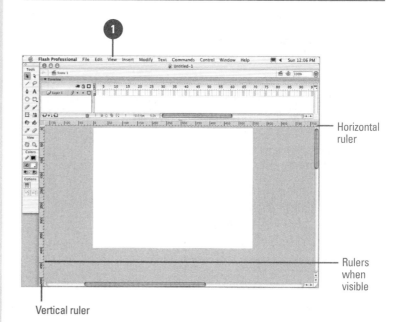

Horizontal ruler

Rulers when visible

Vertical ruler

3

Using Grids and Guides

Flash comes with guides, grids, and rulers to help you lay out artwork and objects with precision. A grid is a series of crisscrossed lines that aid in aligning objects to each other on the Stage. Guides and grids are modifiable. You can change their visibility, position, color, and frequency. These items are invisible by default, but they can be easily turned on and adjusted. Though you see them in the Flash development environment, they are invisible on export. Use guides to align art and objects to each other on vertical or horizontal paths, or turn on the grid for use in designing a layout that is proportional and balanced.

Show and Hide Grids

1. Click the View menu, point to Grid, and then click Show Grid.

   A check mark next to the option means its visibility is enabled.

2. To hide the grid, click the View menu, point to Grid, and then click Show Grid to remove the check mark and hide the grid.

   TIMESAVER *Press*
   ⌘+apostrophe (') (Mac) or
   Ctrl+apostrophe (') (Win) to toggle
   Grid visibility on and off.

See Also

See "Modifying Grid and Guide Settings" on page 92 for information on changing settings.

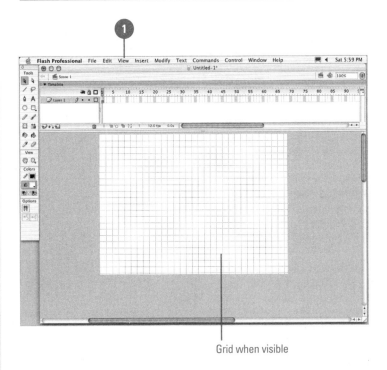

Grid when visible

Create Guides

1. Click the View menu, and then click Rulers to display rulers.

2. Click on the vertical ruler on the left side of the work area with the Arrow pointer and drag to the right, and then release the mouse where you want to place the vertical guide.

    A small directional triangle and line appears next to the pointer as you drag indicating that you are dragging the guide.

3. Click on the horizontal ruler at the top of the work area with the Arrow pointer and drag down, and then release the mouse where you want to place the horizontal guide.

4. Reposition the guides by selecting them with the pointer.

Did You Know?

You can turn guide visibility on and off, lock guides, and enable or disable snapping to guides. Click the View menu, and then click Guides to access these options or use the following keyboard shortcuts: ⌘+; (Mac) or Ctrl+; (Win) toggles between showing and hiding guides Option+⌘+; (Mac) or Ctrl+Alt+; (Win) locks and unlocks guides Shift+⌘+; (Mac) or Ctrl+Shift+; (Win) to turn Snapping on and off.

See Also

See "Displaying Rulers" on page 89 for information on showing and hiding rulers.

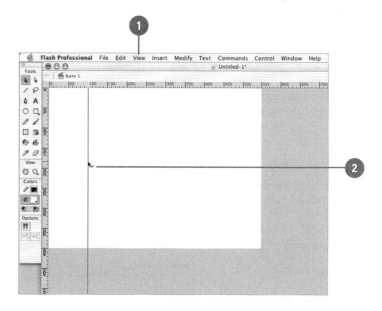

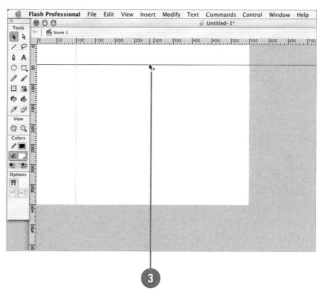

3

Modifying Grid and Guide Settings

The need for grids and guides varies depending upon the type of document you are working on. They are useful for aligning text and graphics to interface elements and are an invaluable tool for creating a well composed and proportioned layout. Every project is different and has different requirements, so Flash allows the display, behavior, and characteristics of guides and grids to be altered to fit your needs. They are only visible in the Flash development environment, and are not exported in the Flash movie.

Modify Grid

 Click the View menu, point to Grid, and then click Edit Grid.

> **TIMESAVER** *Press Option+⌘+G (Mac) or Ctrl+Alt+G (Win) to quickly access the Grid dialog box.*

2 Click the Color popup, and then click a grid line color.

3 Select or clear the Show Grid check box to show or hide grid.

4 Select or clear the Snap To Grid check box to enable or disable snapping.

5 Enter values for horizontal and vertical dimensions for the grid lines.

6 Click the Snap Accuracy popup, and then select a level of sensitivity for snapping to the grid. Select from Must Be Close, Normal, Can Be Distant, and Always Snap.

7 To make the current grid settings the default for new Flash files, click the Save Default button.

8 Click OK.

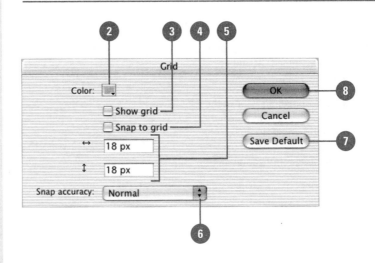

Modify Guides

① Click the View menu, point to Guides, and then click Edit Guides.

TIMESAVER *Press Option+Shift+⌘+G (Mac) or Ctrl+Alt+Shift+G (Win) to quickly access the Guides dialog box.*

② Click the Color popup, and then click a guide line color.

③ Select or clear the Show Guides check box to show or hide guides.

④ Select or clear the Snap To Guides check box to enable or disable snapping.

⑤ Select or clear the Lock Guides check box to enable or disable editing of guides.

⑥ Click the Snap Accuracy popup, and then select a level of sensitivity for snapping to the guides. Select from Must Be Close, Normal, Can Be Distant.

⑦ To remove all guides from the active scene, click Clear All.

⑧ To make the current guides the default guides for new Flash files, click Save Default.

⑨ Click OK.

TIMESAVER *Press ⌘+; (Mac) or Ctrl+; (Win) to toggle between showing and hiding guides; press Option+⌘+; (Mac) or Ctrl+Alt+; (Win) to lock and unlock guides; or press Shift+⌘+; (Mac) or Ctrl+Shift+; (Win) to turn Snapping on and off.*

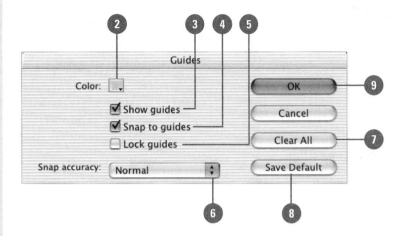

Using Snap Align

Snap Align is a new feature that enables dynamic alignment of art and objects on the Stage. Simply drag an object on the Stage and dashed lines appear that aid you in aligning to the edge or center vertices of other objects on the Stage. In the Snap Align dialog box you can set the distance objects to be from the movie borders and from each other before they snap. Additionally, you can choose to snap objects to edges or vertical and horizontal centers. Using the Snap Align feature enables you to lay out artwork more precisely and dynamically.

Enable Snap Align

1. Click the View menu, point to Snapping, and then click Snap Align.

   A check mark appears next to the menu item when Snap Align is enabled.

2. Drag an object on the Stage.

   Depending on the behaviors set in the Snap Align Settings dialog box, gray dashed lines appear when the edges or center vertices of objects move to within a certain pixel distance.

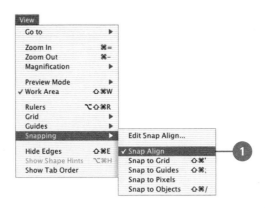

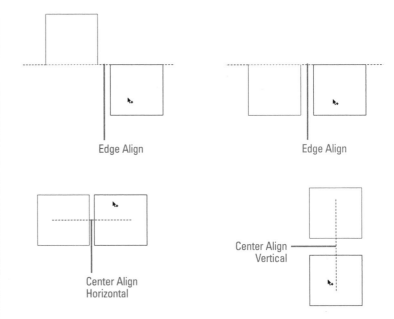

Edge Align

Edge Align

Center Align
Horizontal

Center Align
Vertical

Configure Snap Align

1. Click the View menu, point to Snapping, and then click Edit Snap Align.

2. Select from the following options:

   ◆ **Movie Border.** Enter a value for the distance an object needs to be before it will snap to the boundaries of the movie (in pixels).

   ◆ **Snap Tolerance.** Enter a value for horizontal and vertical edge tolerance (in pixels).

   ◆ **Center Alignment.** Select the check boxes to center alignment on horizontal or vertical vertices or both.

3. Click OK.

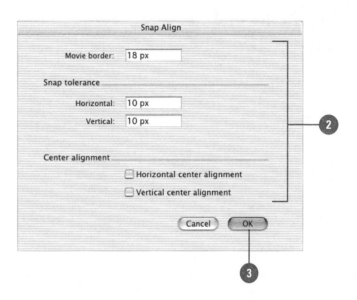

Changing Stroke and Fill Colors

Artwork created in Flash can have strokes and fills. Strokes and fills behave differently and are edited in different ways. A stroke is an outline. It describes the edges of a shape or it can be a simple line. You can create strokes with the Line tool or the Pencil tool. A fill is a solid shape, often contained or surrounded by a stroke. It is the surface area of a shape and can be a color, gradient, texture, or bitmap. Fills can be created with the Paintbrush tool and the Paint Bucket tool. The Oval, Rectangle, and Pen tool can create shapes with either a stroke or a fill, or both. You can edit the characteristics of strokes and fills, such as color, in several ways. If the shape is selected on the Stage, a color change to a stroke or fill can be made in any of the color palettes. Because Flash uses vectors to describe shapes, you can change their properties as much as you want without any loss in quality. It is important to grasp the concept behind them because they are the basis for drawing in Flash.

Change the Stroke Color

1. Click the Arrow tool in the Toolbar.

2. Select the stroke of the shape by double-clicking it.

3. Click the Stroke color box in the Toolbar.

4. Select a new color from the palette.

Did You Know?

You can change the stroke color in three other places. Stroke color boxes are also located in the Property Inspector, the Color Mixer panel, and the Swatches panel. In all cases, select the stroke you want to change and choose a new color from any of the palettes.

You can change the line width and style of a stroke or set the stroke color to None in the Property Inspector. Click the stroke you want to change to select it, and then select any of the options in the Property Inspector. Setting the stroke color to None removes the stroke from the shape.

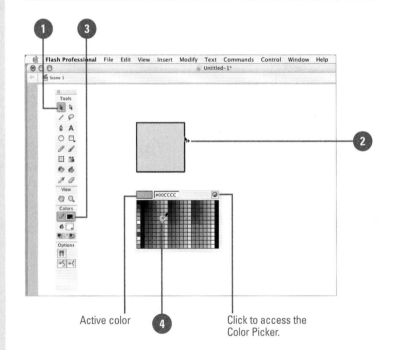

Active color

Click to access the Color Picker.

Change the Fill Color

1. Click the Arrow tool in the Toolbar.

   The pointer becomes an arrow.

2. Click the fill of the shape to select it.

   This is the area inside the stroke.

3. Click the Fill color box in the Toolbar.

4. Select a new color from the palette.

Did You Know?

You can change the fill color in three other places. Fill color boxes are also located in the Property Inspector, the Color Mixer, and the Swatches panel. Just select the fill and choose a new color from one of the palettes by clicking on a new color box.

See Also

See "Editing Fills with the Paint Bucket" on page 103 for information on changing the fill color.

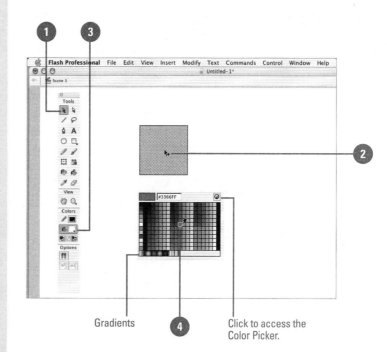

Gradients

Click to access the Color Picker.

3

Creating Custom Colors

Flash allows you to edit and create new colors for strokes and fills in several ways in the Color Mixer panel. You can alter a color's RGB values (assigning it different levels of Red, Green or Blue), Hue, Saturation, Brightness, and Alpha (transparency). You can accomplish this by using sliders, dragging on a color-space, or entering a numeric value that corresponds to a specific color. In each case you can save your color into the palette for easy access.

Create a Custom Color by Entering a Value

1. Open or expand the Color Mixer panel.

2. Enter values between 0 and 255 in the RGB numeric entry boxes.

3. Enter an alpha value between 0 and 100.

4. Click the Options button in the panel, and then click Add Swatch.

Did You Know?

You can alter the RGB values with the sliders located to the right of the numeric entry boxes. Click the small triangles, and then drag the sliders that appear. Additionally, you can drag the cursor over the Color space bar at the bottom of the Color Mixer panel to change the color interactively.

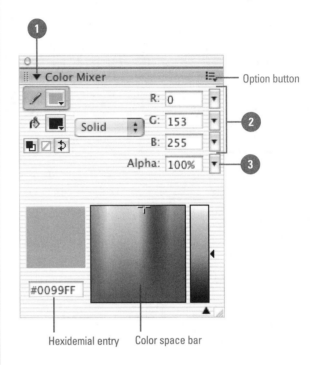

Option button

Hexidemial entry   Color space bar

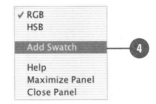

Create a Custom Color with the Color Picker

① Click a Stroke or Fill color box in the Toolbar or the Property Inspector.

② Click the Color Wheel button to the far right of the palette.

③ Click a color from one of the available pickers (Mac) or from the Color Window (Win).

④ Click OK.

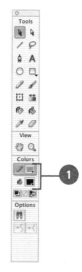

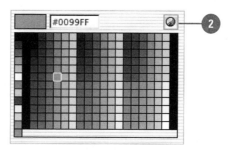

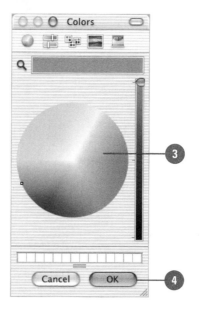

3

Editing Strokes with the Ink Bottle

There are a number of ways to change the stroke of an object. You can select the stroke and change its characteristics in the Property Inspector, the Swatch palettes, and the Color Mixer. If you need to apply the stroke properties of one object to that of another, use the Ink Bottle tool. The Ink Bottle tool holds the properties you've set for strokes in any of the palettes. You can click any object on the Stage to change the properties of its stroke (color, line weight and style) or add a stroke to an object that doesn't have one.

Use the Ink Bottle

1. Select a stroke on the Stage, and then change Stroke attributes in the Property Inspector.

2. Click the Ink Bottle tool in the Toolbar.

   The pointer becomes a small ink bottle.

   TIMESAVER *Press S to select the Ink Bottle tool.*

3. Click on the stroke of the shape to update it with the new attributes.

   The stroke updates to the new color.

Did You Know?

You can click anywhere on the shape with the Ink Bottle to change the stroke. If the object on the Stage is selected (stroke and fill), click down with the Ink Bottle tool to update its stroke.

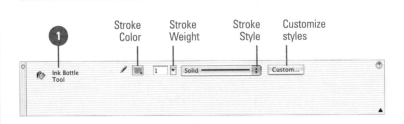

Stroke Color | Stroke Weight | Stroke Style | Customize styles

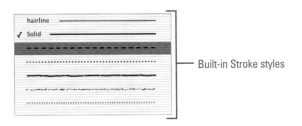

Built-in Stroke styles

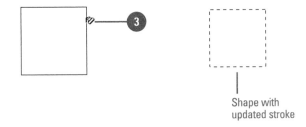

Shape with updated stroke

Editing Fills with the Paint Bucket

You can change the fill of an object with the Paint Bucket tool. The Paint Bucket stores the fill color you've set in the Toolbar or in the Property Inspector. You can change the fill color of any existing shape on the Stage by touching down on the shape with this tool. You can also add a fill to any shape that has a closed stroke.

Use the Paint Bucket

① Change the Fill color box in either the Property Inspector, the Colors area of the Toolbar, or the Color Mixer.

② Click the Paint Bucket tool in the Toolbar.

The pointer becomes a small paint bucket.

TIMESAVER *Press K to select the Paint Bucket tool.*

③ Click in the fill of a shape on the Stage.

The fill updates to the new color.

Did You Know?

You can set the sensitivity of the Paint Bucket tool in the Options areas of the Toolbox. These settings allow the Paint Bucket tool to close gaps in a shape (such as a break in the stroke line) and adjust how large or small a gap needs to be before Flash will close it.

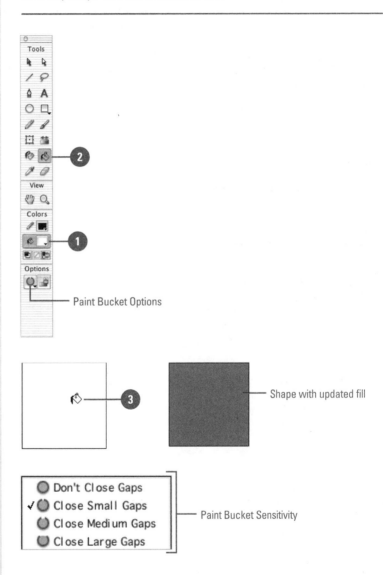

Paint Bucket Options

Shape with updated fill

Paint Bucket Sensitivity

Editing Strokes and Fills with the Eyedropper

The Eyedropper tool allows you to select the attributes of a shape such as fill and stroke color, and line weight and style, and then transfer them to other shapes. This tool detects whether it is a stroke or a fill you are selecting, and then changes into the Ink Bottle (when selecting strokes) or the Paint Bucket (when selecting fills). The Eyedropper provides a quick means for storing and transferring attributes between editable shapes.

Use the Eyedropper Tool to Edit Strokes and Fills

① Click the Eyedropper tool in the Toolbar.

The pointer becomes an eyedropper.

TIMESAVER *Press I to select the Eyedropper tool.*

② Position the eyedropper over the stroke or fill of a shape on the Stage.

- ◆ **Strokes.** When you are positioned over a stroke, a tiny pencil appears next to the tool. When you click on the stroke the Eyedropper becomes an Ink Bottle.

- ◆ **Fills.** When you are positioned over a fill, a tiny paint brush appears next to the tool. When you click on the fill the Eyedropper becomes a Paint Bucket.

③ Click on another shape's stroke or fill to transfer the selected attributes.

The stroke or fill updates to the new color.

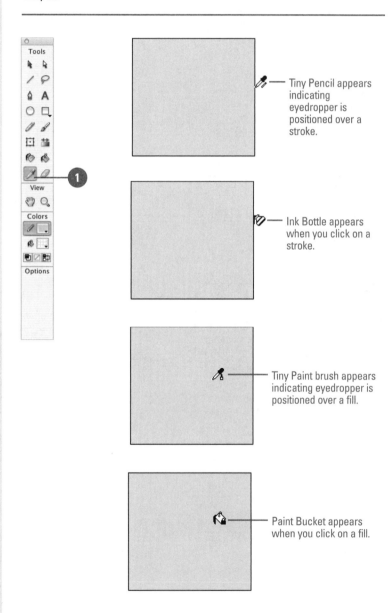

Tiny Pencil appears indicating eyedropper is positioned over a stroke.

Ink Bottle appears when you click on a stroke.

Tiny Paint brush appears indicating eyedropper is positioned over a fill.

Paint Bucket appears when you click on a fill.

Creating Gradients

Flash can create a number of paint effects in addition to solid colors. Gradients are made up of two or more colors that gradually fade into each other. They can be used to give depth to an object or create realistic shadows. The two gradient modes are linear and radial. Linear gradients are made up of parallel bands of color. Radial gradients radiate from a center point. Both can be edited for color, alpha, and position within a fill. A gradient behaves like any other fill. It can be saved to the palette as a swatch and added to other shapes with the Paint Bucket tool.

Create a Three-Color Linear Gradient

1. Select the fill of a shape on the Stage with the Arrow Selection tool.

2. In the Color Mixer panel, click the Fill Style popup, and then click Linear.

3. If necessary, click the small triangle on the bottom of the panel to open the gradient preview and color picker.

4. Position the pointer on the Gradient bar to display a plus (+) sign next to the pointer.

5. Click in the center of the Gradient bar to create a third color proxy indicated by a little box with a triangle on top.

6. Click one of the three color proxy indicators to select it.

7. Click a new color from the Color Picker below.

8. Drag the color proxy indicator along the Gradient bar to adjust the placement of the color along the gradient.

Did You Know?

You can remove a proxy color indicator. In the Color Mixer, drag the proxy indicator down.

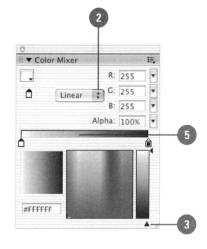

Shape with updated gradient

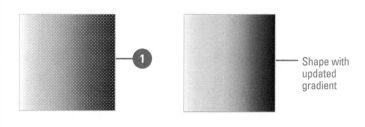

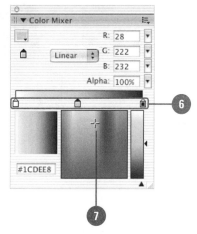

Using the Fill Lock

As you increase the complexity and number of shapes in your movie, it can become tricky to edit each object separately. When using gradient fills on several objects you can choose to span a gradient across several of these objects or give each object its own discreet gradient. The Lock Fill feature allows you to control how a fill is applied, essentially locking its position so that depending on where the shapes are positioned relative to the gradient, the one gradient spans all of the shapes. If you apply the same gradient to multiple shapes with the Fill Lock off, the gradient is applied to each shape independently.

Lock Gradients

1. Create two simple shapes using the Rectangle or Oval tool.

2. Select the first shape on the Stage with the Arrow Selection tool.

3. Click the Paint Bucket tool in the Toolbar.

    TIMESAVER *Press K to select the Paint Bucket Tool.*

4. Click the Lock Fill button in the Options area of the Toolbar.

5. Select a Gradient from the Colors area of the Toolbar or use the Color Mixer or Property Inspector.

6. Click the Eyedropper tool in the Toolbar, and then click on the gradient fill in the first shape.

7. Click down on the second shape to add the gradient fill.

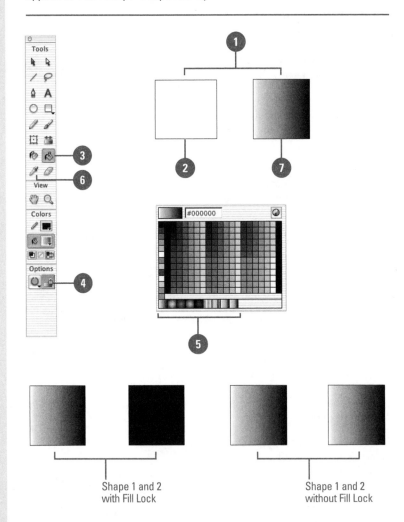

Shape 1 and 2 with Fill Lock

Shape 1 and 2 without Fill Lock

Did You Know?

You can quickly add a gradient that spans all of your shapes. Select all of the objects you want to fill, and then choose a gradient. Click the Paint Bucket tool and make sure the Fill Lock is not selected. With your shapes still selected, touch down on them with the Paint Bucket.

Using Paint Brush Modes

In addition to size, shape, and color settings for the Paint Brush tool, you can control how the brush behaves when painting on existing shapes and objects on the Stage. Paint Brush modes can restrict the area affected by the tool to fills or selections, empty areas of the Stage or specific shapes. When the Paint Brush tool is selected, a popup menu appears in the Toolbar. Select from the following modes: Paint Normal, Paint Fills, Paint Behind, Paint Selection, and Paint Inside. Each performs a specific operation providing you with varying levels of control as you paint. Flash previews your paint path as you paint, but it only affects the areas you've specified in the Paint modes. When you release the mouse, these previews disappear.

Use Paint Brush Modes

1. Click the Paint Brush tool in the Toolbar.

2. Click the Brush Mode popup in the Options area in the Toolbar, and then select from the following:

   ◆ **Paint Normal.** The brush paints over everything including strokes and other fills.

   ◆ **Paint Fills.** Painting only affects existing fills and empty areas of the Stage. Strokes are ignored.

   ◆ **Paint Behind.** The Paint Brush only affects empty areas of the Stage keeping existing lines and fills intact.

   ◆ **Paint Selection.** Painting only affects the selected areas you define with any of the selection tools.

   ◆ **Paint Inside.** The Paint Brush only affects the fill of the shape you started in, ignoring other shapes and empty areas on the Stage.

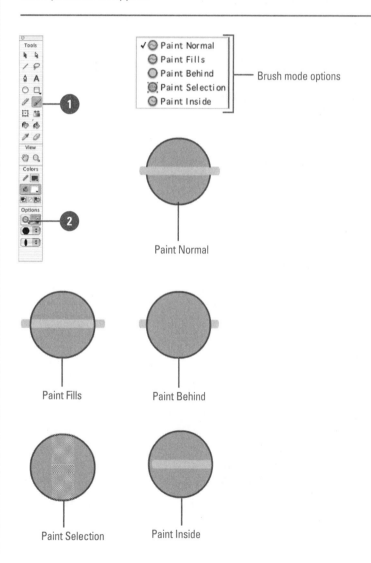

Brush mode options

Paint Normal

Paint Fills

Paint Behind

Paint Selection

Paint Inside

3

Drawing with the Pen Tool

The Pen tool is the basis for vector drawing. Flash provides a number of ways to draw and edit objects that are unique to Flash but the Pen tool utilizes procedures that will be familiar to those who have used other vector drawing programs. The Pen tool utilizes anchor points and Bézier handles to create lines and shapes and behaves in a way that is familiar to those who have used other programs such as Adobe Illustrator and Macromedia FreeHand. You can edit the anchor points and vectors you create by using key modifiers and the Sub-Selection tool. Utilize these tools when you need to create art with more precision.

Use the Pen Tool to Create an Open Path

1. Click the Pen tool in the Toolbar.

   The pointer becomes a pen.

   TIMESAVER *Press P to quickly select the Pen tool.*

2. Click on the Stage.

   An anchor point is created.

3. Move your pointer to another position, and then click again.

   Flash connects the two anchor points.

4. Double-click to end the path.

Did You Know?

You can end an open path using a keyboard shortcut. Press ⌘+click (Mac) or Ctrl+click (Win).

See Also

See "Modifying Shapes with the Sub-Selection Tool" on page 112 for information on using tools.

Open path drawn

Use the Pen Tool to Create a Closed Path

1. Click the Pen Tool in the Toolbar.

   The pointer becomes a pen.

   TIMESAVER *Press P to quickly select the Pen tool.*

2. Click on the Stage.

   An anchor point is created.

3. Move your pointer to another position, and then click again.

   Flash connects the two anchor points.

4. Move the pointer to a third position, and then click again.

   Flash connects the second and third anchor points.

5. Move the pointer back to the first anchor point.

   A small circle appears next to the pen pointer indicating you can close the path of the shape.

6. Click to close the shape.

Did You Know?

You can delete an anchor point with the Pen tool. With the Pen tool selected, click a shape on the Stage to select it. Position the X pointer over the anchor point you want to delete. A small minus (-) sign appears next to the X pointer. Click to delete the point.

You can create horizontal, vertical, and 45 degree lines while you draw. Hold the Shift key while you draw to constrain a line to horizontal, vertical, and 45 degree angles.

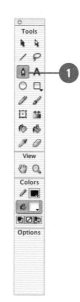

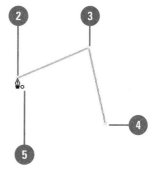

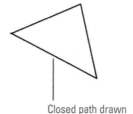

Closed path drawn

Drawing Curves with the Pen Tool

The Pen tool can be used to draw precise and complex curves by simply clicking and dragging it on the Stage. These curves can be modified with precision by adjusting the Bézier handles that extend from the anchor points, or you can move the anchor points themselves. In this way, you can create any number of shape variations. For best results, make the grid visible so aligning anchor points isn't such a mystery.

Create Curved Line Segments

① Click the Pen tool in the Toolbar.

The pointer becomes a pen.

② Click on the Stage without releasing the mouse, drag up, and then release the mouse.

③ Position the pointer to the right of the original point, drag in the opposite direction of the curve, and then release the mouse when the curve is where you want it.

④ Continue adding points as needed. To end the path, double-click or return to the last anchor point drawn and click on it.

> **Did You Know?**
>
> ***You can select to Show Precise Cursors instead of the Tool icons in the General tab of the Preferences dialog box.*** When this option is selected, drawing tools, such as the Pen tool, appear as crosshairs for better precision and alignment to grids and guides.

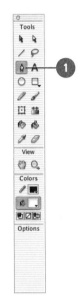

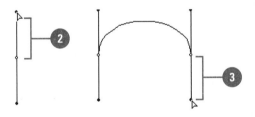

Curved line segment drawn

Create S-Curves

1. Click the Pen tool in the Toolbar.

   The pointer becomes a pen.

2. Click on the Stage without releasing the mouse, drag down, and then release the mouse.

3. Position the pointer to the right of the original point, drag in the same direction as the first drag, and then release the mouse when the curve is where you want it.

4. Continue adding points as needed. To end the path, double-click or return to the last anchor point drawn and click on it.

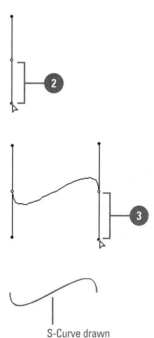

S-Curve drawn

Modifying Shapes with the Arrow Tool

In Flash, unlike other vector drawing programs, you can edit shapes and lines in a unique, freeform way by simply dragging with the Arrow Selection tool. You can quickly adjust the curve or corner of a shape or line without having to select anchor points or use any other tools. This way of editing shapes is also useful for creating shape tweens where amorphous, organic movement is desired. This is what sets Flash apart from other animation tools and gives it its distinctive style. Additionally, you can convert curved line segments into corner points with this simple drag technique.

Use the Arrow Tool to Modify a Shape

① Create a simple oval shape using the Oval tool.

② Click the Arrow tool in the Toolbar.

The pointer becomes an arrow.

③ Make sure the shape you want to modify is not selected.

④ Position the pointer on the edge of the shape, and then drag to modify the shape.

You can pull the curve to any position.

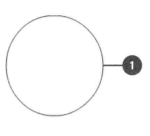

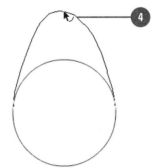

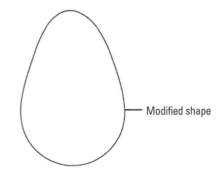

Modified shape

Convert Line Segments with the Arrow Tool

1. Create a simple oval shape using the Oval tool.

2. Click the Arrow tool in the Toolbar.

   The pointer becomes an arrow.

3. Make sure the shape you want to modify is not selected.

4. Position the pointer on the edge of the shape.

5. Press Option+drag (Mac) or Alt+drag (Win) to create a corner point.

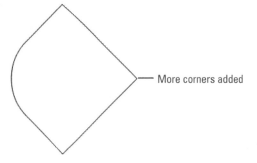

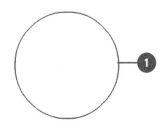

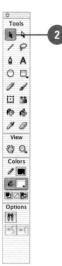

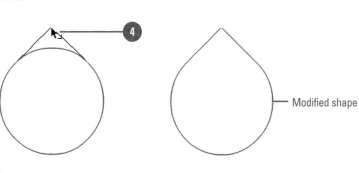

Modified shape

More corners added

Modifying Shapes with the Sub-Selection Tool

Vector shapes are made up of anchor points connected by line segments. There are two types of anchor points: corner points and curve points. Corner points connect two line segments in a sharp angle such as the corner of a square. Curve points define a curve or positions along a straight line and can be modified with Bézier handles. These handles extend out from the curve point and allow for very precise modification of the shape of the curve. The Sub-Selection tool works hand-in-hand with the Pen tool to create and modify shapes and lines in this way.

Use the Sub-Selection Tool to Modify a Shape

1. Create a simple oval shape using the Oval tool.

2. Click the Sub-Selection tool in the Toolbar.

   The pointer becomes an empty (or white) arrow.

3. Click on the edge of the shape to reveal the anchor points, and then click on an anchor point to select it or drag a selection rectangle to select multiple anchor points.

   The anchor points are the little white squares around the edge of the shape. When selected, Bézier handles appear on either side of the anchor point.

4. Grab one of the handles or the anchor points themselves and drag it, and then release the mouse.

Did You Know?

You can also use the arrow keys on the keyboard to move selected anchor points. Select one or more anchor points with the Sub-Selection tool, and then press the arrow keys to move the anchor point and its connected lines in the direction of the key you press.

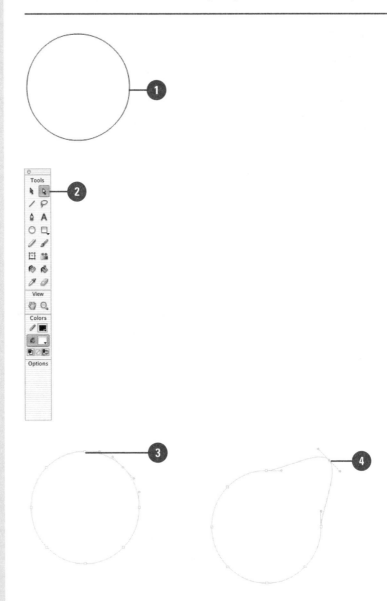

Convert Corner Points to Curve Points

1. Create a simple rectangle shape using the Rectangle tool.

2. Click the Sub-Selection tool in the Toolbar.

   The pointer becomes an empty (or white) arrow.

3. Click on the edge of the shape to select it and then click on one of the corner points to select it.

4. Press Option+drag (Mac) or Alt+drag (Win) the point to convert it to a curve point and create Bézier handles.

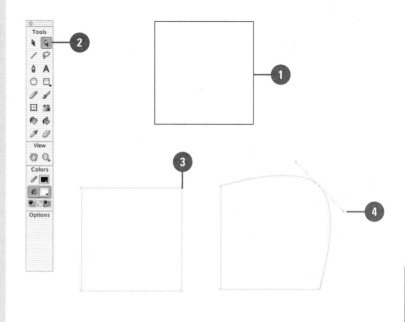

Convert Curve Points to Corner Points

1. Create a simple oval shape using the Oval tool.

2. Click the Pen tool in the Toolbar.

   The pointer becomes a small pen.

3. Click on the edge of the shape to reveal the anchor points.

4. Position the pointer over one of the curve points.

   A small corner icon appears.

5. Click on the point to convert it to a corner point.

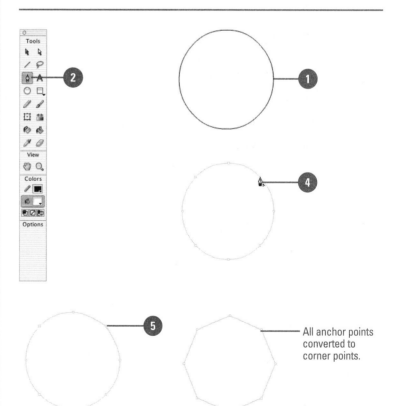

All anchor points converted to corner points.

3

Using the Free Transform Tool

There are a number of ways to change the scale or size of graphics in Flash. The Free Transform tool allows you to interactively scale and rotate any selected object or shape on the Stage. Nearly every object in Flash can be transformed with these two functions of the Free Transform tool including groups, symbols, text, bitmaps, and editable shapes. The Free Transform tool allows you to select an object on the Stage and then interactively change its size or rotate it freely. Both options are available at once depending on where you place your mouse on the bounding box that appears.

Change the Scale of an Object

1. Select the object by clicking on it or by dragging a selection marquee around it with the Arrow tool.

2. Click the Free Transform tool in the Toolbar.

   TIMESAVER *Press Q to select the Free Transform tool.*

3. Click the Scale Modifier button in the Options area of the Toolbar.

4. Drag any of the small handles on the bounding box to change the size of the shape. The corner handles resize proportionally while the handles along the sides resize either horizontally or vertically.

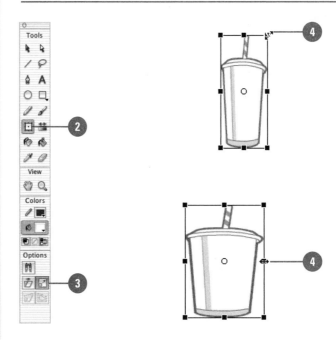

Rotate and Skew an Object

1. Select the object by clicking on it or by dragging a selection marquee around it.

2. Click the Free Transform tool in the Toolbar.

   TIMESAVER *Press Q to select the Free Transform tool.*

3. Click the Rotate/Skew Modifier button in the Options area of the Toolbar.

4. Drag any of the corner handles on the bounding box to rotate the shape. Drag the handles along the side to skew the object.

Did You Know?

You can hold down the Shift key to constrain the rotation scale proportionally. When rotating, it constrains the rotation to 45-degree turns.

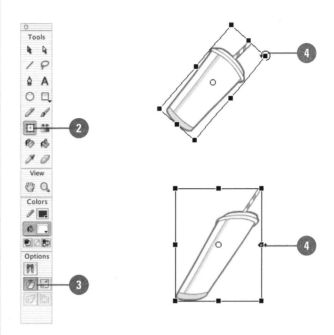

3

For Your Information

Working with Scale and Rotate

In the Default mode, both Scale and Rotate are enabled. Move the pointer to any of the four corner handles in the bounding box to enable the Rotate function. Scale and Rotate work relative to a center point on the shape, which becomes visible when the shape is selected with the Free Transform tool. Move this point if you want to scale or rotate a shape from a different part of the shape. This is especially important when Tweening and animating. You can change the scale and rotate objects by entering values in the Transform panel or in the Property Inspector. You can also access all of the Transform modes and some additional effects, such as Flip Horizontal and Vertical from the Transform submenu in the Modify menu.

Using Transform Options for Shapes

In addition to the scale and rotation changes that can be applied to groups, symbols, bitmaps, and text as well as editable shapes, there are two additional transforms available only to editable shapes. Distort and Envelope are two modes available in the Free Transform tool options that enable you to transform the vectors of editable shapes to varying degrees. Distort transformations work on adjoining edges, tapering them down to vanishing points, similar to perspective. Envelope transformations allow you to warp the edges of a shape by splitting it up into smaller portions each controlled by their own vectors and anchor points.

Distort a Shape

1. Select the object by clicking on it or by dragging a selection marquee around it.

2. Click the Free Transform tool in the Toolbar.

   TIMESAVER *Press Q to select the Free Transform tool.*

3. Click the Distort Modifier button in the Options area of the Toolbar.

4. Drag any of the corner handles on the bounding box to distort the shape.

5. Drag any of the side handles on the bounding box to skew or stretch the shape.

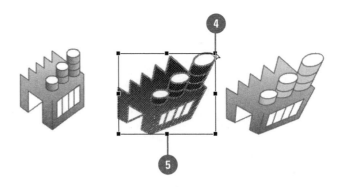

Change the Envelope of a Shape

1. Select the object by clicking on it or by dragging a selection marquee around it.

2. Click the Free Transform tool in the Toolbar.

   TIMESAVER *Press Q to select the Free Transform tool.*

3. Click the Envelope Modifier button in the Options area of the Toolbar.

4. Drag any of the handles on the bounding box to pull the shape in any direction or use the Bézier handles to fine tune the curves.

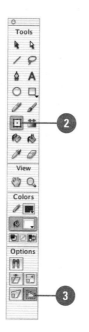

Cutting and Pasting Graphics Between Layers

Unless you lock or hide layers, or lock objects, the graphics on all layers are available for editing. You can select objects on one or more layers, cut or copy them, and then paste them all into a single layer. Flash can have only one layer active at a time. When you create and paste graphics, Flash places them on the active layer of a document. You can paste objects in two different ways: Paste In Center and Paste In Place. Paste In Center puts objects in the center of the open Flash window, which might not be the Stage. If you want to paste to the center of the Stage, you need to center the Stage in the open window. Paste In Place puts objects at the same location it had been when you cut or copied it.

Paste Objects Between Layers

1. Create or open a document with several layers.

2. Select one or more objects on the Stage.

   Flash selects the object's layer in the Timeline.

3. Click the Edit menu, and then click Cut or Copy.

4. Select a destination layer in the Timeline.

5. Click the Edit menu, and then click Paste In Center.

   Flash pastes the objects on the Stage in the middle of the active layer.

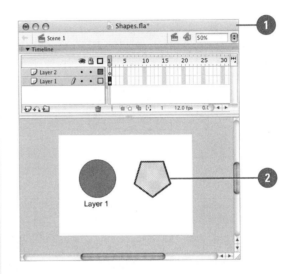

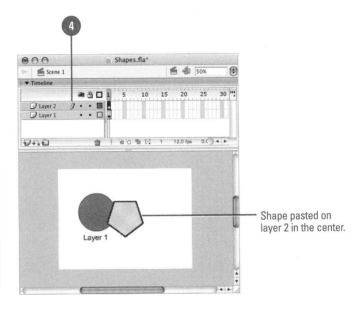

Shape pasted on layer 2 in the center.

Use the Paste In Place Command Between Layers

1. Create or open a document with several layers.

2. Select one or more objects on the Stage.

   Flash selects the object's layer in the Timeline.

3. Click the Edit menu, and then click Cut or Copy.

4. Select a destination layer in the Timeline.

5. Click the Edit menu, and then click Paste In Place.

   Flash pastes the objects into their original locations on the Stage in the middle of the active layer.

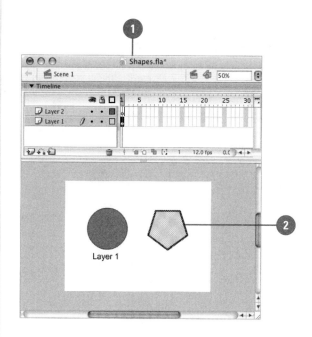

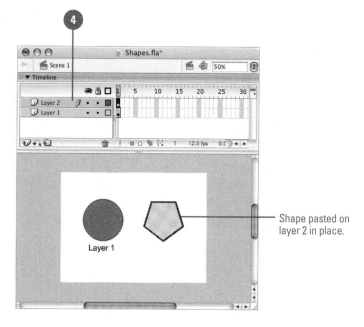

Shape pasted on layer 2 in place.

Working with Graphics on Different Layers

When you select an object on the Stage, Flash selects the object's layer in the Timeline. The reverse is also true. When you select a layer in the Timeline, Flash selects all the objects for that layer on the Stage. As you work with objects on different layers, it helps to know how selections work. Unless you lock or hide layers, or lock objects, the objects on all layers, either active or inactive, are available for editing. You can activate a layer and edit objects on inactive layers.

Edit Object on Inactive Layers

1. Create or open a document with several layers.

2. Click the Selection tool in the Toolbar.

3. Select an object on the Stage.

   Flash selects the object's layer in the Timeline.

4. Click a blank area of the Stage.

   Flash deselects the object but keeps the active layer.

5. Make changes to another object in another layer (inactive layer) without actually selecting the object. You can do any of the following:

   ◆ Drag an object's outline to reshape it.

   ◆ Select a tool on the Toolbar, such as the Paint Bucket tool, and use it to modify the object.

   Flash modifies the object in the inactive layer. The active layer didn't change. Flash changes active layers only if you select an object.

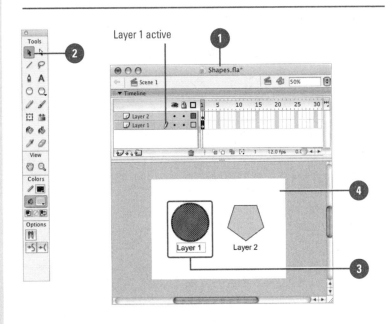

Layer 1 active

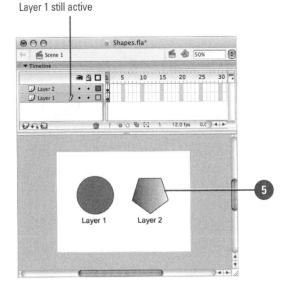

Layer 1 still active

Distributing Graphics to Layers

If you have several objects on a single layer, and need to move them onto separate layers, you can use Cut and Paste in place for each object or you can save time by using the Distribute to Layers command. The Distribute to Layers commands puts each object (shapes, groups, and symbols) in a selection on a separate layer; any unselected objects remain on their original layer. This command comes in handy when you want to create a motion tweening animation, which requires objects to be on individual layers.

Place Selected Objects on Separate Layers

1. Create or open a document with several objects on a single layer.

2. Select all the objects on a single layer you want to distribute to separate layers.

   TIMESAVER *Click the Edit menu, and then click Select All or press ⌘+A (Mac) or Ctrl+A (Win).*

3. Click the Modify menu, point to Timeline, and then click Distribute To Layers.

   TIMESAVER *Press ⌘+Shift+D (Mac) or Ctrl+Shift+D (Win) to distribute to layers.*

   Flash creates a layer for each object. New layers appear at the bottom of the Timeline in the order in which you originally placed them on the Stage. Each object is placed in the same location on the Stage (like the Paste In Place command).

> ### See Also
>
> *See Chapter 8, "Animating with Motion Tweening" on page 215 for information on using motion tweening.*

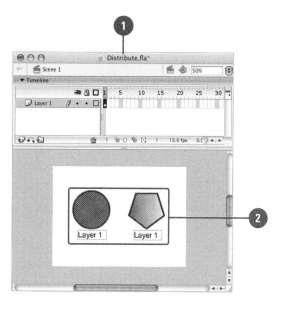

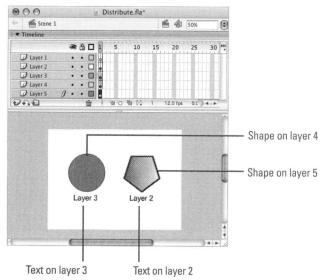

Shape on layer 4

Shape on layer 5

Text on layer 3

Text on layer 2

Working with Groups, Symbols, and Instances

4

Introduction

All vector art and objects are editable. As the complexity of your document increases, you can protect artwork from being inadvertently changed by storing it in special modes called groups and symbols. Groups provide a quick way to seal a shape by storing it in a bounding box that can only be edited by entering a group editing mode. Groups are created on the Stage and are not stored anywhere else. For items that are more global to your movie, you can convert them into symbols. The basis for interactivity and animation in Flash resides in its use of these reusable objects.

You can create artwork and then save that artwork as a symbol that is stored in the Library of your Flash document. Symbols are an efficient way to build your movies because you can reuse these assets as instances on the Timeline, and Flash will only store it in your file once. Apply ActionScript to control a movie clip symbol instance and to add interactivity, place art inside of button symbols to create hit states, or apply a variety of transparency and color effects to instances on the Stage. The Library stores all of the reusable art and objects in your movie including symbols, sounds, video clips, bitmaps, and components. It can be organized and sorted for easy access to your movie's assets. A Library can also be shared with other Flash documents.

Creating Groups

When you group artwork on the Stage, you prevent it from interacting with other artwork on the same layer. **Grouping** essentially stores the artwork in a bounding box that can only be edited by entering a special group editing mode, which you can easily do by double-clicking the group. For example, if you draw a shape over another shape on the same layer, the strokes and fills of the second shape will cut through or replace the strokes and fills of the shape directly beneath it. Grouping your artwork prevents this from happening. You can also use grouping to combine several shapes into one group so you can manipulate them simultaneously. You can ungroup artwork or objects that have been grouped by using the ungroup option or by breaking them apart. Doing so removes the bounding box and the artwork can be freely edited.

Group Artwork on the Same Layer

1. Select the artwork on the Stage that you want to group with any of Flash's selection tools or methods.

2. Click the Modify menu, and then click Group.

   TIMESAVER *Press* ⌘+G *(Mac) or Ctrl+G (Win) to quickly group selected objects or artwork.*

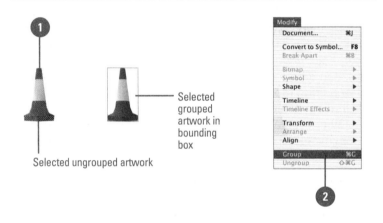

Selected ungrouped artwork

Selected grouped artwork in bounding box

Ungroup Artwork

1. Select the artwork on the Stage that you want to ungroup.

2. Click the Modify menu, and then click Ungroup.

   TIMESAVER *Press Shift+* ⌘+G *(Mac) or Shift+Ctrl+G (Win) to quickly ungroup selected objects or artwork.*

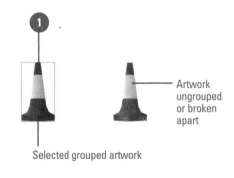

Artwork ungrouped or broken apart

Selected grouped artwork

See Also

See "Breaking Symbols Apart" *on page 145 for information on taking apart elements.*

Arranging Multiple Groups

When objects are grouped they appear on top of shapes that aren't grouped on the same layer. Each subsequent group that is created will appear on top of the last. This is called the stacking order. Flash allows you to change this order with the Arrange command. You can send a group or symbol to the bottom of this stack or bring one at the bottom to the top. Additionally, you can change the order incrementally.

Change the Stacking Order

① Select the group whose stacking order you want to change.

② Click the Modify menu, point to Arrange, and then click:

◆ **Bring To Front**. The selected object is brought to the top of the stack.

   TIMESAVER *Press Option+Shift+Up (Mac) or Ctrl+Shift+Up (Win).*

◆ **Bring Forward**. The selected object is brought up one level in the stacking order.

   TIMESAVER *Press ⌘+Up (Mac) or Ctrl+Up (Win).*

◆ **Send Backward**. The selected object is brought down one level in the stacking order.

   TIMESAVER *Press ⌘+Down (Mac) or Ctrl+Down (Win).*

◆ **Send To Back**. The selected object is brought to the bottom of the stack.

   TIMESAVER *Press Option+Shift+Down (Mac) or Ctrl+Shift+Down (Win).*

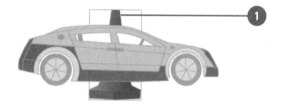

①

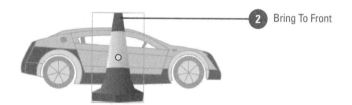

② Bring To Front

4

Using the Library

The **Library** is where all of the reusable assets in your Flash movie are stored. An asset is any artwork or object you have made into symbols, such as fonts, graphic symbols, movie clips, and buttons. Flash also stores bitmaps, sounds, video clips, and components in the Library. You can organize your Library assets into folders, sort the items, duplicate symbols or change their behavior. You can also open libraries from other Flash files to quickly transfer assets from one project to another.

Open the Library

1 Click the Window menu, and then click Library.

TIMESAVER *Press ⌘+L (Mac) or Ctrl+L (Win) to open the Library panel.*

Did You Know?

You can drag Library items in and out of folders. Simply select a Library item from the list and drag it to a folder you would like to store it in.

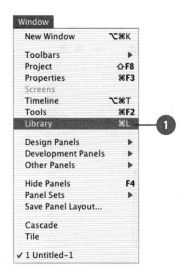

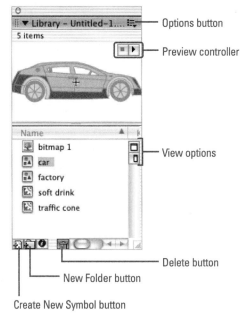

Options button

Preview controller

View options

Delete button

New Folder button

Create New Symbol button

Open Other Libraries

① Click the File menu, point to Import, and then click Open External Library.

TIMESAVER Press ⌘+Shift+O (Mac) or Ctrl+Shift+O (Win) to open the Open As Library dialog box.

② Navigate to the Flash movie containing the Library you want to open.

③ Select the file, and then click Open.

The Library appears docked underneath the Library of the active project.

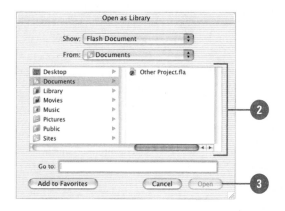

Imported Library

Access Library Options

① Click the Options button on the Library panel.

A menu of options for adding, deleting, and configuring Library items appears.

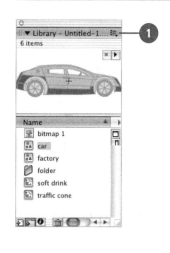

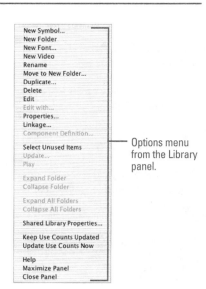

Options menu from the Library panel.

4

Creating Symbols

Using symbols is an efficient way to add artwork or elements to your Flash movie. When you create a symbol, it is stored in the Library where it can be reused as an instance in the Timeline. You can turn graphics or animations you've made into symbols or create a new one from scratch. There are three default behaviors for symbols you can choose from: graphic symbols, movie clips, and buttons. How you use the symbol will determine which of these three behaviors to use. Symbols have their own discrete Timelines. Think of a symbol as a package containing artwork that you can open and close. You enter a symbol editing mode to make changes and when you leave this mode the artwork is protected.

Create New Symbols

1 Click the Insert menu, and then click New Symbol.

   TIMESAVER *Press ⌘+F8 (Mac) or Ctrl+F8 (Win) to create a new symbol.*

2 Type a name for the symbol.

3 Select a Behavior option.

4 Click OK.

   Flash enters a special Symbol editing mode.

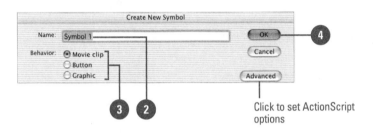

Click to set ActionScript options

Symbol editing mode indicator

Convert Existing Artwork into Symbols

1 Select the artwork on the Stage you want to make into a symbol.

2 Click the Modify menu, and then click Convert To Symbol.

   TIMESAVER *Press F8 to convert the artwork into a symbol.*

3 Type a name for the symbol.

4 Select a Behavior option.

5 Click OK.

   Symbol appears in the Library.

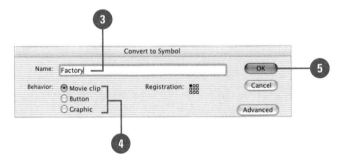

Convert Animations into Symbols

1. In the Timeline, select every frame in the animation that you want to make into a symbol.

2. Click the Edit menu, and then click Copy Frames.

   TIMESAVER *Press Option+⌘+C (Mac) or Ctrl+Alt+C (Win) to copy frames.*

3. Click the Insert menu, and then click New Symbol.

4. Type a name for the symbol.

5. Select a movie clip or graphic symbol behavior.

6. Click OK.

   Flash enters a special Symbol editing mode.

7. Select the first frame of the Timeline.

8. Click the Edit menu, and then click Paste Frames.

   TIMESAVER *Press Option+⌘+V (Mac) or Ctrl+Alt+V (Win) to paste frames.*

See Also

See "Editing in Symbol Mode" on page 130 for information on editing symbols in symbol editing mode.

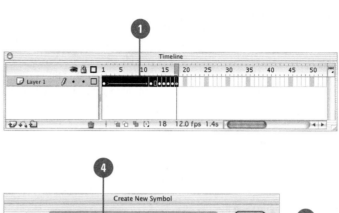

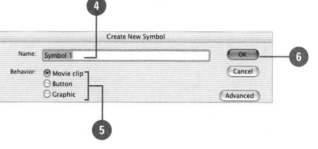

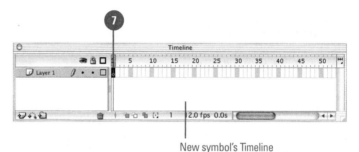

New symbol's Timeline

4

Editing in Symbol Mode

When you need to change or modify a symbol you must enter a special symbol editing mode. Entering this mode allows you to view and edit the symbol's Timeline. Any changes you make are stored in the Library and all other instances of the symbol are updated with these changes. You can choose to enter the symbol mode, entirely replacing the view of the main Timeline, or view the symbol in context to the main Timeline. Additionally, you can open the symbol mode in a new window.

Enter Symbol Editing Mode

1. Select the symbol you want to modify.

2. Click the Edit menu, and then click Edit Symbols.

   Selecting Edit Symbols centers the symbol based on its registration point in the symbol editing work area. The Timeline is not visible.

   TIMESAVER *Press ⌘+E (Mac) or Ctrl+E (Win) to enter symbol editing mode.*

3. Modify the symbol or its Timeline.

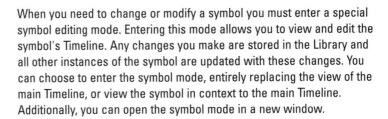
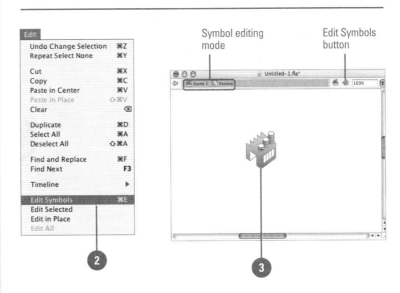

Did You Know?

You can use the Edit Symbols button to access any symbol stored in the Library. When you click the Edit Symbols button in the Edit bar, a list of symbols stored in the Library appears from which you can select.

For Your Information

Entering and Viewing a Symbol's Editing Mode

There are two additional modes for viewing a symbol's editing mode: Edit In Place and Edit In New Window. You can access these options from the Edit menu or from the context-sensitive menus by Control-clicking (Mac) or right-clicking (Win) the instance on the Stage.

Edit In Place. Preserves the view of the symbol's position in the main Timeline, dimming everything else in the main Timeline. This feature is useful when you need to see a symbol's placement relative to other elements in the main Timeline as you edit it. To quickly Edit in Place, double-click the instance on the Stage.

Edit In New Window. Opens the symbol's Timeline in a new window.

Additionally, you can select the symbol from the Edit Symbol popup on the right side of the Information bar above the Timeline.

Exit Symbol Editing Mode

① When you are finished making changes to a symbol, you can return to the main Timeline in several ways:

◆ Click the Back button or the Scene name on the Edit bar to return to the parent scene.

◆ Click the Edit Scene button on the Edit bar, and then click another Scene name.

◆ Click the Edit menu, and then click Edit Document to return to the main Timeline.

◆ Press ⌘+E (Mac) or Ctrl+E (Win).

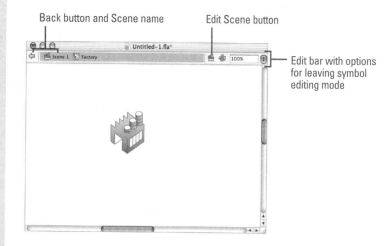

Back button and Scene name   Edit Scene button

Edit bar with options for leaving symbol editing mode

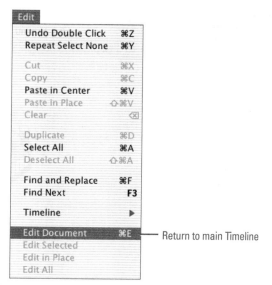

Edit		
Undo Double Click	⌘Z
Repeat Select None	⌘Y
Cut	⌘X
Copy	⌘C
Paste in Center	⌘V
Paste in Place	⇧⌘V
Clear	⌫
Duplicate	⌘D
Select All	⌘A
Deselect All	⇧⌘A
Find and Replace	⌘F
Find Next	F3
Timeline	▶
Edit Document	⌘E
Edit Selected	
Edit in Place	
Edit All	

Return to main Timeline

4

Creating Instances

When you use a symbol in your Timeline you are using an **instance** of it. You can animate an instance of a symbol and apply a variety of effects to it without affecting the original symbol in the Library. You can also use multiple instances of the same symbol. When you change the properties of an instance in the Timeline, you are only applying these changes to that copy, or instance, of the symbol. In this way, you keep the file size down because Flash only keeps track of the changes you've made while preserving the symbol in the form you created. If you have several instances of a symbol in your movie and you want to edit the artwork, you can make changes to the master symbol. When you do this all of the instances of that symbol will be updated with these changes.

Place Instances on the Stage

1 Open or expand the Library panel.

TIMESAVER *Press F11 or ⌘+L (Mac) or Ctrl+L (Win) to quickly open and close the Library panel.*

2 Select the symbol from the list of assets and drag it to the Stage to create an instance of that symbol.

TIMESAVER *Drag the preview image of a symbol selected in the Library item list to create an instance of that symbol on the Stage.*

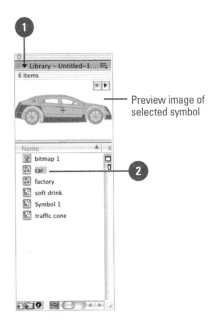

Preview image of selected symbol

Filled keyframe indicates instance is placed on the Stage.

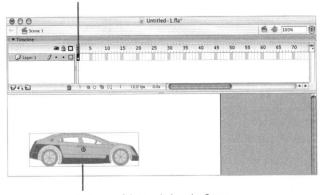

Instance of the symbol on the Stage

Edit Master Symbols

1. Double-click any instance of a symbol you want to edit.

2. Make changes to the symbol artwork or animation.

3. Click the Back button or Scene name on the Edit bar to return to the main Timeline.

   All of the instances reflect these changes.

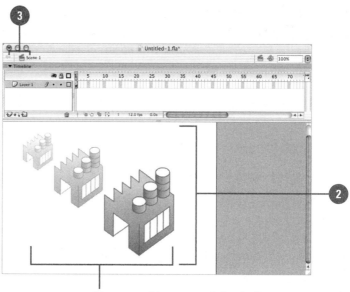

3 instances of the same symbol on the Stage.

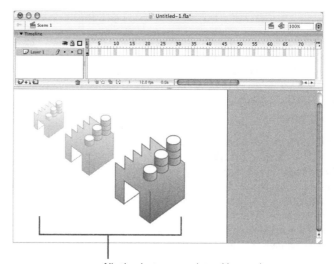

All other instances update with new changes.

4

Changing Symbol and Instance Behaviors

Symbols have three specific behaviors that are set when you first create the symbol: graphic, movie clip, and button. You can change these behaviors on a symbol's instance by selecting it and setting a new behavior in the Property Inspector. Do this when you need the instance to display a behavior different than its parent symbol. Alternately, you can change the behavior of the parent symbol itself in the Library. All subsequent instances that you create from this symbol will exhibit the new behavior.

Change a Symbol's Behavior

1. Open or expand the Library panel.

2. Select the symbol from the list.

3. Click the Properties button at the bottom of the Library window to open the Symbol Properties dialog box.

4. Click a different symbol Behavior option.

5. Click OK.

The symbol displays a new behavior. All subsequent instances will default to this behavior.

Did You Know?

If you are already using instances of a symbol in your movie, they will not be affected by a change in behavior. Flash allows you to change the behaviors of instances separately from your symbol's default behavior. To update the instance to a new behavior, select it on the Stage, and then change the behavior in the Property Inspector.

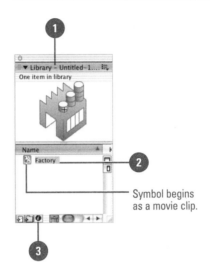

Symbol begins as a movie clip.

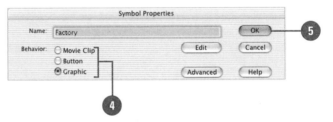

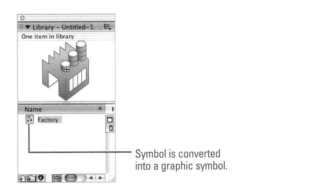

Symbol is converted into a graphic symbol.

Change the Symbol Behavior of an Instance

① If necessary, open the Property Inspector.

② Select the instance on the Stage.

③ Click the Symbol Behavior popup in the Property Inspector, and then select another behavior: Movie Clip, Button, or Graphic.

Did You Know?

You can use a method to change the symbol behavior of any instance. Select from any of the three options: graphic symbol, button, or movie clip. In this way, you can get graphic symbols to behave as movie clips, movie clips to behave like buttons, etc.

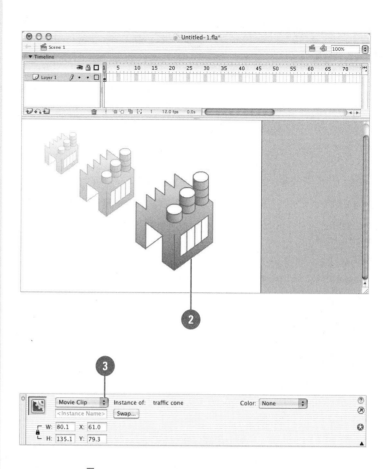

Symbol behavior options for instances

4

Swapping Symbol Instances

Symbols are used in the Timeline as instances. If you apply motion or color effects to an instance, you only affect that instance, not its parent symbol. If you would like to swap the parent symbol for another symbol, while retaining any effects and/or animation that have been applied to the instance, you can use the Swap Symbol feature. All of the effects are preserved but are instead applied to and referencing the new chosen symbol. Alternately, if you are using several instances of a symbol and want to change the content (the master symbol itself) of one of these instances without affecting the other instances, you can duplicate and swap that symbol in the Swap dialog box. Essentially you create a new master symbol linked to your instance that is no longer related to the original master symbol and all its instances.

Swap Instances

1. If necessary, open the Property Inspector.

2. Select the instance on the Stage.

3. Click Swap in the Property Inspector to open the Swap Symbol dialog box.

   TIMESAVER *Control+click (Mac) or right-click (Win) the instance on the Stage, and then click Swap Symbol.*

4. Click a symbol from the list.

5. Click OK.

   The instance is now linked to a new symbol.

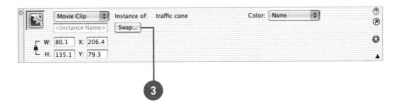

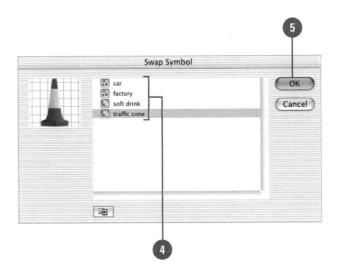

Duplicate Symbols During Swap

1. Select the instance on the Stage.

2. Click Swap in the Property Inspector.

3. Click the Duplicate Symbol icon in the bottom left-hand corner of the dialog box.

4. Enter a new name.

5. Click OK.

    The instance is now linked to a new symbol, copied from the original master symbol.

6. Click OK.

See Also

See "Breaking Symbols Apart" on page 145 for information on breaking symbols apart in symbol editing mode.

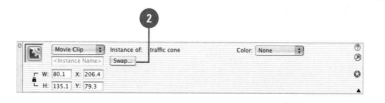

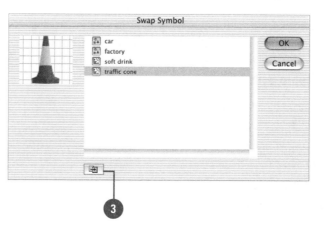

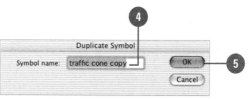

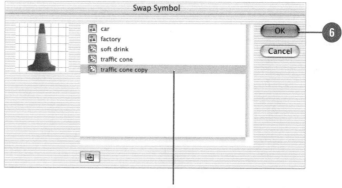

New master symbol created

4

Using Graphic Symbols

Graphic symbols can be used for static images and for animations that are in sync with the main Timeline. There are three instance options available to them: Loop, Play Once, and Single Frame. Set the instance to Loop if you want the symbol's Timeline to play continuously. Play Once plays the Timeline of a graphic symbol once and then stops. Single frame sets the instance to display as a single frame contained in the graphic symbol's Timeline. Unlike movie clip symbols, an animation contained in a graphic symbol can be seen in the main Timeline without having to export the Flash movie. However, any ActionScript and sounds that have been included in a graphic symbol's Timeline will not work.

Create a Graphic Symbol

1. Click the Insert menu, and then click New Symbol.

   TIMESAVER *Press ⌘+F8 (Mac) or Ctrl+F8 (Win) to create a new symbol.*

2. Type in a name for the symbol.

3. Select the Graphic option.

4. Click OK.

   Flash enters a symbol editing mode that contains an empty Timeline for that symbol.

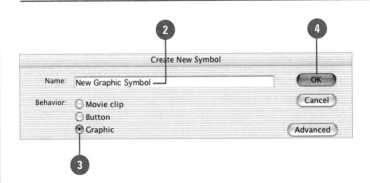

Did You Know?

Graphic symbol animations are synced up to the main Timeline. For example, if the animation in the graphic symbol spans 10 frames, the instance in the main Timeline must also span 10 frames if the entire animation is to be seen.

Change the Options for Graphic Symbol Instances

1. Select a graphic symbol instance on the Stage.

2. Click the popup in the Property Inspector, and then select from the following graphic options:

   ◆ **Loop.** The Timeline in the graphic symbol will loop continuously.

   ◆ **Play Once.** The Timeline in the graphic symbol will play once and stop. If there is no animation in the symbol or if there is only artwork on one frame, it will be treated as a static graphic.

   ◆ **Single Frame.** Sets the instance to a single frame in the Timeline of the master symbol. When this is selected, the graphic symbol is treated as a static graphic.

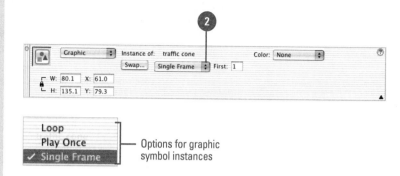

Options for graphic symbol instances

4

Using Button Symbols

Use buttons to add interactivity to your movie. Button symbols have their own four-frame Timeline. The first three frames define the states of the button: up, over, and down. The first frame is the Up state, which is the appearance of the button when in its normal, non-active state. The second frame is the Over state, which is triggered when the user places their mouse over the button. The third frame is the Down state, which appears when the user presses the button with their mouse. The fourth frame—which is invisible outside of the symbol editing mode—defines the active area. This is the area that the user must place their mouse over to activate the other states of the button. You can assign actions to instances of buttons that tell Flash what to do when the button is clicked.

Create a Button

1 Click the Insert menu, and then click New Symbol.

TIMESAVER Press ⌘+F8 (Mac) or Ctrl+F8 (Win) to create a new symbol.

2 Select the Button option.

3 Click OK.

4 Place artwork in the keyframe of the first frame.

This represents the button's Up state, its normal inactive state.

5 Click the Insert menu, point to Timeline, and then click Keyframe to add a keyframe in the second frame (the Over state).

TIMESAVER Press F6 to quickly add a keyframe and press F7 to add a blank keyframe.

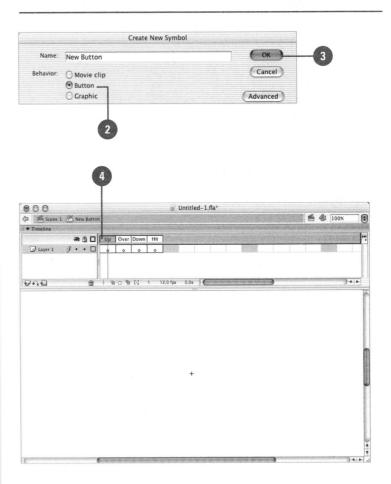

6 Change the artwork or add new artwork in this frame.

7 Click the Insert menu, point to Timeline, and then click Keyframe to add a keyframe in the third frame (the Down state).

8 Alter the artwork or add new artwork in this frame.

9 Click the Insert menu, point to Timeline, and then click Keyframe to add a keyframe in the fourth frame (the active area).

10 Add a simple graphic (a rectangle or oval, for example) to define the active area.

11 Click the Control menu, and then click Test Movie to test your button by exporting the movie.

TIMESAVER *Press ⌘+Return (Mac) or Ctrl+Enter (Win) to test your button.*

See Also

See "Enabling and Disabling Buttons" on page 142 for information on turning buttons on and off.

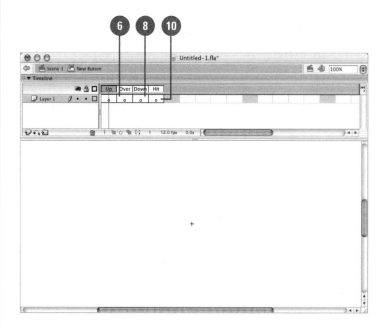

Enabling and Disabling Buttons

Flash allows you to test your buttons within the development environment without having to export the movie. You can test the behavior of simple buttons by toggling the Enable Simple Buttons feature on and off. When buttons are enabled, you can't select them or enter their symbol editing mode normally. Disable this feature if you need to enter the symbol mode. You can quickly see how the different states of your button behave without having to export the whole flash movie. Any ActionScript applied to the button will be ignored.

Enable and Disable Buttons

① Place a button on the Stage.

② Click the Control menu, and then click Enable Simple Buttons to enable the button.

> **TIMESAVER** *Press Option+⌃⌘+B (Mac) or Ctrl+Alt+B (Win) to toggle the enabling and disabling of simple buttons.*

③ Place the mouse over the button to test the Over state.

④ Press down on the button to test the Down state.

⑤ Click the Control menu, and then click Disable Simple Buttons to disable the button.

Did You Know?

Regardless of whether buttons are enabled or disabled, they will be functional when you export your movie. The Enable Simple Buttons command is only relevant to the Flash development environment.

See Also

See "Using Button Symbols" on page 140 for information on creating a button.

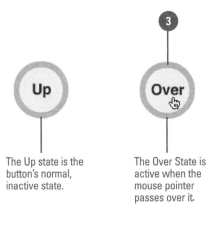

The Up state is the button's normal, inactive state.

The Over State is active when the mouse pointer passes over it.

The Down State is active when the mouse pointer presses down on it.

Creating Invisible Buttons

Buttons do not require graphics to be placed in the hit state frames (the first three frames). As long as the active area contains a shape, the button will be invisible but will be functional and ActionScript can be applied to it. The active area is the fourth frame in the button symbol Timeline. An instance of an invisible button appears as a transparent blue shape in the main Timeline, but will not be visible in the exported movie.

Create an Invisible Button

1. Click the Insert menu, and then click New Symbol.

   TIMESAVER *Press ⌘+F8 (Mac) or Ctrl+F8 (Win) to create a new symbol.*

2. Click the Button option.

3. Click OK.

4. Click the Insert menu, point to Timeline, and then click Keyframe to add a keyframe in the fourth frame (the active area).

   TIMESAVER *Press F6 to create a keyframe.*

5. Add a simple graphic (a rectangle or oval, for example) to define the active area.

6. Make sure the first three frames remain empty.

7. Return to the main Timeline.

8. Drag the invisible button from the Library to the Stage.

   Invisible buttons appear as transparent blue shapes but are invisible in the final export.

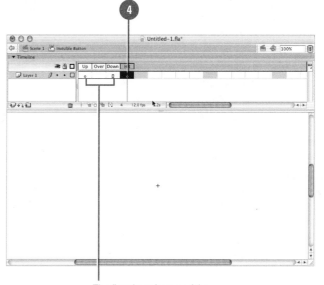

The first three frames of the button remain empty.

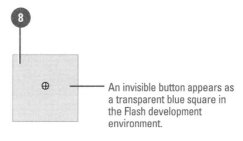

An invisible button appears as a transparent blue square in the Flash development environment.

Using Movie Clip Symbols

Movie clip symbols operate independently on the main Timeline. When you want an animation to loop on a single frame in the Timeline, you can store this animation in the Timeline of a movie clip that will sit on this frame. Movie clip instances can have actions applied to them and can be controlled from anywhere in the Flash movie through ActionScript. They can contain animations, interactive controls, sounds, and even other movie clips. Unlike graphic symbols, you can only see the first frame of the movie clip in the main Timeline. Export your movie to see the movie clip play.

Create and View Movie Clips Symbols

1. Click the Insert menu, and click New Symbol.

2. Click the Movie Clip option.

3. Click OK.

4. Add your content to the Movie Clip Timeline.

5. Return to the main Timeline by clicking the Back button or the Scene name on the Edit bar.

6. Drag the movie clip symbol you just created to the Stage from the Library.

7. Click the Control menu, and then click Test Movie to test the movie clip symbol by exporting the movie.

   TIMESAVER *Press* ⌘+*Return (Mac) or Ctrl+Enter (Win) to quickly test your movie.*

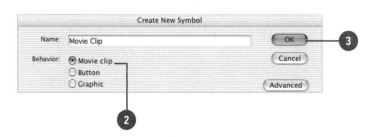

Breaking Symbols Apart

Sometimes you'll need to break a symbol instance so that it is no longer linked to the master symbol. You might do this if you want to add something to the symbol without affecting the other instances. In this way, the content inside the symbol will become a simple graphic that you can adjust without affecting the master symbol you made it from or any of its instances.

Break an Instance

1. Select an instance on the Stage you would like to break.

2. Click the Modify menu, and then click Break Apart.

   TIMESAVER Press ⌘+B (Mac) or Ctrl+B (Win) to quickly break apart a symbol.

See Also

See "Swapping Symbol Instances" on page 136 for information on swapping symbol instances.

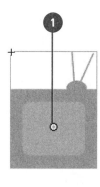

Symbol broken apart into an editable shape.

4

Modifying Instance Properties

You can alter the properties of an instance of a symbol without affecting the master symbol. Any transform applied to an instance can be animated with motion tweening. Flash will gradually draw the frames in between one transform to another. This is how you create movement in Flash. Change the scale of an instance or rotate and skew it. You can perform these functions interactively with the Free Transform tool. You can also add values in the Transform panel, or access additional Transform options in the program's Modify menu. Distort and Envelope cannot be applied to instances and are disabled in the Toolbar options when the Free Transform tool is selected.

Modify the Scale or Rotation

1. Select the instance on the Stage.

2. Click the Free Transform tool in the Toolbar.

   TIMESAVER *Press Q to quickly select the Free Transform tool.*

3. Click the Scale or Rotate Modifier button in the Options section of the Toolbar.

4. Drag the small handles around the bounding box to change the size of the instance or rotate it.

> ### Did You Know?
>
> ***You can select multiple instances and change their properties simultaneously.*** Press Shift+select each instance you would like to alter in tandem. A bounding box will appear around all selected instances.

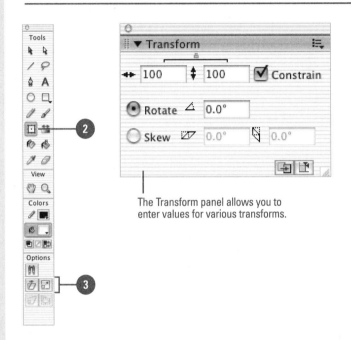

The Transform panel allows you to enter values for various transforms.

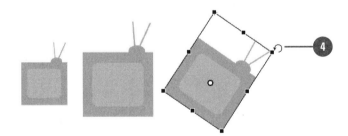

Use Additional Transform Commands

1. Select the instance on the Stage.

2. Click the Modify menu, point to Transform, and then click one of the following:

   ◆ **Free Transform.** Transforms the object freely.

   ◆ **Scale.** Constrains the transform to scale.

   ◆ **Rotate And Skew.** Constrains the transform to rotate and skew.

   ◆ **Scale And Rotate.** Constrains the transform to scale and rotation changes.

   ◆ **Rotate 90° CW.** Rotates the selected object 90° clockwise.

   ◆ **Rotate 90° CCW.** Rotates the selected object 90° counter-clockwise.

   ◆ **Flip Vertical.** Flips the object along a vertical axis.

   ◆ **Flip Horizontal.** Flips the object along a horizontal axis.

   ◆ **Remove Transform.** Removes any transform effects applied to the selected instance.

Transforms objects freely

Constrain transforms

Rotate commands

Flip commands

Removes all applied Transform effects

Did You Know?

Changing the scale or rotation of an instance can also be done in the Transform panel. The Modify menu includes additional transform commands not available anywhere else. Simply select the instance, and then access these panels.

4

Modifying Instance Color Styles

Change the tint, brightness, or transparency of an instance in the Color popup located in the Property Inspector. This feature appears whenever an instance is selected on the Stage. If you would like to add a color to the instance you can do so by selecting the Tint color style. Choose a color and then choose the amount of color that will be applied. You can adjust the Brightness of an instance (that is, how much white or black will be added) by choosing the Brightness color style. An instance can also be made transparent. Altering the Alpha of the instance does this. An Alpha of zero will make the instance invisible though it can still be selected and animated. Use this feature when you want an object to fade on or off the Stage. If you need to apply a color style with alpha you must use the Advanced option.

Modify the Brightness

1. Select the instance on the Stage.

2. Click the Color popup in the Property Inspector, and then click Brightness.

3. Enter a value between -100 and 100 (-100= no brightness, black, 100= maximum brightness, white).

   TIMESAVER *You can use the slider to the right of the field to interactively change the level of Brightness applied.*

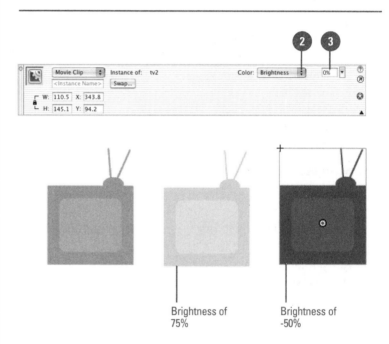

Brightness of 75%

Brightness of -50%

Modify the Tint Color

1. Select the instance on the Stage.

2. Click the Color popup in the Property Inspector, and then click Tint.

3. Click a color from the color box popup or enter an RGB value in the fields.

4. Enter a value between 0 and 100 (0= no color, 100= maximum saturation).

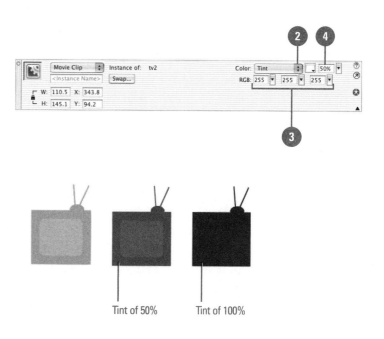

Tint of 50%   Tint of 100%

Modify the Transparency

1. Select the instance on the Stage.

2. Click the Color popup in the Property Inspector, and then click Alpha.

3. Enter a value between 0 and 100 (0= invisible, 100= fully visible).

> **TIMESAVER** *You can use the slider to the right of the field to interactively change the level of Alpha applied.*

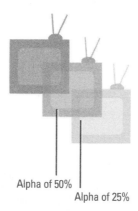

Alpha of 50%
Alpha of 25%

4

Using Advanced Color Options

An instance can only have one color style (Brightness, Tint, or Alpha) applied. To apply multiple color styles you must use the Advanced feature in the Property Inspector's Color popup menu. This option allows you to change the percentage of Red, Green, or Blue (0% -100%) added or subtracted as well as the constant values of RGB (-255 to +255). Additionally there is an Alpha scale that can be applied to each of these options. Apply a color, brightness, or alpha style to an instance and then access the Advanced options to make adjustments. The applied color style is preserved. Experiment with this features until you get the effects that you need.

Modify the Color and Transparency Simultaneously

1. Select the instance on the Stage.

2. Click the Color popup in the Property Inspector, and then click Tint, Brightness or Alpha and apply an effect.

3. Click the Color popup again, and then click Advanced.

4. Click Settings to open the Advanced Effect dialog box.

5. Add or subtract percentages or values of RGB and Alpha.

6. Click OK.

Did You Know?

You can go directly to the Advanced panel to add color effects without having applied any Brightness, Tint, or Alpha. If you have already chosen one of these options and then enter the Advanced settings, your previous applied effect will be preserved and the sliders in the Advanced Settings window will reflect this change. For example, if you have added a tint of red to your instance, the sliders in the Advanced setting will show that red has been added.

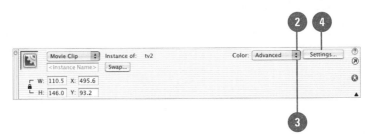

Reduce the color values or alpha by a percentage

Increase or decrease the constant color or alpha values

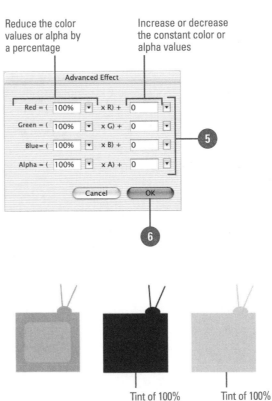

Tint of 100%

Tint of 100%
Alpha of 25%

Working with Text

Introduction

In Flash MX 2004 you can create editable text fields for use as static display text or to implement dynamic text objects with the Text tool. In the program's text menu, as well as the Property Inspector, there are a number of attributes to choose from such as Font type, size, color, indentation, and orientation. Also included are familiar letterform formatting procedures for kerning, tracking, and anti-aliasing. Because text fields are editable, you can change any text attribute—as well as the content in the text field—after it is created.

Use the Break Apart command to break editable text fields into shapes and edit them with any of the selection tools or pen modifiers. This is especially useful for creating new font forms and it also allows you to implement shape tweening. Create dynamic text fields that can be updated from a text file on a server or some other source using ActionsScript. In Flash MX 2004 you can now configure the Find and Replace feature to target text contained in specific elements in your Flash document and swap these out with new entries from the built-in Macromedia dictionaries or from a personal dictionary you create yourself. Find and Replace makes navigating the text in large complex files much simpler. Other new features include new implementation of Cascading Style Sheets for consistent HTML text formatting and the new built-in Spell Checker for enhanced productivity.

What You'll Do

Create Static Text

Change Font Type, Size, and Color

Modify Kerning and Tracking

Change Text Direction and Orientation

Change Text Alignment

Use Break Apart to Modify Characters

Use Alias Text

Use Font Mapping

Set Device Fonts Versus Embedded Fonts

Create Dynamic Text and Input Text

Set Dynamic Text and Input Text Options

Use Cascading Style Sheets with HTML Text

Check Spelling

Use Find and Replace

Creating Static Text

Static text refers to any text field that isn't dynamic or input text. It's generally used for displaying information or for animation. Text created in Flash is editable, which means that you can continue to change it after it is created. This includes changing its attributes as well as the textual content (the letters it contains). The Text tool creates an editable text box wherever you touch down on the Stage. Flash will keep the text on a single line until you hit the Return key. If you need a text box with a predefined width, you can create a text box before you start typing. The entered text will automatically wrap relative to the boundaries of the box and any formatting settings you've applied. To re-enter an existing text box to change the text, simply double-click any character in the Text box or click it with the Text tool to activate it and make it ready to edit.

Create Static Text

1. Click the Text tool in the Toolbar.

   The pointer becomes a crosshair with a small "A" in the corner.

   TIMESAVER *Press T to quickly select the Text tool.*

2. Click the Stage where you want your text box to begin.

3. Begin typing in the box that appears.

4. When you're finished, click anywhere on the Stage outside the text field.

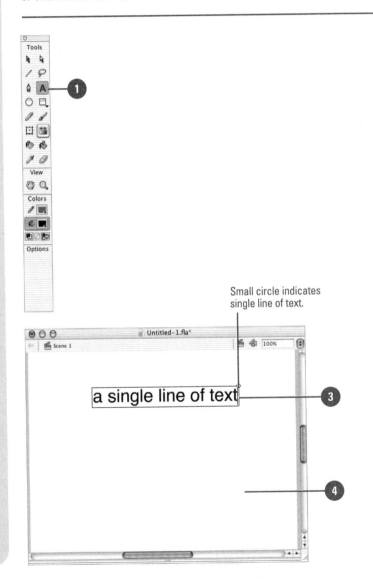

Small circle indicates single line of text.

a single line of text

Create a Text Box

1 Click the Text tool in the Toolbar.

The pointer becomes a crosshair with a small "A" in the corner.

TIMESAVER *Press T to quickly select the Text tool.*

2 Click the Stage where you want your text box to begin and drag until the box is the size you need.

3 Begin typing in the box that appears.

4 When you're finished click anywhere on the Stage outside the text field.

Did You Know?

You can change the size of an existing text box. With the text box active, drag the small circle (single line) or square (text block) to resize. The text in the field wraps to accommodate to the new size.

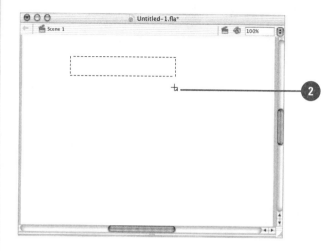

Small square indicates text box

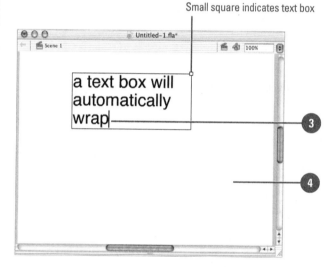

5

Changing Font Type, Size, and Color

Flash includes a number of text properties to choose from. These include a Font type, size, color, and style. You can set these attributes before you create a text field or alter them on existing text. To make changes to the entire text field, select it with the Arrow tool without entering the field (or making it active). Any changes made are applied to the whole field. A text box is considered "active" when the background of the field is an opaque white and text can be entered into it (as opposed to just being selected on the Stage, when it appears in a bounding box). If you only want to change a portion of the field, enter the text field and select only those characters or words you want to change. Attributes such as font type, size, and color as well as more advanced text properties can be easily accessed in the Property Inspector. When the Text tool or any text field is selected, the Property Inspector displays all of the available attributes.

Change the Font Type and Size

1. Select the text field you want to change with the Arrow tool or select text within the text field with the Text tool.

2. Click the Font Name in the Property Inspector, and then select a font size.

3. Enter a point value in the Size entry box or click the Size popup, and then select a font size.

Did You Know?

You can change the font type, size, and style in the Text menu. Click the Text menu, point to Font, Size, or Style, and then select an option.

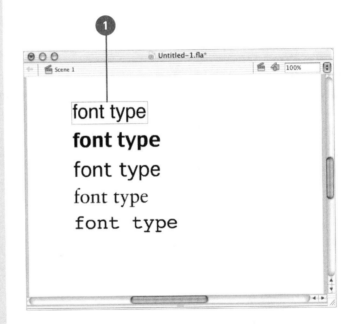

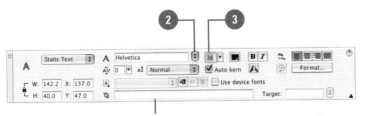

The Property Inspector displays text attributes whenever any text field is selected on the Stage.

Change the Font Color

① Select the text field you want to change with the Arrow tool, or select text within the text field with the Text tool.

② Click the Color popup in the Property Inspector, and then select a fill color.

Did You Know?

You can change the text color in any of the color palettes. Change the fill color of any selected text field by clicking on any of the color palettes. They are located in the Toolbar, the Color Mixer panel, and the Color Swatches panel.

The Property Inspector displays text attributes whenever any text field is selected on the Stage.

5

Modifying Tracking and Kerning

Sometimes the space between text characters can appear awkward or perhaps increasing the space is a creative solution. Flash provides methods for adjusting these spaces, called kerning and tracking. **Tracking** is the space between characters and words on a single line and adjusting tracking affects the entire line. **Kerning** deals with the space between any two characters and adjusting it will only affect that space. Many Fonts contain built-in information about problematic character pairs. Flash makes use of this information when you turn on Auto Kern in the Property Inspector.

Adjust Tracking

1. Select the text in a text field you want to track or you can select the entire text box with the Arrow tool.

2. Click the Text menu, point to Tracking, and then click Increase or Decrease.

   The Tracking increases or decreases in 0.5-point increments.

   TIMESAVER *You can adjust tracking in the Property Inspector with the Character Spacing entry field or slider.*

Did You Know?

You can quickly adjust kerning or tracking using the keyboard. Select the text or text field (to track) or place the cursor between two characters, and then press Option+⌘+right arrow (Mac) or Ctrl+Alt+right arrow (Win) to increase the space or Option+⌘+left arrow (Mac) or Ctrl+Alt+left arrow (Win) to decrease the space. Holding down the Shift key with this keyboard shortcut adjusts the space in larger increments.

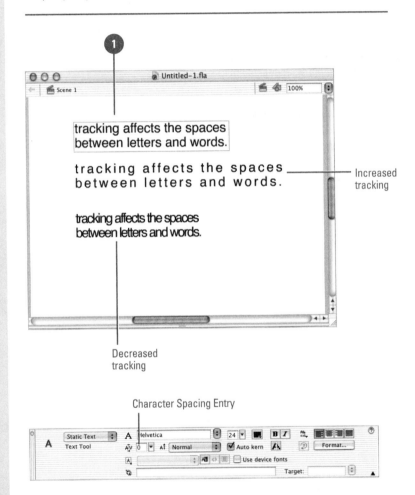

Increased tracking

Decreased tracking

Character Spacing Entry

Adjust Kerning

1. Enter a text field on the Stage by double-clicking on it.

2. Place the cursor between the two characters you want to kern.

3. Click the Text menu, point to Tracking, and then click Increase or Decrease.

Did You Know?

You can reset tracking and kerning to its default value. Click the Text menu, point to Tracking, and then click Reset, or press Option+⌘+Up arrow (Mac) or Ctrl+Alt+Up arrow (Win).

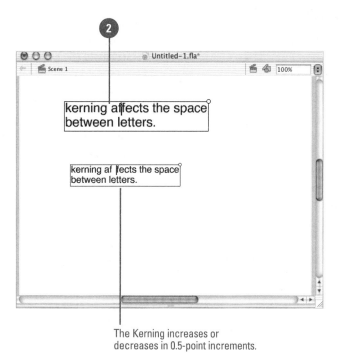

The Kerning increases or decreases in 0.5-point increments.

Set Auto Kerning

1. Select a text field with the Arrow tool.

2. Select the Auto Kern check box in the Property Inspector.

   Auto kern is enabled for that text field.

Auto Kerning can correct problematic character combinations.

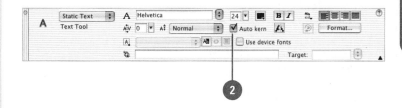

5

Changing Text Direction and Orientation

In addition to a variety of properties that can be applied to text in Flash, there are also procedures for changing the orientation and direction of text. Included is a formatting option for creating vertical text automatically without using any of the Transform commands. When text orientation is set to be vertical, the characters appear in columns though they remain in their normal horizontal orientation. If you need the text to rotate ninety degrees and so follow the orientation of the line, you can set it to rotate automatically in the Property Inspector. This is useful if you are looking for something other than a column. The orientation of the text becomes vertical.

Create a Single Column of Vertical Text

1. Click the Text tool in the Toolbar.

2. Click the Change Direction popup in the Property Inspector, and then click Vertical, Left To Right, or Vertical, Right To Left.

3. Click the Stage where you want your text box to begin, and then start typing in the box that appears.

   TIMESAVER *Press Return (Mac) or Enter (Win) to create a new column.*

4. When you're finished, click on the Stage outside the text field.

Did You Know?

You can convert an existing text field into a vertical text field. Select the text field on the Stage, click the Change Direction popup in the Property Inspector, and then select a vertical option.

You can make vertical text the default orientation. Select the Default Text Orientation check box in the Editing tab of the Preferences dialog box. This can be useful when working in some Asian languages.

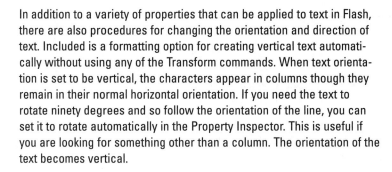

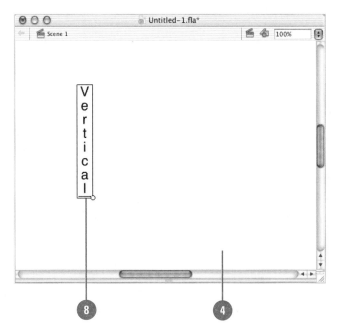

Create a Vertical Text Block

1. Click the Text tool in the Toolbar.

2. Click the Change Direction popup, and then click Vertical, Left To Right, or Vertical, Right To Left.

3. Click the Stage where you want your text box to begin and drag until the box is the size you need.

4. Begin typing in the box that appears.

5. When you're finished, click anywhere on the Stage outside the text field.

Alignment icons update to vertical orientation

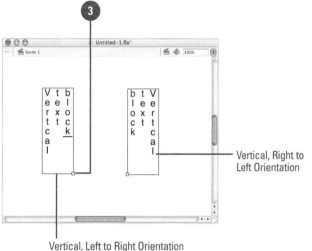

Vertical, Right to Left Orientation

Vertical, Left to Right Orientation

Rotate Characters in a Vertical Text Field

1. Select a character or word in an active vertical text field or select the entire field with the Arrow tool.

2. Click the Rotate Text button in the Property Inspector.

Did You Know?

The Rotate Text button is enabled only for vertical text fields. To rotate horizontal text fields, either convert them to vertical or use the Free Transform tool.

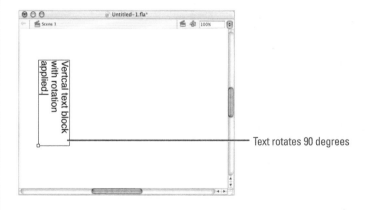

Text rotates 90 degrees

5

Changing Text Alignment

Similar to other text editing tools or word processing programs, Flash includes features for formatting paragraphs with alignment, margins, and indentation. These features can be accessed through the Text menu and in the Property Inspector whenever any text field is selected on the Stage. Each text field can have it's own individual properties assigned to it. Alignment governs the position of the text in a text box, margins are the space between the left and right side of the text and the boundaries of the text box, and indentation sets the amount of character spaces before the first line of text in a paragraph begins.

Align Paragraph Text

① Select the text in a text field you want to align or you can select the entire text box with the Arrow tool.

② In the Property Inspector, click one of the following:

- ◆ **Align Left**. Aligns text to the left margin.

- ◆ **Align Right**. Aligns text to the right margin.

- ◆ **Align Center**. Text is centered between the boundaries of the text box.

- ◆ **Justify**. Each line of text fills the width of the text box boundary.

> ### Did You Know?
>
> *You can quickly select all text in a text field.* If you are inside an active text field, press ⌘+A (Mac) or Ctrl+A (Win) to select all of the text.

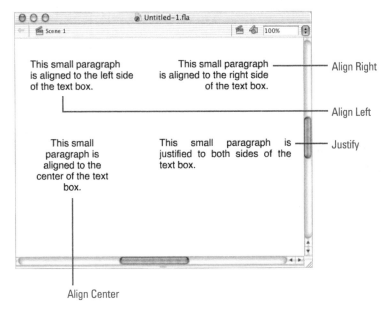

This small paragraph is aligned to the left side of the text box. — Align Left

This small paragraph is aligned to the right side of the text box. — Align Right

This small paragraph is aligned to the center of the text box. — Align Center

This small paragraph is justified to both sides of the text box. — Justify

Set Margins and Line Spacing

① Select a text field with the Arrow tool.

② Click Format in the Property Inspector to open the Format Options dialog box.

③ Enter values for any of the options or access the sliders by clicking on the small triangles next to the following entry boxes:

 ◆ **Indent**. Indents the first line of the paragraph.

 ◆ **Line Spacing**. Adjusts the space between lines of text.

 ◆ **Left Margin**. Adjusts the amount of space between the left barrier of the text box and the left side of the paragraph.

 ◆ **Right Margin**. Adjusts the amount of space between the right barrier of the text box and the right side of the paragraph.

④ When you're finished, click Done (Mac) or OK (Win).

Indentation space affects the first line of text.

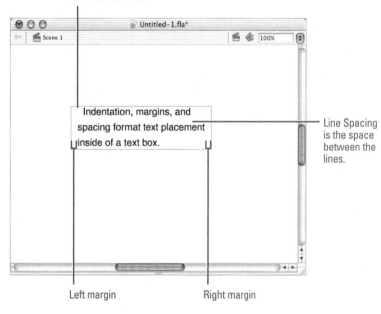

Indentation, margins, and spacing format text placement inside of a text box.

Line Spacing is the space between the lines.

Left margin   Right margin

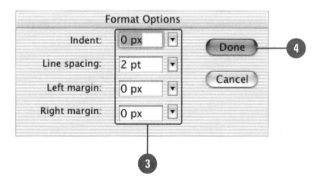

Using Break Apart to Modify Characters

When a line of text is created in Flash it appears in a bounding box that is editable. Sometimes you might need to adjust the characters separately or you might want to modify the shape of the characters themselves to create new character styles. The Break Apart command allows you to do this. There are two levels of breaking that you can utilize. The first break will separate the text field into singular, editable characters. This is useful if you want to reposition or align the letters of a word independently. The second break severs the text from its font reference: in essence it becomes a shape that you can edit with any of the drawing tools or pen modifiers.

Break a Text Field into Single Characters

1. Select the text field on the Stage with the Arrow tool.

2. Click the Modify menu, and then click Break Apart.

    Each character appears in its own editable box.

    TIMESAVER *Press ⌘+B (Mac) or Ctrl+B (Win) to use the Break Apart command.*

Text fields can be broken. — 1

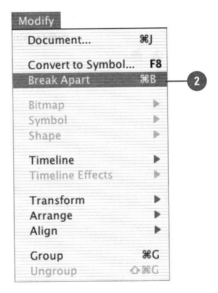

Text fields can be broken. — Broken text field

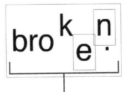

The text field is broken into separate text fields that can be moved and edited separately.

Break a Text Field into Shapes

1. Select the text field on the Stage.

2. Click the Modify menu, and then click Break Apart.

3. Click the Modify menu again, and then click Break Apart.

The characters become simple shapes that you can adjust with Flash's drawing tools.

TIMESAVER *Press ⌘+B (Mac) or Ctrl+B (Win) twice to break text into editable shapes.*

Text fields can be broken. ─1

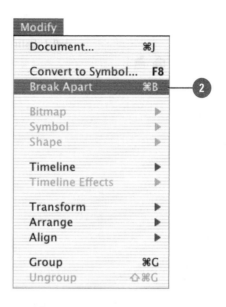

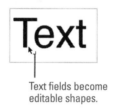

Text fields become editable shapes.

5

Using Alias Text

Anti-aliasing affects the pixels on the edge of a shape by allowing them to blend in with the background. It is a crucial feature when working with some text as it makes it appear smoother and more integrated. The drawback is that at smaller font sizes the text can appear blurry. Flash MX 2004 has added a new feature to the text properties that mimics aliasing even when anti-aliasing is enabled for your Flash movie. When this feature is enabled, Flash aligns the text to the nearest pixel boundary. In this way, the font appears crisp when displayed in the exported Flash movie.

Set a Text Field to Alias Text

① Select the text field with the Arrow tool.

② Click the Alias Text button in the Property Inspector.

> **IMPORTANT** *This feature only supports static text if viewed on earlier versions of the Flash Player (Flash 6 or earlier).*

Did You Know?

Alias Text works best on small font sizes. To achieve the best results with Alias Text, use text below 8 points.

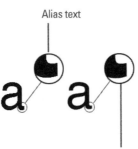

Alias text

Anti-aliasing blends the edge pixels with the background

Anti-alias text at small sizes

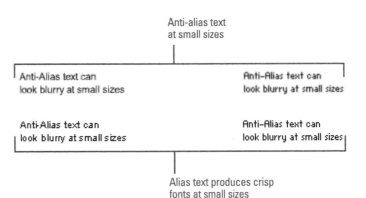

Anti-Alias text can look blurry at small sizes

Anti-Alias text can look blurry at small sizes

Anti-Alias text can look blurry at small sizes

Anti-Alias text can look blurry at small sizes

Alias text produces crisp fonts at small sizes

Using Font Mapping

If you open a document with a missing font on a computer, a Missing Font alert appears, asking you to choose a substitute font. You can open and use the Font Mapping dialog box to map a substitute font to the missing font, view the mapped fonts in the document, and delete a font mapping. After you select a substitute font, text appears with the correct font (if available) or the substitute font (if missing). When you use a substitute font, the text box or attributes might need to be adjusted.

Select Substitute Fonts

1. Open a document.

   ◆ To view all the font mappings saved on your computer, close all documents.

2. Click the Flash (Professional) (Mac) or Edit (Win) menu, and then click Font Mapping.

3. Click a font in the Missing Fonts column.

   TIMESAVER *Press Shift+click to select multiple missing fonts to map to the same substitute font.*

4. Click the Substitute Font popup, and then click a font, or click System Default.

5. Click OK.

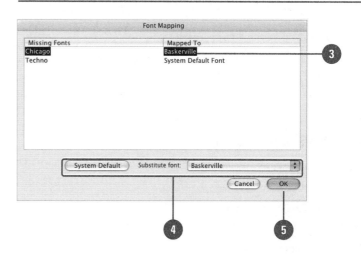

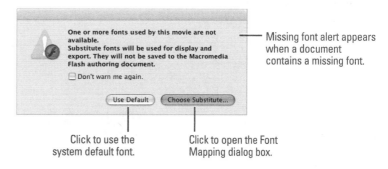

Missing font alert appears when a document contains a missing font.

Click to use the system default font.

Click to open the Font Mapping dialog box.

Did You Know?

You can delete the font mapping. Close all documents, click the Flash (Professional) (Mac) or Edit (Win) menu, click Font Mapping, select a font mapping, click Delete, and then click OK.

You can turn off the Missing Font alert. Click the Flash (Professional) (Mac) or Edit (Win) menu, click Font Mapping, select the Don't Show Again For This Document, Always Use Substitute Fonts check box, and then click OK.

5

Setting Device Fonts Versus Embedded Fonts

When you include a font in your Flash document that is installed on your computer, the font outline information is embedded in the exported Flash movie. This is called an embedded font and it ensures that your fonts will look consistent when displayed on other computers. Of course this adds to the file size, as each character from the selected font family has to be included in the final .swf. If file size is an issue, and the exact character matching is not important, you can choose to use device fonts. When a font is set to device, Flash will not embed the font information in the exported file. Instead the Flash Player will substitute the closest resembling font by name on the computer playing the Flash movie. The drawback is that you won't be able to predict how the fonts will display on every computer. To combat this uncertainty, Flash includes three device fonts. Each is designed with characteristics of typical fonts usually found by default on most computers. You can also choose device fonts when using small font sizes because they are not anti-alias and display clearly.

Set a Text Field to Device Font

① Select a text field you want to set to the device font.

② Select the Use Device Fonts check box in the Property Inspector.

The Device Font has now been changed.

Set a text field to device font.

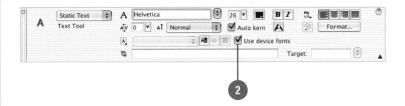

For Your Information

Working with Missing Font Information

If there is incomplete font information on your computer, fonts may appear in the Font list in Flash but will not export in the final movie. To test whether a font is complete, click the View menu, point to Preview Mode, and then click Anti-alias Text. If the text appears jagged, this means the font outlines are missing from the system and the font will not export.

Choose a Built-In Flash Device Font

1. Select a text field you want to set to device font.

2. Click the Font popup in the Property Inspector or click Text, point to Font, and then select one of the following fonts:

   ◆ **_sans**. Matches up with a sans-serif font, such as Helvetica or Arial.

   ◆ **_serif**. Matches up with a serif font, such as Times or Garamond.

   ◆ **_typewriter**. Matches up with a typewritten-looking font, such as Courier.

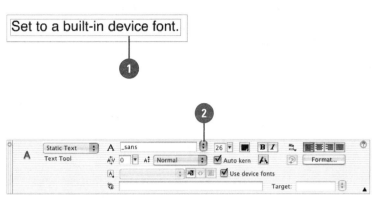

Set to a built-in device font.

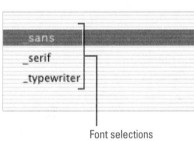

Font selections

5

Creating Dynamic Text and Input Text

When you create text fields in Flash they default to static fields. This means that it is for display only and is hard-coded in the .swf and cannot be changed unless you return to the Flash development environment, edit it, and re-export the file. If you need your text to be updatable from an outside source, such as a text document on a server or if you need the user to input text for you to retrieve and process with ActionScript, you can set your text field to enable this functionality. Setting your text field to dynamic text turns it into an ActionScript object that can be given an instance name or turned into a variable that can be populated from some other source outside of the .swf. This is great when you need to update content on the fly and would rather not have to deal directly with Flash for each update. If you require the user to enter a string of text, such as in a form, you can set a text field to input text. This enables the user to enter information in the text field that can be retrieved and processed.

Set a Text Field to be Dynamic

① Select the text field on the Stage you want to be a dynamic field.

② Click the Text Type popup in the Property Inspector, and then click Dynamic Text.

③ Select from the following properties:

◆ **Instance Name**. Gives the text field an instance name so it can be controlled with ActionScript.

◆ **Character Position**. Changes character position on a line.

◆ **Render Text As HTML**. Preserves Rich Text Formatting, allowing you to include hyperlinks and HTML tags.

◆ **Show Border**. Displays a border around the text field in the exported movie.

◆ **Variable Name**. Gives the text field a variable name for use with ActionScript.

◆ **Character Options**. Allows you to choose which characters you want to embed in the text.

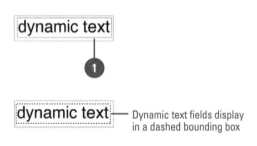

Dynamic text fields display in a dashed bounding box

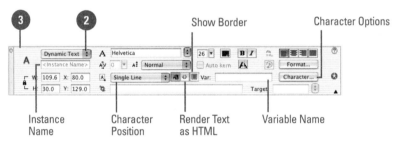

168

Set a Text Field to be an Input Field

1. Select the text field on the Stage you want to be an input field.

2. Click the Text Type popup in the Property Inspector, and then click Input Text.

3. Select from the following properties:

    ◆ **Instance Name**. Gives the text field an instance name so it can be controlled with ActionScript

    ◆ **Character Position**. Changes character position on a line. Choose from Single Line and Multi-Line with or without Wrap, and Password (available only for Input text)

    ◆ **Selectability**. Allows or denies the user the ability to select the text in the exported movie.

    ◆ **Show Border**. Displays a border around the text field in the exported movie.

    ◆ **Variable Name**. Gives the text field a variable name for use with ActionScript.

    ◆ **Maximum Characters**. Limit the amount of characters a user can enter into the field.

    ◆ **Character Options**. Allows you to choose which characters you want to embed in the text.

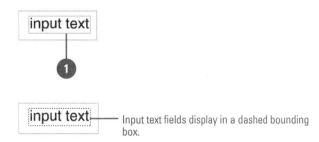

Input text fields display in a dashed bounding box.

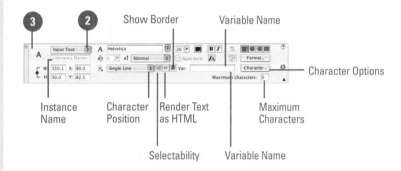

Using Multiple Languages in a Document

When you're working with text in a Flash document, don't forget the global community. Flash now supports multi-language authoring. You could create a document that displays text in Spanish and English, using a variety of methods: The text can be written within an external file, and called using the #include ActionScript within a dynamic or text input field, or the text can be inserted into the document at runtime using an external XML (Extensible Markup Language) file. This allows you to insert different languages that automatically appear to the visitor.

When you're working with multi-language Flash documents, click the Window menu, point to Other Panels, and then click Strings. The Strings panel lets you streamline the process of localizing content into multiple languages, because it collects and tracks all character strings throughout the development process in a central place. In the Strings panel, you can select a language and assign each text string, either a dynamic or input text field, in the document with a unique ID.

5

Setting Dynamic Text and Input Text Options ▶

The Character Options that are available to dynamic and input text allows you to specify which-if any-font outlines you want embedded in the Flash movie for use in these fields. This is a great way to keep file size down because you can include only those characters you need. You can also limit the types of characters a user can enter. For example, if you are asking a user to enter a zip code, you can disable all characters except numbers from being entered.

Use the Character Options Dialog Box

① Select a dynamic or input text field on the Stage.

② Click the Edit Character Options button in the Property Inspector.

③ Click the Specify Ranges option.

④ Select which characters outlines you want to embed in the exported movie.

TIMESAVER *Use ⌘+select (Mac) or Ctrl+select (Win) to select multiple lines from the Character list.*

⑤ Type specific characters into the Include These Characters box to include those outlines.

⑥ Click Auto Fill to include each unique character from the selected text box on the Stage.

⑦ Click OK.

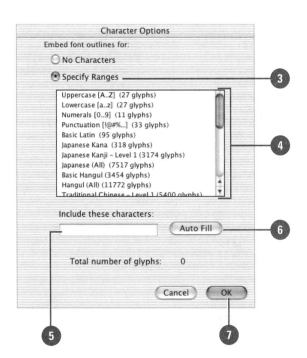

Using Cascading Style Sheets with HTML Text

Cascading Style Sheets (CSS) contain sets of formatting rules for HTML and XML text. CSS allow you to define certain text attributes and give them a style name. This style name, called a selector, can be applied to any implemented text. Each time you need to implement the defined style, you can refer back to the CSS.

This allows for more control over the text displayed on your Web page. Load styles from an external CSS or create them within Flash using the Style Sheet Object. The ActionScript class for CSS is described as: TextField.StyleSheet. This is a new functionality and it is only available to swfs in the Flash 7 Player.

Load an external CSS

In any text or HTML editor, place the following code:

```
// External CSS File: styles.css
headline {
        font-family: Arial, Helvetica, sans-serif;
    font-size: 12 px;
}
bodyText {
        font-family: Arial, Helvetica, sans-serif;
    font-size: 10 px;
}
```

This code is typically found in a CSS. This example defines two styles, one for a sans-serif headline at 12 pixels, the other a sans-serif body text at 10 pixels.

Select the first frame of your Flash movie. Place the following code in the Actions panel:

```
var css_styles = new TextField.StyleSheet();
css_styles.load("styles.css");
css_styles.onLoad = function(ok) {
  if(ok) {
    // display style names
    trace(this.getStyleNames());
  } else {
    trace("Error loading CSS file.");
  }
}
```

The CSS you created, "styles.css" is loaded into this object. A loader is created to ensure the CSS is loaded properly. Make sure the CSS and the swf are in the same directory.

Create a CSS in Flash

Select the first frame of your Flash movie. The following code creates a text style for headline text and body text. Place the following code in the Actions panel:

```
var styles = new TextField.StyleSheet();
styles.setStyle("headline",
   {fontFamily: 'Arial,Helvetica,sans-serif',
   fontSize: '12px'}
);
styles.setStyle("bodyText",
   {fontFamily: 'Arial,Helvetica,sans-serif',
   fontSize: '10px'}
);
```

This CSS code can now be placed in the Actions panel in Flash. This example defines two styles, one for a sans-serif headline at 12 pixels, the other a sans-serif body text at 10 pixels.

5

Checking Spelling

Newly implemented in Flash MX 2004 is a global spell checker that is fully configurable. Search the entire Flash document or isolate specific elements to search in the Spelling Setup dialog box. You can choose from a variety of built-in dictionaries as sources including a personal dictionary you can edit. Additionally you can choose which text characteristics to ignore, such as words with numbers and internet addresses, as well as choose what type of alternative suggestions you want Flash to provide.

Set Up Spell Checking

1 Click the Text menu, and then click Spelling Setup.

2 Select from the following options:

- ◆ **Document Options**. Specify which elements in the Flash document you want to spell check. You can also specify whether you want to live-edit the document during the Check Spelling process.

- ◆ **Dictionaries**. Select a built-in dictionary as a source. At least one dictionary must be selected to activate Check Spelling.

- ◆ **Personal Dictionary**. Specify an option to use a dictionary created and edited by you. Navigate to a text document on your hard drive or edit the default one included by clicking the Edit Personal Dictionary button. Each new entry in the personal dictionary must be on a separate line.

- ◆ **Checking Options**. Set word-level behaviors. You can have Internet addresses ignored, find duplicate words, or specify the types of suggestions you want displayed in the Check Spelling window.

3 Click OK.

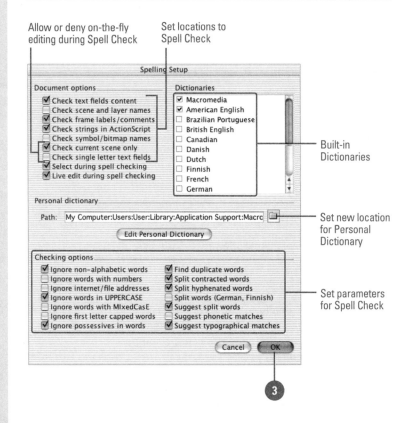

Allow or deny on-the-fly editing during Spell Check

Set locations to Spell Check

Built-in Dictionaries

Set new location for Personal Dictionary

Set parameters for Spell Check

Use Spell Checking

1 Click the Text menu, and then click Check Spelling.

2 If Flash finds suspect words, the Check Spelling dialog box opens. Otherwise, Flash displays a message that the Spell Check is complete.

Word not found (*element*):

This identifies the suspect word and what type of element it was found in parenthesis.

3 Do one of the following:

- ◆ **Add To Personal.** Click to add the word to your personal dictionary.

- ◆ **Ignore.** Click the Ignore and Ignore All buttons to not flag this word again in this Check Spelling session.

- ◆ **Change.** In the Change To and Suggestions fields, Flash displays the closest alternatives to the suspect word.

- ◆ **Delete.** Click to delete the word from the field that contains it.

4 Continue until Flash produces a message that Check Spelling is complete or click Close to stop the Check Spelling process before it is completed.

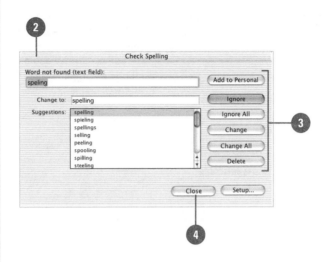

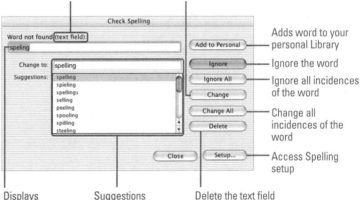

Identifies the location (the element) the misspelled word is located in

Change the word with one from the suggestion list or one you've typed in

Adds word to your personal Library

Ignore the word

Ignore all incidences of the word

Change all incidences of the word

Access Spelling setup

Displays Misspelled Word and allows you to enter a new one to replace it

Suggestions generated from built-in and personal dictionaries

Delete the text field from the document

Did You Know?

You must access the Spelling Setup once to activate Check Spelling. You need to activate Check Spelling to select a dictionary. Click the Text menu, and then click Spelling Setup.

5

Using Find and Replace

Use Find and Replace to locate specific elements in your Flash document. You can specify where to look, what to look for, and what to replace it with. Choose to search the entire Flash document or the current active scene. Each element you search for has its own configurable settings and options. Included is a log that shows the exact locations of the found element.

Locate Items with Find and Replace

1. Click the Edit menu, and then click Find And Replace.

   TIMESAVER *Press* ⌘+F *(Mac) or Ctrl+F (Win) to quickly open the Find and Replace window.*

2. Select where you want to search from the Search In popup menu.

3. Select which element in Flash you want to search for:

   ◆ Text

   ◆ Font

   ◆ Color

   ◆ Symbol

   ◆ Sound

   ◆ Video

   ◆ Bitmap

4. Enter the parameters for your search.

5. Click Find Next or Find All to find the element with the characteristics you've entered.

6. Click Replace or Replace All to update the found element with the new characteristics.

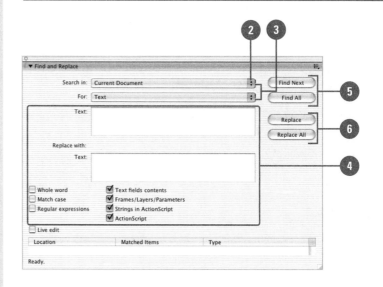

Importing Graphics

6

Introduction

In addition to the vector drawing tools that allow you to create graphics and animation in Flash, you can also import artwork in other formats to use in your Flash movie. The standard bitmapped graphics, Flash now has full native support for PDF, EPS, and Adobe Illustrator 10 files. This extends the versatility of Flash as a comprehensive graphics creation program and allows you to integrate more efficiently non-Macromedia applications into your Flash production process. The use of bitmaps in Flash is particular as there are some limitations in editing them.

Flash drawing tools create and edit vector objects, not pixels, so preparation is necessary for bitmapped graphics in a paint application outside of Flash MX, such as Adobe Photoshop or Macromedia FireWorks. Fortunately, Flash allows you to convert a bitmapped graphic into a vector with the Trace Bitmap function. You can also use a bitmap as a fill for vector objects. An important thing to remember is that any bitmap used in your project can add considerable size to your Flash movie. Flash includes several procedures for optimizing these bitmaps on export, either through global compression settings or applied specifically to each image.

Understanding Vector and Bitmap Graphics

Vector graphics are comprised of anchor points connected to each other by lines and curves, called vectors. These anchor points and vectors describe the contour and surface of the graphic with some included information about color, alpha, and line width. Because they are general descriptions of the coordinates of a shape, they are resolution-independent; that is they can be resized without any loss to the quality of the graphic.

Bitmapped graphics are made up of small, colored squares, called pixels that form a grid. Each pixel is given a specific color and a grid of these pixels forms a mosaic, which is your image. Because of this, bitmaps are dependent on resolution (the number of pixels in the grid). Resizing up or down forces pixels to be created or removed to accommodate the new grid size. The results can be unpredictable and a loss of quality is certain.

Both vector and bitmap graphics have their strengths and weaknesses. Vector shapes are simple and graphic in nature. They are a good choice for creating high-contrast, geometric art or art with limited color shifts. If you need to implement artwork with a richer surface texture, color depth, and shading, like those qualities found in a photograph, a bitmap better suits this purpose. The strength of Flash MX 2004 as a content creator is that you can combine the strengths of both vector art and bitmapped art.

Bitmap Image

Vector Image

Examining Import File Formats

The following files can be imported into Flash:

File Type	Extension	Windows	Macintosh
File Formats			
Adobe Illustrator 10 or earlier	.eps, .ai, .pdf	✓	✓
AutoCAD DXF	.dxf	✓	✓
Bitmap	.bmp	✓	✓ (Using QuickTime)
Enhanced Windows Metafile	.emf	✓	
FreeHand	.fh7-.fh11	✓	✓
Future SplashPlayer	.spl	✓	✓
GIF and animated GIF	.gif	✓	✓
JPEG	.jpg	✓	✓
PNG	.png	✓	✓
Flash Player 6/7	.swf	✓	✓
Windows Metafile	.wmf	✓	✓

The following files can be imported into Flash only if QuickTime 4 or later is installed on your system:

File Type	Extension	Windows	Macintosh
File Formats			
MacPaint	.pntg	✓	✓
Photoshop	.psd	✓	✓
PICT	.pct, .pic	✓ (as a Bitmap)	✓
QuickTime Image	.qtif	✓	✓
Silicon Graphics Image	.sgi	✓	✓
TGA	.tga	✓	✓
TIFF	.tiff	✓	✓

6

Importing PDF, EPS, and Illustrator Files

Flash MX 2004 now includes support for importing Adobe Illustrator 10, EPS, and PDF files. You can now import Adobe Illustrator files created in version 6 through 10, and PDF files created in version 1.4 or earlier (this is the version of the PDF file format, the industry standard, not the version of Adobe Acrobat which is currently at version 6.0). When these files are imported, there are a number of options you can choose from. Some options in the Import options dialog box are context-sensitive; that is, they only appear if they are relevant to the imported file. The dialog box that appears when importing any three of these files is the same expect that if there are multiple pages in the file being imported, an additional option appears so you can choose which pages to import (Adobe Illustrator doesn't support multiple pages). Other than this, they are the same. The "Convert Pages To" option appears regardless of whether there are multiple pages in the document being imported.

Import an Illustrator, EPS, or PDF file

① Click the File menu, point to Import, and then click Import To Stage.

② Click the Show popup (Mac) or Files Of Type (Win), and then select Adobe Illustrator, EPS, or PDF.

③ Navigate to the file on your hard drive.

④ Select the Illustrator, EPS, or PDF file you want to import.

⑤ Click Import (Mac) or Open (Win).

⑥ Click the Scenes (or Screens) or Keyframes option.

If your file has multiple pages (as in the case of a PDF), you can choose to convert these pages into separate scenes or screens, or you can choose to have each page displayed on a separate consecutive keyframe in the same scene.

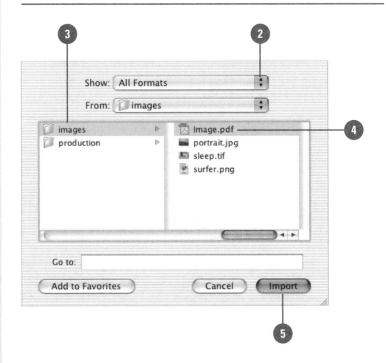

7 Click the Layers, Keyframes, or Flatten option.

- ◆ **Layers**. Select this option to convert the layers in the imported file into corresponding layers in the Flash Timeline.

- ◆ **Keyframes**. Select this option to convert the layers in the imported file into consecutive keyframes.

- ◆ **Flatten**. Select this option to flatten the layers in the imported file onto a single layer in Flash. Each layer is grouped and stacked on top of each other.

8 If necessary, click the All or From option, and then enter a page range.

> **IMPORTANT** *This option only appears if there are multiple pages in the file (as in a PDF document).*

9 Select from the following options:

- ◆ **Include Invisible Layers**. Select this check box to include all layers visible or invisible during the import.

- ◆ **Maintain Text Blocks**. Select this check box to maintain editable text blocks.

- ◆ **Rasterize Everything**. Select this check box to rasterize (convert into a bitmap) all of the art into a single image, and then select a rasterization resolution.

10 Click OK.

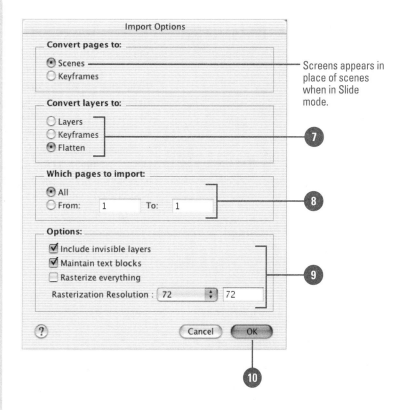

Screens appears in place of scenes when in Slide mode.

6

Importing Bitmaps

You can import bitmaps of several file types directly into Flash to use in your Flash movie. It is important to remember that even though you can edit and resize bitmaps in Flash, the original bitmap will always be embedded in the exported Flash file. If file size is an issue, it is best to bring your bitmapped art in at the size you want to export it. For example, if your image is going to be 160 pixels by 160 pixels in the final movie, it is best to import it at this size and not resize it up or down in Flash. You will end up with higher-quality images and smaller files if you do this. You can import files using the Import To Stage or Import To Library methods. The Import To Stage method stores the bitmap in the Library and places a copy on the Stage, while the Import To Library method stores the bitmap in the Library and doesn't place a copy on the Stage.

Import a Bitmap to the Stage

1. Click the File menu, point to Import, and then click Import To Stage.

2. Click the Show popup (Mac) or Files Of Types list arrow (Win), and then select the format of the file you want to import.

3. Navigate to the file on your hard drive.

4. Select the file you want to import.

5. Click Import (Mac) or Open (Win).

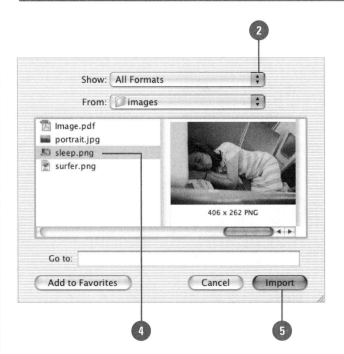

Did You Know?

You may not be able to see the images you've imported to the Stage at certain magnification levels. Flash aligns the top left-hand corner of the image at the 0,0 coordinate. If you are zoomed in, the image may have appeared outside the viewable area. Use the Hand tool to navigate around, zoom out, or press Shift+⌘+W (Mac) or Ctrl+Shift+W (Win) to toggle the Work Area off. This sets the zoom level to 100% and hides the Work Area.

Import to the Library

1. Click the File menu, point to Import, and then click Import To Library.

2. Click the Show popup (Mac) or Files Of Types list arrow (Win), and then select the format of the file you want to import.

3. Navigate to the file on your hard drive.

4. Select the file you want to import.

5. Click Import To Library (Mac) or Open (Win).

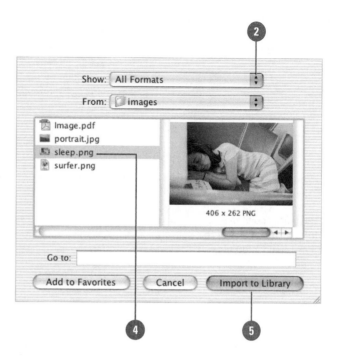

Image is placed in the Library.

Importing Multiple Files

Flash allows you to import multiple files simultaneously to save time. This is useful if you have many files to import. You can select multiple, non-sequential files in the Import dialog box. Choose to import to the Library or to the Stage directly. When you import to the Stage, the file is stored in the Library and a copy is placed on the Stage so you can begin editing it immediately. If you attempt to import a series of files that are numbered sequentially, Flash detects this and produces a dialog box to handle this. When sequential images are imported, they will appear in separate frames by order of the number in their file name. This is extremely useful for image sequences where a series of images forms an animation.

Import Multiple Files

① Click the File menu, point to Import, and then select one of the Import options: Import To Stage or Import To Library.

② Click the Show popup (Mac) or Files Of Types list arrow (Win), and then select the format of the file you want to import.

③ Navigate to the files on your hard drive.

④ Select the file you want to import, and then hold down the ⌘⌥ (Mac) or Ctrl (Win) key and click additional files to select them.

⑤ Click Import (Mac) or Open (Win).

TROUBLE? *You may not be able to see all of the files you've imported because Flash displays them stacked on top of each other.*

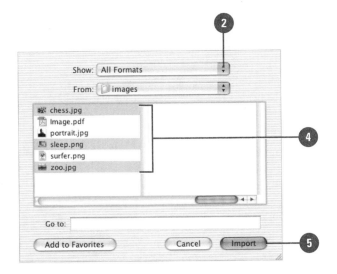

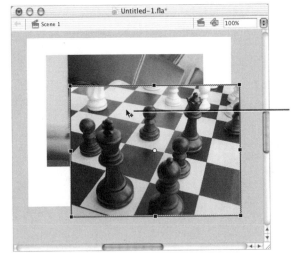

Multiple files imported appear stacked on top of each other. Press down and drag with your mouse to reveal images underneath.

Import a Sequence of Files

1. Click the File menu, point to Import, and then click Import To Stage.

2. Click the Show popup (Mac) or Files Of Types list arrow (Win), and then select the format of the file you want to import.

3. Navigate to the files on your hard drive.

4. Select the first file in the series you want to import.

5. Click Import (Mac) or Open (Win).

   Flash detects that this image is part of a sequence and asks whether you want to import all of them at once.

6. Click Yes.

   The numbered files are imported and placed on separate sequential keyframes on the selected layer in the Timeline.

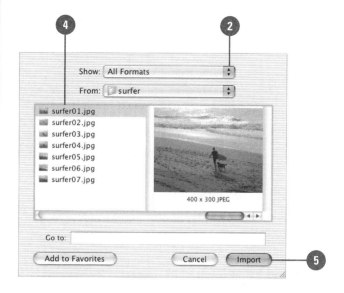

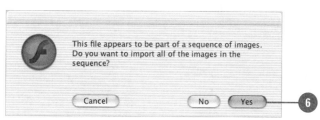

Each imported image appears on a separate frame sequentially.

6

Copying Images from Other Programs

You can paste a bitmap image from other image editing programs, such as Adobe Photoshop or Macromedia FireWorks. Simply use the standard copying procedure in the program of your choice to place the bitmap into the clipboard, which is where the operating system dynamically stores information you copy, and then paste it into Flash directly on the Stage. Copying images from other programs works well for bitmaps. However, results are unpredictable when pasting vector graphics from other programs. Often they become corrupted when they are copied to the clipboard, depending upon the origin program or the operating system. It is best to use the Import command to import vector graphics into Flash.

Paste from the Clipboard

1 Copy the image to the clipboard in an image-editing program.

2 Launch or switch to Flash MX 2004, and then open the Flash document in which you want to paste an image from the clipboard.

3 Select an unlocked layer or keyframe.

4 Click the Edit menu, and then click Paste.

TIMESAVER *Press ⌘+V (Mac) or Ctrl+V (Win) to quickly paste from the clipboard.*

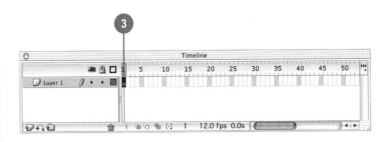

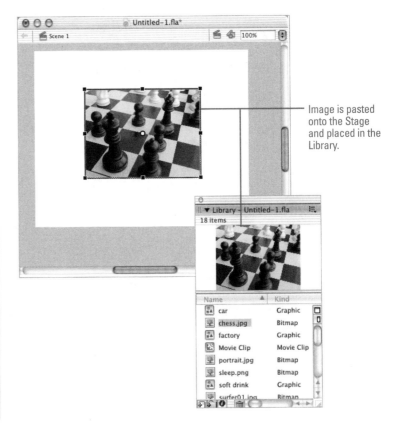

Image is pasted onto the Stage and placed in the Library.

Setting Bitmap Compression

When you export a Flash movie you can decide how much color information to include in each exported bitmap. This is called compression. The more compression you apply, the less color information is included and the lower the size and quality of the image. You can choose to set a global compression for all bitmap files used your Flash movie or you can set a separate compression for each image. In each case there are a number of options available to deal with the relatively large file sizes of some bitmaps. As with all image compression, file size needs to be weighed against image quality. It is always best to experiment until you get the balance you are looking for.

Set Compression for a Single Bitmap

① Open the Library panel.

② Select the bitmap from the Library item list in which you want to set compression.

③ Click the Properties icon in the bottom of the panel or double-click the bitmap file in the list.

④ Select the Allow Smoothing check box to anti-alias the edges of the image, making it appear smoother.

⑤ Click the Compression popup, and then select from the following options:

◆ **Lossless (PNG/GIF).** Image will not compress and will remain in its highest quality.

◆ **Photo (JPEG).** You can choose to use the compression information contained by selecting the Use Imported JPEG Data check box. By deselecting this feature you can set the level of JPEG compression applied to the bitmap. The values are 1-100. The higher the number, the less compression applied, producing a higher quality image.

⑥ Click OK.

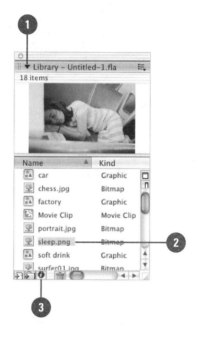

Thumbnail preview

Click to preview in thumbnail

6

Editing Bitmaps in an Outside Editor

You can edit a bitmap in its native program or some other image editing tool. Once it is resaved to the hard drive, you can update the bitmap in Flash. You can also import another image to replace the bitmap in the Library. In either case, every copy of the bitmap used in the Flash movie (including bitmap fills) will update with these changes. This is a convenient way to make global changes to bitmap art included in your project.

Update an Image Edited Outside of Flash

① Import a bitmap into Flash.

② Edit this bitmap in an outside image-editing program of your choice (such as Adobe Photoshop), and then save to the hard drive.

③ In Flash, open the Library panel, and then select the bitmap from the item list.

④ Click the Properties icon in the bottom of the panel or double-click the bitmap file in the list.

⑤ Click Update.

⑥ Click OK.

The bitmap updates to the new version saved to your drive.

Did You Know?

Flash preserves the path when you import a bitmap. When you import a bitmap into Flash, the path to that image is preserved in the Bitmap Properties. If you have moved the image to another directory on your hard drive and you want to update the file in the Library with the new changes, navigate to it by using the Import button in the Bitmap Properties window.

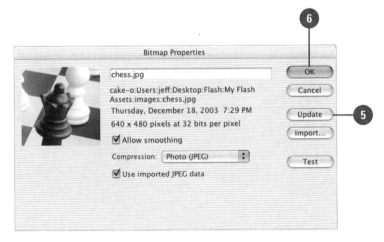

Replace a Bitmap

1. Open the Library panel, and then select the bitmap from the item list.

2. Click the Properties icon in the bottom of the panel or double-click the bitmap file in the list.

3. Click Import.

4. Navigate to the replacement file on your hard drive.

5. Select the replacement file.

6. Click Open.

7. Click OK.

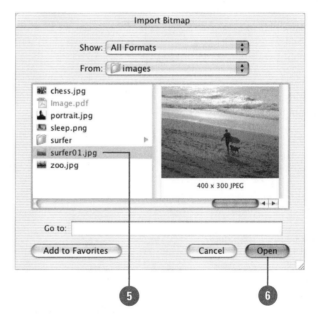

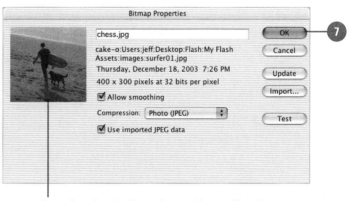

Image is replaced with new imported image. All copies used in the Flash movie update to this new image.

Using Break Apart to Create Fill Patterns

By default, when you import a bitmap into Flash MX and drag it to the Stage, you are limited in how you can edit it. Break Apart the image to remove the image from its bounding box and enables you to cut into the image, remove parts, select regions, and use it as a fill pattern. The bitmap is still linked to its parent in the Library however. Any edit made to a bitmap only affects the copy on the Stage. For example, if you break an image and then edit it down to a tiny portion, in the exported movie the image appears exactly as you edited it. However, it will still have the same file size of the image you imported (less any compression you may have applied). It is always best to do your most severe editing in a bitmap or paint program outside of Flash.

Create a Bitmap Fill Pattern

1 Drag a copy of a bitmap to the Stage from the Library panel; make sure the bitmap is selected on the Stage.

2 Click the Modify menu, and then click Break Apart.

TIMESAVER *Press ⌘+B (Mac) and Ctrl+B (Win) to quickly break apart a bitmap on the Stage.*

3 Click the Eyedropper tool in the Toolbar.

The pointer changes to a small eyedropper.

4 Position the eyedropper over the image, and then click to select it.

The bitmap is now a selected fill that you can use to fill vector shapes.

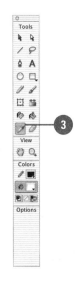

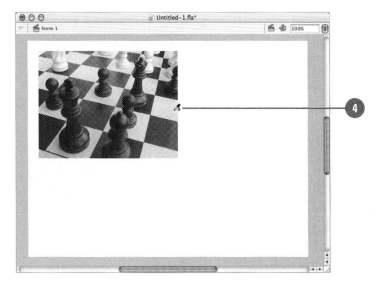

5 Click the Rectangle or Oval tool in the Toolbar.

6 Click and drag on the Stage to create a new shape with the bitmap fill.

Did You Know?

You can use the Paint Bucket tool to add a bitmap fill to an existing shape. A bitmap fill behaves the same as any solid color fill or gradient.

You can select the bitmap fill in the Color Mixer panel. In the panel click Bitmap from the Fill Style popup. All of the bitmaps contained in the Library will appear as thumbnails in the grid below. Select one to make it the active fill.

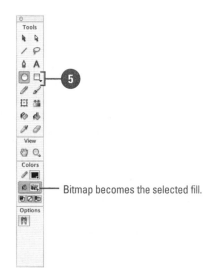

Bitmap becomes the selected fill.

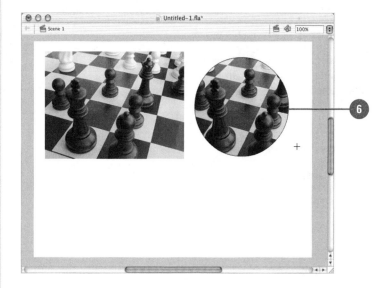

Modifying a Bitmap Fill

Flash defaults to tiling a bitmap fill. Tiling is simply when an image is repeated in a grid until it fills the entire object. If you have applied a bitmap fill to a vector object, you can continue to edit its characteristics and placement. You can resize, skew, or rotate the fill or change its center point within the shape with the Fill Transform tool. This tool allows you to dynamically make these changes when it is applied to any editable shape. As with most of the assets Flash stores in the Library, any change you make to the application of the fill does not affect the master object stored in the Library. In this way, bitmaps like video clips and sounds, behave similarly to symbols in that their master object is not affected, though when you use a bitmap in your movie Flash refers to this as a copy, not an instance, because there are no built-in controls for bitmaps.

Change the Center Point

① Create a shape on the Stage with a bitmap fill.

② Click the Fill Transform tool in the Toolbar.

The pointer changes to an arrow with a small gradient box in the right-hand corner.

TIMESAVER *Press F to quickly select the Fill Transform tool.*

③ Click the shape to select it.

A bounding box appears on the tile.

④ Position the pointer over the white circle in the center of the bounding box.

The cursor becomes a Move icon.

⑤ Click and drag the center point to a new position.

The tile accommodates to the new position of the center point.

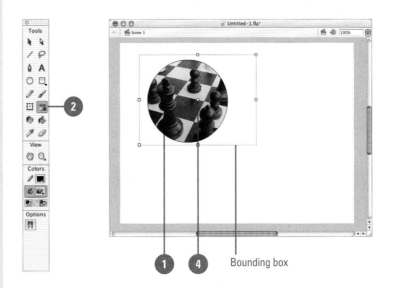

Bounding box

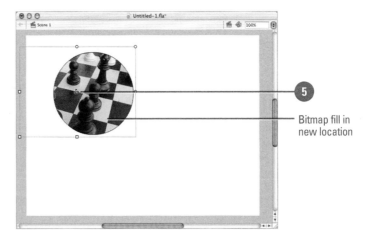

Bitmap fill in new location

Modify the Orientation and Size of a Bitmap Fill

1. Create a shape on the Stage with a bitmap fill.

2. Click the Fill Transform tool in the Toolbar.

   The pointer changes to an arrow with a small gradient box in the right-hand corner.

3. Position the pointer over the shape, and then select it.

   A bounding box appears on the tile.

4. Do one of the following:

   ◆ **Bottom-left-corner square.** Drag this to resize the fill proportionally.

   ◆ **Left-center square.** Drag this to resize width of fill.

   ◆ **Bottom-center square.** Drag this to resize height of fill.

   ◆ **Top-right-corner circle.** Drag this to rotate fill.

   ◆ **Top-center circle.** Drag this to skew fill horizontally.

   ◆ **Right-center circle.** Drag this to skew fill vertically.

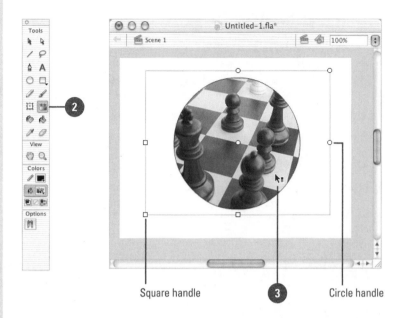

Square handle   3   Circle handle

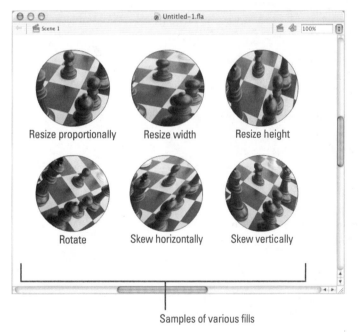

Resize proportionally   Resize width   Resize height

Rotate   Skew horizontally   Skew vertically

Samples of various fills

6

Editing a Bitmap with the Magic Wand

When you use Break Apart on a bitmap, the bitmap becomes a fill and its content is editable. You can select specific regions of it with any of Flash's selection tools and procedures. If you want to remove parts of the bitmap or replace them with different fills you can select those parts with the Magic Wand tool. The Magic Wand tool selects regions of similar colors. Clicking on other parts adds those parts to the selection. The color threshold (or sensitivity) for this tool can be set in the Magic Wand options popup menu.

Use the Magic Wand

① Select a bitmap on the Stage.

② Click the Modify menu, and then click Break Apart.

TIMESAVER *Press* ⌘+B *(Mac) or Ctrl+B (Win) to quickly break apart a bitmap on the Stage.*

③ Click on the Stage to deselect the broken bitmap.

④ Click the Lasso tool in the Toolbar.

⑤ Click the Magic Wand Mode button in the Options section of the Toolbar.

The pointer becomes a small magic wand.

⑥ Position the pointer over regions of the image you want to select.

The color region you clicked on is selected. Subsequent clicks on other regions are added to the selection.

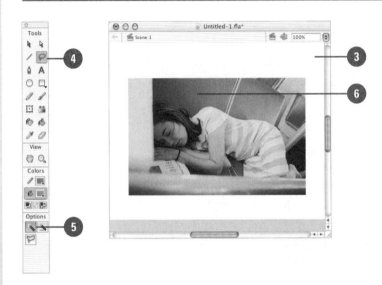

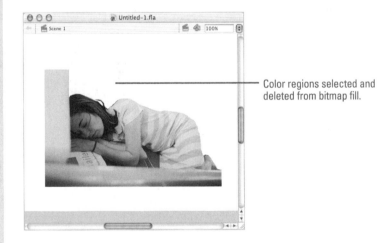

Color regions selected and deleted from bitmap fill.

Set the Magic Wand Options

1. Click the Lasso tool in the Toolbar.

2. Click the Magic Wand Properties button in the Toolbar.

3. Enter a color threshold between 0 and 200.

    This number defines how close adjacent colors have to be to the selected color before they are added to the selection. A higher number selects a broader number of colors.

4. Click the Smoothing popup, and then select from the following options: Pixels, Rough, Normal, and Smooth.

    This sets the smoothness of the edges of the selection.

5. Click OK.

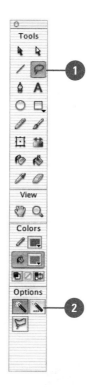

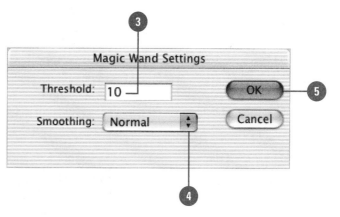

6

Using Trace Bitmap to Create Vector Shapes

Flash provides a procedure to convert bitmaps into vector art. When Trace Bitmap is used, Flash interprets the pixel information in the bitmap and converts it into vector shapes. The results can be unpredictable in quality and have unwieldy file sizes if the bitmaps are very complex. However, there are several parameters in the Trace Bitmap dialog box that can be modified to strike a balance between file size and quality.

Trace a Bitmap

① Drag a copy of a bitmap to the Stage from the Library panel; make sure the bitmap is selected on the Stage.

② Click the Modify menu, point to Bitmap, and then click Trace Bitmap.

TROUBLE? *The Trace Bitmap command is disabled if you select a broken bitmap (a bitmap fill).*

③ Specify values and options to determine how close the vector shape resembles the bitmap:

◆ **Color Threshold.** If the difference in the RGB color value for two pixels is less than the color threshold, the pixel colors are considered the same. Enter a value between 1 and 500.The higher the value, the lower the number of colors.

◆ **Minimum Area.** Determines how many neighboring pixels to include in the threshold calculation. Enter a pixel value between 1 and 1000.

◆ **Curve Fit.** Determines how smoothly Flash creates vector outlines.

◆ **Corner Threshold.** Controls whether to preserve sharp edges or create more smooth contours.

④ Click OK.

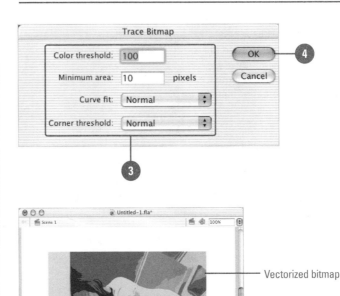

Vectorized bitmap

For Your Information

Creating Vectors Closest to the Original Bitmap

Macromedia recommends using the following settings in the Trace Bitmap feature to produce a vector version that is closest to the original bitmap: Color Threshold = 10, Minimum Area = 1 pixel, Curve Fit = Pixels, and Corner Threshold = Many Corners. However, depending on the complexity of the bitmap, this can produce very large and unwieldy file sizes and in some cases, take a long time for Flash to complete the operation.

Creating Frame-By-Frame Animation

Introduction

Flash provides several methods for creating animation. In addition to shape and motion tweening, you can create frame-by-frame animations. The frame-by-frame method is derived from the traditional animation process whereby the content is redrawn on each frame with slight differences from the last frame. When these frames are played in sequence there is an illusion of movement. In Flash you utilize keyframes in the Timeline to accomplish this. A **keyframe** defines a change to the artwork placed on the Stage. There are a number of ways to create and edit keyframes as they are editable objects. Keyframes can be moved, copied, and pasted to and from any Timeline in your Flash movie or between different Flash documents. Frame-by-frame animations can be previewed in the Flash development environment so you can quickly see the results and check your work as you animate. They can also be viewed in the Flash Player using the Test Movie feature.

Additionally, there is an Onion Skin mode that allows you to see the active frame in context to the frames around it, making it easier to fine-tune keyframe changes. The versatility of the Timeline and the strength of the Flash Player allow you to implement animation in your movie and give it life.

Understanding Frame-By-Frame Animation

Animation is the illusion of movement. It is comprised of a series of pictures, each slightly different from the last, that when played sequentially imply movement. Motion pictures work the same way. What you see when you view a film is a long strip of images played at specific intervals. In this way the content in the pictures moves and seems to imitate real life.

Traditional cell animators draw a picture onto a frame of celluloid and then draw the same thing onto the next frame but with slight changes made to the drawing. Static parts of the scene (such as a background) are copied and only the objects that change are redrawn. In this way the process is more efficient.

The principles for animating in Flash have derived from this process. In Flash you create frame-by-frame animations in the Timeline through the use of keyframes. Each keyframe defines a change on the Stage and when played in succession, the content can seem to evolve, or move. When you export your movie, Flash will play these frames in succession at specific intervals depending on the frame rate you set. A good introduction to this concept, as well as the basics of animation is, the dissection a character walk cycle. When human beings walk, they are essentially repeating the same motion over and over again. In an animated walk cycle, the same thing occurs, though instead of drawing the cycle over and over again, the motion is spaced out so that the last frame (the last image drawn) meets up with the first frame. If this animation is looped, the character will seem to walk perpetually.

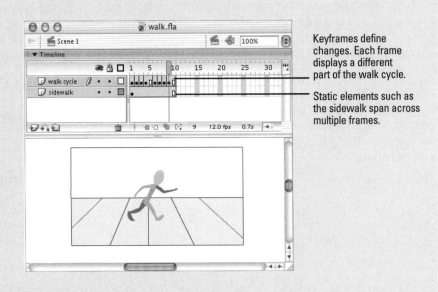

Keyframes define changes. Each frame displays a different part of the walk cycle.

Static elements such as the sidewalk span across multiple frames.

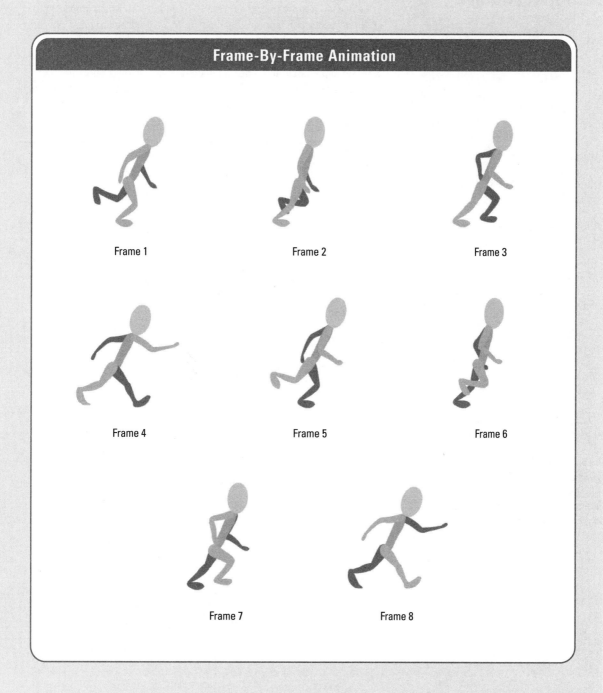

Frame-By-Frame Animation

Frame 1

Frame 2

Frame 3

Frame 4

Frame 5

Frame 6

Frame 7

Frame 8

Creating Keyframes

When art is placed on the Stage it appears in a keyframe in the Timeline. A keyframe is represented as a black-bounded box with a small circle in it. By default, each layer in the Timeline has a keyframe on its first frame. An empty keyframe displays an empty or hollow circle but when you place artwork or objects on the Stage the bounding box becomes shaded and the small circle becomes a filled black dot. A keyframe can span multiple frames when there are no changes to the art. To make a change you create another keyframe. In this way you can create animations or content that seems to move or change over time.

Create a Keyframe

1. Place art or an object on the Stage.

2. Click on a frame later in the Timeline.

3. Click the Insert menu, point to Timeline, and then click Keyframe.

   A new keyframe appears.

   TIMESAVER *Press F6 to add a keyframe or Control+click (Mac) or right-click (Win) the selected frame, and then click Add Keyframe.*

Did You Know?

You can remove content from a keyframe. Select a filled keyframe in the Timeline or the art on the Stage contained in that keyframe, and then press the Delete (Mac) or Backspace (Win) key.

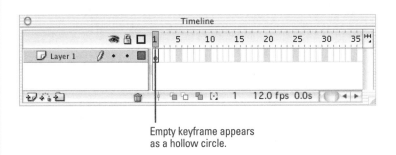

Empty keyframe appears as a hollow circle.

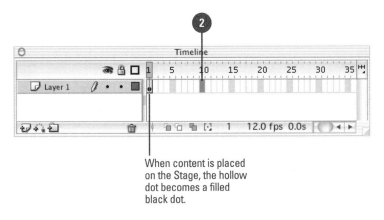

When content is placed on the Stage, the hollow dot becomes a filled black dot.

New keyframe appears

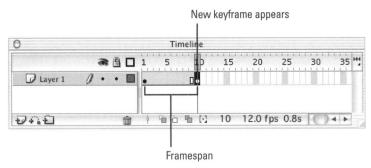

Framespan

Create a Blank Keyframe

1. Click on a frame in the Timeline where you want to add a blank keyframe.

   IMPORTANT *You can only add a blank keyframe to a frame without an existing keyframe (sometimes called an inactive frame or keyspan).*

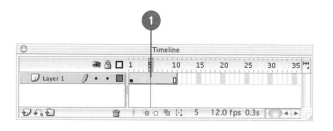

2. Click the Insert menu, point to Timeline, and then click Blank Keyframe.

   TIMESAVER *Press F7 to add a keyframe or Control+click (Mac) or right-click (Win) the selected frame, and then click Add Blank Keyframe.*

Blank keyframe appears

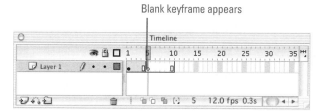

Increase the Keyframe Span

1. Click anywhere in a keyframe span.

2. Click the Insert menu, point to Timeline, and then click Frame.

   Repeat until you've increased the framespan to the length you need.

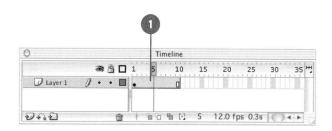

   TIMESAVER *Press F5 to add a keyframe or Control+click (Mac) or right-click (Win) the selected frame, and then click Insert Frame.*

A Framespan increased by 10 frames

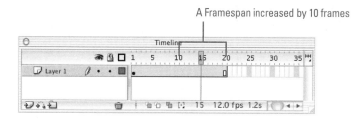

Did You Know?

You can decrease the keyframe span. Press Shift+F5 for each frame you want to remove.

Converting Frames to Keyframes

Any frame can be converted into a keyframe. As a timesaver, you can select a range of frames and convert them all into keyframes simultaneously. This is useful when you have many frames to convert. It is also a good technique for fine-tuning shape and motion tweens. After the tween has been applied, you can convert the frames in the tweened span into keyframes and edit them independently.

Convert Multiple Frames Into Keyframes

1. Click on a frame, and then drag to select a frame span.

2. Click the Modify menu, point to Timeline, and then click Convert To Keyframes.

   TIMESAVER *Press Ctrl+click (Mac) or right-click (Win) the selected frame, and then click Convert To Keyframes or Press F6 after selecting all of the frames you want to convert.*

Did You Know?

You don't have to select a frame to add keyframes. If you place the playhead over a frame and add a keyframe or a blank keyframe, it appears without you having to select the actual frame. However, if you are working with multiple layers, Flash adds a keyframe to all layers at that frame if no frame is selected.

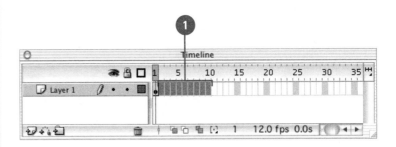

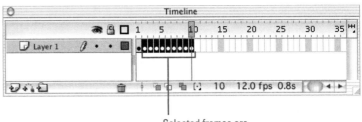

Selected frames are converted into keyframes.

Using Frame-Based Versus Span-Based Selection

Depending upon how you like to work you can choose between two selection modes in Flash. The default mode is frame-based selection. In this mode frames are treated as individual elements. When span-based selection is chosen, Flash treats frames as part of a frame span, which means all of the frames adjacent to a keyframe are selected as a unit. You can accomplish the same tasks in either mode and you can switch between the two depending upon the task at hand.

Set the Frame Selection Style

1. Click the Flash or Flash Professional (Mac) or Edit (Win) menu, and then click Preferences.

2. If necessary, click the General tab.

3. Select the Span Based Selection check box to enable span-based selection or clear it to enable frame-based selection.

4. Click OK.

Did You Know?

You can select a single frame in span-based mode. Press ⌘+click (Mac) or Ctrl+click (Win) the frame. Likewise, to select a span of frames in frame-based mode, click the first or last frame in the span, and then drag until you've selected the entire span.

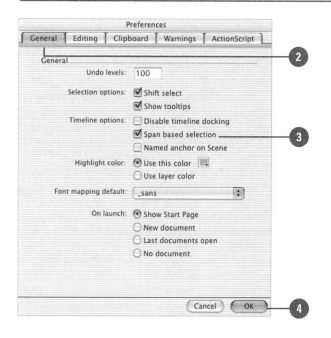

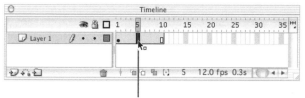

Frame-based selection:
Clicking once on a frame selects that frame

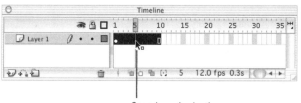

Span-based selection:
Clicking once on a frame selects the entire span

Clearing Keyframes Versus Removing Frames

Clear Keyframes

1 Click on the frame to select it or click and drag to select a range of frames.

2 Click the Modify menu, point to Timeline, and then click Clear Keyframe.

Flash converts the keyframe back into a regular frame.

TIMESAVER *Press Shift+F6 to clear keyframes.*

Depending on what you are trying to accomplish, you can choose to remove a frame's status as a keyframe or remove the frame entirely. Clearing a keyframe preserves the length of the framespan and the overall duration of the animation on the layer. It simply turns the keyframe back into a regular frame and removes any changes the keyframe contained. Conversely, removing frames deletes the entire frame and shortens the framespan as well as the length of your animation in the Timeline.

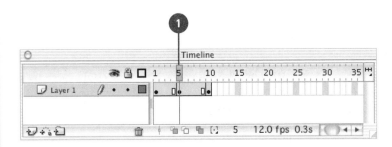

The keyframe is cleared

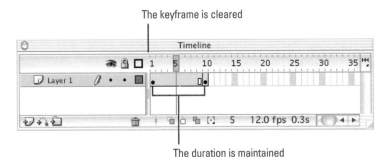

The duration is maintained

Remove Frames

1. Click on the frame to select it or click and drag to select a range of frames.

2. Click the Edit menu, point to Timeline, and then click Remove Frames.

   Flash removes the selected frame(s) and shortens the length of the animation.

   TIMESAVER *Press Shift+F5 to remove frames.*

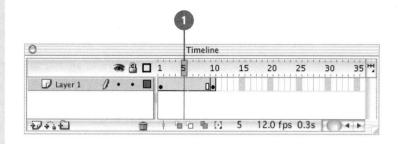

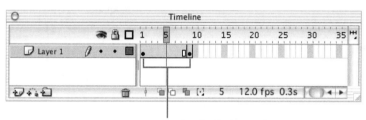

The duration is shortened

Editing Keyframes

Keyframes are editable elements. You can add or remove content from a keyframe, move keyframes around by simply dragging, or copy and paste keyframes in the same Timeline, across scenes and even other Flash documents. Because keyframes are so versatile you can continue to fine-tune your animations after they are created. When the playhead is placed on a frame the content of that frame is displayed on your Stage. Selecting the keyframe in the Timeline selects all of the content on that keyframe on the Stage. Likewise, selecting any of your content on the Stage will select its corresponding keyframe. In this way you can interactively edit the content in a keyframe or the keyframe's position in the Timeline and know what you are affecting.

Copy and Paste Keyframes

1. Click on the keyframe to select it or click and drag to select a keyframe and a range of frames.

2. Click the Edit menu, point to Timeline, and then click Copy Frames.

   TIMESAVER *Press Option+⌘+C (Mac) or Ctrl+Alt+C (Win) to copy frames.*

3. Click on the frame where you want to paste the frames.

4. Click the Edit menu, point to Timeline, and then click Paste Frames.

   TIMESAVER *Press Option+⌘+V (Mac) or Ctrl+Alt+V (Win) to paste frames.*

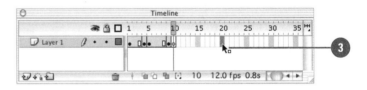

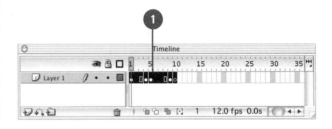

Frames are pasted starting on selected frame.

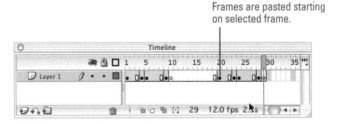

Drag and Drop Keyframes

1 Click on the keyframe to select it or click and drag to select a keyframe and a range of frames.

2 Click again on the selected frame(s), and then drag to a new area of the Timeline.

Did You Know?

It's important to understand the difference between the normal copy and Paste commands and the copy frames and Paste Frames commands. When you copy and paste frames you are copying the keyframes and in-between frames and the content contained in them. Pasting them preserves the structure and layout. If you select a keyframe and use the normal copy and paste commands ⌘+C and ⌘+V (Mac) or Ctrl+C and Ctrl+V (Win), you are only copying the content contained in that keyframe.

You can use drag and drop to copy frames. Press and hold down the Option (Mac) or Alt (Win) key as you drag frames, Flash copies them to a new location.

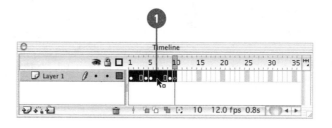

Press the Option key (Mac) or the Alt key (Win) to copy frames as you drag them.

The plus sign (+) modifier indicates a copy has been engaged.

Frames are copied and moved to the new location.

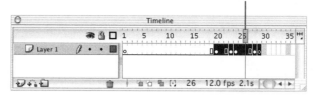

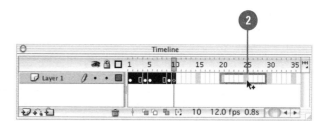

Frames move to the new location.

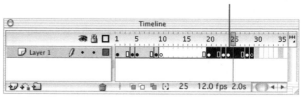

Creating a Simple Frame-By-Frame Animation

Flash incorporates the traditional animation metaphor with its use of keyframe-based animation. Artwork is placed in a keyframe in the Timeline and subsequent keyframes are created to record changes to the artwork. When played consecutively, these minute changes mimic movement as each keyframe describes an altered position or transform effect. Static art that does not change is stored on separate layers and can span the entire animation. In this way, you don't have to redraw the entire frame and you can quickly create complex animations.

Create a Frame-By-Frame Animation

1. Create a new Flash document or open an empty Timeline.

2. Click the first frame to select it.

3. Click the Oval tool in the Toolbar.

4. Click on the Stage, and then drag to draw a circle.

5. Click the second frame to select it.

6. Click the Insert menu, point to Timeline, and then click Keyframe.

   TIMESAVER *Press F6 to insert a keyframe.*

7. Select the second keyframe or double-click the circle on the Stage and drag it slightly to the right.

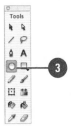

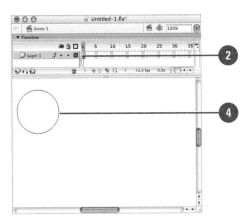

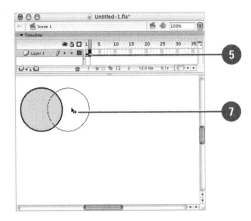

8 Click on the third frame to select it.

9 Repeat step 6.

10 Select the third keyframe or double-click the circle on the Stage and drag it slightly further to the right.

11 Continue to add keyframes and move the circle until it reaches the right edge of the Stage.

IMPORTANT *The more keyframes you add the smoother the animation is.*

12 Click the Playhead and move it across the frames to preview the movement of the circle.

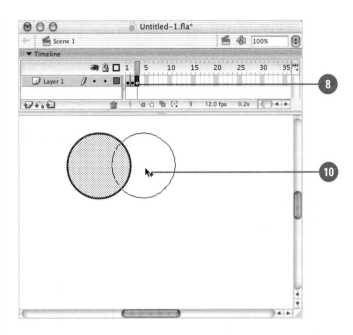

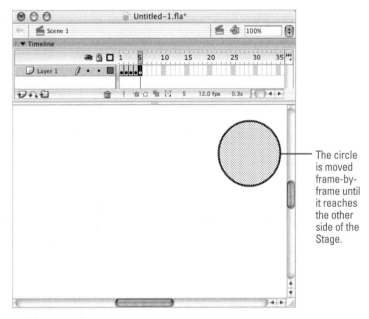

The circle is moved frame-by-frame until it reaches the other side of the Stage.

Playing an Animation

In addition to moving the playhead in the Timeline to view your animation, commonly called scrubbing, Flash provides a controller to navigate the Timeline. The Controller resembles the transport controls on a VCR and can be used in the same way. Additionally, you can export your Flash document into a Flash movie (a .swf file). You do this to see your Flash movie in its final state as there are some elements that are not viewable in the Flash Development environment, such as animations contained in movie clip symbols and ActionScript functionality. To preview basic animations from their own Timeline, you can use the Controller to preview them.

Use the Controller to Play an Animation

1. Click the Window menu, point to Toolbars, and then click Controller.

2. Click Stop to stop the animation.

3. Click Rewind To Beginning to rewind to the first frame of the animation.

4. Click Step Back to step back one frame.

   TIMESAVER *Press the < key to step back a frame.*

5. Click Play to play or stop the animation.

   TIMESAVER *Press Return (Mac) or Enter (Win) to play if stopped or to stop if playing.*

6. Click Step Forward to step forward one frame.

   TIMESAVER *Press the > key to step forward a frame.*

7. Click Go To End to fast-forward to the end of the animation.

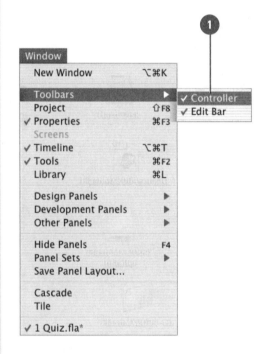

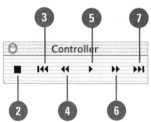

Test Animation in the Flash Player

① Click the Control menu, and then click Test Movie.

Flash exports the entire Timeline and any other scenes you've created into a .swf file that plays in the Flash Player.

TIMESAVER *Press ⌘+Return (Mac) or Ctrl+Enter (Win) to Test Movie.*

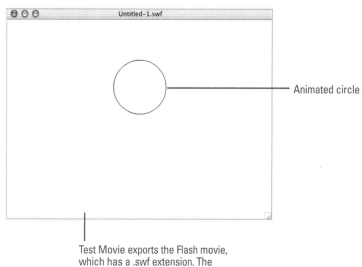

Animated circle

Test Movie exports the Flash movie, which has a .swf extension. The Flash Player plays .swf files.

Using Onion Skinning

Normally the playhead shows one frame at a time—the frame it's placed on. As you play the Timeline the Stage displays the content of one frame at a time forming your animation. Onion Skinning mode allows you to view multiple frames simultaneously. This is useful for fine-tuning your animation because you can see the content on the frames immediately preceding and following the active frame.

Activate Onion Skinning

1 Open a Timeline with a multiple frame animation.

2 Click the Onion Skin Mode button in the Status bar.

Onion skin markers appear in the area above the frame numbers and the area of the range of frames selected dims. The frames that precede the active frame and the frames that follow appear in varying degrees of shading on the Stage, becoming lighter the further they are from the active frame.

In Normal mode, you can only see the content of one frame at a time (the frame the playhead is on).

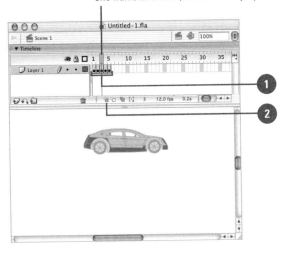

Onion Skin Markers

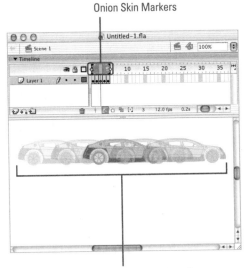

Onion Skinning allows you to see the content on all the frames.

Use Onion Skin Outlines

① Open a Timeline with a multiple frame animation.

② Click the Onion Skin Outlines button in the Status bar.

The frames that precede the active frame and the frames that follow appear as outlines on the Stage.

Did You Know?

You can only edit the active frame.
This is the frame the playhead is on. The art that appears when Onion Skin (regular and outline) is enabled is for preview only.

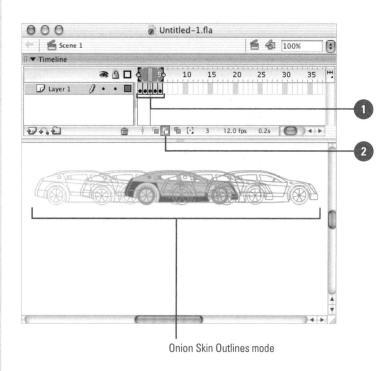

Onion Skin Outlines mode

Modifying Onion Skin Markers ▶

You can adjust the number of frames previewed in the onion skin by manually dragging the onion skin markers. These markers have draggable handles that set the beginning and end of the onion skin. The handles appear as brackets with small dots. Alternately, you can set the range of the markers from the Modify Onion Markers popup menu.

Set Onion Skin Markers Manually

1 Click on the small dot on either end of the onion skin markers and then drag to include or exclude any consecutive frames in the onion skin.

Did You Know?

You can only edit the active frame in the onion skin. To edit other frames and maintain the selected frames, select the Anchor Onion option in the Modify Markers popup menu.

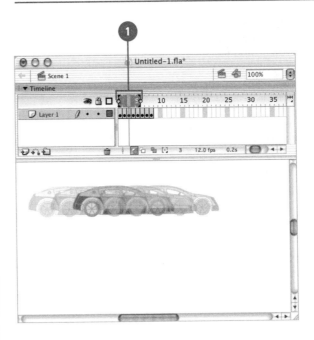

More frames are contained in the Onion Skin Markers, so more of the animation is seen simultaneously.

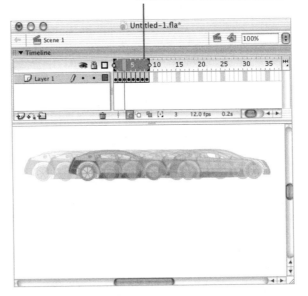

Set Onion Skin Markers in Modify Onion Markers Window

1 Click the Modify Onion Markers button.

The Modify Onion Markers popup appears.

2 Select from the following options:

◆ **Always Show Markers.** Keeps Onion Skin Markers visible in and out of Onion Skin mode.

◆ **Anchor Onion.** Maintains the selected frames even if you move the playhead.

◆ **Onion 2.** Shows two frames before and after the current frame.

◆ **Onion 5.** Shows five frames before and after the current frame.

◆ **Onion All.** Includes the entire duration of the Timeline in the markers.

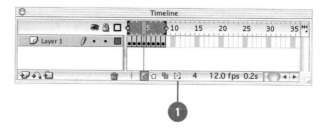

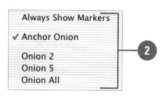

Onion Skin Markers

Command	Description
Always Show Markers	Keeps Onion Skin Markers visible in and out of Onion Skin mode.
Anchor Onion	Prevents the Markers from moving as you move your playhead.
Onion 2	Selects two frames before and after the active frame.
Onion 5	Selects five frames before and after the active frame.
Onion All	Selects all the frames in the Timeline.

Editing Multiple Frames

If you need to make changes to an entire animation or to a multiple series of frames at once, you can select them in Edit Multiple Frames mode. When this feature is enabled, brackets appear similar to those in Onion Skinning mode. Drag them to select the range of frames you want to edit. This works well if you need to make global changes to your animation such as resizing it or changing its location. You can select an entire framespan or layer instead of moving or resizing the content on each individual frame separately.

Select Multiple Frames

1. Open a Timeline with a multiple frame animation.

2. Click the Edit Multiple Frames button in the Status bar.

3. Click and drag the markers until they include all the frames you want to select.

   All of the content in the selected frames appears on the Stage.

4. Click the Arrow tool in the Toolbar.

   TIMESAVER *Press A to select the Arrow tool.*

5. Drag a selection box around the content on the Stage.

   You can make changes to location, scale, effects, etc. All the selected frames will be affected.

   TIMESAVER *Press ⌘+A (Mac) or Ctrl+A (Win) to select all the content on all unlocked layers.*

Did You Know?

When Edit Multiple Frames is activated, it selects all of the frames on all layers contained in the markers. You must lock any layers you don't want included in the selection.

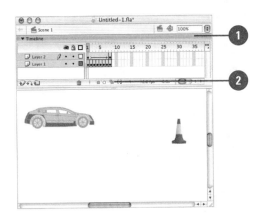

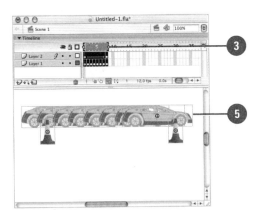

Animating with Motion Tweening

Introduction

In Flash MX 2004, it's not necessary to draw every frame of an animation. You can set the position and attributes of your art in the beginning and ending frames, and Flash will create all of the frames in between. This is called tweening. A motion tween connects two keyframes, each with different effects or characteristics applied to them and then gradually "morphs" one into the other. Tweening allows you to quickly animate objects, apply fades, and gradually alter color, alpha, scale, and any other effect that can be applied to a symbol, group, or text object.

Once an animation is tweened, you can continue to edit it by adding or removing frames to make it move slower or faster, adjust effects, or control the inertia with ease-in and ease-out properties, adding further complexity. Motion tweening produces smaller files than frame-by-frame animation because Flash describes the motion mathematically, incrementally transforming the object in between the two keyframes.

Motion tweening can only be applied to symbols. For editable shapes, groups, and text objects, you must convert them into symbols or Flash will automatically convert them when you apply motion tweening.

What You'll Do

Understand Motion Tweening

Create a Motion Tween

Adjust Motion Tween Properties

Work with Motion Tweening

Understand Frame and Instance Properties

Change the Length of a Tween

Add and Remove Keyframes to a Motion Tween

Change the Frame Rate

Reverse Frames

Animate Scale and Rotation Changes

Add Color Effects to a Tween

Create a Motion Guide Layer

Animate Along a Motion Guide

Orient Objects to a Motion Path

Understanding Motion Tweening

Motion tweening allows you to apply smooth motion and transform effects to symbol instances. Additionally, you can utilize Flash's advanced color effects to apply changes to color, alpha, and brightness.

Because these effects are applied to instances, they only affect the instance placed on the Stage. Its parent (original) symbol in the Library is not affected. Motion tweening produces the smallest file sizes of any of Flash's animation methods.

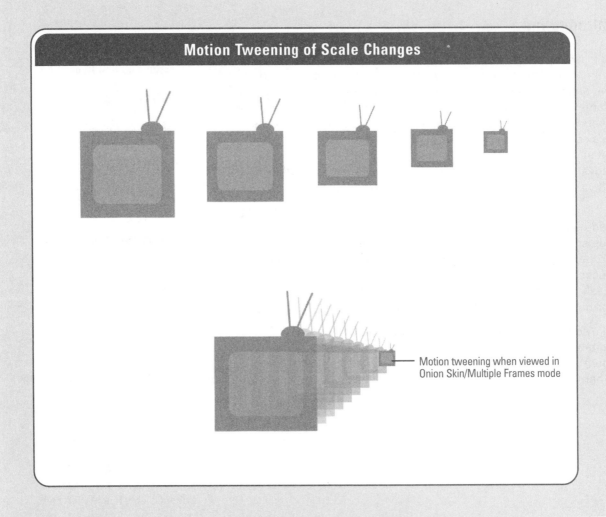

Motion Tweening of Scale Changes

Motion tweening when viewed in Onion Skin/Multiple Frames mode

Motion Tweening of Scale and Alpha Changes

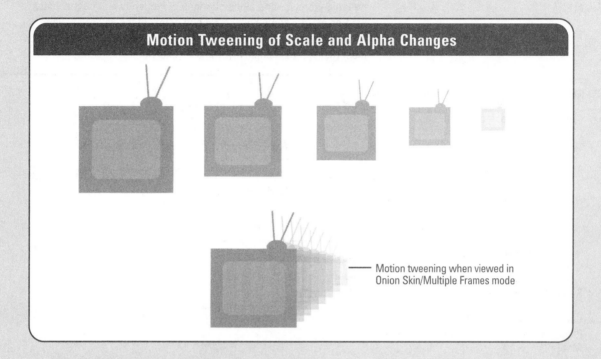

Motion tweening when viewed in Onion Skin/Multiple Frames mode

Motion Tweening of Scale, Alpha, and Rotation Changes

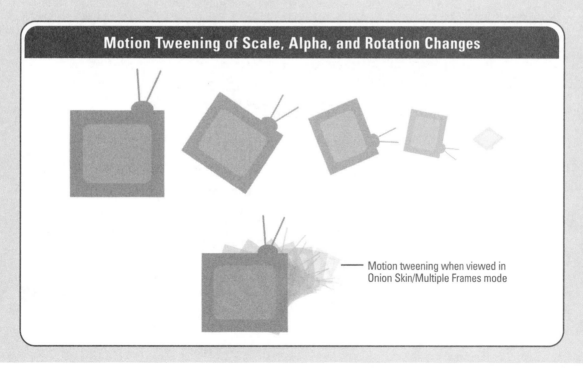

Motion tweening when viewed in Onion Skin/Multiple Frames mode

Creating a Motion Tween

You can tween position, scale, rotation and other transform effects applied to symbols, groups, and text. Additionally, you can apply motion tweening to color and alpha changes. A motion tween connects two keyframes. You should only have one object in the keyframe when you apply the tween or the results will be unpredictable. Tweened frames must reside on the same layer in the Timeline.

Create a Simple Motion Tween

1. Create a new Flash document, and then click on the first frame of the Timeline.

2. Do one of the following:
   - ◆ Draw a shape on the Stage with any of Flash's drawing tools and convert into a symbol.
   - ◆ Drag an instance of a symbol from the Library.

3. Select the first frame.

4. Click the Tween popup in the Property Inspector, and then click Motion.

5. Click frame 10 in the Timeline.

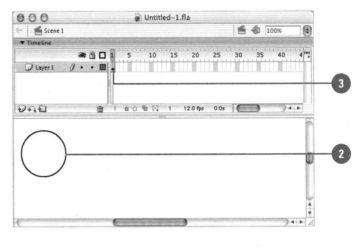

Dotted line indicates a broken or incomplete tween.

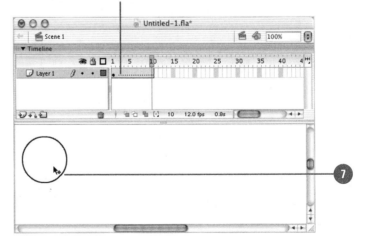

6 Click the Insert menu, point to Timeline, and then click Frame.

Flash displays a dashed line in the framespan to indicate an incomplete or broken motion tween. It also tints the framespan a pale, bluish-purple to indicate that a motion tween has been applied.

TIMESAVER *Press F5 to add frames.*

7 Click and drag the object on the Stage at frame 10 to a new location.

Flash creates a second keyframe that is connected to the first with an arrow. This indicates the motion tween is complete.

8 Click the Control menu, and then click Test Movie to test the animation.

Flash gradually moves the object.

End keyframe is created when object is moved to a new position.

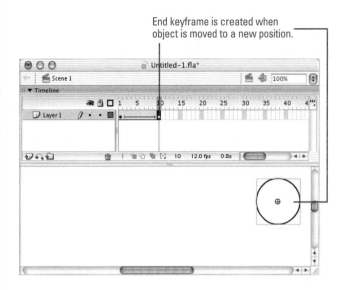

Did You Know?

You can add keyframes and then alter the position of the object on the Stage. Tweening can be applied to any two existing keyframes on the same layer. Select the first keyframe, click the Tweening popup in the Property Inspector, and then click Motion.

You can move keyframes around in the Timeline. Simply click to select it, and then click it again and drag it to a new location.

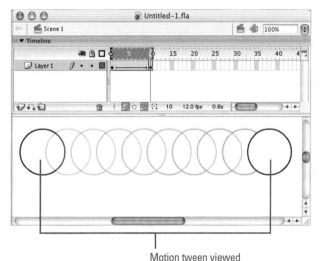

Motion tween viewed in Onion Skin mode.

Adjusting Motion Tween Properties

Motion tweens can be fine-tuned in the Property Inspector. When a tweened frame is selected, a number of options are enabled that you use to add complexity to your motion path. It is also where you remove an applied motion tween. Set the tween to deal with scale, set rotation direction and frequency, or apply inertia by easing in or out of the motion. Additionally, you can set orientation and snapping when using a motion guide.

Set Motion Tween Properties

1. Click the Window menu, and then click Properties to open the Property Inspector.

2. Select a keyframe with motion tween applied.

3. Choose from the following settings:

   ◆ **Tween.** Click this popup to apply motion or shape tweening or to turn these off.

   ◆ **Scale.** Check this when you are tweening scale changes.

   ◆ **Rotate.** Sets the direction and frequency your object rotates.

   ◆ **Orient To Path.** Use this when you have applied a motion guide layer. This keeps your object parallel to the guide relative to its centerpoint.

   ◆ **Sync.** This synchronizes the animation contained in the symbol with the Timeline that contains it. Use this when your symbol's Timeline is not an even number of frames.

   ◆ **Snap.** Check to snap the object's registration point to a motion guide.

   ◆ **Warning Button.** This button only appears if there is a problem with the motion tween. Click it to receive information describing the problem.

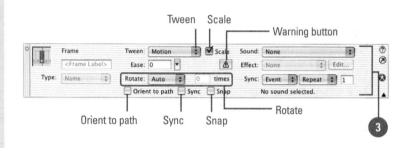

Set Ease Properties in a Motion Tween

1. Click the Window menu, and then click Properties to open the Property Inspector.

2. Select a keyframe with motion tween applied.

3. Click the Ease list arrow, and then select the setting to set the speed at which your object eases in or out of its motion.

   A positive value eases in, a negative value eases out. A zero value evenly distributes motion across each frame.

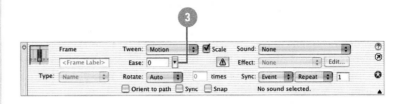

No Easing

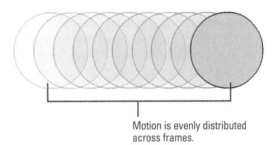

Motion is evenly distributed across frames.

Ease Out

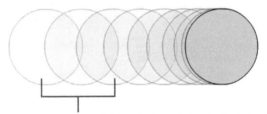

Most of the motion is applied to the beginning frames so the object appears to slow down as it stops.

Ease In

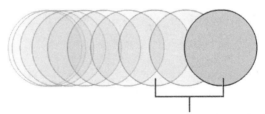

Most of the motion is applied to the end frames so the object appears to slowly accelerate.

Working with Motion Tweening

Motion tweening can only be applied to instances of symbols. When applying motion tweening to groups or text objects, Flash automatically converts them into symbols and stores them in the Library. When this happens, they appear in the Library named as Tween 1, Tween 2, etc. It is a good idea to convert them into symbols as the tweening is applied. When managing large projects with many assets it can become confusing to have assets named in this generic way. Of course you can always rename them by selecting the field in the Library and typing in a new name.

If your tweened animation doesn't behave as expected, there are a few things you can check. If the object disappears when you play the animation and only re-appears on the end keyframe, you may have more than one object on the keyframe. Make sure that only one object, or instance, is on each keyframe in the tweened span. Also, make sure that both instances are of the same object. Flash cannot motion tween two different objects. To "morph" different shapes into each other you must use shape tweening.

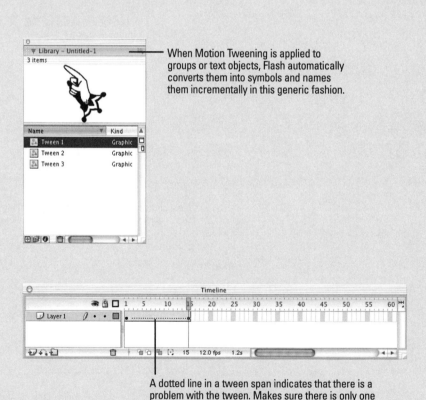

When Motion Tweening is applied to groups or text objects, Flash automatically converts them into symbols and names them incrementally in this generic fashion.

A dotted line in a tween span indicates that there is a problem with the tween. Makes sure there is only one instance (the same instance) on each keyframe.

Understanding Frame and Instance Properties

There is a difference between frame properties and instance properties. This is a source of initial confusion when dealing with animation tweens (both motion and shape). Because the Property Inspector is context-sensitive, it displays properties for many different objects in Flash depending on which of these objects is selected.

Motion (and shape) tweens are applied to keyframes in the Timeline. Color and Transform effects are applied to instances on the Stage. To view the motion tween properties for a specific frame or keyframe, you must select that frame. It is here that you activate tweening and tell Flash what you are going to tween (such as scale or rotation). This needs to be differentiated from the effects you apply to the instances in the tweened keyframes. These are accessed in the Property Inspector and the Transform panel whenever any instance is selected on the Stage. For example, if you check scale as an option in the tween properties for a keyframe, a change in size only results if the size of one of the instances is changed. Conversely, if you want to tween a change in alpha, you can't do this by selecting either of the keyframes in a tween; you must select the instance on the Stage and apply the alpha change when the instance properties appear in the Property Inspector.

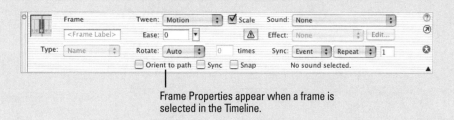

Frame Properties appear when a frame is selected in the Timeline.

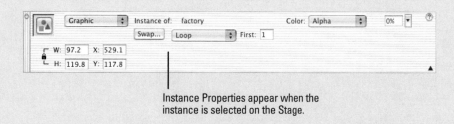

Instance Properties appear when the instance is selected on the Stage.

Changing the Length of a Tween

Tweens in Flash are editable after they have been created. You can continue to change their properties and position in the Timeline, and Flash redraws the tweened frames. To change the length of a motion or shape tween (that is, the time it takes to complete the tween), you can add or remove frames in the framespan. Essentially you are adjusting the amount of frames Flash uses in its calculation of the tween. Adding frames means it takes longer for the transformation to happen, while deleting frames shortens the time.

Add Frames to a Tween

1. Click anywhere except the last keyframe on a motion or shape tweened framespan to place the playhead.

2. Click the Insert menu, point to Timeline, and then click Frame.

TIMESAVER *Press F5 to add frames.*

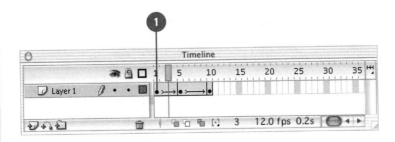

Frame is added to tween span

Duration of other tweens is maintained

Remove Frames from a Tween

1. Click anywhere on a motion or shape tweened framespan to place the playhead.

2. Click the Edit menu, point to Timeline, and then click Remove Frames.

   TIMESAVER *Press Shift+F5 to subtract frames.*

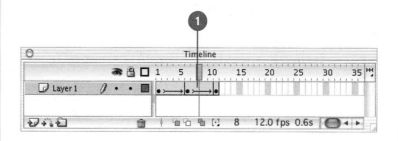

Tween span is reduced by one frame

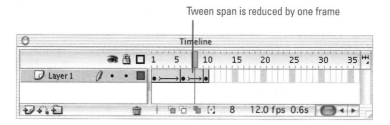

Did You Know?

If no layer is selected, the entire Timeline increases or decreases when you add or remove frames. To constrain this action to one target layer, lock all other layers you don't want to affect, or simply select the frame in the tween you want to adjust.

Tweens with more frames will be smoother. The more frames you add to a tween, the smoother the animation plays, because Flash has more frames to split the motion between. However, if you add too many frames the animation may move so slowly that the illusion of movement could be hampered. It is best to experiment with the length of a motion or shape tween and the frame rate of your Flash movie until you get the results you are looking for.

8

Adding and Removing Keyframes from a Motion Tween

You can add keyframes to a motion tween by simply dragging the object on the Stage on the frame you want the change (or keyframe) to be created or by using the Add Keyframe function in the Insert menu. For example, if you want the object to move to another coordinate before it reaches the end position, you can set another keyframe between them. In this way, you can animate shapes in several directions in the same motion tween. Alternately, you can clear a keyframe from the tween by selecting it and using the Clear Keyframe function in the Modify menu. In either case, the length of the tween is preserved; the frames status as a keyframe is removed and Flash redraws the animation, connecting the keyframes located before and after.

Add a Keyframe to a Motion Tween

1 Click on a frame in a tweened framespan you want to add a keyframe to.

2 Click the Insert menu, point to Timeline, and then click Keyframe.

TIMESAVER *Press F6 to insert a keyframe.*

Did You Know?

You can click and drag the object on the Stage and move it to another coordinate. Flash automatically creates a keyframe on the active frame if the playhead is in a motion tweened framespan.

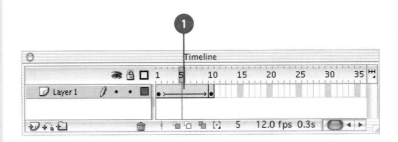

Keyframe is added

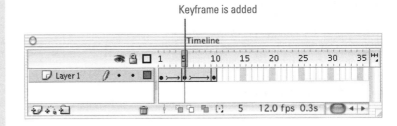

Remove a Keyframe from a Motion Tween

1. Click on the keyframe you want to remove in the motion tween.

2. Click the Modify menu, point to Timeline, and then click Clear Keyframe.

   The keyframe is cleared but the duration of the tween is preserved. The first and last keyframe are automatically reconnected and Flash redraws the tween.

   TIMESAVER *Press Shift+F6 to remove the keyframe.*

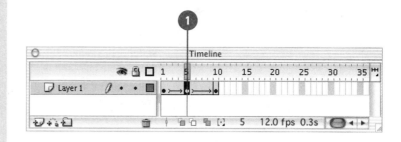

Keyframe is removed

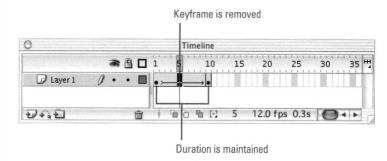

Duration is maintained

8

Changing the Frame Rate

The frame rate describes the amount of frames the Flash Player will play each second. The higher you set the frame rate, the smoother your animations will play. Traditional animations play at a rate of 24 frames per second, the same rate at which film plays, while NTSC video plays at 29.97 frames per second. It is important to keep your audience in mind and what the destination of the Flash movie will be. For delivery via the Web you should consider the processor speeds of the destination computers. If you set the frame rate too high, the computer may not be powerful enough to play all of the frames. When this happens, Flash will drop frames in order to stay in sync. Try to avoid this scenario because it can make your animations play choppy. Consider where your Flash movie is going to be played and choose accordingly. Avoid frame rates over 30 fps and for slower computers, you can go as low as 12 fps, which is the default frame rate in Flash.

Change Frame Rate

1 Click in the Frame Rate field in the Property Inspector.

2 Type in a frame rate.

Document settings appear in the Property Inspector when nothing is selected on the Stage or the Timeline.

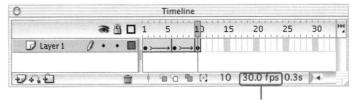

The frame rate is displayed on the Timeline's information bar.

Did You Know?

You can also change the frame rate in the Document options window. Access this window by clicking the Document button in the Property Inspector or in the Modify menu.

Reversing Frames

Use the Reverse Frames command to reverse the frames in the Timeline. You can access this action in the Modify menu and it will be applied to all selected frames. This works for animations created frame-by-frame or with motion or shape tweening applied. Flash changes the order of the frames so your animation plays backwards.

Reverse Frames

1. Click and drag on the range of the frame span or tween you want to reverse.

2. Click the Modify menu, point to Timeline, and then click Reverse Frames.

   TROUBLE? *If the tween is not preserved when you use the reverse frames command, you might not have applied motion or shape tweening to the end keyframe in the tween. Flash only requires you to apply tweening to the starting keyframe in a tween. It is implied that it tweens into the next (or end) keyframe. To fix this, do one of the following: (1) Before you reverse frames, select the end keyframe and apply Motion (for motion tweening) or Shape (for shape tweening) to it from the Property Inspector. (2) After you reverse frames, select the beginning keyframe (which use to be the end keyframe) and apply Motion (for motion tweening) or Shape (for shape tweening) to it from the Property Inspector.*

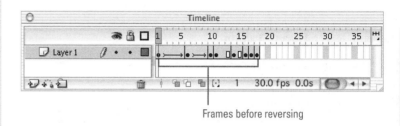

Frames before reversing

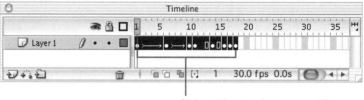

Click and drag to select a range of frames

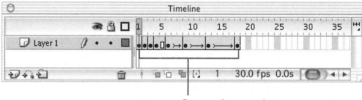

Frames after reversing

Did You Know?

You can select an entire layer and reverse all the frames on that layer. To select an entire layer, click the layer name to select it, and then reverse frames.

Animating Scale and Rotation Changes

Any change made to an object on either keyframe can be tweened. Included are any changes made to the scale or rotation of objects on either keyframes in a tweened span. Simply alter the size or rotation of the instance on either frame and Flash gradually tweens these properties. To change scale, you must select the scale option in the Property Inspector, while rotation has several options to choose from, including clockwise and counter-clockwise rotation, and frequency of rotation.

Change Scale During Tween

① Open a document with a tweened animation or create a new one.

② Select the first keyframe in the tween to open the Motion settings in the Property Inspector.

③ Select the Scale check box in the Property Inspector.

④ Change the size of the object on either keyframe with any of Flash's transform methods including the Free Transform tool, the Transform panel or the transform options in the Modify menu.

⑤ Click the Control Menu, and then click Test Movie to test the animation.

Flash gradually increases or decreases the size of the object.

TIMESAVER *Press ⌘+Return (Mac) or Ctrl+Enter (Win) to test your movie by viewing it in the Flash Player.*

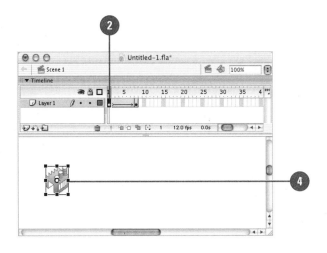

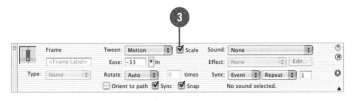

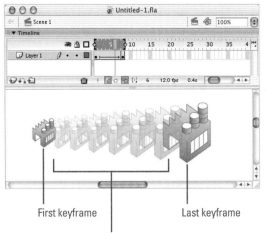

First keyframe

Last keyframe

Scale and position changes tweened

Change Rotation During Tween

① Open a document with a tweened animation or create a new one.

② Change the rotation of the object on either keyframe with any of Flash's transform methods including the Free Transform tool, the Transform panel or the transform options in the Modify menu.

③ In the Property Inspector, select a rotation property:

◆ **None.** This is the default setting. No rotation is applied.

◆ **Auto.** Rotates the object in the direction requiring the least motion.

◆ **CW.** Rotates the object clockwise. Enter the number of times you want the object to rotate.

◆ **CCW.** Rotates the object counter-clockwise. Enter the number of times you want the object to rotate.

④ Click the Control Menu, and then click Test Movie to test the animation.

Flash gradually rotates the object in the direction indicated.

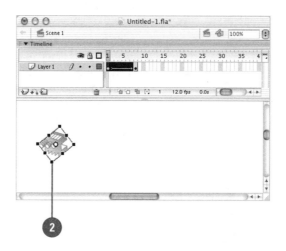

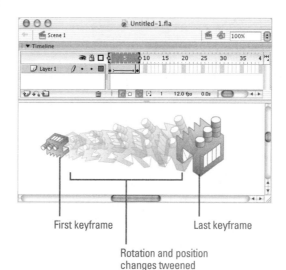

First keyframe   Last keyframe

Rotation and position
changes tweened

Adding Color Effects to a Tween

Any color effect that can be applied to an instance can be transformed in a motion tween. You can tween any color properties applied to either the starting or ending keyframe. For example, if the starting keyframe in a motion tween is tinted red and the ending keyframe is tinted yellow, Flash will gradually change the tint of the object from red, through shades of orange to the final tint of yellow. Use these properties to create any number of color effects in your animations. Additionally, you can tween the alpha of an object to make it appear to fade on and off the Stage.

Tween a Color Effect

1. Open a Timeline with a tweened animation or create a new one.

2. Select the object on the Stage on either keyframe in the tween.

3. In the Property Inspector, select an effect from the Color popup.

4. Click the list arrow to set the percentage of the Color Style applied or enter a value in the entry field.

> **TROUBLE?** *If the Color styles don't appear in the Property Inspector, you may have selected the keyframe in the Timeline and not the object on the Stage.*

5. Play the animation.

   Flash applies the tint gradually between the two keyframes.

See Also

See "Creating a Motion Tween" on page 218 for information on creating a motion tween.

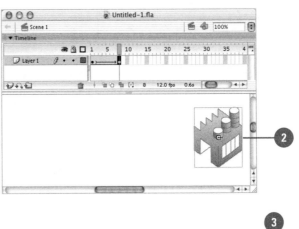

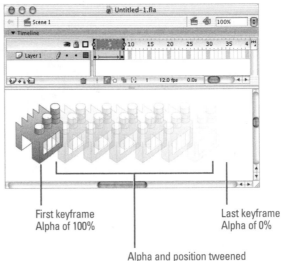

First keyframe
Alpha of 100%

Last keyframe
Alpha of 0%

Alpha and position tweened

Creating a Motion Guide Layer

If you want to implement motion that is smoother, or that follows a curve or some specific path, you can create a motion guide. A motion guide has its own layer just above the layer containing the object. Flash allows you to draw a line that you want your object to follow with any of the built-in drawing tools. Because this layer is a guide, it will be invisible in the exported Flash movie.

Create a Motion Guide

1. Select the layer containing the motion tween.

2. Click the Add Motion Guide button in the Status bar.

   Flash creates a new layer above the selected layer and indents the affected layer.

   TIMESAVER *Press Control+click (Mac) or right-click (Win) the layer you want to add a motion guide to, and then click Add Motion Guide.*

3. Click on the motion guide layer to select it.

4. Draw a line on the Stage with any of Flash's drawing tools to define the path your object will follow.

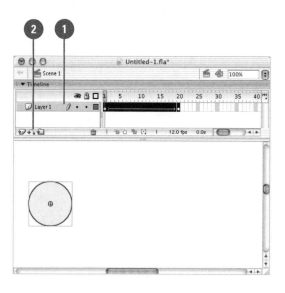

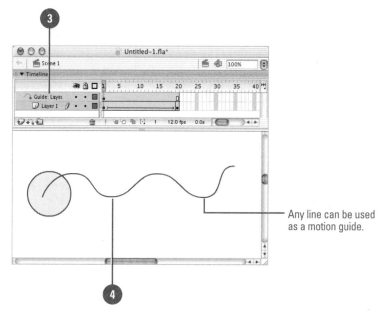

Any line can be used as a motion guide.

8

Animating Along a Motion Guide

Turn snapping on to easily animate along a motion guide. The center point of the object must be on the motion guide path for it to work and snapping ensures that this happens. Once the motion guide is created, all you have to do is drag the object in the first and last frames of the tween to the motion path you drew and Flash will draw the in-between frames along this path.

Animate Along a Motion Path

1. Create a motion guide.

2. Click on the first keyframe of the motion tween, and then click and drag the object on the Stage onto the start of the motion path.

   The object snaps to the motion path.

   TROUBLE? *If the object doesn't snap to the motion path, verify that the Snap setting is turned on in the Property Inspector for this frame. The objects on both the beginning and ending keyframe must be snapped to the motion guide line for the motion to follow the guide line.*

3. Click on the last keyframe of the motion tween, and then click and drag the object on the Stage onto the end of the motion path.

   The object follows the line you drew located in the motion guide layer.

See Also

See "Creating a Motion Guide Layer" on page 233 for information on creating a motion guide.

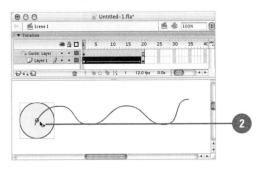

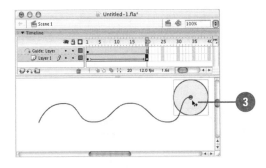

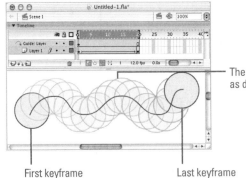

The object follows the path as defined on the guide layer.

First keyframe   Last keyframe

Verify snapping is enabled

Orienting Objects to a Motion Path

When objects are tweened along a motion path, they remain in their native orientation regardless of the path. For certain objects, such as a circle, this is ok. For more complex objects, you must rotate the object so that it follows the path in a more naturalistic way. A good example of this sort of orientation in motion is in the path a car takes while driving down a road-the car must rotate gradually as the road curves to remain parallel with the road, and so, avoid disaster. Flash can do this work for you when you set the Orient To Path option in the motion tween settings.

Animate Along a Motion Path

1. Animate an object along a motion guide.

2. Click on the first keyframe of the motion tween to select it.

3. Select the Orient To Path check box in the Property Inspector.

   The object will automatically rotate to remain parallel with the motion guide.

See Also

See "Animating Along a Motion Guide" on page 234 for information on creating animation using a motion guide.

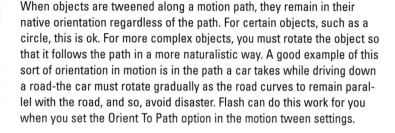

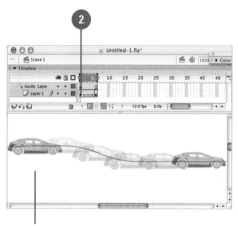

Tweening along a motion guide without orientation can seem unnatural.

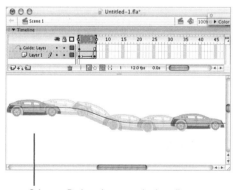

Orient to Path makes sure the baseline is always parallel.

Animating with Shape Tweening

Introduction

Shape tweening works similarly to motion tweening. It follows the same structure of keyframing in the Timeline. You can animate many of the same changes such as alpha, color, scale, and position though its main purpose is to transform the shape of an object into another shape. Whereas motion tweening is applied to groups and symbols, shape tweening must be applied to an editable shape. You can determine whether an object is editable by selecting it with the Arrow tool- if it doesn't have a bounding box when selected, shape tweening can be applied. The reason for this is that when you convert a shape into a symbol, you are essentially protecting it from editing by storing it in its own Timeline. To apply shape tweening to a symbol, you must enter symbol editing mode and apply it to the shape contained inside the symbol. Shapes are created with any of Flash's drawing tools, such as the Oval or Rectangle tools. By making changes to the shape with any of Flash's editing tools, you can change the contours of the shape (for example, turn a circle into a square) and then use shape tweening to make this change happen gradually over time. Because the results of a shape tween can be unpredictable, you can set shape hints to let Flash know how to proceed with the tween. This is useful when you are working with complex shapes such as letterforms. In all cases you should only tween one shape at a time in a tweened span for best results.

Using Shape Tweening

You can use shape tweening when you need to alter the form of any editable shape gradually. Place artwork in a keyframe and then use any of Flash's drawing and editing tools to adjust the contours of a shape on another keyframe. When you apply shape tweening, Flash draws the frames in-between the two keyframes so that the object appears to "morph" between the two states. To provide even more control, you can use shape hints.

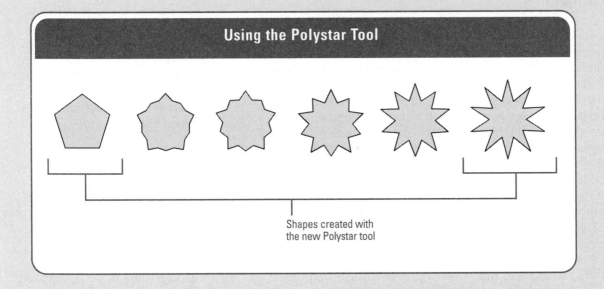

Using the Polystar Tool

Shapes created with
the new Polystar tool

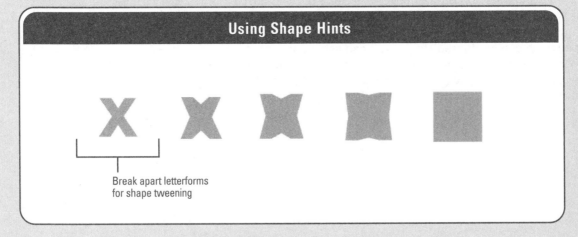

Using Shape Hints

Break apart letterforms
for shape tweening

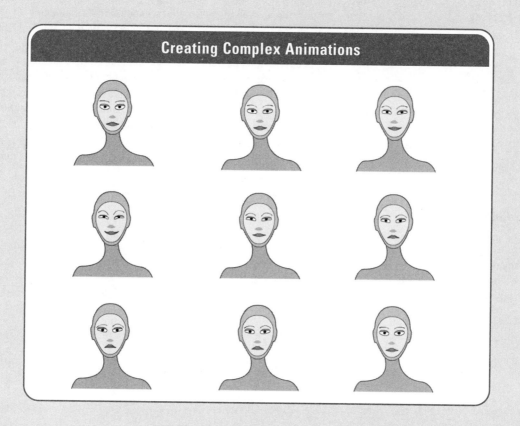

Creating Complex Animations

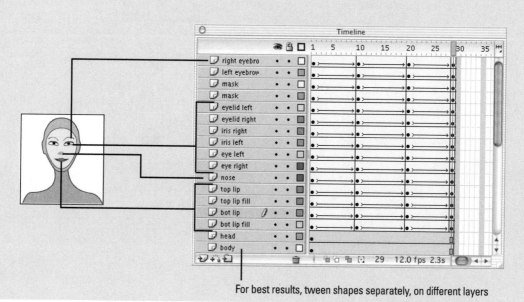

For best results, tween shapes separately, on different layers

Creating a Shape Tween Form

In most cases you can easily shape tween any two simple shapes. Geometric forms such as lines, rectangles and circles yield the best results. Because Flash draws the tweened frames mathematically, the simpler the shape, the more likely it will tween without any problems or without having to apply corrections such as shape hints. Experimentation is the key. As long as both keyframes contain an editable shape, Flash will attempt to "morph" one object into another. Use any of Flash's drawing tools or import a vector shape from another vector drawing program. If you want to apply a shape tween to grouped artwork or a symbol, you can break apart the group or enter symbol editing mode and apply the shape tween to any editable shape in the symbol's Timeline. You can quickly view your animation by exporting it with the Test Movie command. By default, Flash loops animations in the Flash Player.

Create a Shape Tween Form

1. Create a new Flash document.

2. With any of Flash's drawing tools, draw a shape on the Stage at frame 1.

3. Select the first frame.

4. Click the Tween popup, and then click Shape.

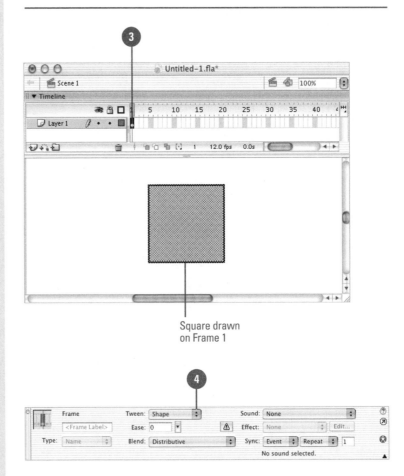

Square drawn on Frame 1

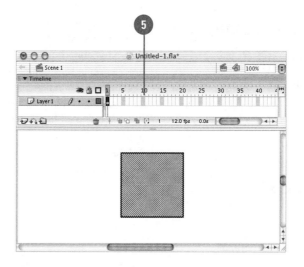

⑤ Select frame 10.

⑥ Click the Insert menu, point to Timeline, and then click Blank Keyframe.

Flash tints a shape tweened span a pale green.

TIMESAVER *Press F7 to add a blank keyframe.*

⑦ With any of Flash's drawing tools, draw a different shape on the Stage at frame 10.

⑧ Click the Control Menu, and then click Test Movie to test the animation.

The shape on frame 1 slowly transforms into the shape on frame 10.

TIMESAVER *Press ⌘+Return (Mac) or Ctrl+Enter (Win) to test your movie by viewing it in the Flash Player.*

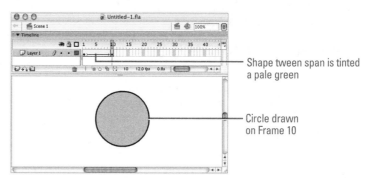

Shape tween span is tinted a pale green

Circle drawn on Frame 10

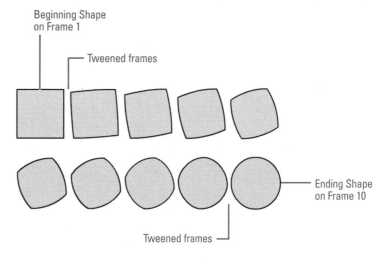

Beginning Shape on Frame 1

Tweened frames

Ending Shape on Frame 10

Tweened frames

9

Adding and Removing Keyframes from a Shape Tween

The procedure for adding or removing keyframes in a shape tween is similar to that of motion tweens except for one crucial difference. In a motion tweened framespan you can drag the object on the Stage and a new keyframe is automatically created. In shape tweened spans, the object is only selectable on a keyframe. To add additional locations or shape changes along a shape tweened span, you must add the keyframe first and then edit the shape. You can do this by using the Add Keyframe function in the Insert menu. Once the keyframe is added, the shape at that point in the framespan becomes editable.

Add a Keyframe to a Shape Tween

1. Place the playhead between any two shape tweened keyframes.

2. Click the Insert menu, point to Timeline, and then click Keyframe.

    TIMESAVER *Press F6 to insert a keyframe.*

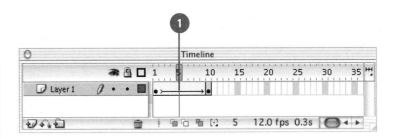

Keyframe is added

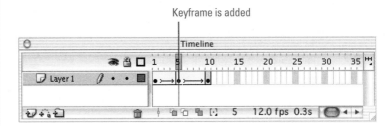

Remove a Keyframe from a Shape Tween

① Click on the keyframe you want to remove in the shape tween.

② Click the Modify menu, point to Timeline, and then click Clear Keyframe.

The keyframe is cleared but the duration of the tween is preserved. The first and last keyframe are automatically reconnected and Flash redraws the tween.

TIMESAVER *Press Shift+F6 to remove the keyframe.*

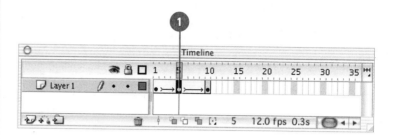

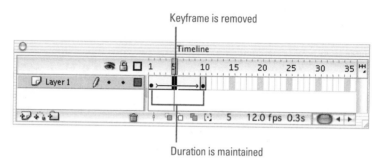

Keyframe is removed

Duration is maintained

9

Changing Shape Positions with Shape Tweening

To create a shape tween you need to draw or place an editable shape in a keyframe. Use any of Flash's drawing tools or import a vector shape from another vector drawing program. If you want to apply a shape tween to grouped artwork or a symbol, you can break apart the group or enter symbol editing mode and apply the shape tween to any editable shape in the symbol's Timeline. You can quickly view your animation by exporting it with the Test Movie command. By default, Flash loops animations in the Flash Player.

Animate a Ball with Shape Tweening

1. Create a new Flash document.

2. Select the Oval tool in the Toolbar.

3. Set the Stroke Color to None.

4. On the first frame, draw a circle on the left side of the Stage.

5. Select the first frame.

6. Click the Tween popup in the Property Inspector, and then click Shape.

7. Click frame 20 in the Timeline.

8. Click the Insert menu, point to Timeline, and then click Keyframe.

   Flash tints a shape tweened span a pale green.

   TIMESAVER *Press F6 to add a keyframe.*

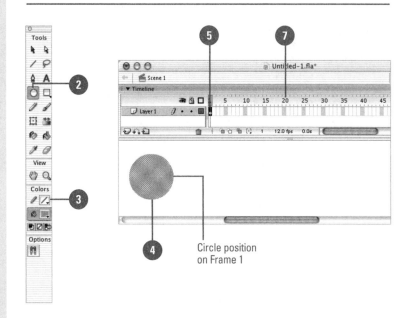

Circle position on Frame 1

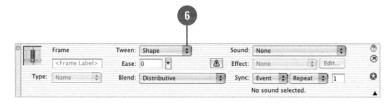

9 Select the Arrow tool in the Toolbar.

10 Select the circle on frame 20 and drag it to the right side of the Stage.

11 Click frame 40 in the Timeline, and then add another keyframe.

12 Select the circle shape on frame 40 and drag it back to the left side of the Stage.

13 Click the Control Menu, and then click Test Movie to test the animation.

The ball animates back and forth across the screen.

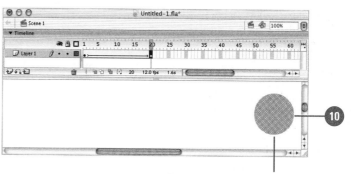

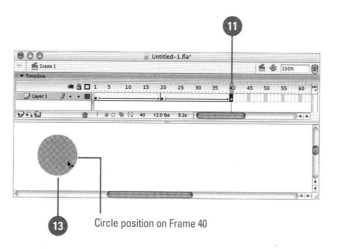

Circle position on Frame 20

Circle position on Frame 40

Changing Shape Position and Form Simultaneously

Many of the same motion effects can be applied using either motion or shape tweening. What differentiates shape tweening from motion tweening is that shape tweening is applied to editable shapes. You can change the form of the shape on either keyframe and these changes will be applied gradually by Flash across the tween, slowly "morphing" one into the other. Additionally, you can combine movement with this tweening process so your shape can change its shape as it changes its location.

Combine Shape Tweening and Movement in a Ball Animation

① Create a shape tween of a moving ball that begins on the left side of the Stage, hits the right side of the Stage, and then returns to the left.

② Click to place the playhead between the first and second keyframes in the shape tween.

③ Click the Insert menu, point to Timeline, and then click Keyframe.

④ Select the Arrow tool in the Toolbar.

⑤ Place the pointer on the left edge of the shape and pull it to create a tail off the circle.

The shape must be deselected on the Stage to pull the edges of the shape.

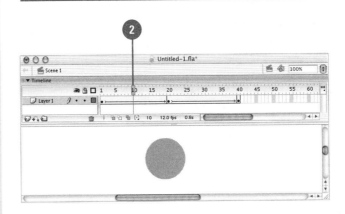

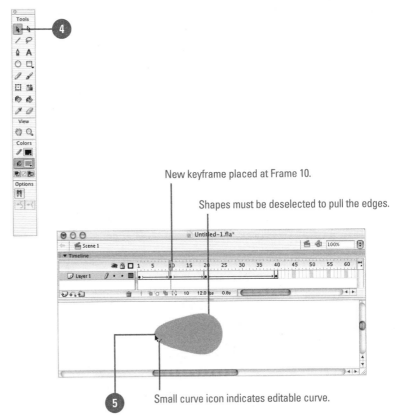

New keyframe placed at Frame 10.

Shapes must be deselected to pull the edges.

Small curve icon indicates editable curve.

6 Click to place the playhead between the second and third keyframes in the shape tween.

7 Click the Insert menu, point to Timeline, and then click Keyframe.

8 With the Arrow tool still selected, place the pointer on the right edge of the shape and pull it to create a tail off the circle.

9 Click the Control Menu, and then click Test Movie to test the animation.

The ball stretches as it animates back and forth across the screen.

See Also

See "Changing Shape Positions with Shape Tweening" on page 244 for information on animating a moving ball.

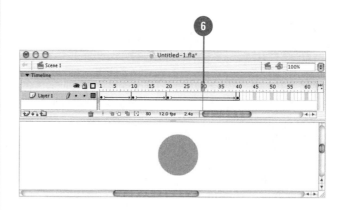

New keyframe placed at Frame 30.

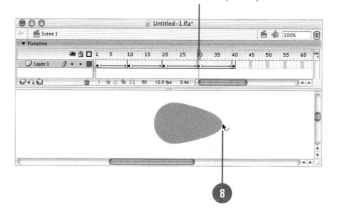

9

Adjusting Shape Tween Properties

When shape tweens are applied to keyframes, the Property Inspector enables several options for controlling how Flash draws the tweened frames. Settings such as easing in and easing out enable you to control how the shape changes are distributed across the frames in the tween. Frame Blending allows you to set preferences to let Flash know which qualities to maintain during the tween.

Set Shape Tween Properties

1. Click the Window menu, and then click Properties to open the Property Inspector.

2. Select a keyframe with shape tween applied.

3. Choose from the following settings:

   ◆ **Ease**. This sets the speed at which your object eases in or out of its motion. A positive value eases in, a negative value eases out.

   ◆ **Blend**. The Distributive option smoothes out the tweened shapes, while the Angular option preserves corners and straight lines in the shape tweens.

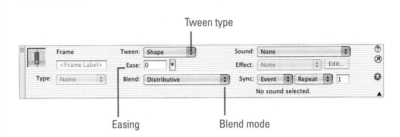

Tween type

Easing

Blend mode

Changing Shape Tweening Color and Alpha Options

Because shape tweening can only be applied to editable shapes, you can't use the same color style effects that are available to instances. Instead, you must make these changes directly to the shape using the color palettes, the Color Mixer, or the Swatches Panel. When shape tweening is applied, differences in color and alpha are tweened along with any shape changes. This applies to strokes as well as fills.

Change Shape Tween Color

1. Select the beginning or ending keyframe in a shape tween or select the shape on the Stage.

2. Click the Window Menu, point to Design Panels, and then click Color Mixer.

   TIMESAVER *Press Shift+F9 to open the Color Mixer.*

3. Make changes to the shape's stroke and fill colors by entering values in the RGB and Alpha fields, or by using the list arrows to the right of these fields.

4. Click the Control Menu, and then click Test Movie to test color tween.

Did You Know?

You can use any palette available to change the color of a shape in a tween. In addition to the Color Mixer, there are palettes located in the Toolbar, Property Inspector, and Swatches panel.

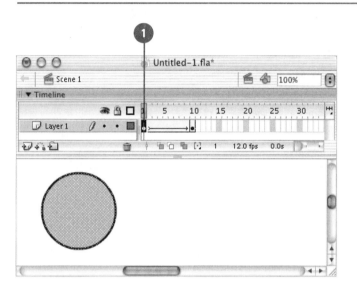

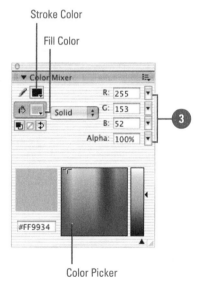

Stroke Color

Fill Color

Color Picker

Using Shape Hints

Sometimes it isn't possible to predict how some, more complicated, shapes will tween. To exercise greater control over the tweening process you can set shape hints to guide how Flash draws the in-between frames. You simply specify a beginning shape hint and then a corresponding end shape hint. In this way, Flash will know which parts of the shape in the first keyframe will transform into which parts in the end keyframe. Even with shape hints enabled the results can be unpredictable but you will have a greater control over the process.

Set Shape Hints

1 Create a shape tween of a simple shape into a complex shape.

2 Click to place the playhead on the first frame of the shape tween.

3 Click the Modify menu, point to Shape, and then click Add Shape Hint.

A small red, circle with a small letter on it appears in the center of the shape. The first letter is "a". Shape hints appear in alphabetical order "a, b, c...". You can use up to 26 hints in one tween.

TIMESAVER *Press Shift+⇧⌘+H (Mac) or Ctrl+Shift+H (Win) to insert a shape hint.*

4 Drag the shape hint to an area of the shape you want to control.

5 Click to place the playhead on the last frame of the shape tween.

The corresponding shape hint appears as a small green circle with a corresponding letter that matches the beginning hint.

Did You Know?

You can remove shape hints. Drag shape hints off the Stage or click the Modify menu, point to Shape, and then click Remove All Hints.

Place start shape hints on problem areas.

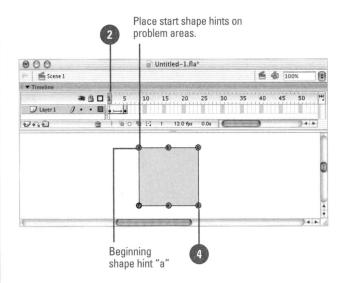

Beginning shape hint "a"

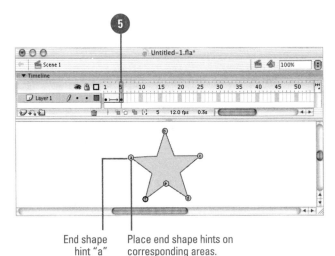

End shape hint "a"   Place end shape hints on corresponding areas.

⑥ Drag the corresponding end shape hints to the part of the shape that corresponds to the placement of the beginning shape hint.

"a" should correspond with "a", "b" should correspond with "b", etc...

⑦ Move the playhead back to the first frame.

⑧ Repeat steps 3, 4, 5, 6, and 7 until you have set and placed shape hints on all areas of the shape you want to control.

⑨ Click the Control Menu, and then click Test Movie to test the animation.

The shape hints help make complex shape tweens more predictable.

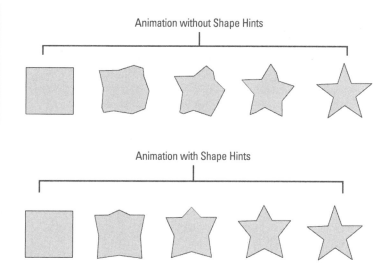

Animation without Shape Hints

Animation with Shape Hints

Did You Know?

You should place your shape hints consecutively in a clockwise or counter-clockwise direction. Placing shape hints out of order can confuse Flash, and often produces unwanted results.

9

Creating Masks

Introduction

You can create mask layers to show and hide parts of your artwork on the Stage. A mask works like a window blocking out everything but a certain area that you define. Any shape, symbol or text object can be used as a mask. The shape you place in a mask layer defines the area that will be visible in the linked layers below it. You can animate a mask to reveal the content on a layer in stages or animate the art in the layer beneath the mask. It is useful for spotlighting and controlling the shape of the viewable area. Masks are great tools for keeping the boundaries of the art on your Stage neat and controlled. They are also useful for cropping, and experimenting with different borders and layouts because you don't have to edit your art, you simply edit the mask. When creating a mask layer it is important not to mix elements. For example, don't use an editable shape and a group on the same mask layer, group everything together or break the groups into editable shapes. However, for the most consistent results, use ungrouped, editable shapes in the mask layer.

Understanding Masks

You use a mask in Flash to control what is viewable on a layer. Whatever you paint or draw onto a mask layer defines the viewable area on any layer it is linked to. Essentially, the shape you place on the mask layer acts like a window to the layers linked beneath it.

To link a layer, you simply drag it into the linked set. When a layer is linked to a mask it displays a tinted icon and is indented underneath the mask layer. Masks are useful for cropping artwork on the Stage and animated masks can create interesting visual effects.

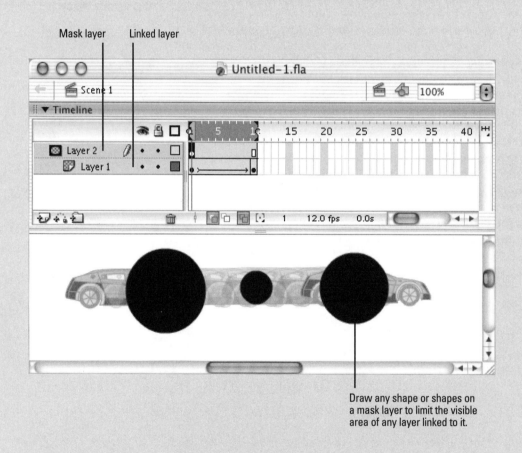

Mask layer   Linked layer

Draw any shape or shapes on a mask layer to limit the visible area of any layer linked to it.

The masked layer and all linked layers must be locked to activate the mask.

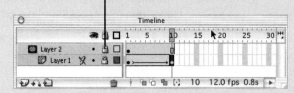

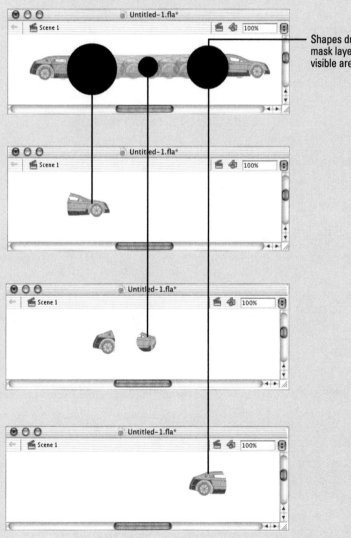

Shapes drawn on the mask layer define the visible area.

Creating a Mask Layer

Any layer can be converted into a mask layer. A **mask layer** only affects the linked layers beneath it and there is no limit to the number of layers that can be included. Once a mask layer is created, you can drag other layers beneath it to link them. It is important to keep in mind that too much masking can affect performance in the Flash Player, especially when objects in the masked layers or the mask itself are animated.

Create a Mask Layer

1. Create a new Layer in the Timeline or select an existing one.

   The layer you select will be the one converted into a mask. If you want to mask the selected layer, create a new layer above this layer and select it.

2. Click the Modify menu, point to Timeline, and then click Layer Properties.

3. Click the Mask option from the Layer Type list.

4. Click OK.

   A blue masking icon appears on the layer.

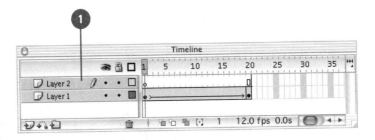

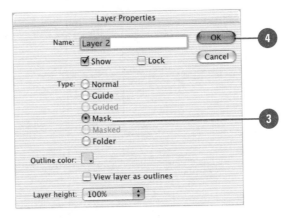

Layer 2 becomes a mask layer indicated by masking icon.

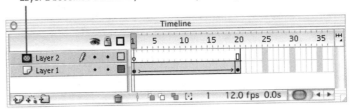

5 Click the layer name of the layer directly beneath the mask layer, and then drag the layer slightly up to link it to the mask.

TIMESAVER *Press Control+click (Mac) or right-click (Win) the Layer Name area of the layer you want to convert into a mask, and then click Mask. When you use this method, Flash converts the layer into a mask and then automatically links it to the layer directly beneath it.*

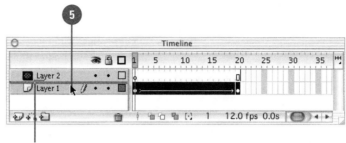

Drag layer 1 slightly up until the gray bar appears. This links it to the mask layer.

Mask layer

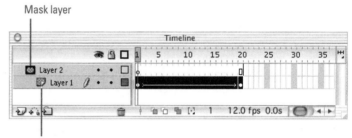

Layer is linked to the mask layer. It appears in the Timeline indented under the mask layer with a tinted icon.

10

Drawing a Mask

Create a Mask Layer

1. Click to select the mask layer.

2. If the mask layer is locked, click on the lock icon in the Lock Layer column to unlock it.

3. Draw a shape with any of Flash's drawing tools or drag a symbol from the Library.

   The area of the shape drawn, or symbol used, is the area that will be visible of the linked layer(s) beneath the layer mask.

You can use any filled shape as a mask. Flash ignores gradients, lines, and the content in bitmaps-in all cases it just deals with the whole shape. Use any of Flash's drawing tools to create a shape that will define the viewable area of the linked layers below. Keep in mind that mixing elements at different levels (editable shapes and symbols, for example) can produce unexpected results. Try to use only one type of element in any one mask: editable shapes, symbols, or groups.

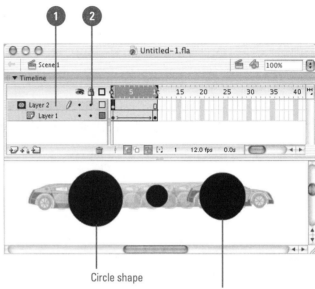

Circle shape

Any shape or shapes drawn on the mask layer defines what is visible in the linked layers beneath.

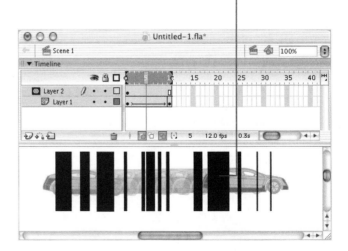

Activating a Mask

To activate a mask, you simply lock it and any of the linked layers beneath it. Linked layers are indented in the Layer Name region and have tinted blue icons. You can lock and unlock a mask and its layers to edit them and see the effects of the mask in the Flash development environment. You can also use the Test Movie command to view the masked effects in the Flash Player.

Activate a Mask

1. Open a document with a masked layer.

2. Click the black dot in the lock column of the mask layer to lock it.

3. Click this dot on each linked layer to lock all of them and see the masking effect.

TIMESAVER *You can click the Lock icon at the top of the lock layers column to lock all the layers in your Timeline simultaneously.*

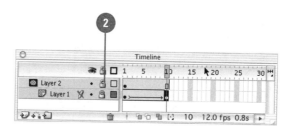

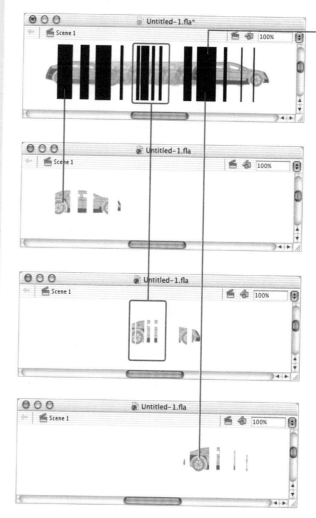

Shapes drawn on the mask layer define the visible area.

10

Editing a Mask

Masks are editable. Which type of element you are using in the mask layer defines the procedure for editing: editable shapes can be modified with Flash's drawing tools, while groups and symbols must be edited in their own editing modes. Regardless, Flash only concerns itself with the fill area. Changes to color, alpha, and other such attributes are ignored. To edit a mask you must first unlock it. To view your changes, simply re-lock the mask layer and all of its linked layers.

Edit a Mask

① If the mask layer is locked, click on the lock icon in the Lock Layer column to unlock the layer and enable it for editing.

② Edit the shape of the mask or if using a group or symbol, enter the group or symbol's editing mode.

③ Relock the mask layer and any linked layers to view changes.

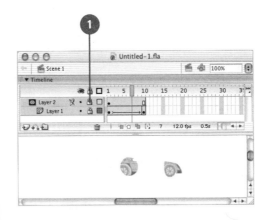

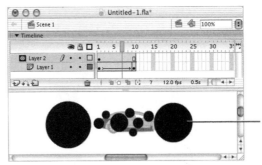

Add or delete shapes, or draw new ones with any of Flash's drawing tools.

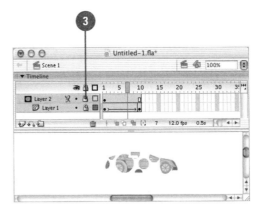

Removing a Mask

To remove a mask layer entirely, you select it, and then click the Delete Layer icon. You can also convert a mask layer back to a normal layer in the Layer Properties dialog. Additionally, you can remove linked layers from a mask layer set by dragging them out of the indented set.

Remove a Mask

① Click on the mask layer to select it.

② Click the Modify menu, point to Timeline, and then click Layer Properties.

③ Click the Normal option from the Layer Type list.

④ Click OK.

The mask layer is converted into a normal layer.

TIMESAVER *Press Control+click (Mac) or right-click (Win) the Layer Name area of the mask layer you want to convert back into a normal layer, and then click Mask to deselect it.*

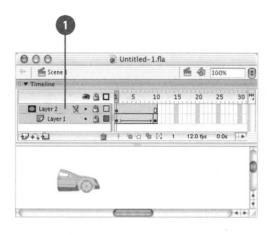

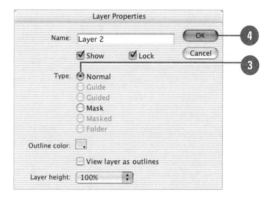

Mask layer becomes a Normal layer

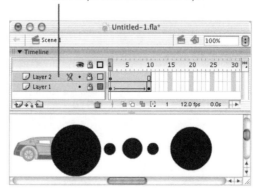

10

Adding Layers to a Mask

Add layers to an existing mask by dragging them to any region within the masked layer hierarchy. Simply drag it between layers already linked, drag it under the mask layer, or drag it slightly up toward the bottom of a masked layer set. There is no limit to the number of layers that can be contained in a mask. Additionally, you can remove linked layers by dragging them out and above the mask layer set.

Link Additional Layers to a Mask

① To add additional layers to a mask, do one of the following:

◆ Click and drag the layer below the mask.

◆ Click and drag the layer until it touches the bottom of a layer already linked to the mask.

> ### Did You Know?
>
> ***You can change the order of the linked layers.*** Masked layers behave the same as other layers. Click and drag the layers to reorder them in the indented set.

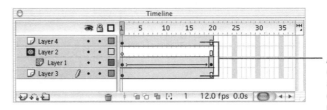

Any layer can be added to an existing mask layer set.

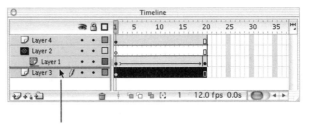

To add a layer to the bottom of the mask set, click and drag slightly up to link it.

To add a layer to the top or between the linked layers of the mask set, click and drag the layer into the indented set.

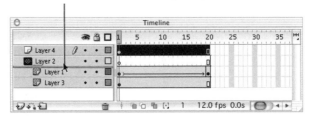

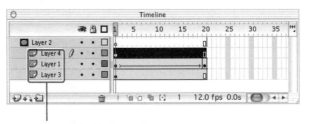

Layers linked to the mask.

Remove a Linked Layer from a Mask

① Click on the linked layer, and then drag it above the masked layer.

The layer will no longer be linked to the mask and the indentation disappears.

Select the layer you want to remove.

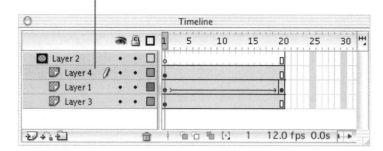

Select the layer you want to remove. Drag it above the mask layer until a gray bar appears.

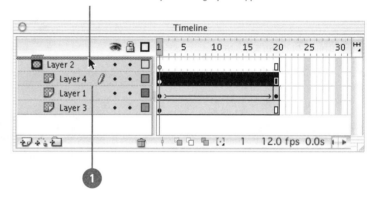

Layer is no longer linked to the mask.

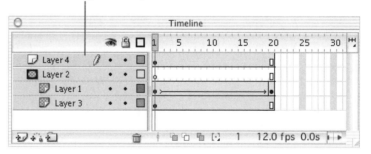

10

Animating a Mask Layer

To create special effects such as a spotlighting effect or a gradual reveal of artwork on the Stage, you can animate a mask. Use any form of animation such as frame-by-frame animation or a shape or motion tween. The path of the shape or object on the mask layer will reveal the art below as it passes over it. Transforms to scale and position work well as well as shape tweens to editable objects. Other effects such as color and alpha will be ignored.

Animate a Mask

1. Place artwork in a linked layer.

2. Click on the first frame of the layer's mask layer in the Timeline.

3. Do one of the following:

   ◆ Draw a shape on the Stage with any of Flash's drawing tools.

   ◆ Drag an instance of a symbol from the Library.

4. Select the first frame.

5 Click the Tween popup in the Property Inspector, and then click Motion (when using symbols) or Shape (when using editable shapes).

6 Click frame 10 in the Timeline.

7 Click the Insert menu, point to Timeline, and then click Keyframe.

TIMESAVER *Press F6 to add a keyframe.*

8 Transform the object with any of Flash's editing procedures: scale, skew, position, or in the case of shape tweening, edit the shape of the object.

9 Lock the mask layer and linked layer to see the effect.

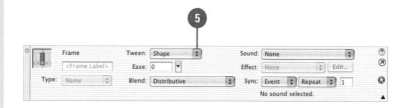

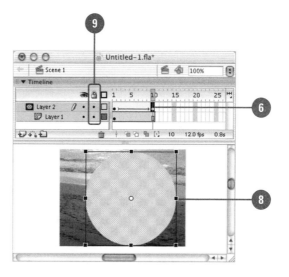

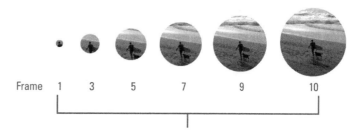

Frame 1   3   5   7   9   10

Tweened scale changes on the masked layer reveal the photograph located on the linked layer beneath the mask in stages.

10

Working with Sounds

Introduction

Incorporating audio can really bring life to a Flash movie; however, the effect is very subtle. For example, most people would not be able to tell you the background music playing behind their favorite movie, but try leaving the sound out and they'll immediately notice. This makes audio a powerful influence on the viewers of your Flash movies. Macromedia understands the power of audio and gives you the ability to import audio in a variety of formats, including MP3, WAV, AIF, and AU. In addition, many formats that are not easy to import can be converted using the QuickTime plug-in. Point your browser to *www.quicktime.com*, and download this free plug-in.

Flash audio can be controlled using Flash's version of JavaScript, called ActionScript, and even gives you the ability to load streaming MP3 files. Add to that the ability to choose between mono and stereo, and you can further reduce the size of your audio files (mono audio files are half the size of stereo). The one drawback to using audio is that it produces a much larger file (even compressed audio files are relatively large), but even this can be reduced to a minimum by using shared audio libraries. Since audio files create large Flash movies, use sounds when they are necessary to the design of the Flash movie, and remember that sometimes silence is golden.

Importing Audio

When working with Flash, understand that Flash will let you import audio in a variety of formats. However, Flash has no way to record or create sounds. Therefore, audio must come from external sources. External sources include companies such as, Digital Juice; where you can download broadcast quality audio. All you need is a credit card, and a computer with an Internet connection, or you can conduct audio searches on the Internet using you favorite search engine, and find a lot of audio files for free. One other consideration is creating you own audio, using your computer, an attached microphone, and a bit of imagination. When you import an audio file to Flash's Stage, you will first need to have a specific layer and keyframe selected. When you work on a Flash project, it might be beneficial to bring audio files directly into Flash's Library. That way you have easy access to them when needed. In addition, any unused audio files are purged when you publish the Flash movie.

Import Audio Files to the Stage

1. Select a keyframe in the Timeline that you want the audio file placed.

    IMPORTANT *You should always place audio files in a separate layer. This gives you easy access and control over the audio file, once it's been placed on the Stage.*

2. Click the File menu, point to Import, and then click Import To Stage.

3. Select the Audio file, and then click Import (Mac) or Open (Win).

Did You Know?

You can import more than one audio file at a time. Click on an audio file, then hold down the Shift key and click on another file to select contiguous audio files, or hold down the ⌘ (Mac) or the Ctrl key (Win), and then click to select non-contiguous audio files.

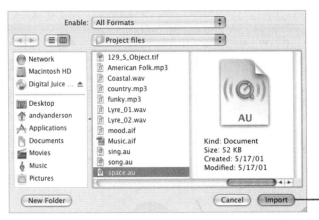

Import Audio Files to the Library

1. Click the File menu, point to Import, and then click Import To Library.

2. Select the audio file or files you want moved into the Library.

3. Click Import To Library (Mac) or Open (Win).

Did You Know?

You can sync sound to a Timeline animation. Select the sound on the Stage, and then change the Sync option on the Properties panel to Stream. Flash will force the animation to sync to the timing of the audio file even if it has to drop video frames to keep up.

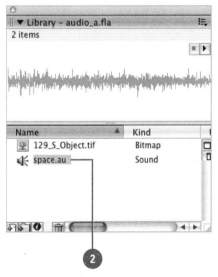

11

Using Audio on the Timeline

Once you've imported audio files into the active document's Library, it's a simple matter to transfer the file to the Timeline. Flash's Timeline is actually a frame-by-frame representation of the Stage. For example, if you select frame 23 on the Timeline, the Stage displays the contents of the 23rd frame on the Stage. Audio, however, does not have a visible Stage object, so when you add an audio file to the Timeline, the effects are only apparent on the Timeline, not the Stage. Flash's Library holds all of the audio files that you've imported into the active Flash document. No matter how many times you use that audio file in the source document, Flash only needs to save it one time in the published Flash movie. One of Flash's powerful features is the ability to draw Flash objects, including audio files, from other Flash libraries. External Flash libraries are simply Flash source documents, which have an active Library. This gives you the ability to create libraries of audio files and use them over and over again.

Add Audio Using the Library

1. Click the Window menu, and then click Library.

   TIMESAVER *Press* ⌘+L (Mac) or Ctrl+L (Win) to open the Library panel.

2. Select a layer and keyframe in the Timeline that you want the audio file placed.

3. Drag the audio file from the Library directly onto the Stage.

   Flash will place the audio file in the selected keyframe.

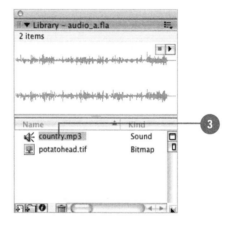

Audio file placed on the keyframe.

Add Audio Using an External Library

1 Click the File menu, point to Import, and then click Open External Library.

2 Select a Flash document that contains an active Library.

3 Click Open.

4 Drag items from the external Library directly to the Stage.

5 Drag items from the external Library to the active document's Library.

IMPORTANT *When you drag an object from an external Library onto the Stage of the active Flash document, it is automatically added to the active document's Library.*

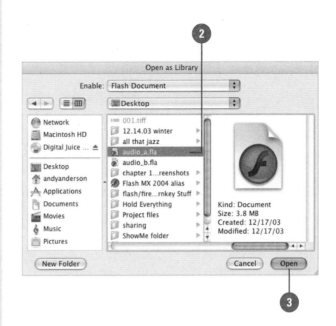

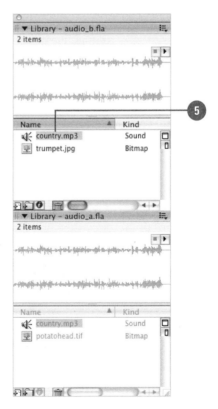

Loading a Sound from a Shared Library

By default, Flash embeds audio files directly into the published (.swf) file. You have the option of loading audio files from a common Library. This gives you the advantage of using the same sounds in several Flash movies at the same time. For example, you create a Web site using fifteen separate Flash movie files, and each one uses the same background music. Rather than embed the same sound fifteen times, you can simply load the sound, when needed, from a common Library. Shared libraries are simple Flash documents that are set up to share their files between several Flash movies. The process is easy, and the rewards are great, and you don't increase the file size of Flash movies using shared Library elements. Once you've created and defined a Flash document as a shared Library, you can use the items in other Flash movies without increasing the size of the Flash published .swf file.

Create a Shared Audio Library

1. Create a new Flash document.

2. Add the audio files to the document's Library. They do not have to be placed on the Stage.

3. Click the File menu, and then click Save. Use a distinctive name for the source document.

4. Select an audio file in the Library.

5. Click the Library Options button, and then click Linkage.

6. Select the Export For Runtime Sharing check box.

7. Enter a distinctive name for the Identifier field or use the default.

8. Enter the name of the published document into the URL field.

9. Click OK.

    Repeat steps 4 through 9 until all the audio files are correctly linked.

10. Click the File menu, and then click Publish to create the Flash .swf file.

11. Close the original source file.

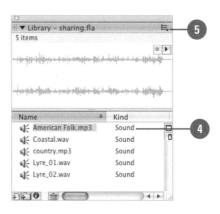

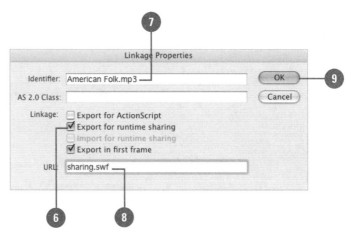

Work with Shared Audio Libraries

1. Click the File menu, point to Import, and then click Open External Library.

2. Select the shared Library, and then click Open.

   The items in the external Library will be grayed out, indicated they are sharable items.

3. Drag the audio files from the external Library to the Library of the active document.

4. When you publish the Flash .swf file, the audio files will be drawn from the common Library, without increasing the size of the Flash movie.

Did You Know?

A Flash Library can be shared with other designers. Since a Library is simply a Flash movie with Library elements, you can create common libraries of often-used elements, and then give them to other designers. When you're working with two or more designers, this is a great way to maintain consistency on a complex project.

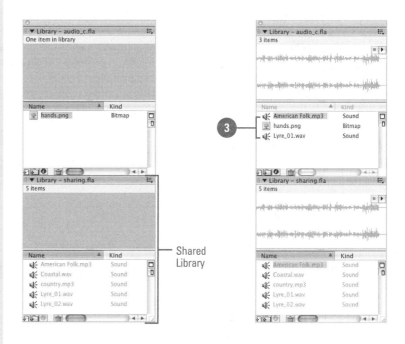

Shared Library

Using Audio with ActionScript Behaviors

Sound is a great motivator. For example, a particular piece of music can make you happy, or it can make you sad. In addition, sounds can pull out childhood memories, and can stir emotions. Sound is a powerful tool, however, different people react differently to sounds, therefore it's important that you think carefully about the sounds you add to your movies, and it's equally important to understand how you can control your movies using ActionScript Behaviors.

Load a Sound from the Library

1. Click the Window menu, and then click Library.

2. Select an audio file from the available Library items.

3. Click the Library Options button, and then click Linkage.

4. Select Export For ActionScript.

5. Enter a distinctive name for the Identifier field or use the default.

6. Leave the other fields at their default values, and then click OK.

7. Click the Window menu, point to Development Panels, and then click Behaviors.

8. Select a button object on the Stage or Timeline keyframe.

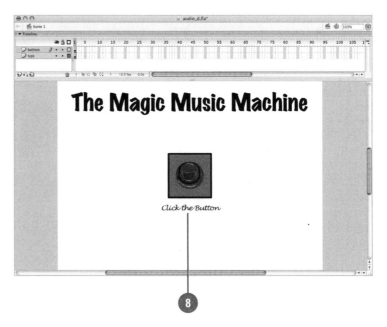

9 Click the plus (+) sign, located in the upper-left portion of the Behaviors panel, point to Sound, and then click Load Sound From Library.

10 Enter the name of the audio file in the Linkage ID field.

11 Enter a unique name in the instance field.

12 Select Play This Sound When Loaded.

13 Click OK.

14 Select an Event to trigger the sound.

IMPORTANT *If the audio file was added to a Timeline frame, the event field will be disabled.*

15 Click the Control menu, and then click Test Movie to test the ActionScript.

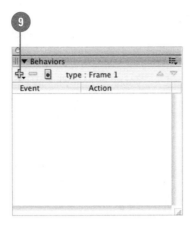

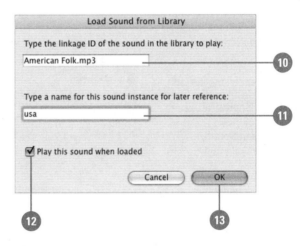

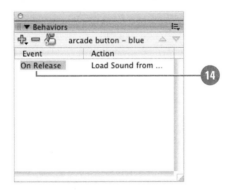

11

Playing and Stopping Sounds

Whenever you place sounds in a Flash document, it's nice to give your visitors control over the playing and stopping of a specific sound. Giving visitors control over a Flash movie gives them more confidence. Most marketing studies show that if a visitor has more confidence over a Flash document, they'll stay longer. If it's a marketing document, that confidence translates into a greater chance that the visitor will buy what you're selling. If it's a training document, the visitor is more likely to listen to what you're saying, and learn from it. Remember, control leads to confidence, and to better Flash documents.

Play and Stop Sounds

1. Select a sound in the Library.

2. Click the Library Options button, and then click Linkage.

3. Check Export For ActionScript, and then click OK.

4. Select a layer to place the sound.

5. Click the plus (+) sign located in the upper-left portion of the Behaviors panel, point to Sound, and then click Load Sound From Library.

6. Enter the name of the sound in the Linkage ID field.

7. Give the file a unique instance name.

8. Clear the Play This Sound When Loaded check box.

9. Click OK.

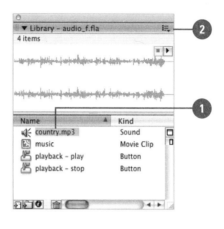

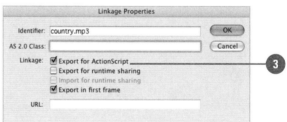

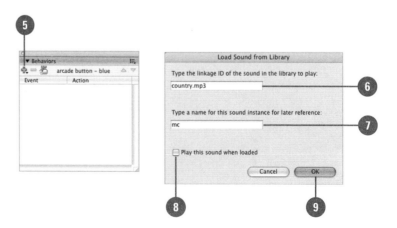

10 Place a Play and Stop button on the Stage.

11 Click the Play button.

12 Click the plus (+) sign, located in the upper-left portion of the Behaviors panel, point to Sound, and then click Play Sound.

13 Enter the name of the sound instance to play.

14 Click OK.

15 Select an Event to play the sound.

16 Click the Stop button.

17 Click the plus (+) sign, located in the upper-left portion of the Behaviors panel, point to Sound, and then click Stop Sound.

18 Enter the name of the sound instance to stop.

19 Click OK.

20 Select an Event to stop the sound.

21 Click the Control menu, and then click Test Movie to test the ActionScript.

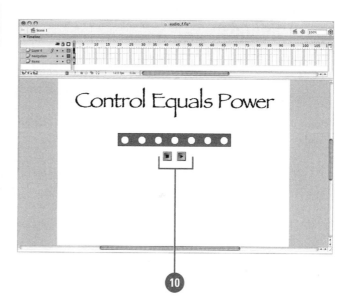

Control Equals Power

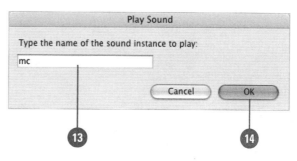

Play Sound

Type the name of the sound instance to play:

mc

Cancel   OK

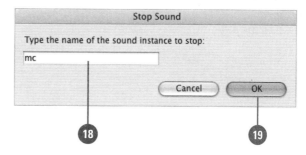

Stop Sound

Type the name of the sound instance to stop:

mc

Cancel   OK

11

Stopping All Sounds

Sound can be a great tool, but it can also be a distraction. For example, you have this wonderful background music playing in your Flash document, unfortunately, the person viewing the Flash movie is at work, surrounded by fellow co-workers. What she needs is a way to stop all the distracting sounds. Flash gives you a generic Behavior that will allow you to do exactly that.

Stop All Sounds

1. Open a Flash source document (.fla) that contains playing audio files.

2. Place a button object on the Stage, and then click it.

3. Click the plus (+) sign, located in the upper-left portion of the Behaviors panel, point to Sound, and then click Stop All Sounds.

4. Click OK.

5. Select an Event to stop the sound.

6. Click the Control menu, and then click Test Movie to test the ActionScript.

   IMPORTANT *When you select the Stop All Sounds behavior, only the sounds playing at that moment will stop. If you have other sounds on the Timeline, they will play when called.*

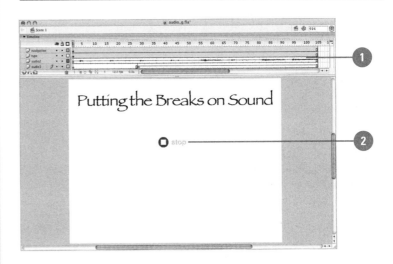

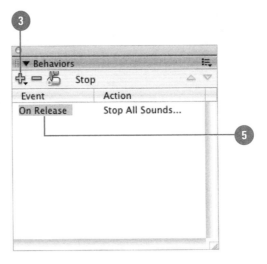

Loading a Streaming MP3 File

You can load a MP3 music audio file using a built in Flash behavior. The advantage to this process is that the file is loaded when needed, and it never increases the size of the original Flash movie. Streaming MP3 files are not part of a pre-existing Flash movie, they're just available from a common location.

Load a Streaming MP3 File

1. Select a button object on the Stage or Timeline keyframe.

2. Click the plus (+) sign, located in the upper-left portion of the Behaviors panel, point to Sound, and then click Load Streaming MP3 File.

3. Enter the URL to the source MP3 file.

4. Enter a unique name in the identifier field.

5. Click OK.

6. If you selected a button object, select an Event to trigger the sound.

7. Click the Control menu, and then click Test Movie, to test the ActionScript.

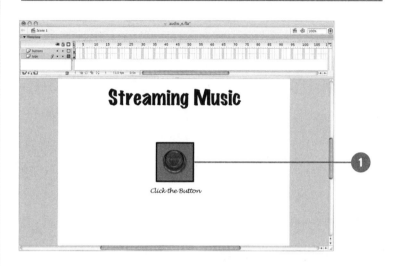

Did You Know?

Streaming MP3 audio files play before they're completely loaded. Flash performs a calculation on the files as it's loading, when it has enough of the audio file; it begins playing, while it continues to download the remaining information in the background. For large audio files, this cuts down on long wait times, and keeps the visitor from becoming bored.

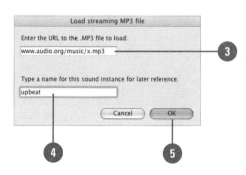

Syncing Sounds to the Timeline

When you sync a sound to the Timeline you're essentially instructing Flash how to play the sound. Syncing sounds is a fundamental operation because choosing the wrong sync operation can drastically change how the sound plays out during the execution of the Flash movie. Flash gives you the ability to choose a separate sync operation for each individual sound file. When you place the sound on the Timeline, the Properties panel displays the audio properties for the selected sound, and lets you define individual properties for every sound in your Flash document. For example, you have a background music sound that's located in several scenes, and you want to make sure it doesn't play on top of itself (Sync: Stop). In addition, you have a narration that you want perfectly synced to an animation on the Timeline (Sync: Stream).

Sync Sounds to the Timeline

1. Select a sound file on the Timeline.

2. Click the Window menu, and then click Properties.

3. Click the Sync popup, and then select from the following options:

   ◆ **Event.** When you select Event (default) the sound plays when the record head reaches the keyframe containing the sound, and continues to play until the end of the sound. If the record head reaches another keyframe that contains the same sound, it will begin playing on top of the original sound.

   ◆ **Start.** Doesn't allow the sound to play on top of itself.

   ◆ **Stop.** Stops a sound if it is already playing, without affecting any other sounds.

   ◆ **Stream.** The Stream Sync creates sounds synchronized to the Timeline. Useful for matching sounds to a particular visual event in the movie. If the video can not keep up with the audio, Flash will automatically drop video frames to keep the audio synchronized.

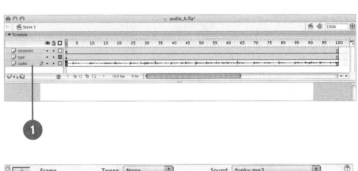

Looping Sounds

When you loop a sound, you're instructing the Flash movie to repeat the sound a given number or times, or to loop the sound forever. Some sounds loop better than others. For example, you create some background music, and you want it to continue to play for as long as the visitor is on that particular page, but you don't want the sound to have a definable beginning or end. Creating looping sounds requires another program such as Sonic Foundry, or Acid Pro. Once the sound is imported into Flash and placed on the Timeline, you can determine the number of loops.

Loop Sounds

1. Click the File menu, point to Import, and then click Import To Library, Import To Stage, or Open External Library.

2. Add the looping sounds to the open document.

3. Click the Window menu, and then click Properties.

4. Select the keyframe containing the sound you want to loop.

5. Click the popup to select Repeat.

6. Enter the number of times you want the sound to loop (up to 9,999).

7. Click the popup to select a Loop option to force the sound into an infinite loop.

    IMPORTANT *The effects applied (including Sync and Looping) will only modify the selected audio file. Each copy of an audio file dragged into a Flash movie is controlled independently.*

11

Editing Sounds

Flash is not a major sound editing application. For example, you can't trim or cut audio files, nor can you enhance audio or reduce hum and background noises. Flash expects all that to be done before you import the file. However, you do have some control over when the sound begins and ends (time in, and time out), and you do have control over the volume (fade in and fade out). Making sure that your audio file is clean and smooth flowing, will help with the quality of your audio file.

Work with Edit Envelope

1. Select a keyframe on the Timeline that contains an audio file.

2. Click the Window menu, and then click Properties.

3. Click the Edit button.

4. Click the Effect popup, and then select from the following options:

   ◆ Left Channel

   ◆ Right Channel

   ◆ Fade Left To Right

   ◆ Fade Right To Left

   ◆ Fade In

   ◆ Fade Out

   ◆ Custom

5. Drag the Time In marker to the right to change where the audio file begins.

6. Drag the Time Out marker to the left to change where the audio file ends (the Time Out marker appears at the end of the audio file).

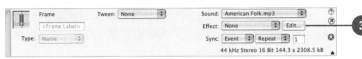

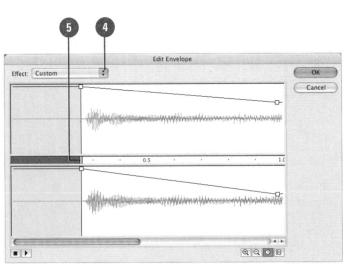

7 Click the Envelope lines to adjust the volume on the right or left channels.

8 Use the Zoom buttons to increase or decrease the size audio file in the edit window.

9 Click the Play or Stop buttons to test the changes to the audio file.

10 Click the Time Marker buttons to change the marker code from frames to seconds.

11 Click OK to save your changes.

IMPORTANT *Adjusting an audio file using Edit Envelope only impacts the select instance of the audio file. The original audio file (in the Library) is unaffected by these changes.*

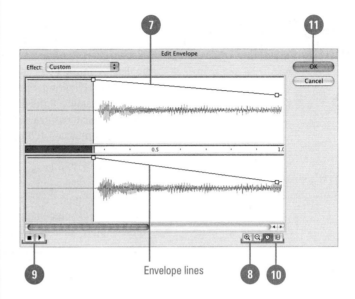

Envelope lines

Publishing Documents Containing Audio

Sooner or later, you're going to want to export your Flash movie that contains audio as an SWF file. The process of publishing is relatively painless; however, there are a few considerations as to the compression of the files, which will be important to the size and playability of the Flash movie. Publishing requires knowledge of where the document will be used. For example, if the document is to be streamed over the Internet, and you're visitors have relatively low bandwidth; you would want to choose compression settings that would significantly reduce the size of the audio files. It's possible that the Flash document is intended for playing off a CD; in that case, you could increase the compression settings. When you're designing a Flash document it's imperative that you understand the end game, and design the document toward that goal. Always remember that you can design a Flash document, but it's your visitors that ultimately will see, and use it.

Publish Sound Documents

1. Click the File menu, and then click Publish Settings.

2. Check Flash (default) on the Formats tab.

3. Click the Flash tab.

4. Click the Set buttons for Audio Stream or Audio Event.

5. Click the Compression popup, and then select from the following options:

   ◆ **Disable.** Turns off all sound compression options, and instructs Flash not to export sounds.

   ◆ **ADPCM.** Performs minor compression to the audio files.

   ◆ **MP3.** Creates audio files, especially music files with excellent quality in a small file size.

   ◆ **Raw.** Leaves the sounds intact without any compression schemes applied.

   ◆ **Speech.** Creates optimized files for the human voice.

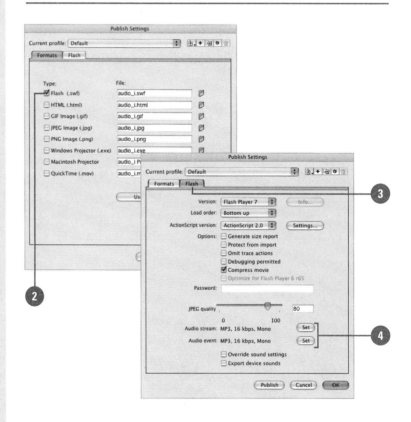

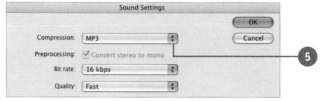

284

6 Select the Convert Stereo To Mono checkbox for the ADPCM and RAW compression formats.

7 Based on your Compression selections from step 5, select the following options:

◆ **Sample Rate.** Available for ADPCM, Raw, and Speech compression. The higher the sample rate the better the quality, but the bigger the file.

◆ **ADPCM bits.** Higher bit values translate into better quality audio, but larger file sizes.

◆ **Quality.** Available for MP3 compression. The Best option gives the finest quality, but produces a larger file.

◆ **Bit Rate.** Available for MP3 compression. The higher the value the better the quality and the bigger the file.

8 Click OK.

9 Select the Override Sound Settings check box to take priority over the individual settings applied to the audio files.

10 Select the Export Device Sounds check box to export device sounds with the published Flash movie.

11 Click OK.

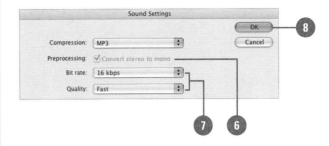

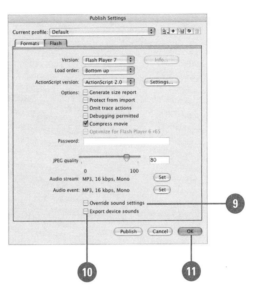

For Your Information

Audio File Quality

You cannot publish a Flash movie with audio files that are better quality than the originals. For example, if the MP3 audio files you're using have a Bit rate of 16kbps, increasing that to 48kbps does not create a better quality audio file. In fact, that's true of most Flash objects, not just audio. To increase the quality of an audio file would require the use of an audio application, such as Sound Forge.

11

Working with Video

Introduction

It wasn't too long ago that Flash and video did not mix. Macromedia introduced Flash to video in MX, and enhanced the feature set in MX 2004. Not only does Flash allow you to import video, it gives you the ability to compress the video using user-defined, or preset values, and lets you trim excess video without the need of using a video-editing application. It's important to understand that although Flash can import, trim, and compress a video file, it can't make the quality of the video any better than the original. If you receive your video from outside sources, there is little you can do; however, if you're the one shooting the footage, pay close attention to lighting, camera angles, and distractions within the video. The more time and attention you spend taking the video, the better the video will be when imported into Flash. However, if you do need to tweak a video file, applications such as Adobe's Premiere (Mac/Win), and Apple's Final Cut Pro (Mac), are excellent choices for the budding movie director.

What You'll Do

Use the Video Import Wizard

Work with Video on the Timeline

Use Movie Clips with Video Files

Use Video with ActionScript Behaviors

Control Video Through Movie Clips

Work with Media Player for Streaming Video

Work with Media Display Component

Work with the Media Controller Component

Export FLV Files from Video-Editing Applications

Working with the FLV File Format

Using the Video Import Wizard

Importing video into Flash is not much more difficult than importing a graphic or audio file. The difference is that Flash will help guide you through the process of choosing the correct compressor for the final movie. It's important that you know the final destination of the Flash movie with video. For example, if you were preparing the .swf file for presentation on the Internet, your compressor setting would be different than, say preparing the same file for burning onto a CD. The Video Import Wizard is Flash's way of helping you through the process of importing video files into Flash. When you import video, the Wizard automatically opens, and guides you through the steps. You can choose to accept the Wizard's recommendations, or you can make changes.

Use the Video Import Wizard

1. Click the Import menu, point to Import, and then click Import To Library.

   IMPORTANT *Although you can import a video directly to the Stage, it is recommended that you import videos first into the Library for ease of access and control, and then into a Library movie clip or to the Stage.*

2. Select the video file, and then click Import To Library.

3. If necessary, select Embed Video In Macromedia Flash Document. If you select the Link To External Video File option you will have to publish the flash movie in the QuickTime format, and then click Next.

4. Select Import The Entire Video or Edit The Video First.

5. Click Next.

6. If you select Edit The Video First, select from the following video editing options:

   ◆ Click the Play, Stop, and Step buttons to preview the video.

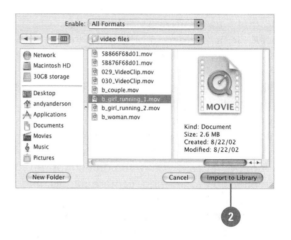

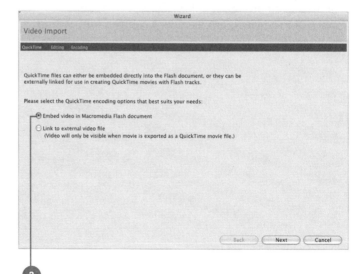

- ◆ Drag the Play Head to quickly position the video to any viewable point.

- ◆ Click the Set In Point and Set Out Point arrows to crop the video file based on the current position of the Play Head.

- ◆ Click the Preview Clip button to preview the edited clip.

- ◆ Click Create Clip to save the current version of the clip in the Edit Clip list.

- ◆ Select a clip from the Edit Clip list, and then click the Update Clip button to edit the clip.

- ◆ Use the arrows to reorder the clips in the Edit Clip list.

- ◆ Click the Trash Can button to delete a selected clip.

- ◆ Check the Combine List option to combine all of the clips into a single file, otherwise they are created in separate files.

7 Click Next.

IMPORTANT *You must have at least one clip, even if it's the entire video file, to continue.*

8 Click the Compression Profile popup, and then select from the available options, or click the Edit button and create your own compression profile.

9 Click the Advanced Settings popup, and then select from the available user-defined profiles, or click the Edit button to edit a user-defined profile.

10 Click the Delete buttons, to delete a compression profile or an advanced settings file.

11 Click Finish.

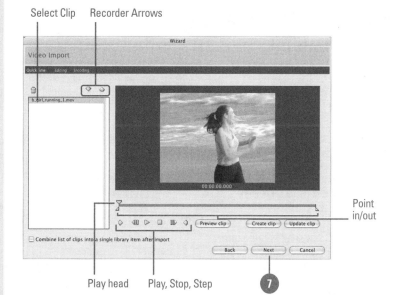

Select Clip   Recorder Arrows

Point in/out

Play head   Play, Stop, Step

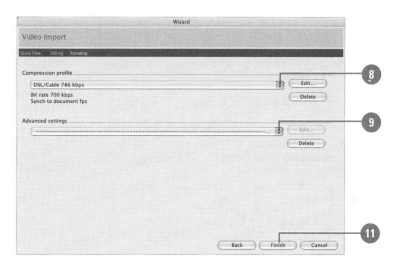

For Your Information

Customized Compression Settings

When you create you own compression settings, you have the option to change the file size, and frame rate of the video file. Since both of these options impact quality, it is recommended that your video files be originally saved at the frame rate, and size needed for the Flash movie.

12

Working with Video on the Timeline

When you import video into a source document, Flash stores a copy of the video in the active document's Library, even if you import the video directly to the Stage Flash will still place a copy in the Library. It's always best to import video files, first into the Library; that way you have control of the video, and how it's brought onto the Stage. Moving a video file directly to the Stage is the easiest way to incorporate video into a Flash movie. In fact, once the video file has been imported into Flash, it's a simple drag and drop operation. However, video files should always be held within a separate layer. That gives you control over the display of the video, and lets you place other Flash elements in other layers.

Move a Video File Directly to the Stage

1. Open a Flash source document (.fla) that contains one or more video files in the Library.

2. Click the Window menu, and then click Library.

3. Click the Insert Layer button, and then name the new layer video_1.

4. Select the new layer.

5. Drag the video file from the Library onto the Stage.

   A dialog box opens indicating how many frames the video file will occupy on the Stage.

6. Click Yes.

7. Click Control, and then click Test Movie to view the video file as it will appear in the Flash movie.

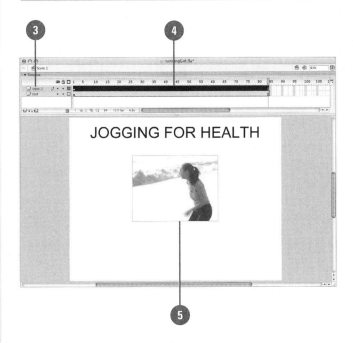

Did You Know?

You can increase the number of video formats you can import into Flash. For free downloads, go to *www.quicktime.com*, and download QuickTime 6 or later (Mac) or go to *www.microsoft.com/directx/* and download DirectX 9 or later (Win).

Using Movie Clips with Video Files

While placing a video file directly onto the Stage may be an easy way to bring a video file into a Flash movie, the best way to control video is to first place it into a movie clip, and then drag the movie clip onto the Stage. That gives you control of the clip with two Timelines: the Timeline on the Stage, and the Timeline of the movie clip.

Use Movie Clips with Video Files

1. Click the Window menu, and then click Library.

2. Click the Insert menu, and then click New Symbol.

3. Name the new symbol, and then click the Movie Clip Option.

4. Click OK.

5. Drag a video file from the Library into the movie clip Library.

6. Click Yes when Flash instructs you as to how many frames the video file will occupy in the movie clip.

7. Return to the current scene by clicking the Scene button, located in the upper-left corner of the Flash window.

8. Click the Insert Layer button, and name the new layer video_1.

9. Select the new layer.

10. Drag the movie clip from the Library onto the Stage.

    The movie clip occupies a single frame.

11. Click Control, and then click Test Movie to view the video file as it will appear in the Flash movie.

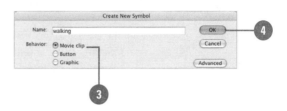

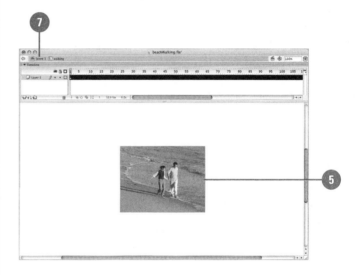

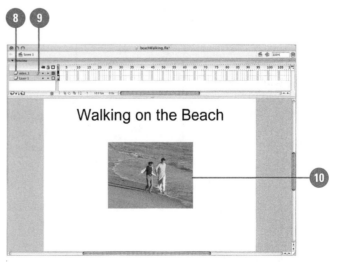

12

Using Video with ActionScript Behaviors

Playing a video file inside a Flash movie is one thing, controlling the movie, or better yet, letting your visitor's control the movie is something quite different. Control of a movie requires knowledge of Flash's ActionScript language. **ActionScripting** is a control language that instructs Flash what to do, and when to do it. For example, you could create an ActionScript that instructs Flash to play or stop a movie, or you could add buttons to move the video backward or forward, one frame at a time. One way to display video in a Flash Movie is to drag it directly from the Library to the Timeline. Once the video is on the Timeline, ActionScripts can be created to start and stop the video. Since you're using the active document's Timeline to control the video, any other layers containing animation sequences on the Timeline will stop and start along with the video.

Control Video from the Timeline

1. Create a new layer to hold the video file, and then select the layer.

2. Drag the video file from the Library to the Stage.

3. Create a new layer to hold the navigation buttons, and then select the layer.

4. Drag a Play, Stop, and Rewind button into the Navigation layer, and then place them underneath the video.

5. Click the Window menu, point to Development Panels, and then click Actions.

> **Did You Know?**
>
> *You can check the syntax of any script with the click of a button.* Click the Check Syntax button, located at the top of the Actions panel, and Flash will check the syntax of the your script.

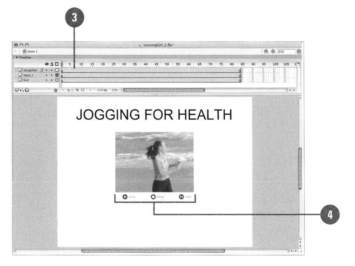

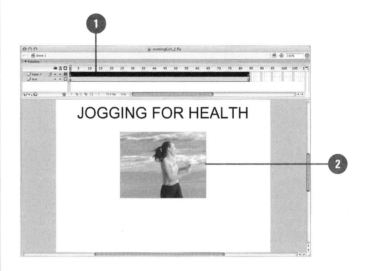

6 Select the Play button, and then enter the script as shown in the illustration.

7 Select the Stop button, and then enter the script as shown in the illustration.

8 Select the Rewind button, and then enter the script as shown in the illustration.

9 Click the Control menu, and then click Test Movie.

Flash tests the ActionScript.

Did You Know?

Flash contains several sets of pre-designed buttons. Click the Window menu, point to Other Panels, Common Libraries, and then click buttons. Flash's button Library contains nine folders with dozens of impressive buttons; including arcade buttons, and buttons for controlling a Flash movie. So, the next time you need a button, check out what's available in Flash's common button Library.

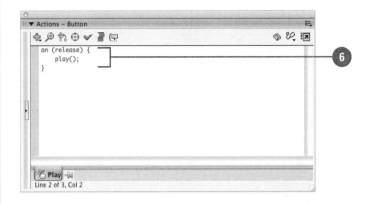

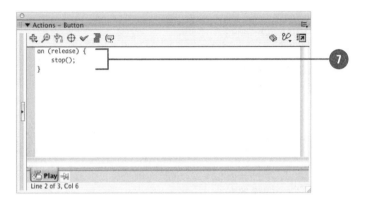

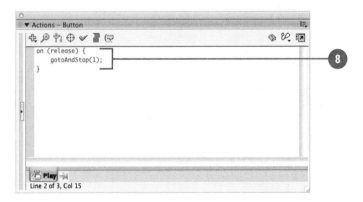

12

Controlling Video Through Movie Clips

While it's an easy matter to drag a video file onto the Stage and then use start and stop ActionScripts to control the playing of the video, it's better to create a movie clip, and then load the video file into the clip. It's a bit more work, but the additional rewards are great. For example, you can instruct a movie clip to stop playing without affecting anything else on the Stage. As a matter of fact, you can have as many movie clips on the Stage as you want, and each one can be controlled individually. It's exactly that kind of control that leads to awesome Flash movies. To control a video using a movie clip you will need to have a flash document that contains one or more video files, in the Library.

Control Video Through Movie Clips

1. Click the Insert button, and then click New Symbol.

2. Name the symbol, and then select the Movie Clip option.

3. Click OK.

4. Drag a video file from your Library into the movie clip symbol.

5. Click the Scene button, to return to the Stage of the active scene.

6. Create a new layer to hold the video, and then select the layer.

7. Drag the movie clip to the Stage, and then select the clip.

8. Enter a unique Instance name in the Property Inspector.

   IMPORTANT *The Instance name you enter will be used in the ActionScript to identify the movie clip to the button object "with (instance name)".*

9. Create a new layer to hold the navigation buttons, and then select the layer.

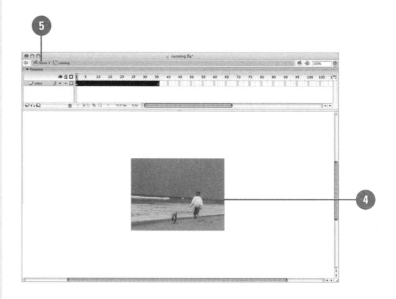

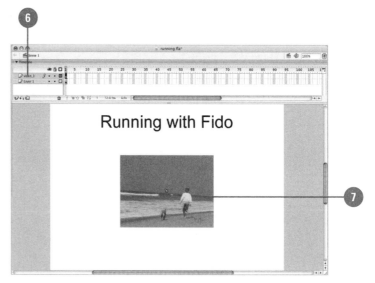

10 Drag a Play, Stop, and Rewind button into the Navigation layer, and then place them underneath the video.

11 Click the Window menu, point to Development Panels, and then click Actions.

12 Select the Play button, and then enter the script as shown in the illustration.

13 Select the Stop button, and then enter the script as shown in the illustration.

14 Select the Rewind button, and then enter the script as shown in the illustration.

15 Click the Control menu, and then click Test Movie.

Flash tests the ActionScript.

IMPORTANT *ActionScripting is a relatively easy language to learn, but it is also a very unforgiving language. For example, the gotoAndStop script must be written exactly as shown, including the capital "A" and "S". While ActionScripting, remember to keep an eye on syntax.*

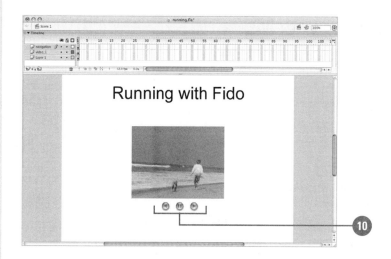

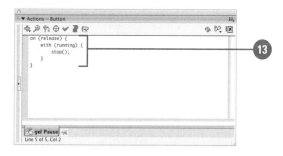

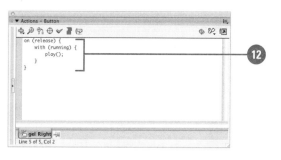

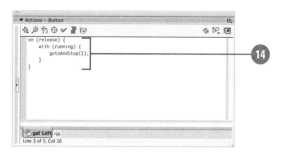

12

Working with Media Player for Streaming Video

It seems obvious that you would want to keep Flash movies that contain video relatively small, in order to minimize the download time of the file. However, since Flash uses streaming technology (the file begins playing before it's totally downloaded), it's more important to think about the amount of time before the movie plays. For example, a Flash movie that might take 3 minutes to download may only take about 15 seconds before it starts playing. That's what streaming is all about. The Flash Media Player component lets you load and control streaming media files in the FLV, or MP3 formats, into a Flash movie.

Work with the Media Playback Component

1. Click the Window menu, and then click the Components and Component Inspector panels.

2. Click the Media Components Expand triangle.

3. Drag the MediaPlayback Component onto the Stage, and then select the component.

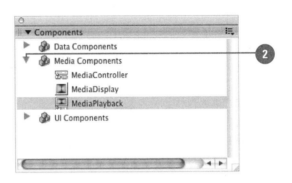

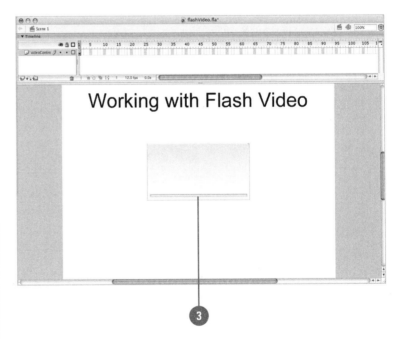

Working with Flash Video

④ In the Component Inspector panel, click the Parameters tab.

⑤ Click FLV.

⑥ Enter the URL of the Flash movie file.

⑦ Select the Automatically Play check box to have the video automatically play when loaded.

⑧ Select the Use Preferred Media Size check box to display the video using the original files width and height.

⑨ Select the Respect Aspect Ratio check box to keep the videos width and height in proportion.

⑩ Select Top, Bottom, Left, or Right for the placement of the control panel.

⑪ Select Auto, On, or Off to control when the control panel appears with the video.

⑫ Click the plus sign (+) to add cue points to the video file, using hours, minutes, seconds, and milliseconds.

⑬ Click the Control menu, and then click Test Movie to test the video in the Flash player.

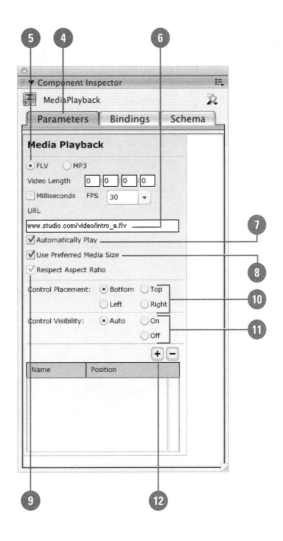

See Also

See "Working with the FLV File Format" on page 304 for information on creating FLV video files.

For Your Information

Streaming Video

Flash gives you three ways to control streaming video files using the Media Player, Media Controller, and Media Display. Each of these components let you control video (or audio) as a separate file that is loaded into the Flash movie. Flash media components support files in the FLV (video), or MP3 (audio) formats, and since the components must use Macromedia Flash Communications Server technology, the Flash files must be saved in the Flash 7 player.

12

Working with the Media Display Component

The Flash Media Display component lets you load an FLV or MP3 file into a Flash movie. The Media Display component gives you an easy way to create a placeholder for a video file, without any play, pause, or rewind buttons. This component is an excellent choice for inserting self-running video files into a Flash document such as an introduction, or slide show.

Work with the Media Display Component

1 Click the Window menu, and then click the Components and Component Inspector panels.

2 Click the Media Components Expand triangle.

3 Drag the Media Display component onto the Stage, and then select the component.

Did You Know?

You can use more than one Media Display component. Drag two or more Media Display components on the screen to load and run more than one video file. However, since running multiple video files may cause a slowdown of the entire movie, use them only if they're necessary.

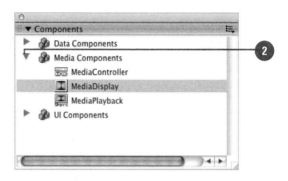

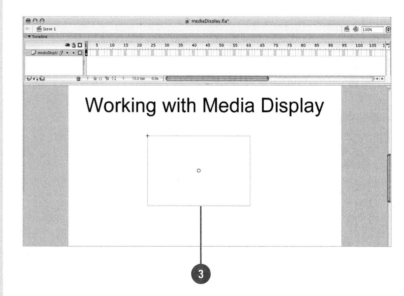

4 In the Component Inspector panel, click the Parameters tab.

5 Click FLV.

6 Enter the URL of the Flash movie file.

7 Select the Automatically Play check box to have the video automatically play when loaded.

8 Select the Use Preferred Media Size check box to display the video using the original files width and height.

9 Select the Respect Aspect Ratio check box to keep the videos width and height in proportion.

10 Click the plus sign (+) to add cue points to the video file, using hours, minutes, seconds, and milliseconds.

11 Click the Control menu, and then click Test Movie to test the video in the Flash player.

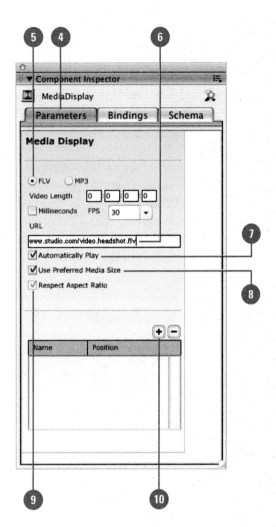

Working with the Media Controller Component

The Flash Media Controller component lets you control a streaming media file that has been loaded using a Media Display component. The Media Controller component lets you easily create play, pause, and rewind controls for any video on the screen. The Media Controller component is an excellent choice for controlling video files placed on the screen using the media data component.

Work with the Media Controller Component

1. Click the Window menu, and then click the Components and Component Inspector panels.

2. Click the Media Components Expand triangle.

3. Drag the Media Display component onto the Stage, and then select the component.

4. In the Property Inspector, enter a unique instance name for the Display component.

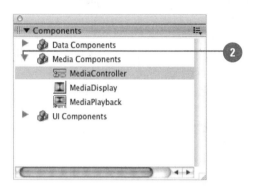

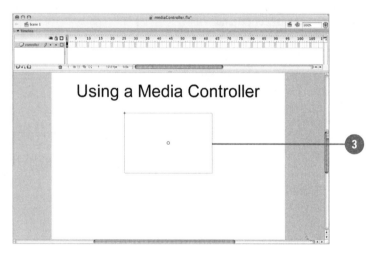

Using a Media Controller

Did You Know?

You can use the Media components to give you control over precise placement of the controller. Drag the Media Controller on the Stage and place it anywhere you like. The advantage of the Media Controller is that you decide the placement of the controls in relationship to the player. This gives you a distinct design advantage over using the Media Player component.

5 In the Component Inspector panel, click the Parameters tab.

6 Click FLV.

7 Enter the URL of the Flash movie file.

8 Deselect the Automatically Play check box to pause the video when loaded.

9 Select the Use Preferred Media Size check box to display the video using the original files width and height.

10 Select the Respect Aspect Ratio check box to keep the videos width and height in proportion.

11 Click the plus sign (+) to add cue points to the video file, using hours, minutes, seconds, and milliseconds.

12 Drag the Media Controller component onto the Stage, and select the component.

13 In the Property Inspector, enter a unique instance name for the Controller component.

14 Click the Add Behavior button (+), in the Behaviors panel, point to Media, and then click Associate Display.

15 Select the instance name given to the Media Display component, and then click OK.

This associates the controller with the correct video.

16 Click the Control menu, and then click Test Movie to test the video in the Flash player.

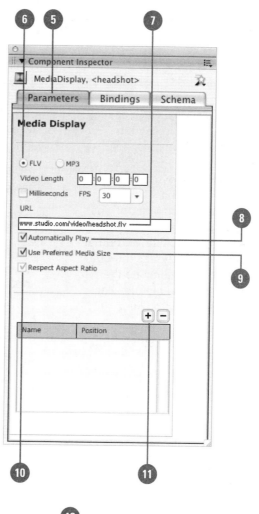

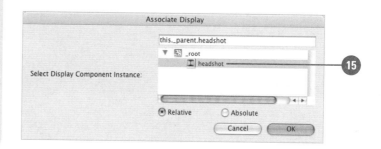

12

Export FLV Files from Video-Editing Applications

Flash MX Professional 2004 along with QuickTime 6.1.1 let you use the FLV Export plug-in to export FLV files from various supported video-editing applications. Once saved, you can import these FLV files directly into Flash for use in your Flash documents, just like any other video files. An advantage to FLV files is that they can be played back dynamically at runtime to give you a streamlined workflow. For example, you can select encoding options for video and audio content as you export, including frame rate, bit rate, quality, and other options. Then you can import FLV files directly into Flash without needing to re-encode the video after import. Since large video files can take several minutes to import into Flash, this saves time.

Some video applications currently supporting the FLV Plug-in are:

♦ Adobe After Effects (Win and Mac)

♦ Anystream Agility (Win)

♦ Apple QuickTime Pro (Mac)

♦ Avid Xpress DV (Win and Mac)

♦ Adobe After Effects (Win and Mac)

♦ Discreet Cleaner (Win and Mac)

♦ Discreet Cleaner XL (Win and Mac)

When you install Flash MX 2004 you will have the option to install the FLV Plug-in into the QuickTime folder. Then when you open any supported program, you can step through the following instructions to export FLV files for use in Flash.

1. Click the File menu, point to Export, and then click QuickTime.

2. Select Macromedia Flash Video (FLV), and then click Options.

3. Click an Encoding Method popup, and then select from the available encoding options:

♦ **Baseline** (1 Pass) is the most basic method of encoding.

♦ **Better** (1 Pass VBR) is the same as Baseline but encodes using Variable Bitrate with the Baseline option, but the file size may be smaller.

♦ **Screen Recording Codec** is for recording screen operations with a lossless compression.

4. Click the Frames Per Second popup, and then select a value or enter a frame rate.

5. Click the Limit Data Rate popup, and then select Normal, Better, or Best.

6 Click the Kilobits/Sec Rate popup, and then select a rate.

7 Enter a Keyframe value to control the frequency of keyframes.

8 Click the Motion Estimation popup, and then select Faster or Best.

9 Select an Audio Encoding option:

- ◆ **Audio.** Exports audio content with the video file.

- ◆ **Mono.** Exports all audio content in one channel.

- ◆ **Stereo.** Exports audio content in stereo.

10 Select one of the Other options:

- ◆ **Resize Image To Preset.** Select a preset image size from the pop-up menu.

- ◆ **Width and Height.** Specify values for Width and Height or a percentage of the original.

11 Select the Lock Aspect Ratio check box to keep the aspect ratio the same size as the original clip.

12 Click the Deinterlacing popup, and then click None, Lower, or Upper.

13 Click OK.

FLV Plug-In Exporter dialog box

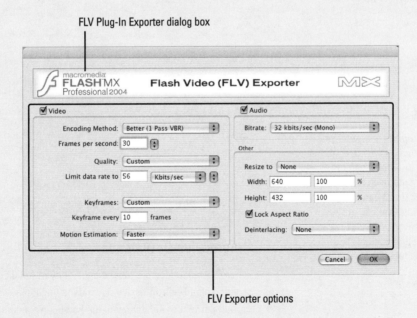

FLV Exporter options

Working with the FLV File Format

The FLV or Flash Video file format allows you to import or export a static video stream including encoded audio. For example, you could use the FLV format to save video for use with communications applications, such as video conferencing. When an FLV clip is exported with streaming audio, the audio is compressed using the Streaming Audio settings in the Publish Settings dialog box, and the files is compressed with the built-in Sorensen codec. FVL files can be used with Flash's new media components to create streaming video files directly in a Flash movie. In order to use the FLV format you must first setup the video files for exporting. Any Flash document that contains video clips will work.

Export Video Clips into the FLV File Format

1. Select a video clip in the Library panel.

2. Click the Libraries Options button, and then click Properties.

3. Click Export.

4. Enter a name for the exported file.

5. Enter a location where it will be saved.

6. Click Save.

7. Click OK.

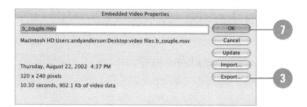

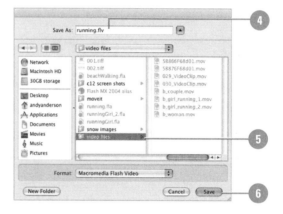

Did You Know?

You can use the Property Inspector to modify a Flash FLV video clip. Drag the FLV video file onto the Stage, select the video clip, and then open the Property Inspector. The Property Inspector lets you give the clip an instance name; change the width, height, and registration point of the clip; even swap a video clip with another video clip.

Applying Timeline Effects

Introduction

When Macromedia unveiled Flash MX 2004, they added a lot of new features to make the process of creating complex Flash movies easier for the novice, and at the same time, give the experienced user more power to control the Flash environment. An example of ease with power is Flash's new Timeline effects. Timeline effects allow you to change shapes over time, such as explode and object, or create a blur or drop shadow. Since these effects are part of the Timeline, they're animated effects. Timeline effects are similar to motion tween effects without all the hassle. You start with an object in a specific keyframe, and then work through an effects dialog box, to instruct Flash exactly how you want the effect to appear. Once the effect is created, you can modify how the effect appears on the screen, at any time during the design process.

One more bit of news about Flash MX 2004 is that it's extensible. That means other companies and 3rd party vendors can create add-on products to help to further automate your workflow. As time goes by, you will see more and more automation features and Timeline effects, being offered free, or for a small fee. What that means to you as a Flash designer is that you will be able to do more complicated Flash animations, in less time, and have more control over the effects.

What You'll Do

Use the Explode Effect

Use the Blur Effect

Use Copy To Grid

Apply the Drop Shadow Effect

Use the Expand Effect

Use the Distributed Duplicates Effect

Apply the Transform Effect

Use the Transition Effect

Modify Timeline Effects

Convert Timeline Effects into Keyframes

Remove Timeline Effects

Using the Explode Effect

The Explode effect is probably one of the more impressive of the Timeline effects. The steps to creating an Explode effect are simple—Flash, through the Explode dialog box, will do all the hard work for you. This particular effect will work on any vector object, simple or complex. All you have to do is decide what you want to explode.

Use the Explode Effect

1. Select a keyframe.

2. Draw a shape on the Stage using the oval, rectangle, or polystar tools, and then select the shape.

3. Click the Insert menu, point to Timeline Effects, point to Effects, and then click Explode.

4. Decide the length of the effect in the frames.

5. Click the arrow buttons to decide the direction of the explosion.

6. Change the X and Y Arc Size (in pixels).

7. Enter a rotation value.

See Also

See Chapter 3, "Creating Graphics" on page 73 for information on creating shapes to use with Flash's new Timeline Effects.

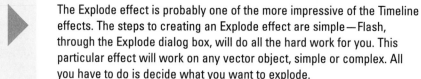

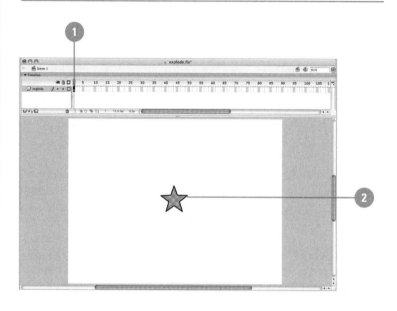

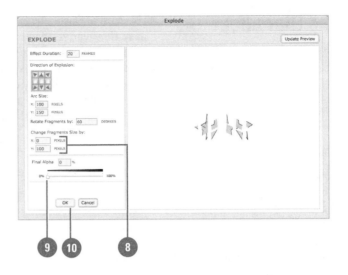

8. Change the X and Y Fragments Size (in pixels).

9. Drag the slider to adjust the Final Alpha (transparency) of the effect.

10. Click OK.

This adds the effect to the Timeline.

11. Click the Control menu, and then click Test Movie.

Flash displays the Timeline effect.

IMPORTANT *Every time you change one of the Timeline effect parameters, you will need to click the Update Preview button to see the effects demonstrated in the Preview window.*

Did You Know?

You can create a Flash movie with multiple effects. Remember that you can only have one effect per layer. If you want to create two exploding objects, you will need a separate layer for each effect.

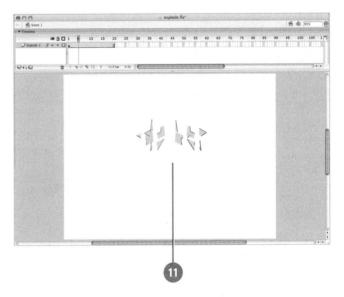

Using the Blur Effect

Like most of Flash's Timeline effects, the process of creating the effect is easy. However, you don't have to create Timeline effects from objects drawn on the Stage. Timeline effects can be created from imported vector objects, as well as graphic behavior Library symbols. The Blur Timeline effect has many uses. For example, you could use the Blur Timeline effect to create a fader used in a slide show, or you could use it to simply have items on the Stage slowly fade to transparent.

Use the Blur Effect

1. Select a keyframe.

2. Draw a shape on the Stage or move a graphic symbol out of the Library.

3. Click the Insert menu, point to Timeline Effects, point to Effects, and then click Blur.

4. Enter a resolution value.

   The lower the value, the less complex the blur effect.

5. Enter a Scale value.

   Scale determines the size difference between the starting and ending shapes in the blur effect.

6. Select the Allow Horizontal and Vertical Blur check boxes.

   Unchecking both options will cause the object to slowly fade to transparent.

7. Click the arrow buttons to decide the direction of the blur.

8. Click OK to add the effect to the Timeline.

9. Click the Control menu, and then click Test Movie.

   Flash displays the Timeline effect.

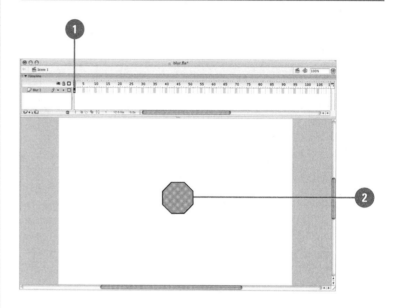

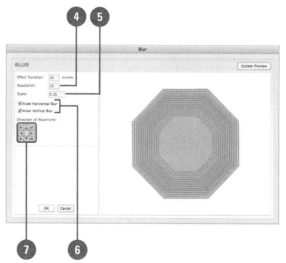

Using Copy To Grid

The Copy To Grid Timeline effect lets you select an object and copy it over and over again, using a grid-like pattern to control the placement of the objects. Use the Copy To Grid effect to create a tiled pattern from a single shape, or use it to generate a maze-like array of similar elements. In fact, it's not necessary to limit this effect to one shape; you can select one, two, or as many shapes as you want to include within the grid.

Use Copy To Grid

1. Select one or more shapes.

2. Click the Insert menu, point to Timeline Effects, point to Assistants, and then click Copy To Grid.

3. Enter values in the Rows and Columns Grid Size input fields.

   Higher values increase the number of objects in the grid.

4. Enter values in the Rows and Columns Grid Spacing input fields.

   Higher values increase the space between items within the grid.

5. Click OK to add the effect to the Timeline.

6. Click the Control menu, and then click Test Movie.

   Flash displays the Timeline effect.

Did You Know?

You can apply Timeline effects to more than just a simple graphic. Timeline effects can be applied to text, complex graphics, shapes, groups, symbols, bitmap images, and even button symbols. When you apply a Timeline effect to a movie clip, Flash nests the effect within the movie clip.

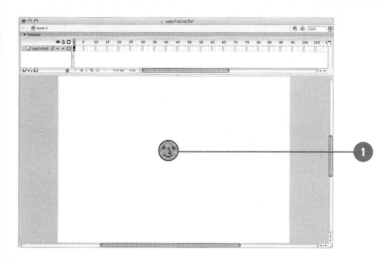

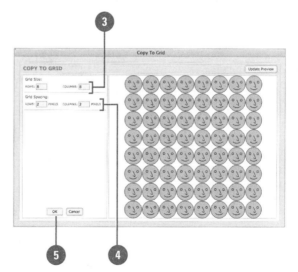

Applying the Drop Shadow Effect

The Drop Shadow Timeline effect adds a visual sense of three dimensions to a Flash movie. The effect creates an offset copy of the original image, and reduces its alpha (transparency) to create a hard-edged shadow effect. The Drop Shadow effect can be applied to any Flash objects, and since they are not an animated effect, they only occupy one frame on the Timeline.

Apply the Drop Shadow Effect

1. Select a keyframe.

2. Draw a shape using the oval, rectangle, or polystar tools, and then select the shape.

3. Click the Insert menu, point to Timeline Effects, point to Effects, and then click Drop Shadow.

4. Click the Color button to change the color of the drop shadow.

5. Drag the slider to adjust the Final Alpha (transparency) of the effect.

6. Enter the X and Y value (in pixels) to change the Shadow Offset.

7. Click OK to add the effect to the Timeline.

8. Click the Control menu, and then click Test Movie.

   Flash displays the Timeline effect.

   IMPORTANT *If an object contains a stroke, the drop shadow will contain a line surrounding the shape that emulates the stroke on the original object.*

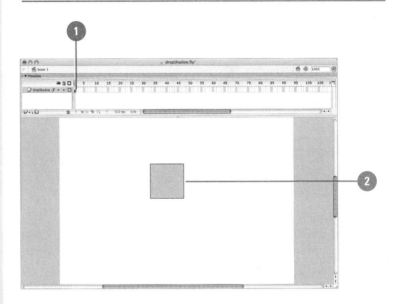

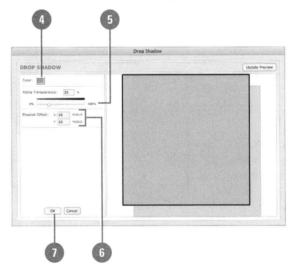

Using the Expand Effect

The Expand Timeline effects is similar to creating a shape or motion tween, where the object expands or contracts over a predetermined time. This particular effect requires that the object be grouped (click the Modify menu, and then click Group), or in a Library as a graphic behavior symbol.

Use the Expand Effect

1. Draw a shape using the oval, rectangle, or polystar tools, and then group or drag a graphic behavior symbol from the Library.

2. Click the Insert menu, point to Timeline Effects, point to Effects, and then click Expand.

3. Enter the Duration of the effect in frames.

4. Select Expand, Squeeze, or Both.

5. Click the arrow buttons, to decide the direction of the explosion (left or right only).

6. Enter the X and Y values (in pixels), to adjust the center value of the changing shape.

7. Enter the Width and Height values (in pixels), to change the size of the expansion of the image as it changes.

8. Click OK to add the effect to the Timeline.

9. Click the Control menu, and then click Test Movie.

   Flash displays the Timeline effect.

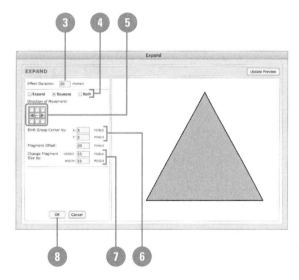

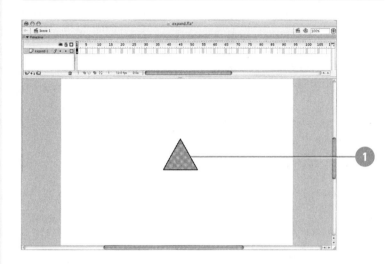

Using the Distributed Duplicate Effect

The Distributed Duplicate Timeline effect produces a cascading grouping of objects based on a selected shape. As the shape cascades, you can choose to have the shape get smaller, change color, rotate, slowly go transparent, or a combination of any options. It should be noted that when Flash creates any of its animated Timeline effects, a copy of the effect is automatically stored in the Library of the active document. If you open the Library, you can view each of the frames Flash created to produce the effect.

Use the Distributed Duplicate Effect

1. Draw a shape using the oval rectangle or polystar tools, and then select the shape.

2. Click the Insert menu, point to Timeline Effects, point to Assistants, and then click Distributed Duplicate.

3. Enter the number of copies.

4. Enter the X and Y Offset Distance (in pixels).

5. Enter an Offset Rotation value to cause the duplicated objects to rotate.

6. Enter an Offset Start Frame value, to animate the Distributed Duplicate effect.

Did You Know?

You can use effects more than once. Since Flash stores a copy of the effect in the Library, you can open another Flash document, and then move the effect into the other document. Remember to move the Effects Folder, and the graphic symbol. In addition, if the effect occupies 20 frames, you will have to add 20 frames to the layer in the new document that you're moving the effect to.

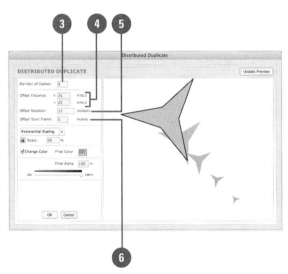

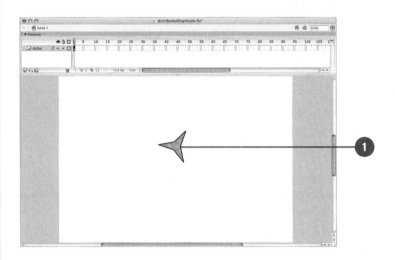

7 Click to select between Linear and Exponential Scaling.

8 Enter a Scale value to have the shapes change size as they are duplicated.

9 Select the Change Color check box, and then select an ending color for the final duplicate.

10 Drag the slider to adjust the Final Alpha (transparency) of the effect.

11 Click OK.

12 Click the Control menu, and then click Test Movie.

Flash displays the Timeline effect.

See Also

See "Modifying Timeline Effects" on page 318 for information on how to adjust the settings of an effect after it's applied.

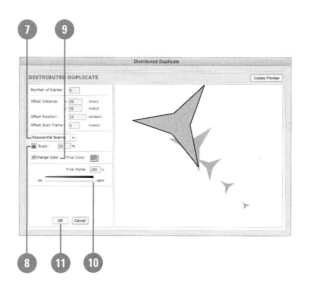

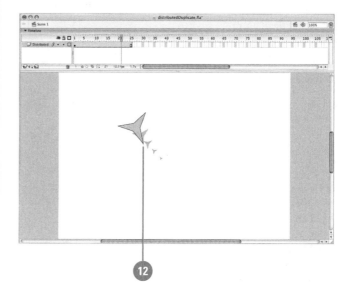

Applying the Transform Effect

The Transform Timeline effect lets you select an object, and over time, change its size, rotational value, position, and alpha. As with the other Timeline effects, this effect can be created from scratch using standard Flash options. The difference is: The Timeline effect can be created in seconds, as opposed to minutes.

Apply the Transform Effect

1 Draw a shape using the oval, rectangle, or polystar tools, and then select the shape.

2 Click the Insert menu, point to Timeline Effects, point to Transform/Transition, and then click Transform.

3 Enter the Duration of the effect in frames.

4 Select Change Position By or Move To Position.

5 Enter the X and Y values (in pixels) to shift the object.

6 Enter a Scale value to change the size of the object as it transforms.

Did You Know?

You can use Flash's new Timeline effects to save file size. Since Flash uses motion tween animation techniques to create a Timeline effect, they're more efficient, occupy less file space, and are faster to generate than creating the effect using normal frame-by-frame animation techniques.

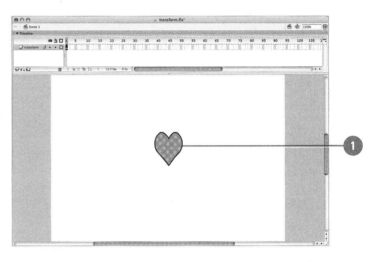

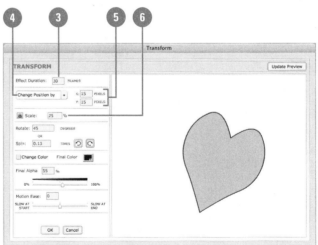

7. Enter a rotation value, and then click the clockwise or counter-clockwise buttons to rotate the object.

8. Select the Change Color check box, and then click the Final Color box. This changes the color of the object over time, as it transforms.

9. Drag the slider to adjust the Final Alpha (transparency) of the effect.

10. Drag the Motion Ease slider to change how the object transforms: Slow At Start, or Slow At End.

11. Click OK to add the effect to the Timeline.

12. Click the Control menu, and then click Test Movie.

Flash displays the Timeline effect.

Did You Know?

You can increase or decrease the number of frames in a Timeline effect, after it's been applied. Click on the last frame of the effect, hold down the ⌘ (Mac) or Ctrl (Win) key, and then drag right to increase or left to decrease.

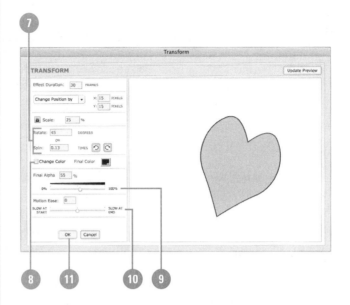

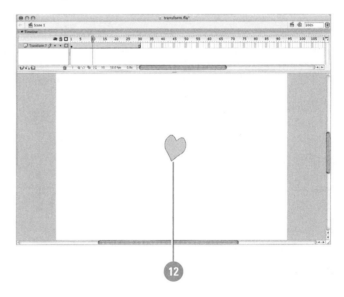

13

Using the Transition Effect

The Transition Timeline effect changes an objects alpha (transparency), and lets you incorporate a transitional effect called Wipe, which collapses the object from the top, bottom, left or right. The Transition effect can be used as a transition between images in a slide show, or as a novel way to have an object disappear from the Stage. In truth, the uses for Timeline effects are as varied as the designers that use the Flash application.

Use the Transition Effect

1. Draw a shape using the oval, rectangle, or polystar tools, and then select the shape.

2. Click the Insert menu, point to Timeline Effects, point to Transform/Transition, and then click Transition.

3. Enter the Duration of the effect in frames.

4. Select from the following Direction options:

   ◆ **In/Out.** Click In or Out to determine how the transition begins. For example, if the Fade option is selected, does the transition fade In, or fade Out.

   ◆ **Fade.** Select the Fade check box to have the object fade (determined by the In or Out option).

   ◆ **Wipe.** Select the Wipe check box to have the object wipe left, right, up, or down (determined by the arrow buttons).

   ◆ **Arrows.** Click the arrow buttons to determine the direction of the Wipe effect.

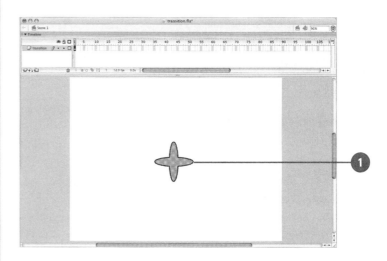

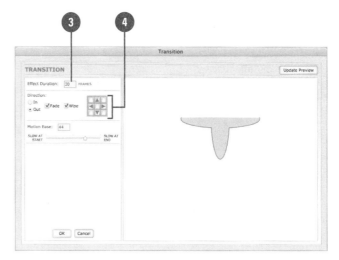

⑤ Drag the Motion Ease slider to accelerate or decelerate the transition.

⑥ Click OK to add the effect to the Timeline.

⑦ Click the Control menu, and then click Test Movie.

Flash displays the Timeline effect.

Did You Know?

Timeline effects are not limited to the latest version of the Flash plug-in. Since Timeline effects are created as standard Library items, they will successfully play, even if your visitors are still using version 3 of the Flash plug-in.

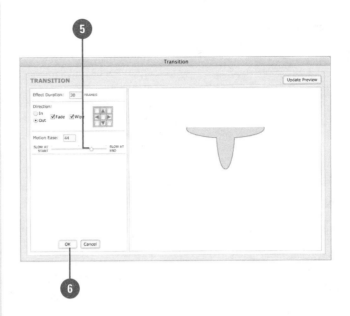

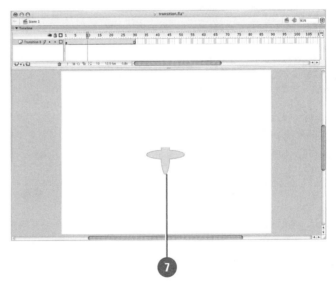

Modifying Timeline Effects

Once you create a Timeline effect, you cannot return to the Insert menu, and edit the effect. For example, what if you use the Explode Timeline effect, and you want to increase the effects duration: Macromedia understands that you want help in creating Timeline effects, and they also understand that you might change you mind, and modify the effect. When you modify a Timeline effect, you can change any of the options available from the original effect dialog box; however, you can't change one effect into another. To change to a different effect, first remove the current effect, then click the Insert menu, point to Timeline Effects, and then select another effect.

Modify Timeline Effects

 Select the Timeline effect.

2 Click the Modify menu, point to Timeline Effects, and then click Edit Effect.

You can also click the Edit button, located on the Property Inspector.

3 Make the necessary changes to the effect.

4 Click OK to add the effect to the Timeline.

5 Click the Control menu, and then click Test Movie.

Flash displays the modified Timeline effect.

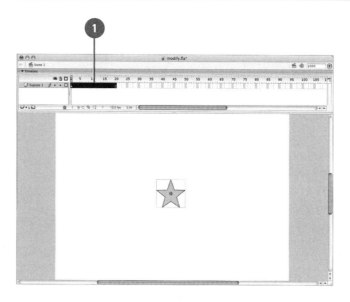

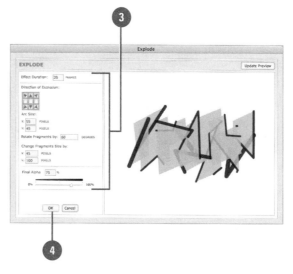

Converting Timeline Effects into Keyframes

Once you add a Timeline effect to a Flash object, the layer the effect resides in holds the frames required to display the effect. If you scrub the Timeline (drag the play head left to right), you can see the results of the Timeline effect, but you can't access or edit the individual frames. Flash gives you the option of converting the Timeline effect into individual keyframes. This will give you frame-by-frame control over the effect (which is good), but you will never be able to modify the effect with Flash's Modify Effect command.

Convert Effects into Keyframes

1. Select all the frames in the effect layer.

2. Click the Modify menu, point to Timeline, and then click Convert To Keyframes.

   IMPORTANT *Flash warns you that proceeding will prevent you from further editing the effects settings.*

3. Click OK.

   Each frame on the Timeline now contains a keyframe that holds a portion of the original Timeline effect.

See Also

See Chapter 7, "Creating Frame-by-Frame Animations" on page 195 for more information on working with animations created on separate frames.

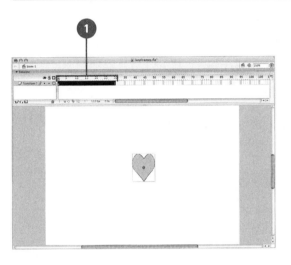

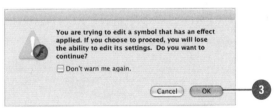

Keyframes contain the elements of the converted effect.

Removing Timeline Effects

It's possible that, once created, you will want to remove a Timeline effect from a Flash object. Flash will not only remove the Timeline effect, in addition, it will restore the object to its original state. While, in many cases it might be just as easy to delete the layer containing the Timeline effect and start over, it's possible that the graphic used in the creation of the effect is an important element, and you don't wish to redraw it. In addition to restoring the original object, Flash will also purge the Library of all the elements it used in the creation of the Timeline effect.

Remove Timeline Effects

1. Select the Timeline effect.

2. Click the Modify menu, point to Timeline Effects, and then click Remove Effect.

   Flash removes the Timeline effect, and restores the object to its original state.

   IMPORTANT *When you remove a Timeline effect, Flash removes the effect in two steps. If you change your mind and want to restore the effect, remember that you will have to use the undo command ⌘+Z (Mac) or Ctrl+Z (Win) twice, or the effect will not be restored.*

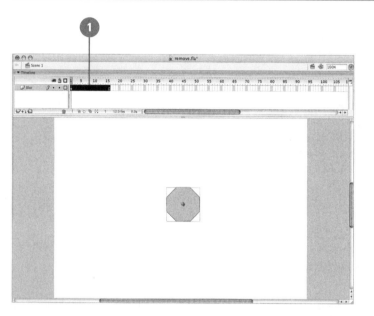

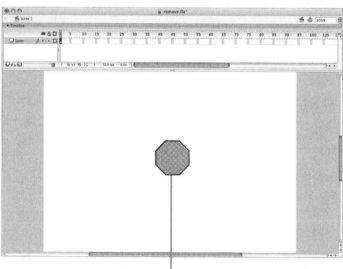

Object restored to original state

Using ActionScript Behaviors

Introduction

ActionScript Behaviors are Flash's way of simplifying some of the more common ways you control a Flash movie. Think of ActionScripting as the language you use to communicate with Flash. For example, if you were in Paris, and you needed directions to the Eiffel Tower, knowing the French language would be the best way to find your final destination. Knowing how to ActionScript gives you the ability to navigate through Flash and create a movie that reacts to the visitor through interactive buttons and screens. ActionScripting literally brings life to a Flash movie. ActionScript Behaviors are pre-written sections of ActionScript that help you perform some of the more commonly used Actions in Flash, such as: opening a Web Page, or playing and stopping a movie clip. Flash has Behaviors that help you control the Web, movie clips, video, and audio files. In addition, Flash's extensible application architecture, allows for the creation of even more Behaviors, so occasionally point your browser to the Macromedia Exchange at: *www.macromedia.com/cfusion/exchange/index.cfm*, and see what's new from the creators of Flash.

Adding Behaviors

Behaviors are timesavers because they give you sections of ActionScript code for common Flash tasks. In addition, behaviors are a great way to introduce yourself to the wonderful world of ActionScripting without having to write all the code. For example, if you want to add a Play ActionScript to a button, you can do it using the Add button in the Behaviors panel, or you can write out the code on your own; see the example code below. Using Behaviors, as opposed to writing the code by hand, is not better, they're simply faster. The more time you save doing common Action-Scripting tasks using Behaviors, the more time you will have for the creative process.

Using the Behaviors Panel

You use the Behaviors panel to apply the behavior to a triggering object, such as a button. You specify the event that triggers the behavior, such as releasing the mouse, select a target object, such as the movie clip instance, and then select settings for behavior parameters, such as a frame number or label, or a relative or absolute path. Flash comes with built-in behaviors, such as Load Graphic, Duplicate Movieclip, and GotoAndPlay At Frame Or Label. To add and configure a behavior, select a trigger object, and then step

through the following general instructions (steps may vary depending on the behavior):

1. Click the Window menu, point to Development Panels, and then click Behaviors.

2. Click the Add (+) button, and then select a behavior from the menu.

3. If necessary, select settings for the behavior parameters, and then click OK.

4. Under Event, click On Release (the default event), and then select a mouse event from the menu.

Add button   Click to select a mouse event.

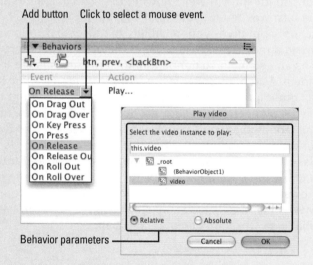

Behavior parameters

Example Play ActionScript code

```
on (release) {
    if(this.video_1._parent._currentframe == this.video_1.parent._totalframes){
        this.video_1parent.gotoAndPlay(1);
    } else {
        this.video_1._parent.play();
    }
}
```

Understanding the Load Graphic Behavior

The Load Graphic Behavior lets you load .jpg images into a running Flash movie. The advantages to loading a graphic, as opposed to embedding a graphic is huge. You can create what is called a Flash front-end movie. A front-end movie is a small Flash movie that contains areas to load different graphics images. For example, you have several graphics that you want to incorporate into a slide show. You can create a Flash movie with a scene for each graphic, and then embed the images into each scene; you can create a timeline with individual keyframes, each holding a graphic; or you can create a single scene and use Behaviors such as Load Graphic to add the images, when required.

Planning the Project

Since you are loading (not embedding) images, the setup is important to the successful completion of the project. You will need to create a specific folder to hold all of the images that you'll use for your project, and then you'll need to know their height and width. Since you might be loading more than one image into your project, it's important that all the images are the same height and width. After you create the folder, drag the images you want into the folder. The Load Graphic Behavior requires that all the images be saved in the .jpg format.

Project Folder

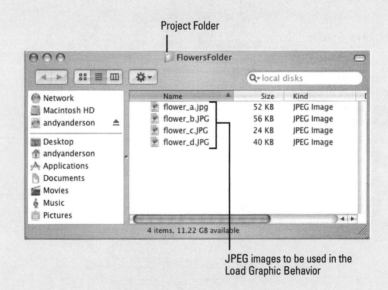

JPEG images to be used in the
Load Graphic Behavior

Using the Load Graphic Behavior

Once you have the JPEG images safely tucked away in their own folder, you can turn your attention to the design of the front end. For starters, you will need a defined area that is the same width and height of the graphics, and a button object to attach the Load Graphic Behavior. When you insert the Load Graphic behavior, Flash will need to know the full path name to the image file. For example, if the images reside in a folder named photos, on the server *www.images.com*, the full path name would be: *http://www.images.com/photos/filename.jpg*, with *filename.jpg* being the name of the image file.

Use the Load Graphic Behavior

1. Click Insert, and then click New Symbol.

2. Select the Movie Clip option, and then name the Symbol.

3. Click OK.

4. Leave the Movie Clip behavior untouched, and click the Scene button to return to the active scene.

5. Select the layer to hold the movie clip.

6. Drag the movie clip onto the Stage, and position it in the upper-left corner of the box reserved for the image, and then select the movie clip.

7. Enter a unique instance name for the movie clip.

8. Select the Button object.

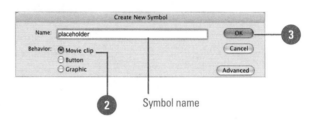

Symbol name

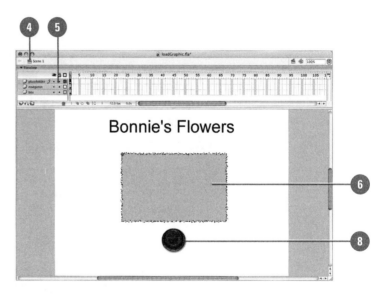

9 Click the Add button (+) in the Behaviors panel, point to Movieclip, and then click Load Graphic.

10 Enter the full path name to the .jpg file.

11 Select the unique instance name for the movie clip.

12 Click OK.

13 Click the Event list arrow, and then click an event to trigger the Load Graphic Behavior.

14 Click the Control menu, and then click Test Movie to test Load Graphic.

Flash displays the graphic.

Did You Know?

You can use the Load Graphic Behavior on the Timeline. When Load Graphic is placed in a black keyframe on the Timeline, it's the play head that triggers the loading of the graphic. You can place Load Graphic in a blank keyframe every twenty frames, and then load a different graphic. If the frame rate is set to 5fps you can create a slide show where an image changes every 4 seconds.

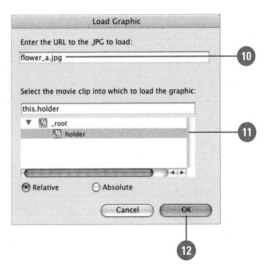

14

Using the Goto Play and Stop Behaviors

The Goto Behaviors give you control over the Timeline of a movie clip that's embedded within the active movie. For example, you can create a Flash movie clip that holds several images spaced equally on the Timeline, and use the Goto and Play options to let the visitor control the slideshow. The Play/Stop Goto Behaviors are different then the Play and Stop Behaviors. With the Goto portion of the behavior, you can direct the playhead to a specific point on the Timeline, and then continue to play, or stop the movie clip.

Use the Goto Play and Stop Behaviors

1. Select the layer to contain the movie clip.

2. Drag the movie clip onto the Stage.

3. Enter a unique instance name for the movie clip.

4. Select the Play Button object (a button object you designate to play the movie).

5. Click the Add button (+) in the Behaviors panel, point to Movieclip, and then click Goto And Play At Frame Or Label.

6. Select the unique instance name for the movie clip.

7. Enter a frame number where the movie clip begins playing.

8. Click OK.

9. Select the Stop Button object (a button object you designate to stop the movie).

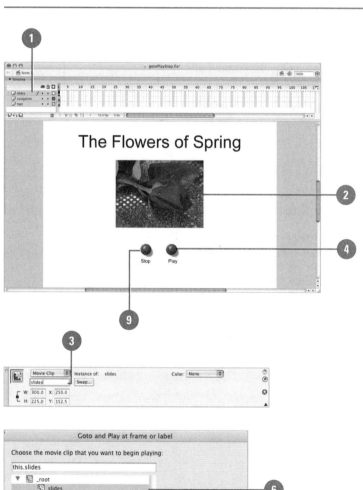

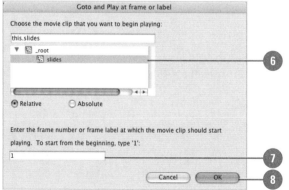

10 Click the Add button (+) in the Behaviors panel, point to Movieclip, and then click Goto And Stop At Frame Or Label.

11 Select the unique instance name for the movie clip.

12 Enter a frame number where the movie clip will stop playing.

13 Click OK.

14 Click the Event list arrow, and then select an event to trigger the behavior.

15 Click the Control menu, and then click Test Movie.

Flash displays the movie clip.

See Also

See Chapter 12 "Working with Video" on page 278 for more information on creating videos for using Flash's ActionScript Behaviors.

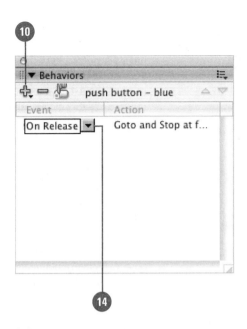

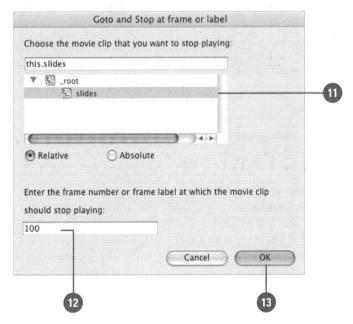

Using the Load External Movieclip Behavior

The Load External Movie Clip Behavior gives you the ability to load external .swf files into the active Flash movie. The most efficient way to utilize this behavior is to create a blank or placeholder movie clip in the active document. The placeholder movie clip is empty and is used to load and position the external movie clip. The ability to load external movie clips lets you create small Flash movies because the movie clips are only loaded when needed. In addition, as a designer, it lets you create modular elements, almost like actors in a movie, and lets you load them when needed, and remove them when they're no longer needed. For example, you could create a button object and use the Load External Movie Clip Behavior to load a specific Flash movie, or you could place the behavior directly on the timeline, and load (or unload) movie clips based on the playback of the movie. To utilize this behavior, you will need one or more external Flash movie files (.swf), and a Flash movie to hold the movie clips as they are called. In addition, you'll need one or more button objects (if you're planning on letting the user control the action), and a blank movie clip to hold the external clips.

Use the Load External Behavior

1. Select the layer to contain the placeholder movie clip.

2. Drag the movie clip from the Library onto the Stage.

3. Enter a unique instance name for the movie clip.

4. Select the Load Button object (a button object you designate to load the external movie clip).

5. Click the Add button (+) in the Behaviors panel, point to Movieclip, and then click Load External Movieclip.

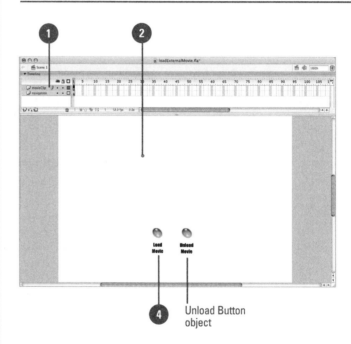

Unload Button object

6. Select the unique instance name for the movie clip.

7. Enter the path to the external .swf file.

8. Click OK.

9. Select the Unload Button object (a button object you designate to unload the external movie clip).

10. Click the Add button (+) in the Behaviors panel, point to Movieclip, and then click Unload Movieclip.

11. Select the unique instance name for the movie clip you want to unload.

12. Click OK.

13. Click the Control menu, and then click Test Movie.

Flash displays the movie clip.

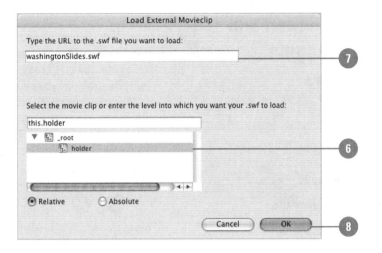

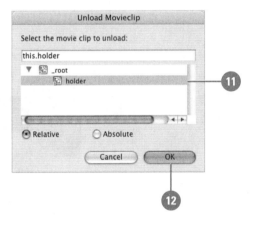

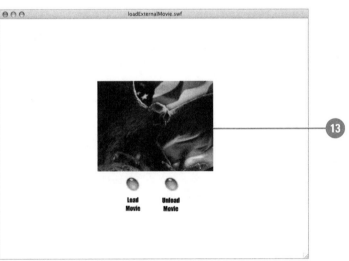

Using the Start and Stop Dragging Behaviors

The Start and Stop Dragging Movieclip Behaviors are a novel way to give Flash visitors the chance to interact with your site. The behaviors can be attached to objects on the screen, when the visitor clicks and drags; the object is dragged along for the ride. The ideas here are endless. For example, you could create a house with furniture (each piece of furniture being a movie clip), and let the visitor rearrange the furniture. Or, you could create a puzzle, and let the visitors assemble the puzzle. To begin the process, you will need a Flash document that contains one or more movie clips (for dragging).

Use the Start and Stop Dragging Behaviors

1. Select the layer to contain the movie clip or clips.

2. Drag the movie clips from the Library onto the Stage.

3. Enter a unique instance name for each movie clip.

4. Select one of the movie clips.

5. Click the Add button (+) in the Behaviors panel, point to Movieclip, and then click Start Dragging Movieclip.

6. Select the unique instance name for the movie clip.

7. Click OK.

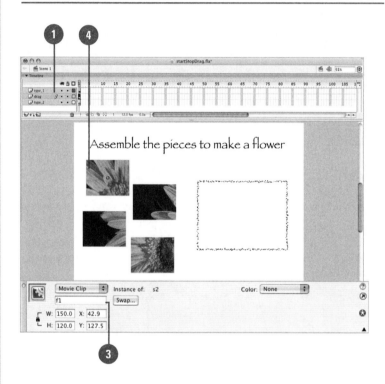

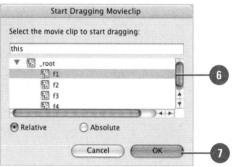

See Also

See Chapter 6 "Importing Graphics" on page 175 for more information on importing graphics into Flash to be used with the Start and Stop Dragging Behaviors.

8 Click the Event list arrow, and then change the event that triggers the behavior to On Press.

9 Leave the movie clip selected.

10 Click the Add button (+) in the Behaviors panel, point to Movieclip, and then click Stop Dragging Movieclip.

11 Click OK.

12 Click the Event list arrow, and then change the event that triggers the behavior to On Release.

Repeat steps 4 through 12 until all of the movie clips have the Start and Stop Dragging Movieclip Behaviors attached.

13 Click the Control menu, and then click Test Movie.

Flash displays the movie clip.

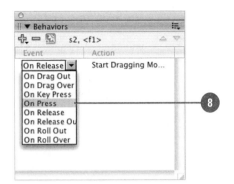

Did You Know?

You have to attach both the Start and Stop Dragging Movieclip Behaviors to each object. If you do not attach the Stop Dragging Movieclip Behavior, once you select the object to drag, you will not be able to get rid of it. The Stop Dragging Movieclip Behavior instructs Flash to release the object, based on the selected event.

14

Using the Goto Web Page Behavior

The Goto Web Page Behavior gives you the ability to link a Flash document to the Web, with the use of interactive button objects. For example, you can create a Web site entirely in Flash, and then use the Goto Web Page Behavior to direct visitors to other sites and pages, or you could create a set of interactive buttons for use on a standard HTML driven Web site. Whichever option you choose, the ability to direct a visitor to other Web sites is essential to creating Internet-oriented documents.

Use the Goto Web Page Behavior

1. Drag a button object from the Library onto the Stage, and then select the button.

2. Click the Add button (+) in the Behaviors panel, point to Web, and then click Go To Web Page.

3. Enter the full URL path to the Web page.

4. Click OK.

5. Click the Event list arrow, and then select an event to trigger the Goto Web Page Behavior.

6. Click the Control menu, and then click Test Movie.

   Flash connects to the Web page.

Did You Know?

You can create an entire menu bar and save it as a single Flash movie file. Drag all the button objects on the Stage and arrange in a logical navigation order. One at a time, apply the Goto Web Page Behavior to each button object, and then shrink the Stage to match the buttons and publish the movie. Use Dreamweaver to add the Navigation bar to any Web page.

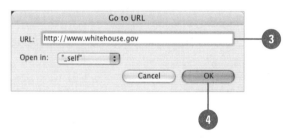

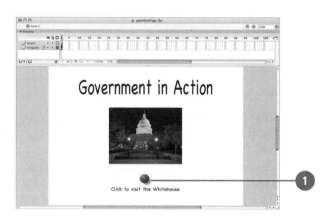

Using Basic ActionScripts

Introduction

Flash's programming language is called ActionScript. **ActionScript** lets you create detailed instructions on how the Flash movie will perform. ActionScripts require an event to trigger the specific action. Say, you create a button, and you want the ActionScript to trigger an instruction that will stop the movie, but only when the user clicks the button object. The defined event is the user clicking his mouse, and the action would be to stop playing the movie. ActionScript is not that difficult to learn because it uses logical phrases. For example the command to stop playing a Timeline is:

```
stop () ;
```

That's pretty simple, but remember that syntax is very important. For example, the ActionScript for moving to a specific frame on the Timeline is:

```
gotoAndPlay (2) ;
```

Notice the capitalization of the letters—A and P—and how the words are grouped together without any spaces. ActionScript is a relatively easy language to learn, but a very precise language to code, so pay close attention to the syntax.

The good news is that once you master the language and the syntax, the full power of Flash is available to you. You can create ActionScripts that are triggered (the event), by specific data, or information typed in by a visitor. You can even create ActionScripts that are sensitive to variables such as: date and time. Flash helps you by giving you functions (English-like script) and as your ActionScript skills grow, you can even create and call your own functions. Flash MX 2004 utilizes ActionScript 2.0, which moves the scripting language closer to JavaScript. The power of Flash is fully realized when you write ActionScripts, and incorporate them in your Flash documents.

Using Object-Oriented Programming

Objects are the key to understanding object-oriented programming. In object-oriented programming, an object is just as real as an object in this world. For example, your dog, or even your computer are objects that exist in the real world. Real-world objects share two characteristics with objects in the computer world: They have a specific state and behavior. For example, dogs have a state such as their name, color, breed, and if they're hungry. Dog behaviors would be: barking, fetching, and wagging their tails. All objects in the real and computer world have a behavior and a state.

Computer objects are modeled after real-world objects in that they also have a specific state and behavior. A software object maintains its state using one or more variables. A **variable** is an item of data named by an identifier, and a software object performs its behavior with methods. A **method** is a function associated with an object. Everything a software object understands (its state) and what it can do (its behavior) is expressed by the variables and the methods within that object.

A software object that represents a speeding car would have variables that instruct the object as to speed, direction, and color. These variables are known as instance variables because they contain the state for a particular object, and in object-oriented terminology, a particular object is called an instance. In addition to its variables, the car would have methods assigned to change speed, and turn on the lights. These methods are formally known as instance methods because they inspect or change the state of a particular instance.

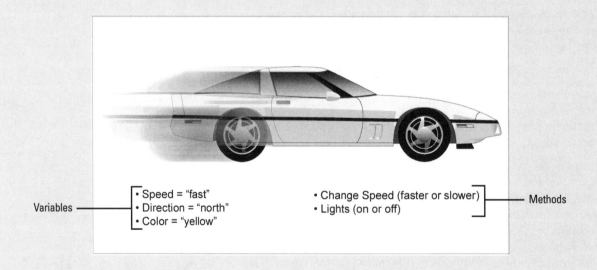

Variables
- Speed = "fast"
- Direction = "north"
- Color = "yellow"

- Change Speed (faster or slower)
- Lights (on or off)
Methods

Viewing the Actions Panel

The Action panel is where the Flash designer gains control of a Flash document, by allowing you to create and edit actions for an object or frame. To use the Actions panel, first select an object on the stage, or select a frame on the Timeline, then click the Window menu, point to Development Panels, and then click Actions. Scripts can be typed directly into the Actions panel using the Script pane, or augmented by using a list of installed Actions in the Toolbox.

◆ **Toolbox.** Supplies a list of all installed actions, organized into a folder.

◆ **Script pane.** Enter the Actions into the Script pane.

◆ **Script Navigator pane.** Gives reference to all the Scripts in the active movie.

◆ **Current Script tag.** Indicates which script is being edited.

◆ **Pin Script.** Adds a tab for a selected script.

◆ **Options menu.** Contains options that control and format the Actions panel.

◆ **Reference.** Provides online help.

◆ **Add Statement.** Lets you add script elements to the current action.

◆ **Find, and Find and Replace.** Searches the active script.

◆ **Insert Target Path.** Inserts a specific target clip into the action.

◆ **Check Syntax.** Checks the current action for syntax errors.

◆ **Auto Format.** Cleans up the script by auto indenting.

◆ **Show Code Hint.** Gives you hints to the syntax of the action, as you type.

◆ **Debug Options.** Let's you add or remove breakpoints into the action, which causes Flash to pause on the specified line of code.

◆ **View Options.** Gives you formatting options on how the scripts appear in the Script pane, such as: line numbers, and word wrap.

15

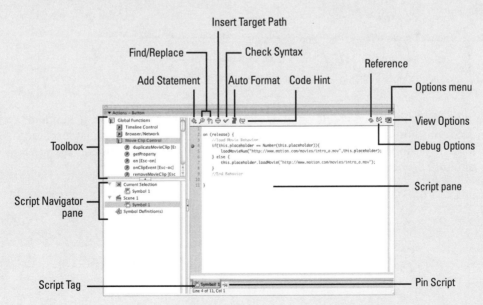

Understanding Properties and Methods

Objects in Flash are defined using two primary identifiers: properties and methods. The **properties** of an object define its characteristics. For example, in the real world a house would be an object, and its properties would be things like its color, style, and number of windows and doors. In Flash it would be written something like this:

```
house.color = "green";
house.style = "ranch";
house.windows = "12";
house.doors = "2";
```

In this example, the word *house* is a unique instance name for the house object, and the words *color*, *style*, *windows*, and *doors* represent the properties assigned to this instance. Think of an instance as a copy of a Library item. For example, when you create a movie clip, the object is created in Flash's Library. When you return to the Stage, you can then drag the movie clip from the Library to the Stage (technically, you're moving a Library symbol, created using the movie clip behavior). Once the movie clip is moved to the Stage, it is defined as an instance of the original Library item. When you select an instance on the Stage, Flash's Properties panel lets you give it a unique name. In the previous example "house" is the unique name defined in the Properties panel.

Giving a Library symbol a unique name gives you a lot of control. For example, you could move two instances of the same movie clip onto the Stage, give each of them their own unique names (house1, house2) in the Property Inspector, and then define different properties for each one. Something like this:

```
house1.color = "green";      house2.color = "blue";
house1.style = "ranch";      house2.style = "tudor";
house1.windows = "12";       house2.windows = "8";
house1.doors = "2";          house2.doors = "4";
```

As a matter of fact, you could create an entire town, using one Library item. The advantage to this approach is enormous. You could create a Flash movie with 100 different instances of the same movie clip, and the Flash movie would only need to save a single copy, and then change that one copy using different properties.

In Flash, most objects have properties. For example, the MovieClip object has property values such as transparency, horizontal and vertical position, and visibility. You might define properties loosely as the physical appearance of a movie clip, as it appears on the Flash Stage. A **method** instructs the object to perform some task. For example, if a DVD player is an object, then the methods would be something like: play, record, and stop. Flash methods are written like this:

```
play();
record();
stop();
```

Some methods require parameters within the parenthesis. For example, the following method instructs the play head to move to frame 6 on the Timeline and stop:

```
gotoAndStop(6);
```

Attaching the method to a specific object requires identifying the object in the ActionScript code:

```
myDVD.gotoAndStop(6);
```

ActionScript is a language, and just like learning any foreign language, all the words and syntax might seem strange at first; however, the longer you work with the language, the simpler it becomes.

15

Applying Properties and Methods to an Object

Once you've gotten the hang of writing ActionScripts, the next step is to apply properties and methods to objects in a Flash document. You can have an object, and let your visitor control its color. Changing the color is an example of changing an object's properties. To make an object change color, you will need a Flash document that contains a MovieClip and button symbols. An easy script translation would be: Flash, when my visitor clicks (release) on the button, I want you to assign a new color to an object that I gave a unique instance name (changeit), and I'm defining that property as objectColor, and change the color (setRGB) to red (0x990000). When you attach ActionScripts to buttons, you're not limited to just a single use. For example, you could drag three instances of the same button symbol on the Stage, and repeat the previous code with one exception: change the SetRGB value of one to (0x990000) for red, another to (0x009900) for green, and the third one to (0x000099) for blue.

Apply Properties and Methods

1. Drag the movie clip onto the Stage.

2. Enter a unique instance name in the Property Inspector.

3. Drag the button symbol onto the Stage, and then select the symbol.

4. Click the Window menu, point to Development Panels, and then click Actions.

Did You Know?

You can now edit ActionScript code using external editor applications. MetaData (Windows), BBEdit (Macintosh), or any editor that saves files using the .as (ActionScript) extension gives you the ability to edit and save ActionScript code. The file can then be opened in Flash (click the File menu, and then click Open), or imported into the Flash Actions panel (click the Actions Options button, and then click Import Script).

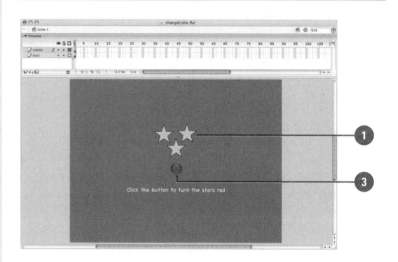

⑤ Enter the script as shown in the illustration.

⑥ Click Control, and then click Test Movie.

⑦ Click the button to change the color of the object to red.

IMPORTANT *Button objects can have triggering events other than a user click. You can create a button instance that uses the rollover event, and have an object change color as the user rolls over the button. Or, you can create an invisible button with a rollover event that triggers a property change when the user rolls over a specific portion of the image.*

See Also

See "Creating an Invisible Button" on page 143 for information on creating invisible buttons.

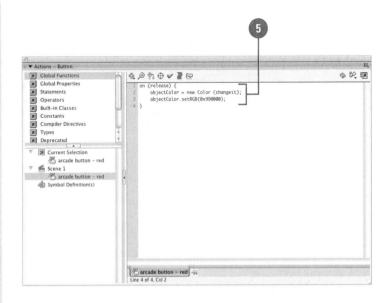

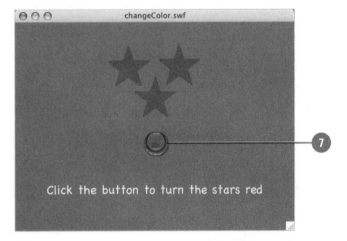

Setting ActionScript Preferences

Flash's Actions panel lets you bring a Flash document to life by writing ActionScripts. Since ActionScripting is so important, Flash gives you the ability to control the Actions panel through preferences. ActionScript preferences give you the ability to control the font and size of the text typed into the Actions panel, as well as using syntax coloring to help you visualize the code.

Set ActionScript Preferences

1 Click the Flash (Professional) (Mac) or Edit (Win) menu, and then click Preferences.

2 Click the ActionScript tab, and then select from the following options:

◆ **Automatic Indentation.** Instructs Flash to perform syntax indentation.

◆ **Code Hints.** Gives you onscreen hints as you type.

◆ **Tab Size.** Enter a value for the number of spaces used.

◆ **Delay.** Delay before showing a code hint. Drag this slider to select a value (0 to 4) in seconds.

◆ **Open/Import and Save/Export.** Select UTF-8 or Default encoding, for open and import operations (UTF-8 is best).

◆ **Text.** Select a font and size for the ActionScript text.

◆ **Syntax Coloring.** Choose the syntax-coloring scheme.

◆ **Language.** Click ActionScript 2.0 to modify the ActionScript sub-settings.

3 Click the Reset To Defaults button to reset the settings.

4 Click OK.

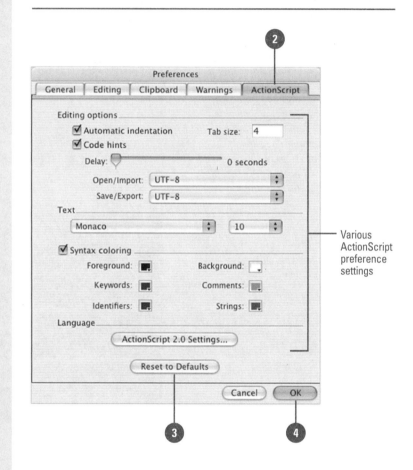

Various ActionScript preference settings

Using Dot Syntax

Since ActionScripts are the heart and soul of a Flash movie, it's important to understand the syntax required to create good scripts. ActionScripts, just like any human language, has rules you should follow. However, in ActionScripts, you have to follow the rules or it won't work.

One of the more important rules to follow is the use of dot syntax. The use of dots (.) in a script serve several purposes. First, is to specify the target path to a particular Timeline. For example, **_root.america.kansas.wichita** defines a movie clip on the main (_root) Timeline with the name america, containing a movie clip named kansas, which in turn contains a movie clip named wichita. Dot syntax is used to create a road map for Flash to follow.

Another use of dot syntax is to change the properties and methods for a specific object. Since ActionScript, by definition is an object-oriented language; Flash performs its responsibilities by instructing an object to do something (method), or by changing a property. For example, **star._rotation = 90;** instructs Flash to rotate the MovieClip instance named *star*, 90 degrees (property). To instruct the star MovieClip instance to play (method), you would enter the following code: **star.play();**

Simply stated, dot syntax is a separator between two or more parts of a Flash script, and gives the ActionScript a road map, or path to follow to complete its command.

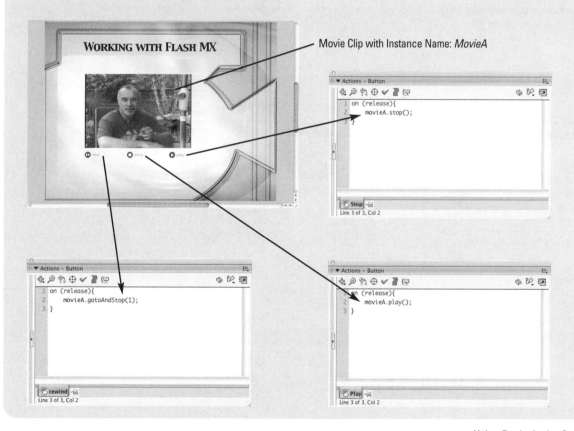

Movie Clip with Instance Name: *MovieA*

Applying Dot Syntax to a Movie Clip

When you use dot syntax, you gain control over a Flash ActionScript. For example, you have a movie clip of a car, and the wheels of the car are separate movie clips. In other words, you've dragged a movie clip symbol (the wheels), into a movie clip (the car), and you want to use a button to stop and start the wheels movie clip. To do this will require using dot syntax to identify the path to the correct movie clip, and then use the play or stop methods on the wheels.

Use Dot Syntax

1. Open the file *movingCar.fla,* and then open the car movie clip symbol in the Flash Library.

    See "*Real World Examples*" on page xviii in the Introduction for information on downloading practice files from the Web.

2. Create a new layer, and then select the new layer.

3. Drag the wheel movie clip symbol into the car movie clip, and then place one copy for the front and one copy for the back wheels.

4. Select and give each of the wheel symbols a unique name in the Property Inspector.

See Also

See Chapter 14, "Using ActionScript Behaviors" on page 321 for additional information on creating scripts in the ActionScript panel.

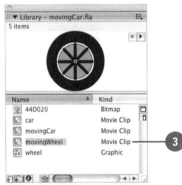

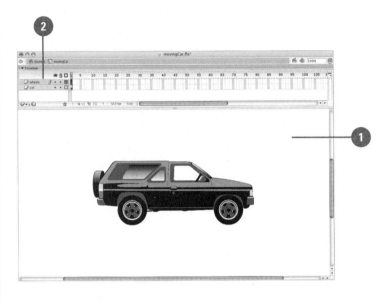

5. Return to the Stage, drag the car movie symbol onto the Stage, and then select the symbol.

6. Give the car movie symbol a unique name in the Property Inspector.

7. Drag the Play button symbol onto the Stage, and then select the symbol.

8. Enter the script as shown in the illustration.

   IMPORTANT *Transportation is the instance name of the car symbol on the Stage, and front wheel and back wheel, are the instances names for the wheel movie clips as defined in the Library.*

9. Drag the Stop button symbol onto the Stage, and then select the symbol.

10. Enter the script as shown in the illustration.

11. Click the Control menu, and then click Test Movie.

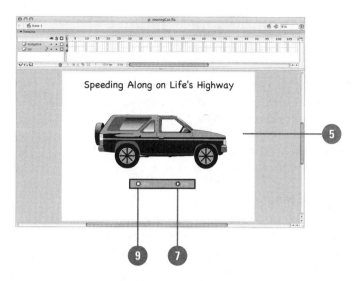

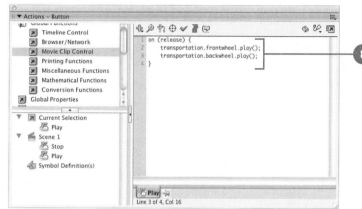

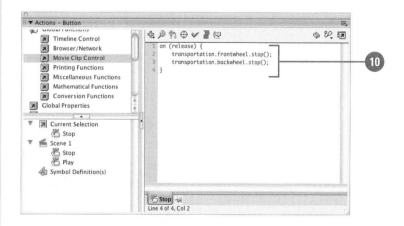

Understanding Event Handlers

Event handlers control when events in Flash occur. When you create a script, some event will be invoked to trigger that particular action. Event handlers come in three different types: mouse events, frame events, and clip events. Choosing the correct event handler will make all the difference in the world.

Work with Mouse Events

Mouse events trigger actions when the mouse interacts with a button or movie clip instance. The following events can be associated with mouse events:

- **on (press).** The acton is triggered when the mouse is pressed.

- **on (release).** The action is triggered when the mouse is pressed, and then released.

- **on (releaseOustide).** The action is triggered when the mouse is pressed on a object (button), and then released outside.

- **on (keyPress).** The action is triggered when the visitor presses a pre-defined key.

- **on (rollOver).** The action is triggered when the visitor rolls over an object.

- **on (rollOut).** The action is triggered when the visitor rolls out of an object.

- **on (dragOver).** The action is triggered when the visitor clicks and then drags into an object.

- **on (dragOut).** The action is triggered when the visitor clicks on an object, and then drags out.

Mouse Handlers in the Actions panel

Mouse Handlers in the Behaviors panel

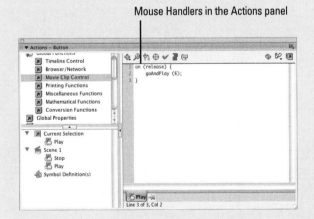

Attaching a Mouse Event to a Button

Attaching a mouse event to a button is probably the easiest of all the events handlers. For example, you have a movie clip of a dog that contains a barking audio file. When the movie clip plays, the dog barks. However, the trick is you want to have the dog bark when the visitor rolls their mouse over the dogs face. To do this, you will need to create an invisible button, and then attach the mouse event to the invisible button.

Attach an Event to a Button

1. Click the Insert menu, and then click New Symbol.

2. Select the Button option, and then name the Symbol.

3. Click OK.

4. Create a blank keyframe in the Hit state of the button, and then create a shape.

   Leave the Up, Over, and Down states blank.

5. Exit the Symbol editing mode, and then return to the Stage.

6. Drag a movie clip onto the Stage.

7. Create a new layer, and then name the layer.

8. Drag the invisible button onto the Stage, and then place it over the area of the image you want to use as a button.

9. Enter the script as shown in the illustration.

   When the visitor rolls into or out of the invisible button, the rollOver or rollOut event handlers will trigger the playing or stopping of the dog movie clip.

10. Click the Control menu, and then click Test Movie.

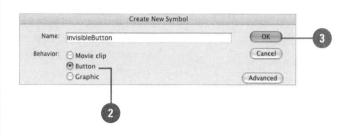

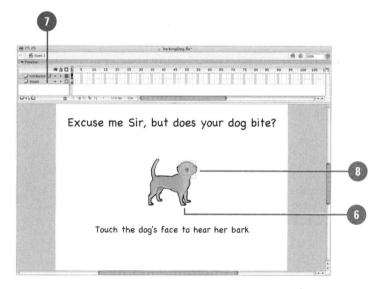

Excuse me Sir, but does your dog bite?

Touch the dog's face to hear her bark

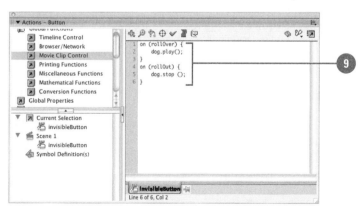

Working with Frame Events

Frame event handlers are easy to understand. When an action is attached to a frame, the action is triggered when the play head hits the frame. For example, you want to create a frame event that swaps images on the Stage, and you want the images to swap every 40 frames. You can attach an ActionScript that swaps the image, and place the action every 40 frames. When the play head hits the frame, the action executes. When you attach an ActionScript to a frame, you'll need a blank keyframe on the Timeline, and it is strongly recommended that you always place ActionScripts in a separate layer from access, and control. In addition, if you're planning to swap images in a Flash movie, it's always best to use a blank movie clip (called a placeholder), to hold the images.

Attach an ActionScript to a Frame

1. Drag a blank movie clip onto the Stage, and then select the clip.

2. Give the movie clip a unique instance name, in the Property Inspector.

3. Create a new layer, and then name the layer.

4. Create blank keyframes at frame numbers 1, 21, 41, and 61.

5. Select a frame, click the Insert menu, point to Timeline, and then click Blank Keyframe.

6. Select frame 1, and then enter the script as shown in the illustration.

7. Select frames 21, 41, and 61, and then repeat the script, except change the name of the image you want to load (image_b.jpg, image_c.jpg, image_d.jpg).

8. Click the Control menu, and then click Test Movie.

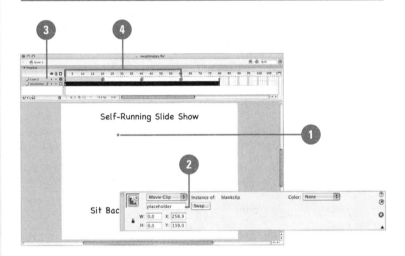

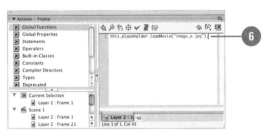

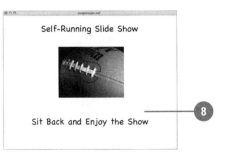

Understanding a Clip Event

Since clip events are attached to movie clips, the action is triggered by the event specified in the onClipEvent handler. You might want a specific movie clip to stop playing when another movie clip loads on the Stage, or when the user clicks or moves their mouse. The Clip Event is one of a series of event handlers that Flash uses to create actions within a Flash movie. You can attach event handlers directly to a button or movie clip instance by using the onClipEvent() or the on() handlers. The onClipEvent() handles movie clip events, and on()handles button events. To use an on() or onClipEvent() handler, attach it directly to an instance of a button or movie clip on the Stage, and then specify the event you want to handle for that instance. For example, the following on() event handler executes whenever the user clicks the button the handler is attached to.

```
on(press) {
    trace("The button has been pressed.");
}
```

You can specify two or more events for each on() handler, separated by commas. The ActionScript in a handler executes when one of the events specified by the handler occurs. For example, the following on() handler attached to a button will execute whenever the mouse rolls over or out of the button.

```
on(rollOver, rollOut) {
    trace("mouse rolled in or out");
}
```

If you want different scripts to run when different events occur, you have the option to attach more than one handler to an object. You can attach onClipEvent() handlers to the same movie clip instance. The first would execute when the movie clip first loads (or appears on the Stage); the second executes when the movie clip is unloaded from the Stage.

```
onClipEvent(load) {
  trace("loaded");
}
onClipEvent (unload) {
  trace("unloaded");
}
```

15

Working with Clip Events

Clip events are movie clips with attached scripts. For example, you can have a specific action happen when the movie clip enters the Stage, or when it leaves, or even when the mouse moves around the Stage.

The following clip events can be attached to a movie clip:

◆ **onClipEvent (load).** The action is triggered when the movie clip loads to the Stage.

◆ **onClipEvent (unload).** The action is triggered when the movie clip unloads.

◆ **onClipEvent (enterFrame).** The action is triggered when the movie clip loads at the current frame rate.

◆ **onClip Event (mouseMove).** The action is triggered by movement of the

mouse. You have the ability to receive absolute values as to the position of the visitor's mouse.

◆ **onClipEvent (mouseDown).** The action is triggered by moving the mouse down.

◆ **onClipEvent (mouseUp).** The action is triggered by moving the mouse up.

◆ **onClipEvent (keyDown).** The action is triggered when you press the cursor Down key.

◆ **onClipEvent (keyUp).** The action is triggered when you press the cursor Up key.

◆ **onClipEvent (data).** The action is triggered when a specific piece of data is received.

Assigning a Clip Event using the Behaviors panel

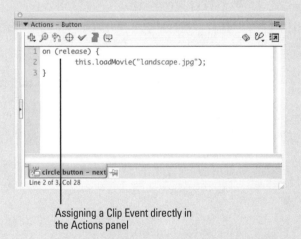

Assigning a Clip Event directly in the Actions panel

Attaching a Clip Event to a Movie Clip

You can only attach an onClipEvent() to a movie clip instance that has been placed on the Stage. You can't attach an onClipEvent() to a movie clip instance that is created at runtime; for example, using the attachMovie() method. Using different event handlers within the same Flash document do not conflict with each other. For example, you could have a button with an on(press) handler that tells the .swf file to play, and the same button can have an onPress method, for which you define a function that tells an object on the Stage to rotate. When the button is clicked, the SWF file plays, and the object will rotate. Being able to consolidate different event handlers with a single instance, gives you greater control, as well as less Stage clutter.

Attach an onClipEvent to a Movie Clip

1. Place a movie clip on the Stage, and then select the movie clip.

2. Give the movie clip a unique instance name in the Properties panel.

3. Move down the Timeline and add a keyframe at frame 80.

4. Click the Insert menu, point to Timeline, and then click Keyframe.

5. Add a second movie clip to the Stage, and then select the second movie clip.

6. Enter the script as shown in the illustration.

7. Click the Control menu, and then click Test Movie.

   When the playhead hits frame 80 it loads the second movie clip. The loading of the movie will trigger the onClipEvent handler, and stop the playing of the movie clip with the unique instance name of movie2.

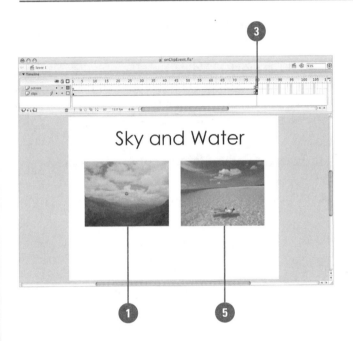

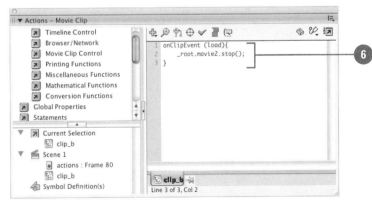

15

Understanding Data Types

When you use ActionScripts, you have the ability to work with data. Data can be information entered in by a visitor in an input data field, or it can be computer information such as, the current position of the mouse, or the date and time. When you work with data, you have 4 possible data types:

- **String.** Allows for the entering of text values.

- **Number.** Allows for the entering in of numeric values.

- **Boolean.** A Boolean state has two values; typically true or false.

- **Object.** Serves as a storage device for any data type, including other objects.

Use Data Types to Control Information

Since data types control the type of information that can be entered into a data field, you can use them to validate the data someone is entering. For example, you want to create a calculator to convert Fahrenheit into Celsius. To do this, you will need an input field for someone to enter the current temperature in Fahrenheit, a button that would perform the calculation, and then a dynamic text field for the result, and one for an error message.

1. Select the Input Field, and then give it a unique variable name in the Property Inspector.

2. Select the Error Dynamic Text Field and give it a unique variable name in the Property Inspector.

3. Select the Results Dynamic Text Field, and then give it a unique variable name in the Property Inspector.

4. Select the button instance, and then enter the following script into the Actions panel (see the next page).

Error Message using text

Error Message using a blank field

Correct data...no error message

```
on (release) {
        result = ""
        if (!input.length) {
                err = "Please Enter a Number"
        }
        else {
                n = new Number(input)
                if(isNaN(n)){
                        result = ""
                        err = "Enter Numbers ONLY"
                }
                else{
                        err = ""
                        if(fah_type.getValue(true)){
                                n = (5 / 9) * (n - 32)
                                s = n.toString(10)
                                result = s.substring(0,7) + " DegreesC"
                                }
                        else{
                                n = (9 / 5) * n + 32
                                s = n.toString(10)
                                result = s.substring(0,7) + " DegreesF"
                        }
                }
        }

}
```

When the movie is played, the visitor will enter a value into the data field, and it will be evaluated as to whether it's pure numeric. If it isn't, an error message will display in the dynamic error field. If the field contains numbers, then the calculation will perform the conversion, and the results displayed in the output field.

15

Creating Loops

Loops allow Flash to perform an action repeatedly. You can use a loop to create a dynamic drop-down menu, validate data, search for text, duplicate movie clips, and even to detect collisions in games that have projectiles and objects. **Conditional statements** let you execute an action based on a specific condition. You can have a specific action continue to loop until a certain condition was met. For example, continue to search for a specific text string until it is found, or the end of the text document is reached. Loops come in two forms—While loops and For loops—it doesn't matter what type of loop is chosen, they will both require a conditional statement to start and stop the loop.

◆ **While Loops.** While loops continue to execute while a certain condition exists (keep looping or searching) until the specific value is reached.

```
i = 4;
while (var i > 0) {
    my_mc.duplicateMovieClip("newMC" + i, i );
    i--;
}
```

◆ **For Loops.** For loops are self-contained counters. For example, loop (repeat the action), ten times, and then stop.

```
on (release) {
    for (x=0; x<=10, ++x);
    myClip.duplicateMovieClip ("myClip" + x, x);
    myClip._rotation =45 + x * 10;
    }
}
```

Working with For Loops

The For loop works with an increasing or decreasing numeric value. For example, you could use a For loop to create several copies of a movie clip on the Stage. Letting the For loop control movie clips to the Stage is far more efficient than having to move them one at a time. In addition, the visitor can control when the items appear on the Stage using a button.

Work with For Loops

1. Drag a movie clip from the Library to the Stage, and then select the movie clip.

2. Enter a unique instance name for the movie clip in the Property Inspector.

3. Place a button on the Stage, and then select the button.

4. Enter the script as shown in the illustration.

   When you play the movie, clicking on the button causes the action to loop 10 times. Each time it loops, it duplicates the original movie clip and rotate it by a 45 degrees plus the current value of x times 10.

Did You Know?

You can use a For Loop to pause a Flash movie. Select a value, instruct the loop to increment by 1, and then loop until the value is reached. Use a loop timer for such items as a Flash slide show, where you want the slides to display on the stage for a given number of seconds before moving to the next slide.

See Also

See "Working with While Loops and Using Loop Exceptions" on page 354 for information on using other looping actions.

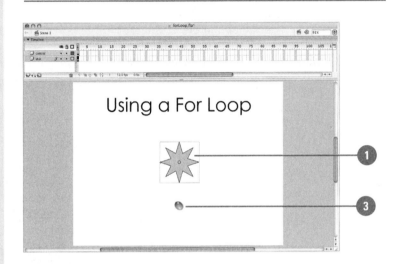

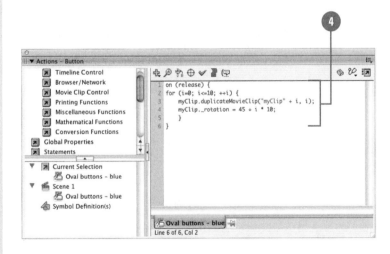

15

Working with While Loops and Using Loop Exceptions

While loops wait for a specific condition to start or stop the loop. That may sound similar to the For loop, with one exception: The For Loop is self-contained, and the While loop works with an external condition, or one outside the scope of the loop. For example, to have a While loop perform the same action as the previous For loop, you would use the following script:

```
on (release) {
  while (x<10);
  myClip.duplicateMovieClip ("myClip" + x, x);
  myClip._rotation =45 + x * 10;
  x=x+1;
  }
}
```

When you create a Looping action, you can further control the loop by using the following loop exceptions:

◆ **Continue.** The continue exception lets you stop the current loop from performing its actions, and jump directly to the next cycle of the loop.

◆ **Break.** The break exception is used to exit a loop, even if the original condition that is driving the loop is still true.

For example, If you create a While loop using the following script:

```
total = 0;
i = 0:
while (++i <=20) {
  if (i == 10) {
    continue;
  }
  total +=i;
}
```

The results would be a script that executes and added 1 to total; unless the value of i equaled 10. This would create a sequence of numbers 1 2 3 4 5 6 7 8 9 11 12 13 14 15 16 17 18 19 20. If you had used the break exception in place of continue, the values would read: 1 2 3 4 5 6 7 8 9. Therefore, it loops whether For or While are controlled by internal or external conditions, and using a break or continue exception gives you further control over the loop.

Using Conditional Statements

Conditional statements in ActionScript are a critical part of interactivity. It lets you program a script based on any number of conditions. For example, in the morning, you say good day, or good morning to someone you meet. In doing so, you made a conditional choice.

ActionScript does the same thing. You can create an ActionScript that checks the time of day. If it's before noon, Flash responds with a Good Morning message, if it's from noon to 5, say Good Afternoon, or after 5 till midnight, say Good Evening. This type of condition is known as an if/else condition. If this happens do this... else do that. Since a variable can be almost anything you can measure on a computer, and a conditional statement is made up of two or more variables, ActionScript can be taken to a point where it almost thinks for itself. The previous example could be expressed in flow charting the following way:

Typically, when you're creating a conditional statement, you're comparing one element against another using operators. The following operators are available to create conditional statements:

- **==** Checks for equality between two values (is time of day greater than 5).

- **!=** Checks for inequality between two values.

- **<** Checks for less than (is value A less than value B).

- **>** Checks for greater than (is value A greater than value B).

- **<=** Checks for less than or equal to between two values.

- **>=** Checks for greater than or equal to between two values.

- **&&** Checks for a logical AND (if day == "Friday" && time > 5).

- **||** Checks for a logical OR (if day == "Saturday" || day == "Sunday").

Using these operators to check between two or more values, you can create complex ActionScripts that react differently based on the available data. To create a dynamic field that checked the time, and responded with the appropriate answer, you would enter the following code:

```
if (time > "0000 &&  time < 1200) {
    response = "Good Morning";
} else if (time >1200 && time < 1700) {
    response = "Good Afternoon";
}else if (time > 1700 && time < 2400);
    response = "Good Evening"
}
```

Using Functions

A **function** is a block of ActionScript code that can be reused anywhere in a SWF file. If you pass values as parameters to a function, the function will operate on those values. A function can also return values. Flash MX contains built-in functions that let you access certain information and perform certain tasks, such as getting the version number of Flash Player hosting the SWF file (getVersion()). Functions that belong to an object are called methods. Functions that don't belong to an object are called top-level functions and are found in the Functions category of the Actions panel.

Each function has its own characteristics, and some functions require you to pass certain values. If you pass more parameters than the function requires, the extra values are ignored. If you don't pass a required parameter, the empty parameters are assigned the undefined data type, which can cause errors when you export a script. To call a function, it must be in a frame that the playhead has reached.

To call a function, simply use the function name and pass any required parameters. The following code describes a common syntax for creating functions:

```
function firstFunction (x, y, z) {
    // place all actions here;
}
```

Calling a Function

Functions begin with the word function, followed by the name of the function (user-defined). The area enclosed by parenthesis; used for passing parameters to the function actions. If the parameters are left blank, you're essentially creating a generic function that will function the same way every time it's called. If however, the function contains parameters, it will perform in a unique way, each time it's called. When you call a function, you're instructing Flash to execute all of the actions within that function. Therefore, if firstFunction contained 20 actions, all of them would be executed by using a single line of script. To call a function simply, add this line to the action:

```
myFunction ();
```

Passing Parameters to a Function

If the function has been defined to accept parameter information, you can use the following line of script:

```
myFunction (parameter 1, parameter2);
```

Once a Function is defined, it can be called any time it's needed. Therefore, it's a good practice to define all of your functions in frame 1 of the active Flash document, that way they can be called any time after that.

Debugging a Movie

Introduction

Flash MX 2004 and Flash MX Professional 2004 provide several enhancements that make it easier for you to debug scripts using the ActionScript language. The new features include new language elements, improved editing and debugging tools, and the introduction of a more object-oriented programming language; however, not all debugging problems reside in an ActionScript. Debugging a Flash movie is similar to a mechanic attempting to fix the engine on a car. He can hear a knocking or pinging sound, but he's not sure what's causing it, so he brings out his debugging tools to help locate the problem.

A Flash movie is not a car, however, there are similarities; for example, if the movie is not doing what you want: Maybe it's running too slow, or your movie crashes after playing a specific scene; you can bring out Flash's debugging tools to help locate (and fix) the problem. When you design a Flash movie, the fonts, colors, video and audio (if any), along the overall construction of the movie are very right-brain techniques (your creative side at work). When you debug a Flash movie, you're using a very logical approach to the problem. Flash's debugging tools include the Actions panel, the Movie Explorer, and even the ability to view variables and how they react during the play of the movie. Like the car mechanic, you're listening for that annoying pinging sound. Flash will not only help you locate the problem, its array of debugging tools will help you fix it, and get you back speeding down the electronic highway.

Debugging Concepts

When you debug a movie, you're not just looking for the obvious problems; you're attempting to see if you can find anything that might happen. Depending on the complexity of the movie, hidden problems can be difficult to find. For example, if you're calling video files into a Flash movie, are all your paths to the files correct? It may function fine when you're testing on your computer, but will it still work when you move it to a CD or Web server? Test it and find out. Here are a few things to consider when going into the debug phase of a Flash Movie:

◆ **Paths to file.** I've already mentioned this, but it needs repeating. If you're importing external .swf files, image files, video, or audio files into a Flash movie, the best approach is to create a folder to hold the entire Flash project, and then create subfolders within that folder to hold the movie assets. When you move the Flash project, move the entire folder. That way all the path names stay correct, and you always know where everything is, at all times.

◆ **Short descriptive file names.** Computers allow for file names of unlimited length; however, that does not mean that you need to use large file names. Large file names are harder for you to type in, and there is a greater chance that you will mistype the name. Use short descriptive names.

◆ **Use smart naming conventions.** Since file names display alphabetically, it's not a bad idea to come up with similar names for similar file types. For example, car_1.jpg, car_2.jpg, car_3.jpg. The name and extension describe (in general terms), the content of the file, and file type, and will display one after the other. Smart naming conventions won't make your

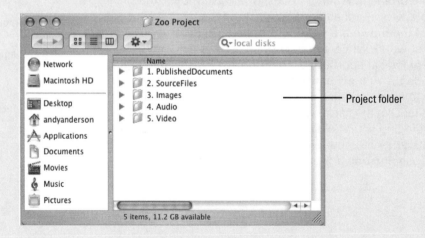

Project folder

flash project any better, but they will help to organize some of the confusion that comes with a complicated Flash project.

◆ **Test and test often.** Debugging does not start at the end of a project, it begins as soon as you click the File menu, and then click New. As a matter of fact, Flash lets you test a movie whenever you choose. Just click the Control menu, and then click Test Movie (to test the entire Flash movie), or click Test Scene (to test just the active scene).When you test a scene or movie, Flash creates a temporary .swf file, and then runs the movie in a version of the Flash plug-in. Flash publishes the test movie using the settings in the Publishing dialog box.

◆ **Bandwidth.** If this project is going out to the Internet, make sure that the size of the finished movie isn't so large, that your visitors have to wait a long time for it to

download. It's possible you might want to include a pre-loader to entertain the audience while they're waiting.

◆ **Planning is the key.** If you want your Flash movie to look good, work without error, and be completed in the least amount of time, then plan, plan, and then plan some more. Use the carpenter's adage: Measure Twice... Cut Once. University studies show that planning a project, before you start, cuts the project completion time by 20 percent. Planning involves thinking about what you want to accomplish (what's the message), research and gather all the files, and things you'll need to get the project complete, and think about where the project will be used (Internet, CD). In addition, a well-planned project will cut down your debugging time by over half.

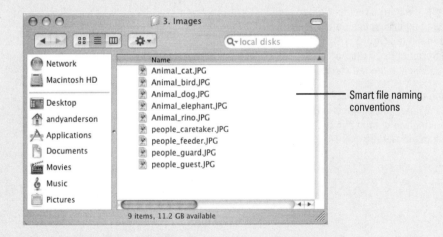

Smart file naming conventions

Debugging with the ActionScript Editor

The ActionScript editor has been updated in a number of ways to make it easier to use edit and debug scripts. When you're debugging a Flash movie, the traditional wisdom is to try to push it until it breaks, and then figure out why it broke. However, once you find out what's broke, it's very possible that you're going to have to work on the ActionScript's that drive the movie. That's where the Actions panel comes into play. The designers of Flash MX 2004, have added a few new editing and debugging features, as well as enhanced some old ones.

Use the ActionScript Editor

1. **Word wrapping**. Click the Options pop-up menu in the Script pane, to enable or disable word wrapping.

2. **Viewing context-sensitive Help**. When your pointer is positioned over an ActionScript element in the Actions toolbox or in the Script pane, you can click the Reference button in the context menu to display a help page about that element.

3. **Importing scripts**. When you select Import Script from the pop-up menu in the Actions panel, the imported script is copied into the script at the insertion point in the active code file.

4. **Single-click breakpoints**. To add a debugging breakpoint before a line of code in the Debugger panel or the Script pane of the Actions panel, click in the left margin.

5. **Pinning multiple scripts**. You can pin multiple scripts within a FLA file along the bottom of the Script pane in the Actions panel.

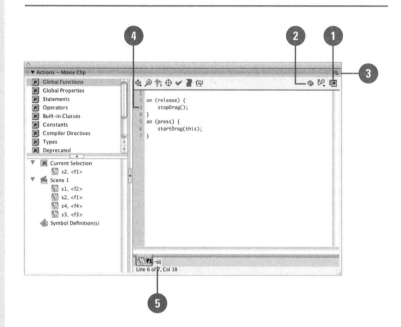

6 **Script navigator.** The Script navigator is a visual representation of the structure of your Flash (.fla) file; you can navigate through the file to locate the ActionScript code.

7 **Integrated Script window for editing external files.** (Flash Professional only). You can use the ActionScript editor in a Script window (separate from the Actions panel) to write and edit external script files.

8 **Syntax coloring.** Syntax coloring utilizes a user-defined set of colors to display the code entered into the Script pane. Click the Flash menu, and then click Preferences (Mac), or click the Edit menu, and then click Preferences. Click the ActionScript Preferences tab to modify the syntax coloring, font and size, or the scripting text.

9 **Instant Syntax Checking.** Click the Check Syntax button to get an instant evaluation of the current script.

10 **Code Hint.** Click the Show Code Hint button, and then Flash will give you a hint of what to do next.

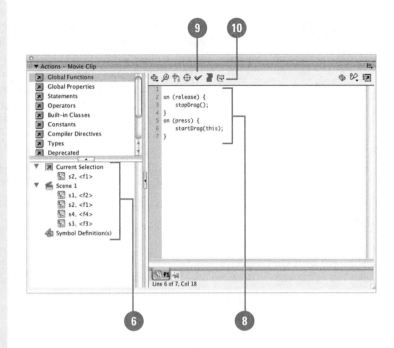

Did You Know?

Normal mode is gone from Flash MX 2004. In previous versions of Flash, you could work in the Actions panel in Normal mode, in which you filled in options and parameters to create code. It was a great way for novice ActionScript coders to learn programming. However, in Flash MX 2004 and Flash MX Professional 2004, you can work in the Actions panel only by adding commands directly to the Script pane.

16

Using the Movie Explorer

Flash's Movie Explorer gives you an easy way to view and organize the contents of an .fla document, and even select elements for modification. It contains a display list of currently used elements, arranged in a tree hierarchical structure. The Movie Explorer gives you the ability to filter which categories of items in the document are displayed; choosing from text, graphics, buttons, movie clips, actions, and imported files. You can even display selected categories as individual scenes, concise symbol definitions, or both. When you select an item in the Movie Explorer panel, the item will be selected in the Flash document. If you double-click on an ActionScript, Flash will open the script in the Actions panel, or if you double-click on a Library item, Flash will open the item in the Library.

Use the Movie Explorer

1. Click the Movie Explorer Options button, and then select from the following options:

   ◆ **Go To Location.** Takes you to the selected layer, scene, or frame in the active document.

   ◆ **Go To Symbol Definition.** Takes you to the symbol definition for a symbol that is selected in the Elements area.

   ◆ **Select Symbol Instances.** Takes you to the scene containing instances of a symbol that is selected in the Definitions area.

   ◆ **Find In Library.** Select to highlight the selected symbol in the document's Library.

   ◆ **Rename.** Select to enter a new name for a selected element.

   ◆ **Edit In Place.** Select to edit a selected symbol on the Stage.

   ◆ **Edit In New Window.** Select to edit a selected symbol in a new window.

   ◆ **Show Movie Elements.** Displays the elements in your document organized into scenes.

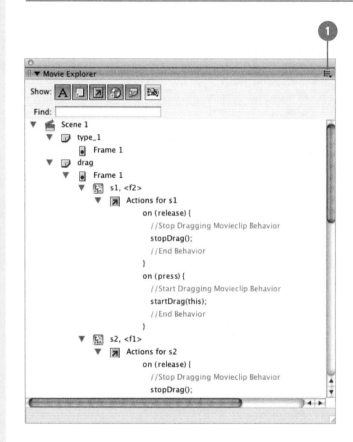

- ◆ **Show Symbol Definitions.**
  Select to display all the
  elements associated with a
  symbol.

- ◆ **Copy All Text To Clipboard.**
  Select to copy selected text to
  the Clipboard.

- ◆ **Cut, Copy, Paste, And Clear.**
  Select to perform these
  functions on a selected
  element.

- ◆ **Expand Branch.** Select to
  expand the navigation tree at
  the selected element.

- ◆ **Collapse Branch.** Select to
  collapse the navigation tree at
  the selected element.

- ◆ **Collapse Others.** Select to
  collapse the branches in the
  navigation tree not containing
  the selected element.

- ◆ **Print.** Select to print the
  hierarchical display list
  currently displayed in the
  Movie Explorer.

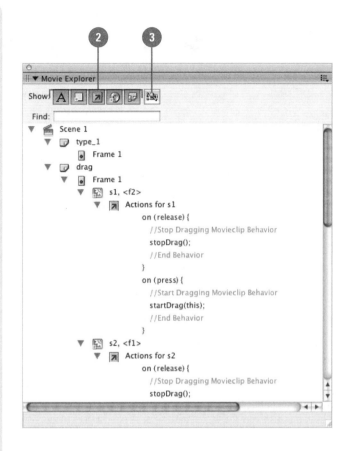

2 The Show buttons gives you the
option to show or hide different
elements of the movie. These
options will only impact the Movie
Explorer, not the Flash Stage.

- ◆ **Show Text**

- ◆ **Show Buttons, Movie Clips,
  and Graphics**

- ◆ **Show ActionScripts**

- ◆ **Show Video, Sounds, and
  Bitmaps**

- ◆ **Show Frames and Layers**

3 Click the Customize Which Items
To Show button, to customize what
items display in the Movie Explorer
window.

16

Debugging Manually

Debugging a Flash movie manually means exactly what it implies. You can open the movie and take it for a test drive. Debugging a movie manually gives you a chance to be the visitor, and experience your movie exactly as they would. When you manually test a Flash movie, you want to experience the wait time for downloading, you want to forget that you created this masterpiece, and you want to come at it just as if you were a first time viewer. A Flash movie is composed of various design elements: Text, video, audio, images, and animation, all of which go into the production of a Flash movie, and the glue that binds the whole thing together; ActionScripting. Your visitors will never see the ActionScript code, and most do not care how it was written; but they will care if it doesn't work properly. For example, your visitor clicks a button to load a video file, and the video never loads, or it takes so long to load that they get bored and leave. It's problems like these that manual debugging can solve.

Debug Manually

1 Click the Control menu, and then click Test Movie (to test the entire Flash movie), or click Test Scene (to test the active scene).

> **IMPORTANT** *Flash uses the settings described in the Publish Settings dialog box to test the movie. Use different settings such as Flash plug-in, to test the movie against earlier versions of the Flash plug-in.*

2 Test the movie for any structural failures. Click all the buttons, and then do all the things you think a visitor would do.

3 Note any problems on paper (remember this is manual); called a debug, or edit list. The list can then be used to edit the document, using Flash's standard editing tools.

See Also

See Chapter 21 "Publishing a Movie" on page 445 for information on modifying publishing settings.

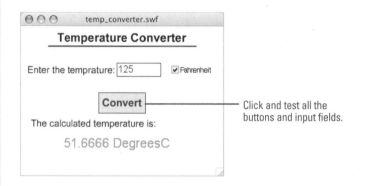

Click and test all the buttons and input fields.

For Your Information

Debugging Flash Player

When Macromedia Flash MX is installed, the debug version of the Macromedia Flash Player is installed for the application as well as any browser specified. While this debug version of the player can be very useful when authoring, there may be situations where the standard player is desired. If you would like to uninstall the debug player, point your browser to: *http://www.macromedia.com/support/flash/ts/documents/remove_player.htm*, and then follow the onscreen instructions. You can then point your browser to: *http://www.macromedia.com/shockwave/download/download.cgi?P1_Prod_Version=ShockwaveFlash*, and download the current version of the player.

Using the Flash Debugger

Flash provides several tools for testing ActionScript in your SWF files. The Debugger panel lets you find and locate errors hidden in an .swf file, while it's running in the Flash Player. You must view your SWF file in a special version of Flash Player called the Flash Debug Player (installed automatically when you install the Flash application). The Debugger panel, shows a hierarchical display list of movie clips currently loaded in the Flash Player. You can then use the Debugger to display and modify variables and property values as the .swf file plays. In addition, you can insert breakpoints to stop the .swf file and step through the ActionScript code line by line. In fact, you can even use the Debugger panel to test files on a Web server in a remote location. The Debugger lets you set breakpoints in your ActionScript that stop the Flash Player, and then lets you step through the code as it runs. You can then go back to your scripts and edit them so that they produce the correct results. The Debugger will show you where the problems are, but it doesn't fix them.

Use the Flash Debugger

1. Click the Control menu, and then click Debug Movie.

2. The Code View panel displays a message indicating the movie is paused.

3. Click the Play button to start the movie.

4. Click Stop Debugging to turn off the Debugger panel.

5. Click inside the code, and then click the Toggle Breakpoint to add or remove a breakpoint at the insertion point of the cursor.

   Breakpoints stop the movie from playing and allow you to step through the code line by line.

6. Click Remove All Breakpoints to remove all the breakpoints from the code.

7. Click the Step Over, Step In, and Step Out buttons to step through each line of an ActionScript.

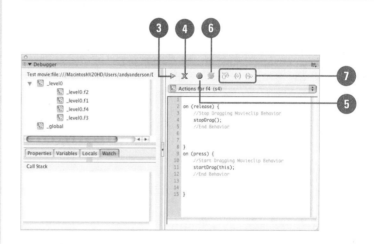

16

For Your Information

Test Your Movie

When you use the Test Movie command to test movies that implement keyboard shortcuts, click the Control menu, and then click Disable Keyboard Shortcuts. This prevents Flash from interpreting keystrokes, and lets them pass through to the player. For example, you can have a Flash document that uses Ctrl+U to display a file, or video. However, Flash uses Ctrl+U to display the Preferences panel. If you don't Disable Keyboard Shortcuts, pressing Ctrl+U in the Flash player will actually open Flash Preferences.

Viewing Variables

When you work in the Debugger panel, you have the option of viewing any variables used in the Flash movie. The Variables tab in the Debugger panel displays the names and values of any global and Timeline variables in the .swf file. If you change the value of a variable on the Variables tab, you can see the change reflected in the .swf file while it runs. This gives you the ability to test new data variables and their impact on the Flash player document.

View Variables

1. Click the Control menu, and then click Debug Movie.

2. Select the movie clip containing the variable from the display list.

3. Select an item in the display frame to view the variables names and values.

4. Click the Continue button to observe the variables as the Flash movie runs.

5. Click the Variables tab.

   IMPORTANT *The display list updates automatically as the .swf file plays. When a movie clip is removed from the .swf file at a specific frame, the movie clip, variable and variable name, are removed from the display list in the Debugger panel. This lets you focus on the current variables. When you're viewing a complex Flash movie that contains a lot of variables, only having to view the current variables cuts down on the visual clutter, and helps you to focus on the immediate problem.*

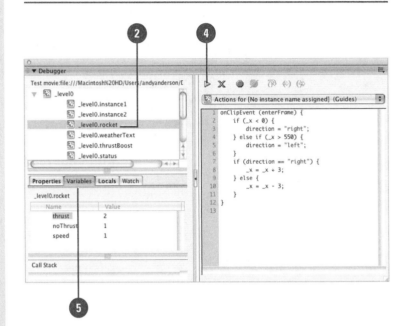

Adding Variables to the Watch List

In any complex Flash movie there will probably be a set of critical variables that you want to keep an eye on. You can monitor critical variables in a controllable way, by marking them to appear in the Debugger panel Watch list. The Watch list displays the absolute path to the variable and its current value, and just like the Variables tab, you can enter a new variable value at any time during the debugging process. If you add a local variable to the Watch list, its value appears only when Flash Player is stopped at a line of ActionScript where that variable is in scope. All other variables appear while the .swf file is playing. If the Debugger can't find the value of the variable, it will list the value as undefined.

Add Variables

1. Click the Control menu, and then click Debug Movie.

2. Click the Variables or Locals tab, and then select a variable.

3. Click the Debugger Options button, and then click Watch.

4. Click the Watch tab.

5. Click the Debugger Options button, and then click Add Watch.

6. Enter the target path to the variable name and the value in the fields.

   IMPORTANT *To remove variables from the Watch list, select a variable on the Watch tab, click the Debugger Options button, and then click Remove Watch.*

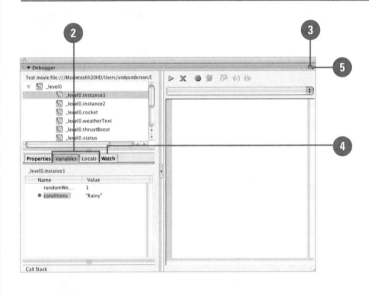

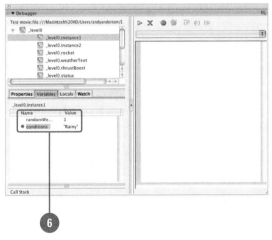

16

Viewing Properties

The Properties tab in the Debugger panel displays all property values of any movie clip on the Stage. Properties are modifiable script elements such as _alpha (controls transparency), or _rotation (controls the rotation of an object). The Properties tab will list all the properties including their current values. You can then adjust the values as the Flash movie is running to judge their impact. This gives you a tremendous amount of control over the debugging process. For example, changing the transparency value of a Flash object, and then observing how that change impacts performance and design.

View Properties

1. Click the Control menu, and then click Debug Movie.

2. Select an available movie clip from the Display list.

3. Click the Properties tab to view all the properties, and their associated values.

4. Double-click on a value, and then enter a new value in any available property.

5. Click the Continue button to view how the Properties change as the Flash movie executes.

   IMPORTANT *The Property value is picky about what you enter. For example, you can enter a value of 100 or text within quotes such as: "newvalue", but you cannot enter expressions such as: y + 12, or an array of values such as: 1, 2, 3.*

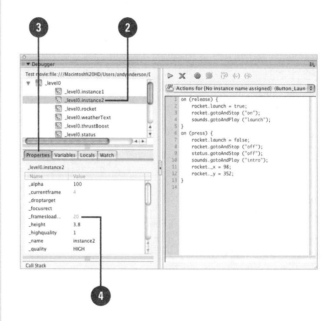

Setting Breakpoints

Breakpoints are instructions to the Debugger to halt the running of a Flash movie. For example, you're watching how the .swf file plays using the debugger, however, it's moving so fast it's difficult to watch everything. By inserting a breakpoint, you instruct the Debugger to halt the movie, and any variables and properties will display the values associated with that point in time. You can then change the values, and instruct the Debugger to continue playing the movie, using the modified values.

Set Breakpoints

1. Click the Control menu, and then click Debug Movie.

2. Select a line of script where you want to place a breakpoint.

3. Click the Toggle Breakpoint button above the code view to add a breakpoint, or remove a previously inserted breakpoint.

4. Click the Play button to begin playing the Flash .swf file.

5. The Debugger will stop the movie at each breakpoint.

Did You Know?

You can set breakpoints with the click of your mouse. Click in the left margin next to the line you want to set a breakpoint. A red dot indicates a breakpoint. You can also click the red dot to remove the breakpoint.

You cannot set a breakpoint on a comment line. If you set a breakpoint in a comment (or empty line) in the Actions panel, the breakpoint will be ignored by the Debugger.

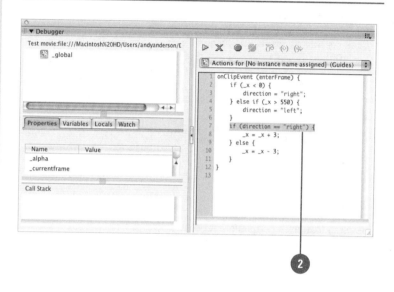

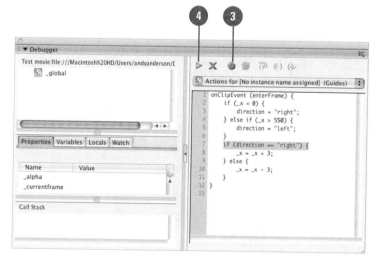

16

Stepping Through Code

When you open the Debugger panel, the Flash Player is automatically paused. This gives you the opportunity to set breakpoints in the script (see previous lesson: Setting Breakpoints). Once the breakpoints are set, you can click the Continue or Play button, and the Debugger will play the .swf file until it encounters a breakpoint. When a breakpoint is reached, the Debugger again pauses the movie. You now have the option to step in, out, or through the breakpoint script.

Step Through Code

① Click the Control menu, and then click Debug Movie.

② Add (or remove) breakpoints by clicking directly in the code, and then click Toggle Breakpoint.

③ Click the Continue button.

④ Flash will stop at the first breakpoint.

⑤ Select from the step options:

◆ **Step In**. Click to step into and execute a function (works only for user-defined functions).

◆ **Step Out**. Click to move out of a function (works only if you are currently stopped in a user-defined function).

◆ **Step Over**. Click to skip over a line of code.

◆ **Continue**. Click to leave the line at which the player is stopped and continues playing.

◆ **Stop Debugging**. Click to inactivate the Debugger, but continue to play the SWF file.

IMPORTANT *If you want to know where the Debugger stopped, keep an eye on the yellow arrow. A yellow arrow along the left side of the Debugger's code view indicates the line at which the Debugger stopped.*

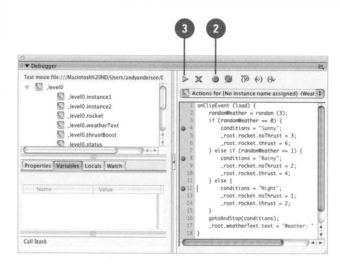

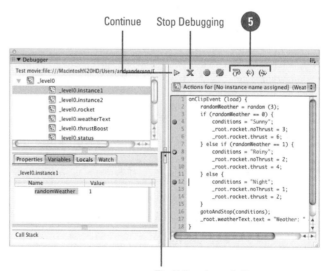

The Yellow Arrow indicates where the Debugger stopped.

Adding Display Components

Introduction

Components are building blocks than you can use to create interactive, dynamic Flash documents. Think of a component as a movie clip with modifiable parameters, which are set during the design of a Flash document, and ActionScript APIs (APIs allow you to customize the component at runtime). Since components are reusable, they give developers the ability to share code between projects.

You can use components created by Macromedia, download components created by other developers or, with a bit of practice create your own components. Flash MX 2004 comes packaged with many components: They include the ability to add check boxes, radio buttons, and even create sophisticated menus and labels with a minimum of scripting experience.

For example, you want to create list of options, which a visitor would then be able to click and choose. You can open the Actions panel, and then create the list by typing in about 40 or more lines of script, or you can use Flash's built-in component to create the list. The difference is not in the quality of the list, but the amount of time it took to create it. Spending less time on creating dynamic, interactive Flash elements gives you more time to concentrate on design features; and to a Flash visitor, it's not about the code or how long it took you to create it... it's about the design, and it will always be about the design.

Understanding Basic Components

If you're the type of Flash designer that wants to create Rich Internet Application, while writing as little ActionScript as possible, then Flash components are just what you've been looking for all these years. You can drag components into a document, set a few parameters in the Property or Component Inspector panel, attach an on() handler directly to a component in the Actions panel to handle component events, and you're finished. If you think components sound too good to be true, then think again. Components are not just a way to get out of coding, they're an excellent way to create consistency in your design; and since components are based on pre-tested code, they will work the same way every time.

When you work with Flash components, you can create Flash content that is accessible to users with disabilities using Flash accessibly features. As you design accessible Flash applications, consider how your users will interact with the content. For example, visually impaired users might rely on additional technology, such as screen readers, while hearing-impaired users might read text and captions in the document. To make a Flash Component accessible, click the Window menu, point to Other Panels, and then click Accessibility to open the Accessibility panel. For more information on creating assessable compliant documents, open your browser and visit *www.w3.org/WAI/*, or for information on Flash, open your browser and visit *www.macromedia.com/*, go to the Flash Exchange, and then type the word "accessibility" in the keyword field. To open an accessibility sample document, open the file AccessibleApplications.fla from the Samples folder; see "*Opening Sample Documents*" on page 14.

Components panel

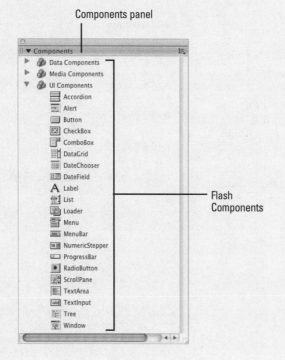

Flash Components

Accessibility panel

Components are added to the Stage using the Components panel. For example, to add an Alert component to the Stage, you would open the Components panel, expand the UI Components list, and then drag the Alert icon onto the Stage.

There are five categories of components: user interface components, data components, media components, managers, and screens. **User interface components** allow you to interact with an application (RadioButton, Checkbox, and TextInput). **Data components** allow you to load and manipulate information from data sources (WebServiceConnector and XMLConnector). **Media components** allow you to play back and control streaming media (MediaController, MediaPlayback, and MediaDisplay). **Managers** are defined as nonvisual and let you to manage a feature, such as focus or depth, in an application (FocusManager, DepthManager, PopUpManager, and StyleManager).

Screens come in two versions: slide screens and form screens. A Flash Slide Presentation uses the slide screen, and a Flash Form Application uses the form screen.

Once the component is on the Stage, it is controlled through the Component Inspector panel. The Component Inspector panel has three tabs: Parameters, Bindings, and Schema. Each tab gives you modifiable elements to help control the look and functionality of the component. The Parameters tab lists the most commonly used properties and methods; others parameters can be added using the ActionScript panel. The Bindings tab gives you a way to bind, or link two or more components together. For example, you can bind an external database to a display component, for onscreen viewing of the data. The Schema tab contains a list of a component's bindable properties, data types, internal structure, and other special attributes.

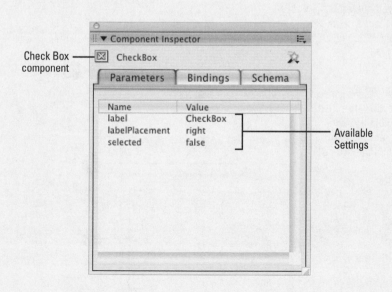

Check Box component

Available Settings

17

Adding a Text Input

The TextInput component works with the ActionScript TextField object. Once a TextInput component is added to the Stage, you can use styles to customize font, size, and color. In addition, a TextInput component can be formatted using HTML, or even as a password field that disguises the text. When a TextInput field has focus, the visitor can use the arrow keys to move through information in the field, and they can use the tab key to move the focus to the next object, or Shift+Tab to move to the previous object. TextInput fields can be used to hold information. For example, you could use a group of TextInput components as the basis for creating an interactive form for fields such as: name, address, city, state, and zip code.

Add a TextInput Component

1 Open the Components panel.

2 Click the UI Components Expand triangle.

3 Drag the TextInput component onto the Stage, and then select the component.

4 Open the Component Inspector panel, and then select the Parameters tab.

5 Select from the following Text Input parameters:

◆ **editable**. When you click the value field, and select true, the field can be edited. If you select false, the field can be selected but not edited.

◆ **password**. When you click the value field, and select true, text entered into the field appears as dots. If you select false, text typed into the field appears as typed.

◆ **text**. Click the value field, and then enter the text that will appear in the field when the Flash document opens.

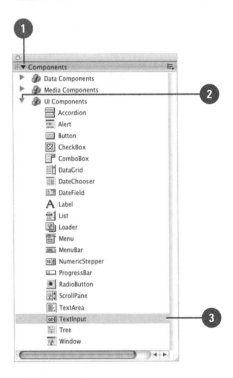

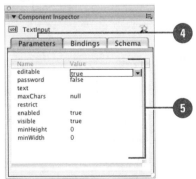

- **maxChars.** Click the value field, and then enter a numerical value indicating the max characters allowed in the TextInput field.

- **restrict.** Click the value field, and then enter any characters that cannot be entered into the TextInput field.

- **enabled.** When you select true, the field can be edited. If you select false, the field appears grayed out and is not selectable, or editable.

- **visible.** When you click the value field, and select true, the field can be viewed. If you select false, the field is invisible.

- **minHeight.** Click the value field, and then enter a minimum height for the TextInput box.

- **minWidth.** Click the value field, and then enter a minimum width for the TextInput box.

6 Click the Control menu, and then click Test Movie.

IMPORTANT *Although you can change the size of any component using the Free Transform tool, since the TextInput component is a single-line component, changing its height does not impact how many lines of text you can type.*

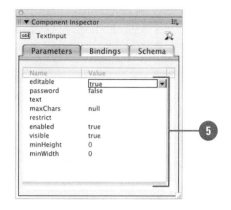

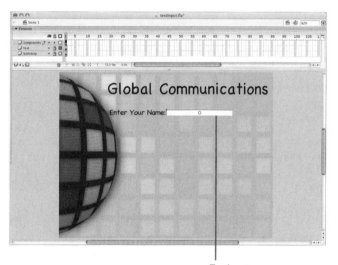

TextInput component

17

Adding a Combo Text Box

The ComboBox component creates a drop-down list of selectable options. They can be either static or editable. The static ComboBox component allows a user to make a single selection from a drop-down list. An editable ComboBox component lets users enter text into a text field located at the top of the list, as well as selecting an item from a drop-down list. A ComboBox component is composed of three subcomponents: Button, TextInput, and List components. When a visitor selects an item, the label of the selection is automatically copied to the text field at the top of the combo box. The ComboBox component is an excellent way to offer several choices to a user, without the necessity of them having to type in a response. For example, a ComboBox could be used to list all of the states in the union in a drop-down box; giving the user the chance to select his home state. When the ComboBox displays in a Flash document, it appears as a single line; clicking the triangle to the right of the line, expands the box and displays all the available options.

Add a ComboBox Component

1. Open the Components panel.

2. Click the UI Components Expand triangle.

3. Drag the ComboBox component onto the Stage, and then select the component.

4. Open the Component Inspector panel, and then select the Parameters tab.

5. Select from the following ComboBox parameters:

   ◆ **data.** Click the value field, and then enter an array in the Values dialog box. Click the plus (+) sign to add values, and the minus sign (-) to remove a value. Data values are used to populate the drop-down list.

   ◆ **editable.** When you click the value field, and select true, the field can be edited. If you select false, the field can be selected but not edited.

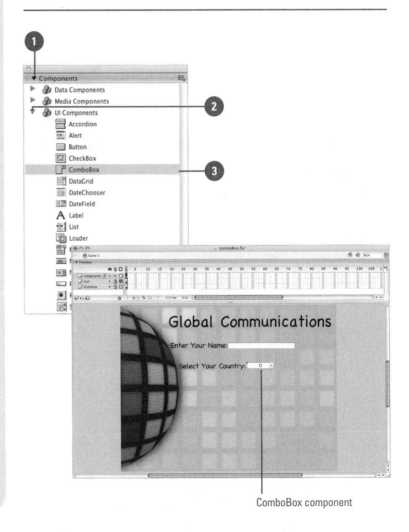

ComboBox component

376

◆ **labels.** Click the value field, and then enter an array in the Values dialog box. Click the plus (+) sign to add values, and the minus sign (-) to remove a value. Data values are used as the selectable items in the list.

◆ **rowCount.** Click the value field, and then enter a number to determine the maximum height of the drop-down list.

◆ **enabled.** When you click the value field, and select true, the items in the list can be selected. If you select false, the field appears grayed out and is not selectable.

◆ **visible.** When you click the value field, and select true, the field can be viewed. If you select false, the field is invisible.

◆ **minHeight.** Click the value field, and then enter a minimum height for the ComboBox box.

◆ **minWidth.** Click the value field, and then enter a minimum width for the ComboBox box.

IMPORTANT *If there is not enough room for the ComboBox to open without hitting the bottom of the document, it will open up instead of down.*

6 Click the Control menu, and then click Test Movie.

When you click the Select Your Computer list arrow, the list will open, and a selection can be made by clicking on one of the available options.

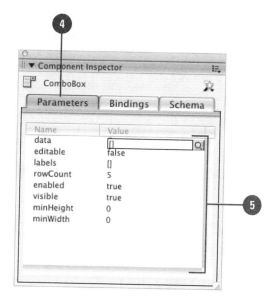

17

Adding a Check Box

A check box is simply a square box that the user can select or deselect. When it is selected, a check mark appears in the box. When a selected check box is clicked, the check mark is removed. The state of a CheckBox component does not change until the mouse is released over the component.

Add a CheckBox Component

1. Open the Components panel.

2. Click the UI Components Expand triangle.

3. Drag the CheckBox component onto the Stage, and then select the component.

Did You Know?

You can control the state of a CheckBox component without the mouse. If the CheckBox component has focus (selected), pressing the Spacebar selects or deselects the check mark.

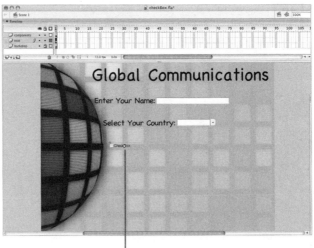

CheckBox component

4 Open the Component Inspector panel, and then select the Parameters tab.

5 Select from the following CheckBox parameters:

◆ **label.** Click the value field, and then enter a label for the check box.

◆ **labelPlacement.** Click the value field, and then select between right, left, top, or bottom for the placement of the label text.

◆ **selected.** Click the value field and select between true (field appears with a checkmark), or false (field appears without a check mark).

6 Click the Control menu, and then click Test Movie.

Click in the CheckBox component to add a check mark, and then click a second time to remove the check mark.

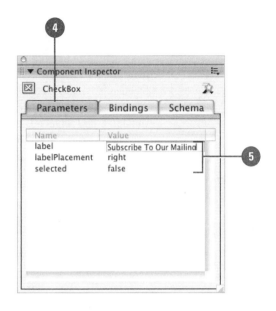

Adding a Radio Button

The RadioButton component lets you do something that the CheckBox component cannot do: force a user to make a single choice within a set of choices. The RadioButton component must be used in a group of at least two RadioButton instances, and only one member of the group can be selected at any given time. Selecting one radio button in a group will deselect the currently selected radio button in the group. For example, Gender: Male, Female. There can be only one answer to that question, so you would group the two items using RadioButton components.

Add a RadioButton Component

1. Open the Components panel.

2. Click the UI Components Expand triangle.

3. Drag one or more RadioButton components onto the Stage, and then select one at time.

Did You Know?

A visitor can control a radio button selection with the keyboard. Click the Tab key until one of the buttons within the group receives focus (is selected), and then use the left and right arrow keys to change the selection within the group. Having the ability to use the keyboard makes Flash components compliant with the current rules on accessibility as set by the U.S. Congress.

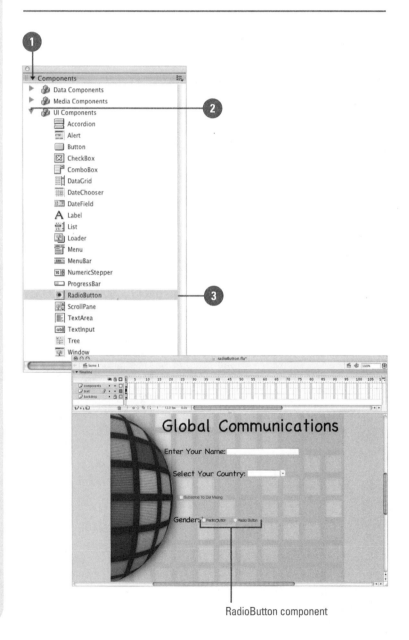

RadioButton component

④ Open the Component Inspector panel, and then select the Parameters tab.

⑤ Select from the following RadioButton parameters:

◆ **data.** Click the value field, and then enter a value that will be used to populate the RadioButton.

◆ **groupName.** Click in the value field, and then enter a group name for the button. When you associate a group name to several RadioButton components, the visitor will only be able to select one button in the group.

◆ **label.** Click the value field, and then enter a label for the RadioButton.

◆ **labelPlacement.** Click the value field, and then select between right, left, top, or bottom for the placement of the label text.

◆ **selected.** Click the value field, and then select between true (field appears selected), or false (field appears unselected).

⑥ Click the Control menu, and then click Test Movie.

Since the RadioButton components both use the same Group name, you can only select one button.

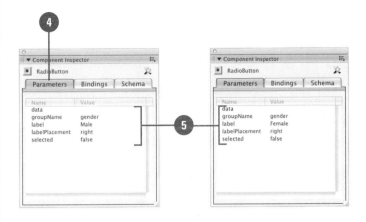

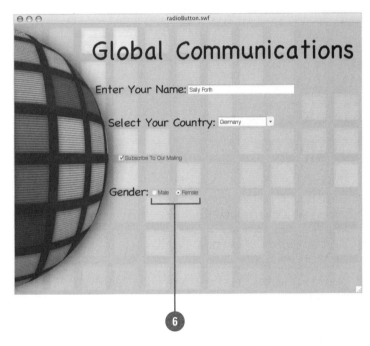

Adding a Text Area

The TextArea component works with the ActionScript TextField object. Once a TextArea component is added to the Stage, you can use styles to customize font, size, and color. In addition, a TextArea component can be formatted using HTML. If this sounds similar to the TextInput component, you're right. In fact, the major difference between a TextInput, and Text Area field is the ability of the TextArea field to generate multiple lines. TextArea fields can be used to hold information. For example, you can use a TextArea component to create a comment, or suggestion field on an interactive form.

Add a TextArea Component

1. Open the Components panel.

2. Click the UI Components Expand triangle.

3. Drag the TextArea component onto the Stage, and then select the component.

4. Open the Component Inspector, and then select the Parameters tab.

5. Select from the following TextArea parameters:

   ◆ **editable.** When you click the value field, and select true, the field can be edited. If you select false, the field can be selected but not edited.

   ◆ **html.** When you click the value field, select true, to allow HTML to control the formatting of the data. If you select false, the field cannot be modified using HTML.

   ◆ **text.** Click the value field, and then enter the initial text that will appear in the TextArea component.

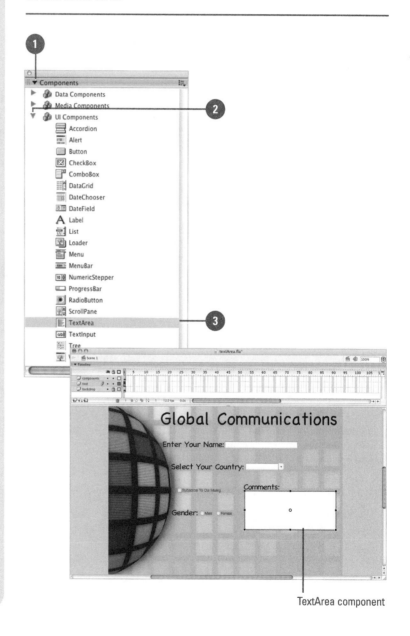

TextArea component

- ◆ **wordWrap.** When you click the value field, and select true, the text typed by the visitor wraps in the TextArea box. If you select false, the text will not wrap.

- ◆ **maxChars.** Click the value field, and then enter the maximum number of characters that can be typed into the TextArea component.

- ◆ **restrict.** Click the value field, and then enter any characters that cannot be entered into the TextArea field.

- ◆ **enabled.** When you click the value field, and select true, the field can be edited. If you select false, the field appears grayed out and is not selectable, or editable.

- ◆ **visible.** When you click the value field, and select true, the field can be viewed. If you select false the field is invisible.

- ◆ **minHeight.** Click the value field, and then enter a minimum height for the TextArea.

- ◆ **minWidth.** Click the value field, and then enter a minimum width for the TextArea.

6️⃣ Click the Control menu, and then click Test Movie.

Visitors can type as much information as needed, and when the box fills up, scroll bars appear to the right of the box; allowing them to maneuver up and down through the document.

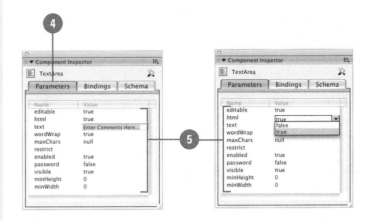

17

Adding a Button

The Button component is a clickable rectangular button, which can be resized. If you desire, you can add a custom icon to the Button component. In addition, you can change the behavior of a Button component from push to **toggle**. A toggle button stays pressed when clicked and returns to its up state when clicked again. All of these options are accomplished through the Component Inspector panel.

Add a Button Component

1. Open the Components panel.

2. Click the UI Components Expand triangle.

3. Drag the Button component onto the Stage, and then select the component.

4. Open the Component Inspector panel, and then select the Parameters tab.

5. Select from the following Button parameters:

   ◆ **icon.** Click the value field, and then enter the full path name to an icon file.

   ◆ **label.** Click the value field, and then enter a label for the Button component.

   ◆ **labelPlacement.** Click the value field, and then select between right, left, top, or bottom for the placement of the Button component text.

   ◆ **selected.** When you click the value field, and select true, the button appears selected. If you select false, the button is normal or deselected.

Button component

◆ **toggle.** When you click the value field, and select true, the button, when selected returns a true value. If you select false the button returns false when selected.

◆ **enabled.** When you click the value field, and select true, the button can be clicked. If you select false, the button is grayed out and cannot be clicked.

◆ **visible.** When you click the value field, and select true, the Button can be viewed. If you select false, the Button is invisible.

◆ **minHeight.** Click the value field, and then enter a minimum height for the Button.

◆ **minWidth.** Click the value field, and then enter a minimum width for the Button.

6 Click the Control menu, and then click Test Movie.

When you click the button, it changes color; just like a typical rollover button. You could now attach an ActionScript to the button to load another scene or movie.

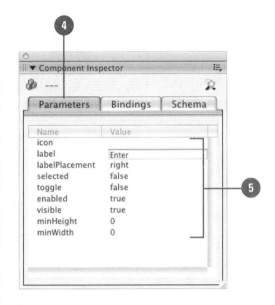

Adding a Menu Bar

The Menu component lets a visitor select items from a popup menu. The Menu component opens in an application when a user rolls over or clicks a button-like menu activator. Flash conserves valuable space by creating Menu components dynamically at runtime. Menu components have an obvious advantage over static menus: They only display information when requested, and they give a sense of order to a site that requires the visitor to select from many choices.

Add a MenuBar Component

1 Open the Components panel.

2 Click the UI Components Expand triangle.

3 Drag the MenuBar component onto the Stage, and then select the component.

4 Open the Component Inspector panel, and then select the Parameters tab.

IMPORTANT *Menus represent the navigation, or steering wheel of your Flash document. Visitors require a powerful, yet easy-to-understand way to navigate. Not only should your menu systems be easy, it should be designed to allow visitors to get to any page, scene or document within three clicks. It's called the 3-click rule (of course), and it keeps visitors from getting frustrated trying to navigate through your site. Remember, build it, and they will come... make it easy to navigate, and they will stay.*

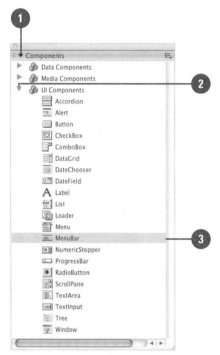

MenuBar component

5 Select from the following MenuBar parameters:

◆ **labels.** Click the Zoom button to the right of the value field, and then enter the labels used in the Menu Bar. Click the plus (+) sign to add a label, and the minus sign (-) to remove a label. Click the up and down arrow keys to reorder the values.

◆ **enabled.** When you click the value field, and select true, the menu can be used. If you select false, the menu is grayed out and cannot be used.

◆ **visible.** When you click the value field, and select true, the menu can be viewed. If you select false the menu is invisible.

◆ **minHeight.** Click the value field, and then enter a minimum height for the menu.

◆ **minWidth.** Click the value field, and then enter a minimum width for the menu.

6 Click the Control menu, and then click Test Movie.

When you roll over the menu, the buttons change color. You can now attach an ActionScript to the button to load another scene or movie.

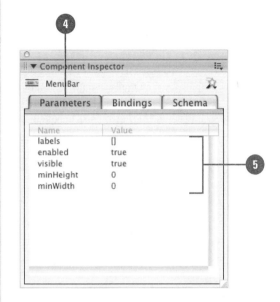

17

Adding an Alert

The Alert component lets you create a popup a window that presents the user with a message and response buttons. An Alert window can have any combination of Yes, No, OK, and Cancel buttons. Alert components are used when it's important to get a piece of information to the user. For example, a data validation routine indicates that the user is not entering in their zip code; you can create an Alert component that informs them of their error, and makes them go back and type in their zip code.

Add an Alert Component

① Open the Components panel.

② Click the UI Components Expand triangle.

③ Drag the Alert component onto the Stage, and then select the component.

④ Press the Backspace key to delete the Alert window from the Stage. This removes the Alert component from the Stage, but keeps the component as a complied clip in the Library.

⑤ Select the first keyframe in the Flash document.

> **See Also**
>
> *See Chapter 15 "Using Basic ActionScripts" on page 333 for more information on writing ActionScripts.*

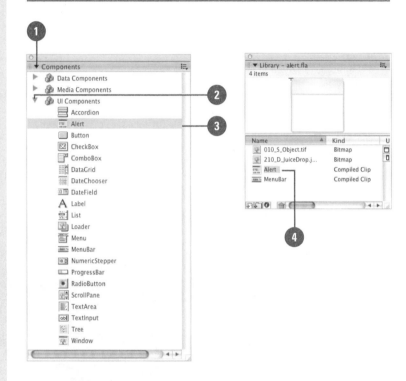

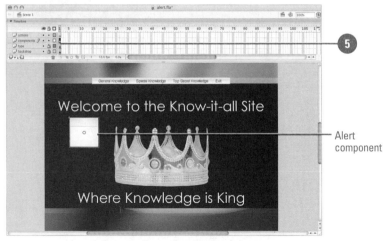

Alert component

Open the Actions panel, and then enter the script as shown in the illustration.

This code creates an Alert window with OK and Cancel buttons. When either button is pressed, the myClickHandler function is called. But when the OK button is pressed, the startKnowledgeApplication() method is called. In this test, a trace box opens and displays the message Launch Knowledge Application.

Click the Control menu, and then click Test Movie.

IMPORTANT *Since Alert components are only visible when called, it is standard procedure to first drag the Alert component to the Stage, and then delete it. It is the Alert component in the Library that is called, not the one on the Stage.*

17

Adding a List

The List component is a scrollable box that lets users select one or more items in the list. Lists are similar to the ComboBox component except List components can be formatted to display all of the available items at once; where the List component uses a drop-down (or up) feature to only display the items when requested (clicking the triangle button to the right of the list).

Add a List Component

① Open the Components panel.

② Click the UI Components Expand triangle.

③ Drag the List component onto the Stage, and then select the component.

④ Open the Component Inspector panel, and then select the Parameters tab.

IMPORTANT *The List component reduces the clutter of a typical data screen by allowing you to control the height of a data box. For example, if you wanted a visitor to select their home State, from a list, you wouldn't want all 50 States permanently displayed on the screen. You would create a more manageable size box, and make the visitor scroll up or down to select the correct State.*

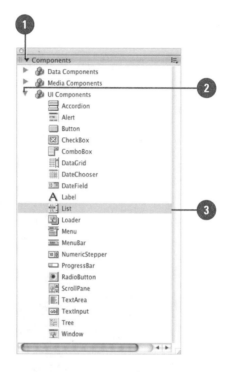

List component

5 Select from the following List parameters:

◆ **data.** Click the value field, and then enter an array in the Values dialog box. Click the plus (+) sign to add values, and the minus sign (-) to remove a value. Data values are used to populate the list labels.

◆ **labels.** Click the value field, and then enter an array in the Values dialog box. Click the plus (+) sign to add values, and the minus sign (-) to remove a value. Data values are used as the selectable items in the list.

◆ **multipleSelection.** When you click the value field, and select true, the visitor can select more than one item in the list. If you select false, the visitor can only select a single item.

◆ **rowHeight.** Click the value field, and then enter a number to determine the spacing between items in the list. The higher the value, the more space between items.

6 Click the Control menu, and then click Test Movie.

Click on a Chapter, and then select that chapter. You can now attach an ActionScript to the list to load the correct chapter.

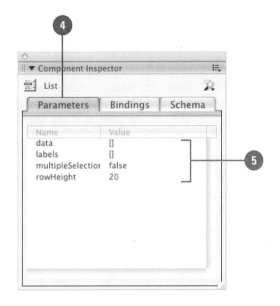

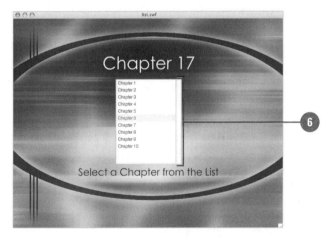

Adding a Label

A Label component consists of a single line of text. You can specify that a label be formatted with HTML. You can also control alignment and sizing of a label. Label components do not have borders, nor do they contain input that can be changed by the user. They are simply text information. Labels can be used to identify data input fields, or they can contain visitor information important to the understanding of a form. In addition, Labels can change what they display, as the Flash movie plays.

Add a Label Component

① Open the Components panel.

② Click the UI Components Expand triangle.

③ Drag one or more Label components onto the Stage, and then select the component, one at a time.

④ Open the Component Inspector panel, and then select the Parameters tab.

Did You Know?

You can use the Label component to display short help messages, when needed. Locate a blank label component on the Stage, and then create an ActionScript to instruct the Label component to display information when a problem occurs. For example, you could have the Label component display a message such as: Please Enter Your Name, if the visitor does not fill out the required Name field on an order form.

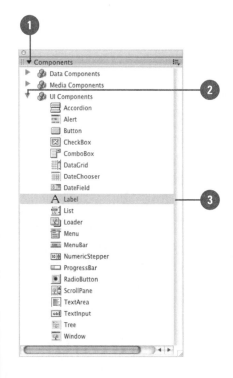

Label component

5 Select from the following Label parameters:

- ◆ **autoSize.** Click the value field, and then select between left, center, right, or none. The autoSize parameter uses this information when automatically resizing the text.

- ◆ **html.** When you click the value field, select true, to allow HTML to control the formatting of the text. If you select false, the field cannot be modified using HTML.

- ◆ **text.** Click the value field, and then enter the text that will appear in the field when the Flash document opens.

- ◆ **visible.** When you click the value field, and select true, the field can be viewed. If you select false, the field is invisible.

- ◆ **minHeight.** Click the value field, and then enter a minimum height for the Label.

- ◆ **minWidth.** Click the value field, and then enter a minimum width for the Label.

6 Click the Control menu, and then click Test Movie.

The Label components represent visitor information. For example, labeling fields that require visitor input.

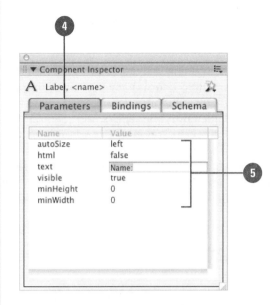

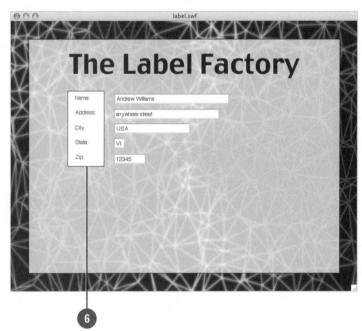

Using Components to Build a Form

When you create a form, you're incorporating all the various Flash components onto the Stage. Flash components make creating a form easy; however, there are still design considerations to be made. For example, what information do you need to extract from your visitors, and how will you receive it? Does your audience primarily speak and read English, or do you need to make the form multi-lingual (that's possible by creating label components that display text in a language selected by the visitor). And what about handicap, and accessibility standards, how do you handle them? Yes, Flash does make the creation of a form easy, but you are still responsible for the overall design, and that includes images, backgrounds, colors, fonts and sizes, readability, and accessibility. The following Flash document is an example of incorporating multiple components to create an interactive form.

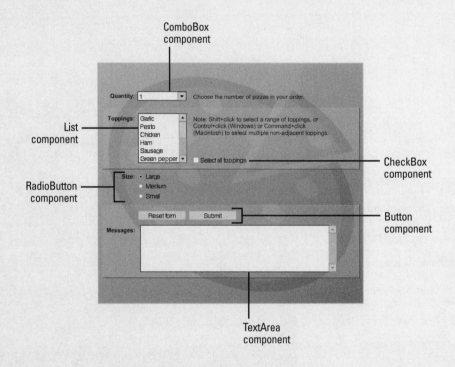

When you create a form, it is a good programming practice to isolate components onto separate layers. That way they're easier to locate and edit, and you can always lock the components layer, to prevent accidental tampering.

Adding Advanced Display Components

Introduction

Components are composed of two elements: a movie clip and parameters, allowing you to modify the components appearance and behavior. Components run the gamut from a radio button to a scroll pane. Components equalize the designer's playing field: enabling anyone to build complex applications, even if they do not have a complete understanding of the ActionScript language. And as easy as it is to simply drag the component you need from the Components panel onto the Stage, it is just as easy to customize the look and feel of components to suit your design needs.

Components let you easily and quickly build strong applications with a consistent appearance and behavior. Each component comes with predefined parameters, located in the Component Inspector panel, which let you control how the object looks and operates. Each component also includes a set of API (application programming interface), methods and properties that allows you to set parameters and additional options at runtime. This is typically accomplished by adding the scripts to Frame 1 in the Flash Timeline. It is said that Flash components finally allow for the separation of coding and design.

Components allow ActionScript writers to create functionality that designers can use in applications, and designers with little programming skill can incorporate Rich Media Content to their Flash documents with a minimum of coding experience. And if the components that shipped with Flash MX 2004 are not enough, you can always download additional components built by members of the Flash community by pointing your browser to: *http://www.macromedia.com/cfusion/exchange/index.cfm* at the friendly Macromedia Exchange.

Adding a Data Grid

The DataGrid component allows you to create strong data-enabled displays and applications. You can use the DataGrid component to create a recordset (retrieved from a database query in ColdFusion, Java, or .Net) using Macromedia Flash Remoting and display it in columns. You can also use data from a data set or from an array to fill a DataGrid component. The DataGrid component includes horizontal scrolling, event support (including event support for editable cells), sorting capabilities, and performance optimizations. The data for a grid can come from a recordset that is fed from a database query in Macromedia ColdFusion, Java, or .Net using Flash Remoting, a data set or an array. To pull the information into a DataGrid, you set the DataGrid.dataProvider property to the recordset, data set, or array.

Add a DataGrid Component

1. Open the Components panel.

2. Click the UI Components Expand triangle.

3. Drag the DataGrid component onto the Stage, and then select the component.

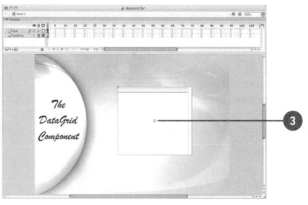

4 Enter a unique instance name for the DataGrid component in the Property Inspector.

5 Select Frame 1, open the Actions panel, and then enter the script as shown in the illustration.

The Flash Remoting recordset recordSetInstance is assigned to the dataProvider property of myDataGrid.

See Also

See "Modifying DataGrid Options" on page 412 for more information on changing DataGrid parameters.

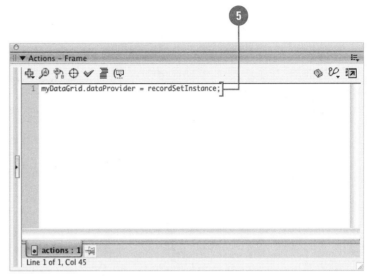

```
1 myDataGrid.dataProvider = recordSetInstance;
```

For Your Information

Dragging a DataGrid

When you drag a DataGrid onto the Stage, the component displays at a pre-defined width and height. If you want to resize the instance, just select the Transform tool from the toolbox, and then use the resize nodes to change the width and height. If you drag another DataGrid component onto the Stage, it will display using the default width and height. If you want an exact copy of the one you first placed on the stage, select the Arrow tool, hold down the Alt key (Win), Option key (Mac), and then drag the component. Flash will create an exact copy of the modified component.

18

Using a Local Data Provider

The DataGrid component lets you provide data using a local (embedded in the document) data provider. The data is read into the grid from a pre-written ActionScript, and since Flash components are on the Stage, the ActionScript would typically be entered into the first frame of the Flash Timeline.

Use a Local Data Provider

1 Open the Components panel.

2 Click the UI Components Expand triangle.

3 Drag the DataGrid component onto the Stage, and then select the component.

4 Enter a unique instance name for the DataGrid component in the Property Inspector.

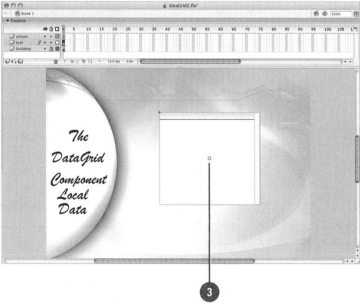

⑤ Select Frame 1, open the Actions panel, and then enter the script as shown in the illustration.

⑥ Click the Control menu, and then click Test Movie.

The name and home fields are the column headings for the DataGrid component, and the values fill the cells in each row.

IMPORTANT *It's smart programming to create a separate layer to hold the ActionScript for the DataGrid. That way you have much easier access to the script.*

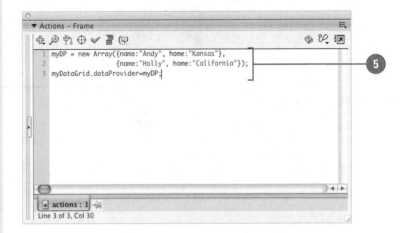

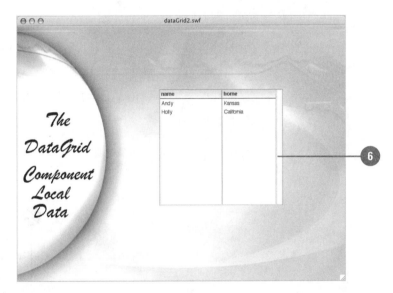

For Your Information

Data Provider

Data Provider such as: adding data within an ActionScript, makes the Flash document display the same data every time the Flash document is displayed. You can always modify the data as the movie plays, by adding additional ActionScript instructions on the Timeline, and therefore, creating a more dynamic Data Provider.

18

Adding a Loader

The Loader component is a container that can display a .swf or a .jpg. In addition, you can scale the contents of the loader, or resize the loader itself, to accommodate the size of the contents. By default, the contents are scaled to fit.

Add a Loader Component

1. Open the Components panel.

2. Click the UI Components Expand triangle.

3. Drag the Loader component onto the Stage, and then select the component.

4. Select the Free Transform tool to size the Loader to the dimensions of the image file.

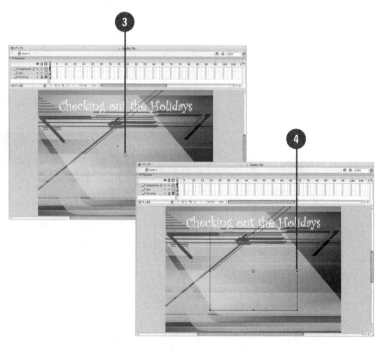

5 Open the Component Inspector panel, and then click the Parameters tab.

6 Enter the path to the .jpg or .swf file in the contentPath value field.

7 Click the Control menu, and then click Test Movie.

Flash displays the selected image in the Loader component.

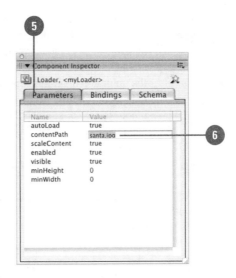

18

Adding a Numeric Stepper

The NumericStepper component allows a user to step through an ordered set of numbers. The component consists of a number displayed beside small up and down arrow buttons. You can decide the maximum and minimum values along with the step value. When the visitor clicks the up or down buttons, the value changes until the maximum or minimums are reached. The numeric stepper, its name implies it only handles numbers, text or special characters are not allowed. The NumericStepper component has many uses; for example, a site that books rooms for a major hotel chain would use a stepper for letting the visitor indicate how many people are staying, or an airline for how many people are flying.

Add a NumericStepper Component

1 Open the Components panel.

2 Click the UI Components Expand triangle.

3 Drag the NumericStepper component onto the Stage, and then select the component.

4 Open the Component Inspector panel, and then select the Parameters tab.

IMPORTANT *The NumericStepper component can be used to change the properties of items on the stage. You could link a NumericStepper instance to the property value of a dynamic text box, and then use the stepper to change the size of the text. This can be useful for people who require larger, readable text.*

⑤ Select from the following NumericStepper parameters:

◆ **maximum.** Click the value field, and then enter the maximum value associated with the NumericStepper.

◆ **minimum.** Click the value field, and then enter the minimum value associated with the NumericStepper.

◆ **stepSize.** Click the value field, and then enter a numerical value for stepping between numbers. For example, a stepSize value of 2, would cause the values to step by 2 (2, 4, 6, 8).

◆ **value.** Click the value field, and then enter the first number value that appears in the NumericStepper.

◆ **enabled.** When you click the value field, and select true, the field can be selected. If you select false, the field appears grayed out, and is not selectable.

◆ **visible.** When you click the value field, and select true, the field can be viewed. If you select false the field is invisible.

◆ **minHeight.** Click the value field, and then enter a minimum height for the NumericStepper.

◆ **minWidth.** Click the value field, and then enter a minimum width for the NumericStepper.

⑥ Click the Control menu, and then click Test Movie.

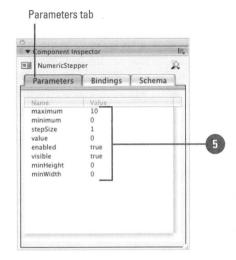

Adding a Progress Bar

The ProgressBar component is a necessity for Flash documents that require a long time to download because they display the loading progress while a user waits. Web designers live under what is called the "ten-second rule." What that implies is that visitors to your Web site have very little patience, and they want to see things happening. When you add a ProgressBar component, the visitor sees a moving representation (a bar), letting them know the information is being downloaded.

Add a ProgressBar Component

① Open the Components panel.

② Click the UI Components Expand triangle.

③ Drag the ProgressBar component onto the Stage, and then select the bar.

④ Give the ProgressBar component a unique instance name in the Property Inspector.

⑤ Open the Component Inspector panel, and then select the Parameters tab.

⑥ Click the Mode list arrow, and then click Event.

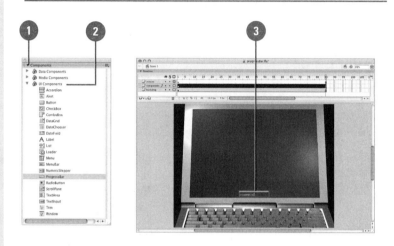

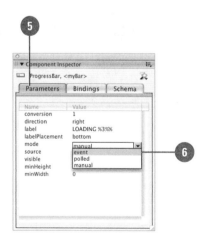

(7) Drag a Loader component from the Components panel onto the Stage.

(8) Give the Loader component a unique instance name in the Property Inspector.

(9) Select the ProgressBar component.

(10) Click the Parameters tab in the Component Inspector panel, and then enter the instance name of the Loader into the Source value field.

(11) Select Frame 1 in the Timeline of the Actions panel.

(12) Enter the script as shown in the illustration that will load a .jpg, or .swf file into the Loader component.

When executed, the ProgressBar component will display a horizontal bar, and the percentage of the file that's loaded.

(13) Click the Control menu, and then click Test Movie.

When executed, the ProgressBar component will display a moving horizontal bar, and a percentage which displays how much of the file has loaded.

IMPORTANT *Notice that you're not adding scripts to the components on the Stage. The key is that these components are activated by scripts in Frame 1 on the Timeline, and are identified by using unique instance names for each component.*

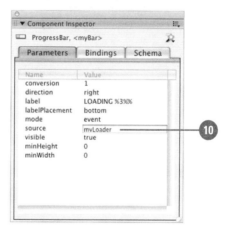

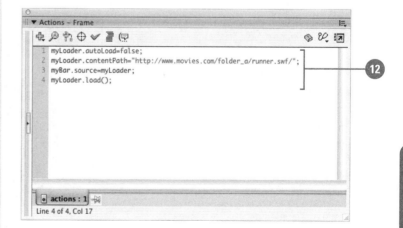

18

Adding a Scroll Pane

The ScrollPane component can be used for displaying large movie clips, .jpg files, and .swf files that need a scrollable area to display, or that you want to confine to a specific area on the Flash Stage. You have the ability to display images in a limited area, using scroll bars, and the content loaded into the ScrollPane can be from a local location, or over the Internet.

Add a ScrollPane Component

1. Open the Components panel.

2. Click the UI Components Expand triangle.

3. Drag the ScrollPane component onto the Stage, and then select the pane.

4. Open the Component Inspector panel, and then select the Parameters tab.

5. Select from the following ScrollPane parameters:

   ◆ **contentPath.** Click the value field, and then enter the full path name to the movie, clip, .jpg, or .swf file.

   ◆ **hLineScrollSize.** Click the value field, and then enter the number of pixels to move the content when the left or right arrow in the horizontal scroll bar is pressed.

   ◆ **hPageScrollSize.** Click the value field, and then enter the number of pixels to move the content when the track in the horizontal scroll bar is pressed.

   ◆ **hScrollPolicy.** Click the value field, and then select whether the horizontal scroll bar is always present (on), never present (off), or appears automatically according to the size of the image (auto).

- **scrollDrag.** Click the value field, and then select whether there is scrolling when a user presses and drags within the ScrollPane (true), or no scrolling (false).

- **vLineScrollSize.** Click the value field, and then enter the number of pixels to move the content when the up or down arrow in the vertical scroll bar is pressed.

- **vPageScrollSize.** Click the value field, and then enter the number of pixels to move the content when the track in the vertical scroll bar is pressed.

- **vScrollPolicy.** Click the value field, and then select whether the vertical scroll bar is always present (on), never present (off), or appears automatically according to the size of the image (auto).

- **enabled.** When you click the value field, and select true, the field can be selected. If you select false, the field appears grayed out, and is not selectable.

- **visible.** When you click the value field, and select true, the field can be viewed. If you select false, the field is invisible.

- **minHeight.** Click the value field, and then enter a minimum height for the ScrollPane.

- **minWidth.** Click the value field, and then enter a minimum width for the ScrollPane.

6 Click the Control menu, and then click Test Movie.

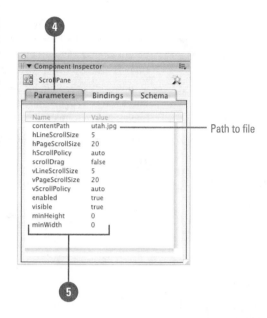

Path to file

18

Adding a Tree

The Tree component allows a user to view hierarchical data. The tree appears within a box like the List component, but each item in a tree is called a node and can be either a leaf or a branch. By default, a leaf is represented by a text label beside a file icon and a branch is represented by a text label beside a folder icon with a disclosure triangle that a user can open to expose children. The children of a branch can either be leaves or branches themselves.

Add a Tree Component

1. Open the Components panel.

2. Click the UI Components Expand triangle.

3. Drag the Tree component onto the Stage, and then select the tree.

4. Open the Component Inspector panel, and then select the Parameters tab.

5. Select from the following Tree parameters:

   ◆ **multipleSelection.** Click the value field, and then select whether the visitor can select multiple items (true), or single items (false).

   ◆ **rowHeight.** Click the value field, and then enter a numerical value for the height of each row in pixels.

6. Create a unique instance name for the Tree component in the Property Inspector.

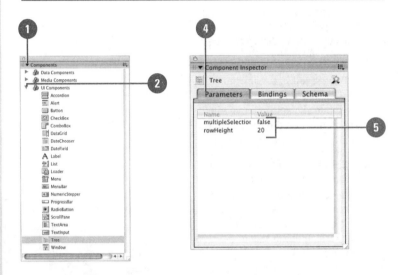

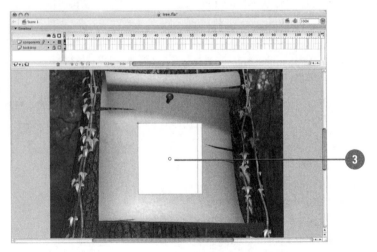

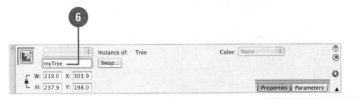

7 Open the Actions panel, and then enter the script as shown in the illustration into Frame 1 on the Timeline.

This Script creates a trace action inside the handler and sends a message to the Output panel every time an item in the tree is selected.

8 Add the remaining script to Frame 1 in the Timeline to complete the Tree component structure.

The previous code creates an XML object called myTreeDP. Any XML object on the same frame as a Tree component automatically receives all the properties and methods of the TreeDataProvider API. The second line of code creates a single root node called Local Folders.

9 Click the Control menu, and then click Test movie.

In the .swf file, you can see the XML structure displayed in the Tree. Click the triangle next to Local Folders to expand the list. Each time you click on an item in the list, the trace action in the change event handler sends the data "was selected" to the Output panel.

See Also

See Chapter 19 "Adding and Modifying Data Components" on page 413 for information on working with data components.

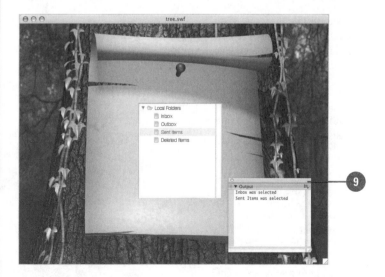

Adding a Window

The Window component lets you display the contents of a movie clip inside a window using a title bar, a border, and an Close button (optional). The Window component lets you create complex Flash documents with one or more windows controlling the viewing of multiple movie clips. Since a movie clip can contain anything from a static image to video, the Window component gives you the creative freedom to choose what design elements best suit your Flash document, and then incorporate them on the Stage. In addition, since movie clips can contain their own play, stop, and rewind buttons, you can use the Window component to load the movie clip, and then use the clip's internal controls to play the movie. Finally, use the Close button on the Window component to unload the clip when finished.

Add a Window Component

1. Open the Components panel.

2. Click the UI Components Expand triangle.

3. Drag the Window component onto the Stage, and then select the window.

4. Open the Component Inspector panel, and then select the Parameters tab.

5. Select from the following Window parameters:

   ◆ **closeButton.** Click the value field, and then select whether the Close button is available (true) or disabled (false).

   ◆ **contentPath.** Click the value field, and then enter the full path name to the movie clip you want to display.

   ◆ **title.** Click the value field, and then enter the name that will appear in the title bar.

   ◆ **enabled.** Click the value field, and select true, the Window can be accessed. If you select false, the Window appears grayed out and is not usable.

- ◆ **visible.** When you click the value field, and select true, the Window can be viewed. If you select false, the Window is invisible.

- ◆ **minHeight.** Click the value field, and then enter a minimum height for the Window.

- ◆ **minWidth.** Click the value field, and then enter a minimum width for the Window.

- ◆ **skinCloseDisable.** The value field represents the name of the formatting .fla document used for the Close button, when disabled.

- ◆ **skinCloseDown.** The value field represents the name of the formatting .fla document used for the Close button, when down.

- ◆ **skinCloseOver.** The value field represents the name of the formatting .fla document used for the Close button, when the mouse is over.

- ◆ **skinCloseUp.** The value field represents the name of the formatting .fla document used for the Close button, when Up.

- ◆ **skinTitleBackground.** The value field represents the name of the formatting .fla document used for the title background.

- ◆ **TitleStyleDeclaration.** Click the value field, and then enter the path to a style declaration that formats the title bar of a window (CSS).

6 Click the Control menu, and then click Test Movie.

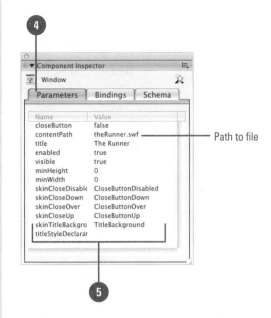

Path to file

Modifying DataGrid Options

Just like any other Flash component, the DataGrid has parameters that can be modified. However, as the previous example illustrates, using the Actions panel and entering scripts can give you further control over the modification of a Flash component. The Parameters available from the Component Inspector panel, give you a start at how you can modify a component.

Modify DataGrid Options

 Open the Component Inspector panel.

2 Select the Parameters tab.

3 Select from the following DataGrid parameters:

◆ **editable.** When you click the value field and select true, the field can be edited. If you select false, the field can be selected but not edited.

◆ **mutipleSelection.** When you click the value field, and select true, the visitor can select more than one item in the list. If you select false, the visitor can only select a single item.

◆ **rowHeight.** Click the value field, and then enter a number to determine the spacing between items in the list. The higher the value, the more space between items.

See Also

See "Adding a DataGrid" on page 396 for more information on using DataGrid components.

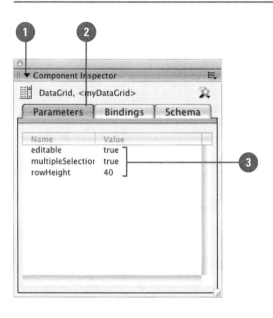

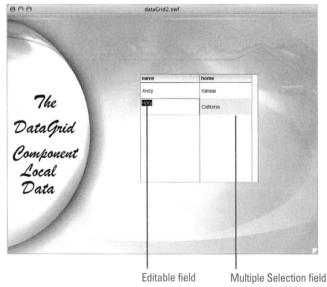

Editable field   Multiple Selection field

Adding and Modifying Data Components

Introduction

Flash MX 2004, and Flash MX Professional 2004 come packaged with various components. To provide Rich Internet Applications to developers, Macromedia provided developers with new tools, better support for video and advanced data components. The Data Connection Kit contained 3 components—Connector, Dataset, and Resolver. The Connector component was used to connect to and retrieve data from a remote data source, the Dataset component was used to manage the data in Flash, and the Resolver sent the updated data back to the original data source.

In Flash MX 2004, these components have been expanded and improved, and include support for XML, and Web Services (WSDL). In fact, any visual component in Flash MX Professional 2004 can be bound to data. **Data binding** is a concept where the property of one component can be bound to the property of another component—if the property of the one component changes, so will the property of the other component or components. Flash MX comes with several Data components such as the DataHolder, the WebServicesConnector, and the XMLConnector. In fact, you can point your browser to *www.macromedia.com*, and then go to the Flash Exchange to download even more components.

The power of a component is its ability to change. Components can be modified directly in the Component Inspector panel, or they can be modified dynamically, as the Flash movie runs. The Component Inspector panel has three areas to modify a component—Parameters, Bindings, and Schema. These three tabs allow you to attach components to data files, change or modify the text on a button, or create drop-down menus, and lists. Components are powerful tools in Flash; knowing how to modify them, gives you the control you need to create dynamic Flash sites.

Using the Data Holder

The DataHolder component holds various types of data and lets you generate events based on how the data changes. The main function of the DataHolder component is to hold data and act as a conduit between other components utilizing data binding. You can assign any type of data to a DataHolder property, either by creating a binding between the data and another property, or by using your own ActionScript code. Whenever the value of that data changes, the DataHolder component generates an event with a name equal to the property name. Any bindings associated with that property are executed. You could have a DataHolder that keeps the current system time, and have several display fields bound to that information. One of the fields is simply a display of the time in hours, minutes, and seconds, and another field might be a calculated field that displays good morning, afternoon, or evening, depending on the data sent from the DataHolder field. When you create a DataHolder it comes with one bindable property named data; you can add more properties to create a group of data information fields, which can transmit their data to other components.

Use the DataHolder Component

1. Open the Components panel.

2. Click the Data Components Expand triangle.

3. Drag the DataHolder component onto the Stage, and then select the component.

4. Give the DataHolder component a unique name in the Property Inspector.

5. Click the UI Components Expand triangle.

6. Drag a DataGrid component onto the Stage, and then select the component.

7. Give the DataGrid component a unique name in the Property Inspector.

8. Select the DataHolder component.

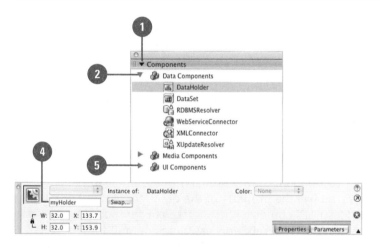

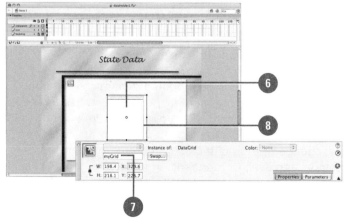

9. Open the Component Inspector panel, and then click the Schema tab.

10. Click the Add Component Property button (+) located at the top of the Schema tab.

11. Enter a unique name in the Field Name field.

12. Select Array from the Data Type popup menu.

13. Click the Bindings tab in the Component Inspector panel, and then add a binding between the property of the DataHolder component and the data provider property of the DataGrid component.

14. Click OK.

15. Select Frame 1 on the Timeline, and then enter the script as shown in the illustration.

16. Click the Control menu, and then click Test Movie.

See Also

See Chapter 19, "Adding and Modifying Data Components" on page 413 for more information on using Schema and Binding options.

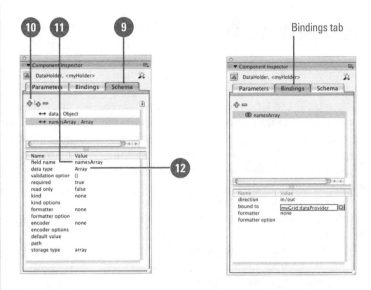

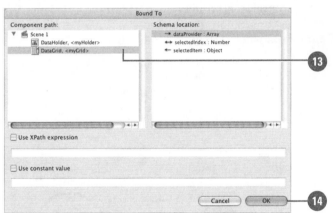

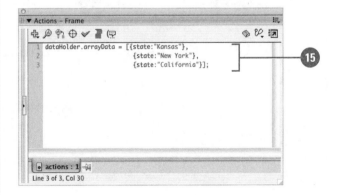

Understanding Web Services

Communications is an important part of our daily life. Think of a society where everyone spoke a different language. While most people that live in a country have a single language to communicate with, the Internet is still struggling with standardizing many of its communication features. However, as communication protocols and message formats become more and more consistent, it becomes possible to be able to describe the exchanges between two or more computer systems in a structured way. WSDL (Web Services Descriptive Language) addresses this need by defining an underlying XML grammar (a standard communication system) for describing network services as collections of communication standards capable of exchanging messages.

A Flash WSDL compliant document defines Web services to be a collection of network endpoints. This translates into a better system of transferring data between two endpoints, or ports; components therefore are more reliably bound, and can move easier between systems.

The protocol and data format specifications for a particular endpoint become a reusable binding. An endpoint, or port is defined by associating a network address with a reusable binding, and collections of ports define a Web service. Think of the endpoints as the connection between two computers: Two computers connected together by a communications cable. When one computer speaks to the other, Web Services ensures that they are speaking the same language.

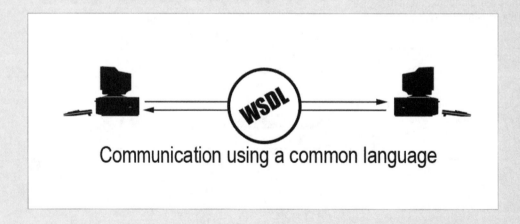

Communication using a common language

Flash WSDL compliant documents use the following elements to define a Web service:

♦ **Types.** A container for data type definitions using some type system (such as XSD).

♦ **Message.** An abstract, typed definition of the data being communicated.

♦ **Operation.** An abstract description of an action supported by the service.

♦ **Port Type.** An abstract set of operations supported by one or more endpoints.

♦ **Binding.** A concrete protocol and data format specification for a particular port type.

♦ **Port.** A single endpoint defined as a combination of a binding and a network address.

♦ **Service.** A collection of related endpoints.

While all of this may seem a bit overwhelming, it translates into an easier way to move data between two points. Eventually, transferring information on the Internet will be as easy as talking over the fence to your next-door neighbor. For more information on Web Services, point your browser to *http://www.w3c.org*, and type in "*Web Services*" into the search field.

The good news about Web Services is that Macromedia Flash MX 2004 takes care of all the hard stuff with the WebServicesConnector component which is detailed in the next section: Using the WebServiceConnector Component.

Using the Web Service Connector

The WebServiceConnector component enables you to access remote methods offered by a server using the industry-standard SOAP (Simple Object Access Protocol) protocol. This gives a Web service the ability to accept parameters and return a result back to the generating script. By using the Flash MX Professional 2004 authoring tool and the WebServiceConnector component, you can access and bind data between a remote Web service and your Flash application. To save programming time, a single instance of WebServiceConnector component can be used to make multiple calls to the same operation. All you would have to do is to use a different instance of the WebServiceConnector for each different operation you wanted to call. You can use the WebServiceConnector to connect to a Web service, and make the properties of the Web service available for binding to properties of Flash UI components within your application. Think of a Web Service as a database of information, which can be downloaded—using the WebServiceConnector—and then displayed inside a Flash movie. For example, the Virginia Department of Parks and Recreation has a Web service (large database) that contains information in the WSDL format that you can download and display within a Flash document. Since the connection to the service is live, every time the Park Service changes information such as, the opening and closing times for the park, the Web Service would send that information to your Flash document (called listening) and automatically update the page.

Use the WebServiceConnector Component

1. Click the Window menu, point to Development panels, and then click Web Services.

2. Click the Define Web Services button, and then click the Add (+) button to add the path for a Web service WSDL file.

3. Add a call to a method of the Web service by selecting the method, Control-clicking (Mac) or right-clicking (Win), and then selecting Add Method Call from the context menu.

4. Click OK.

   This will create a WebServiceConnector component instance in your application.

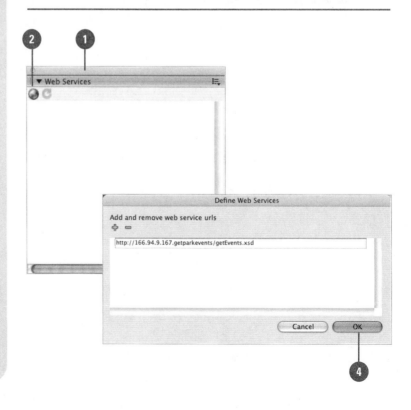

5 Click the Parameters tab in the Component Inspector panel to edit these properties as needed. For example to provide additional formatting or validation settings.

6 Use the Bindings tab in the Component Inspector panel to bind the Web service parameters and the results that are now defined in your schema to UI Components within your application, such as a DataGrid.

7 Click OK.

8 Add a trigger to initiate the data binding operation by attaching the trigger to a button.

You can add an ActionScript on the WebServiceConnector component or create a binding between a Web service parameter and a UI control. Set its Kind property to AutoTrigger.

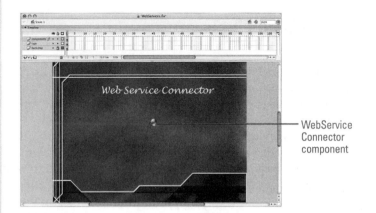

WebService Connector component

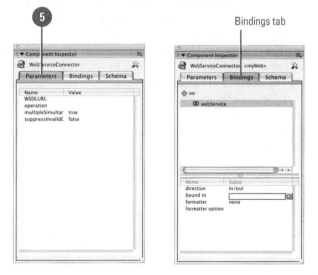

Bindings tab

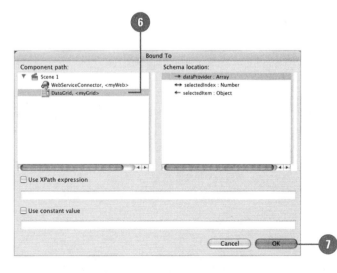

Adding and Modifying Data Components **419**

Using XML in Flash

Extensible Markup Language (XML) is a simple, but very flexible text information system. Originally designed to meet the challenges of large-scale electronic publishing, XML also plays an important role in the exchange of a wide variety of data on the Web and elsewhere; including Flash documents.

The main difference between XML and HTML, is that XML was designed to carry data. XML is not a replacement for HTML. XML and HTML were designed with different goals: XML was designed to describe data and to focus on what data is, and HTML was designed to display data and to focus on how data looks. In other words, HTML is about displaying information, while XML is about describing information. It was created to structure, store and to send information.

The following is an example of XML:

```
<memo>
<to>Holly</to>
<from>Andy</from>
</description>Reminder</description>
<body>Keep up the great work!</body>
</memo>
```

The note has a header and a message body. It also contains a sender and receiver. Understand that the XML document doesn't do anything. It's simply information wrapped in programmer-defined XML tags. To make all this work, someone must write a piece of software to send, receive or display the information, and that's where Flash's XMLConnector component comes into play. XML is simply a cross-platform, software and hardware independent tool for transmitting information.

XML is a tool for transmitting information in a way that all systems can understand. Again, it's all about communication. When computers were born (followed closely by the birth of the Internet), everyone spoke a different language, and the moving of information was a difficult venture. With the inception of XML and WSDL, all of those communication problems are quickly becoming a thing of the past, and Flash is at the forefront of implementing these new technologies.

Modifying a Component's Attributes

You can write ActionScript code to change the properties for any Flash component instance. For example, you can change the color of text of a label instance named myLabel using the following code:

myLabel.setStyle("color", "0x990000")

The preceding code would instruct Flash to change the color of the text used in the Label component instance named: myLabel, to red. Changes to the properties of a component can be attached to the instance on the Stage (influences only the one instance), or they can be used to globally change all instances, by placing the script in Frame 1 on the Timeline.

Modify Attributes

1. Open the Actions panel.

2. Select an instance or Frame 1 on the Timeline.

3. Enter the script as shown in the illustration.

4. Click the Control menu, and then click Test Movie.

The following table is a list of the available ActionScript options for changing the attributes of a component instance.

Available Flash Attributes

backgroundColor	borderColor
borderStyle	buttonColor
color	disabledColor
fontFamily	fontSize
fontStyle	fontWeight
highlightColor	marginLeft
marginRight	scrollTrackColor
shadowColor	symbolBackgroundColor
symbolBackgroundDisabledColor	symbolBackgroundPressedColor
symbolColor	symbolDisabledColor
textDecoration	textIndent

Using the XML Connector

The XMLConnector component is designed to read or write XML documents using standard HTTP protocol, get operations or post operations. It acts as the connector between other Flash components and external XML data sources. For example, you could use a DataGrid component to format and display information received from a remote site containing an XML document. Since XML (Extensible Markup Language) is a hardware independent language, it's easy to work with, and can be modified to fit a specific purpose. The XMLConnector communicates with components in a Flash application using data binding features, or ActionScript code. It has properties, methods, and events but no runtime visual appearance. In fact, all of Flash's connector components have no visual presence; they are simply the gateway for passing information from one source to another. The XMLConnector component implements a set of methods, properties, and events that define a simple way to send parameters to, and receive results from an external data source.

Use the XMLConnector Component

1. Open the Components panel.

2. Click the Data Components Expand triangle.

3. Drag the XMLConnector component onto the Stage, and then select the component.

4. Give the XMLConnector component a unique name in the Property Inspector.

5. Open the Component Inspector panel, and then click the Parameters tab.

6. Enter the full path name to the external XML file.

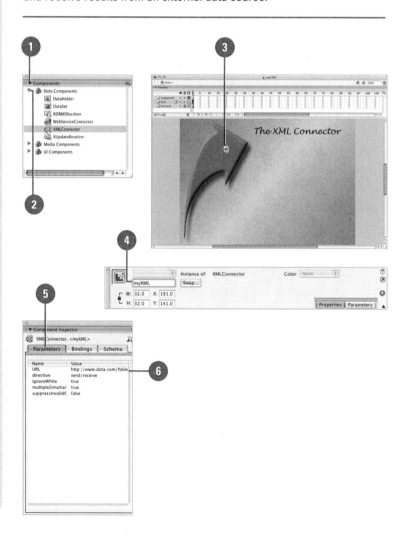

7 Click the Schema tab, and then specify a schema for the XML document.

The schema tab lets you create fields to format the XML data.

8 Click the Bindings tab to bind the data elements from the XML document to properties of the visual components in your application.

For example, you can connect to an XML document that provides weather data, and bind the Location and Temperature data elements to Label components in your application, so that the name and temperature of a specified city appears in the application at runtime.

9 Click OK.

10 Add a trigger to initiate the data binding operation by attaching the trigger behavior to a button, and then add your own ActionScript.

You can also create a binding between an XML parameter and setting a UI component's Kind property to AutoTrigger.

11 Click the Control menu, and then click Test Movie.

Bindings tab

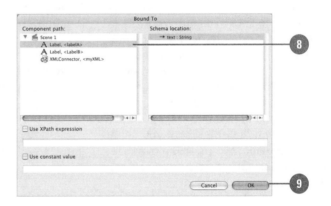

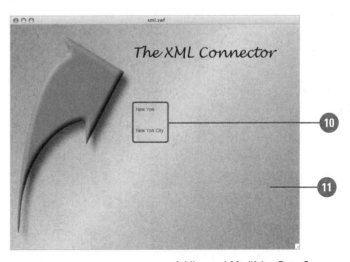

Using the Component Inspector

The Component Inspector panel represents the focus of control for most of Flash's components. After you add an instance of a component to a Flash document, you can use the Component Inspector panel to set and view information for the instance. You can drag a component from the Components panel to the Stage, and then give the component a unique instance name, using the Property Inspector.

Once a component and instance name are established, you can use the Component Inspector panel to set and modify parameters for that particular instance. Parameters represent the instance's appearance and behavior. Parameters that appear in the Component Inspector panel are known as authoring parameters. **Authoring parameters** represent common things such as the label attached to a Button component, or items displayed when using the MenuBar component. There are other parameters that can be set using ActionScript. In addition, authoring parameters can also be set with ActionScript. If you set a parameter using ActionScript, it will override any value set while authoring. Each Flash component has its own unique set of parameters.

The Component Inspector panel has two additional tabs: Bindings and Schema. The Bindings tab defines a link between two endpoints, a source (external data file, movie clip, graphic) and a destination component (DataGrid, Loader, Label). It listens for changes to the source endpoint and copies the changed data to the destination endpoint each time the source changes. The Schema tab lets you view the schema for the selected component.

Schema is basically a list of the component's binding properties, their data types, their internal structure, and other special attributes, depending on the selected component. This is the information that the Bindings tab needs in order to handle your data correctly. You can drag the DataGrid component onto the Stage, and then use the XMLConnector to pull in data from an external Web site. You can click the Schema tab, define the binding component (DataGrid), and then use the Bindings tab to link the DataGrid component to the external XML file.

Once connected, the XMLConnector would listen for changes to the external XML file, and then pass that information on to the DataGrid component. Since the DataGrid displays visible information in a Flash document, the result would be information that performs live updates to the Flash screen.

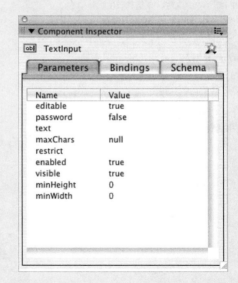

Working with Parameters

After adding an instance of a component to a Flash document, you can name the instance in the Property Inspector, and then specify the parameters for the instance using the fields on the Parameters tab in the Component Inspector panel.

Each component has parameters that you can set to change its appearance and behavior. A **parameter** is a property or method that appears in the Property Inspector and Component Inspector panel. The most commonly used properties and methods appear as authoring parameters; others can be set using ActionScript. Think of authoring parameters as the most common parameters.

Additions parameters include the ability to change an instance's font, color, and size. Additional parameters are added by selecting the instance on the Stage, and typing the script into the Actions panel. Adding parameters directly to the component instance will only impact the selected instance. If you add the script to Frame 1 in the Timeline, you can create global changes to instance parameters.

Components panel

Component Inspector panel

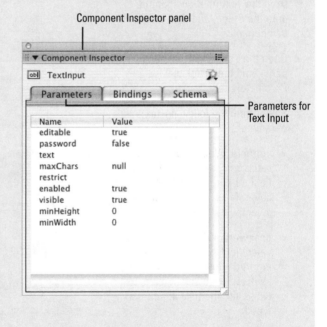

Parameters for Text Input

Modifying Parameters

To modify the parameters of a component, you must first create an instance of the component. For example, if you want to modify a TextInput field, you would first open the Components panel, and then drag a TextInput component onto the Stage. Next, you would give the component a unique instance name by selecting the component, and then entering the name in the Property Inspector. Finally, you would open the Component Inspector panel, click the Parameters tab, and then make the changes. Understand that each component will have its own unique parameters, and changing parameters in the Component Inspector panel only changes the selected instance.

Modify Parameters

1. Open the Components panel.

2. Click the UI Components Expand triangle.

3. Drag the TextInput component onto the Stage, and then select the component.

4. Open the Component Inspector panel, and then click the Parameters tab.

5. Select from the following TextInput parameters:

   ◆ **editable.** When you click the value field, and select true, the field can be edited. If you select false, the field can be selected but not edited.

   ◆ **password.** When you click the value field, and select true, text entered into the field appears as dots. If you select false, text typed into the field appears as typed.

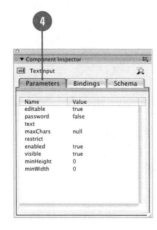

◆ **text.** Click the value field, and then enter the text that will appear in the field when the Flash document opens.

◆ **maxChars.** Click the value field, and then enter a numerical value indicating the max characters allowed in the TextInput field.

◆ **restrict.** Click the value field, and then enter any characters that cannot be entered into the TextInput field.

◆ **enabled.** When you click the value field, and select true, the field can be edited. If you select false, the field appears grayed out, and is not selectable or editable.

◆ **visible.** When you click the value field, and then select true, the field can be viewed. If you select false, the field is invisible.

◆ **minHeight.** Click the value field, and then enter a minimum height for the TextInput box.

◆ **minWidth.** Click the value field, and then enter a minimum width for the TextInput box.

6 Click the Control Menu, and then click Test Movie.

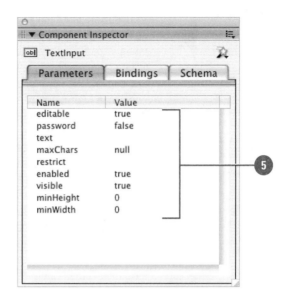

Did You Know?

You can change the properties of an instance from the Properties panel. Select an instance of a component on the Stage, and then open the Property Inspector. Click the Window menu, and then click Properties.

Creating Bindings

Data binding is a simple way of connecting Flash components to each other. Components can be viewed as containers that transfer information (images, text, numbers, video, graphics) from one to the other. In the Component Inspector panel, the Bindings tab controls the two containers, so that when property X of component Y changes, it will copy the new value to property Y of component B. You can do data binding within the Component Inspector panel using the Bindings tab. The Bindings tab lets you add, view, and remove bindings for the selected component. Although data binding works with any component, its main purpose is to connect Component panel UI components to external data sources such as Web Services and XML documents. These external data sources are available as components with properties, which you can bind to other component properties. The Component Inspector panel is the main tool that is used within Flash for data binding. It contains a Schema tab for defining the schema for a component and a Bindings tab for creating bindings between component properties. The following example demonstrates how to create basic data binding by connecting one UI component to another.

Create Bindings

1. Open the Components panel.

2. Click the UI Components Expand triangle.

3. Drag the NumericStepper component onto the Stage, and then select the component.

4. Give the NumericStepper a unique instance name in the Property Inspector.

5. Drag a second NumericStepper onto the Stage, and then give it a unique instance name.

6. Select the first NumericStepper component.

See Also

See Chapter 19 on "Adding and Modifying Data Components" on page 413 for more information on XML and Web Services.

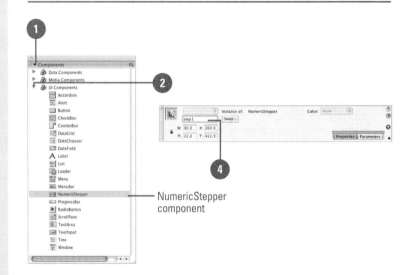

NumericStepper component

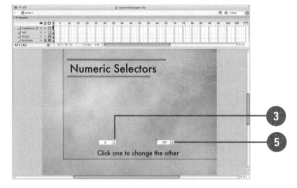

7. Open the Component Inspector panel, and then click the Bindings tab.

8. Click the Add Binding (+) button to add a binding.

9. In the Add Binding dialog box, select Value.

10. Click OK.

11. Move to the Name/Value section, located at the bottom of the Bindings tab.

12. Click the Bound To item under Name, and then click the Magnifying Glass icon.

13. In the Bound To dialog box, select component B.

14. Click OK.

15. Click the Control menu, and then click Test Movie.

When you click the up and down buttons on the first NumericStepper, the value changes automatically in the second NumericStepper.

IMPORTANT *You can use the Bindings tab to link two or more components together. If you want to add another component, just click the Add Binding (+) button to bind a second, or third component. There is no limit to the number of components that can be bound together.*

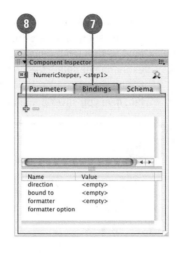

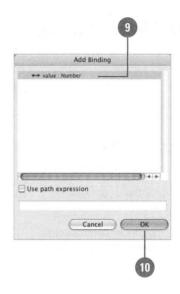

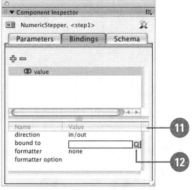

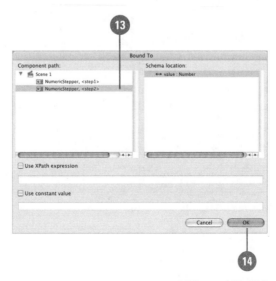

19

Modifying Bindings

Once you create a binding between two components or between a component, such as a DataGrid, and an external file, you can control the binding through the binding options. For example, you may not want the exchange of data either way, or you may wish to control what type of data is entered or received. The Binding options, located on the Bindings tab, give you several author controllable options.

Modify Bindings

① Open the Components panel.

② Click the UI Components Expand triangle.

③ Drag the NumericStepper component onto the Stage, and then select the component.

④ Give the NumericStepper a unique instance name in the Property Inspector.

⑤ Drag a TextInput component onto the Stage, and then give it a unique instance name.

⑥ Select the NumericStepper component.

⑦ Open the Component Inspector panel, and then click the Bindings tab.

⑧ Click the Add Binding (+) button to add a binding.

⑨ In the Add Binding dialog box, select Value.

⑩ Click OK.

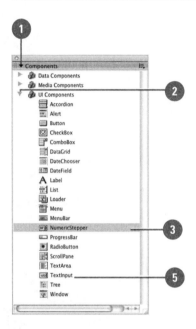

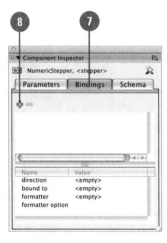

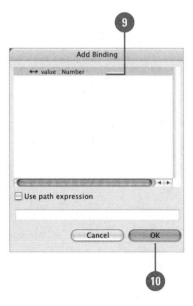

11 Move to the Name/Value section, located at the bottom of the Bindings tab.

12 Click the Bound To item under Name, and then click the Magnifying Glass icon.

13 In the Bound To dialog box, select the TextInput component.

14 Click OK.

15 Click the Control menu, and then click Test Movie.

If you click the up and down arrows on the NumericStepper, the value in the TextInput field change. If you enter a value into the TextInput field, and press Return or Tab, the value in the NumericStepper changes.

16 Close the Flash movie, and then select the NumericStepper.

17 Click the Value field at the top of the Component Inspector panel, click the Direction option, and then change the value from in/out to out.

18 Click the Control menu, and then click Test Movie.

If you click the up and down arrows on the NumericStepper, the value in the TextInput field changes. If you enter a value into the TextInput field, and press Return or Tab, the value in the NumericStepper no longer changes.

IMPORTANT *Data binding is supported only between components that exist in Frame 1 of the main Timeline, Frame 1 of a movie clip, or Frame 1 of a screen.*

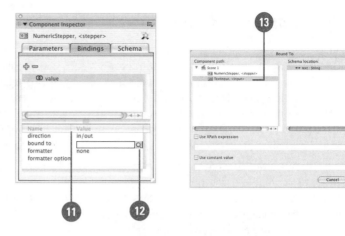

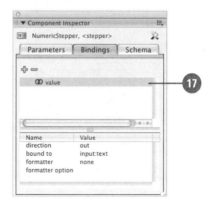

19

Understanding Schema

The Schema tab in the Component Inspector panel lets you view the schema for a selected component. The schema tab contains a list of what are known as a component's bindable properties, along with data types, internal structure, and special attributes.

The Bindings tab uses this information to handle data correctly. The top portion of the Schema tab displays bindable properties associated with the selected component. The bottom portion of the Schema tab, displays detailed information about the selected schema item (selected from the top portion of the Schema tab).

A component's schema describes the structure and type of data, independent of exactly how the data is stored. For example, the Schema tab identifies data, but not if the data is stored using XML objects, or possibly ActionScript code.

Schemas are important because they help create a communication link between other components, using the Bindings tab. For example, you can use the XMLConnector and DataGrid components to pull data from an XML document, and then display that information on the Stage. The XMLConnector provides the communication link to the external data file, and the DataGrid provides you with an easy way to organize and display the information, but not until you define the data using the Schema tab, and then bind the XMLConnector to the DataGrid using the Bindings tab.

A component's schema simply represents the properties and fields that are available for data binding. Each property or field contains settings that control validation, formatting, type conversion, and other features that affect how data binding and the data management components handle the data of a field. The bottom pane of the Schema tab presents these settings, and gives you the ability to view or edit them.

Schema tab

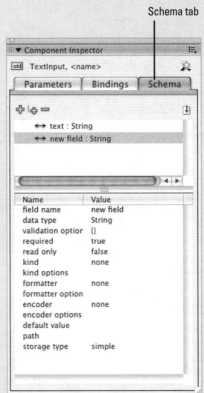

Modifying Schema

To modify the schema of a component, you must first select an instance of the component. For example, if you want to modify the schema of a DataGrid component panel, you first select the component, open the Component Inspector panel, click the Schema tab, and then make the changes. Each component has its own unique schema, and changing parameters in the Component Inspector panel only changes the selected instance.

Modify Schema

1. Select a unique instance of a component on the Stage.

2. Open the Component Inspector panel.

3. Click the Schema tab.

4. Click the Add A Component Property button (+) to add additional fields to the schema list.

5. Click the Add A Field Under The Selected Field button (+) to add an additional field that's nested with the selected field.

6. Click the Delete The Selected Field Or Property button (-) to remove the selected field or property from the schema.

7. Select an item in the upper portion of the Schema tab, and then modify its options in the lower portion of the Schema tab.

Did You Know?

The Schema tab displays data based on the selected component. Although all components have properties, by default, the Schema tab only displays properties that contain dynamic data. Dynamic data properties are called bindable properties. Flash lets you bind to any property by adding it to the schema panel yourself (using the Add Field (+) button), or using ActionScript code.

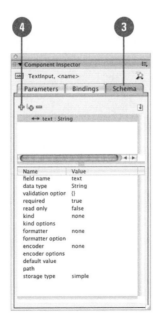

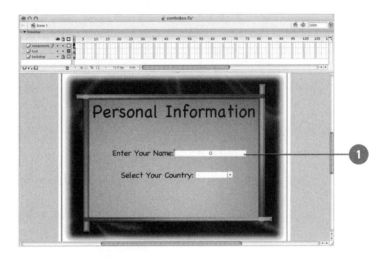

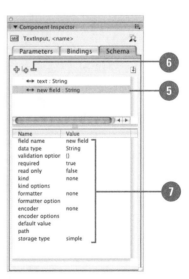

Automating Your Work

20

Introduction

The History panel helps you work more efficiently in Flash. As you work, the History panel tracks all the steps you take in Flash. With the History panel, you can undo or redo steps to correct mistakes, replay selected steps for new tasks to streamline repetitive work, and record steps for replay from the Commands menu to automate your work.

You can open the History panel from the Other Panels submenu on the Window menu. Each step you take in the active document during a work session appears on a separate line in the History panel. You can undo or redo a single step or series of steps quickly with the Undo/Redo slider, which you can drag up to undo a series of steps or drag down to redo a series of steps. You can also select a series of steps in the History panel and replay them to the same object or to a different object in the document.

Do you often repeat the same series of steps? Rather than repeat the same actions, you can work faster by saving the entire series of steps as a command on the Commands menu, which you can reuse again and again. Flash stores the commands you save for future use. After you save steps as a command, you can select the command name on the Commands menu to run it, or use the Manage Saved Command dialog box to rename or delete commands.

Due to the complex nature of some steps, such as adding a gradient to a shape or modifying document size, Flash cannot replay or save (as a command) all steps in the History panel. For these steps, a red X appears in the icon for a step in the History panel. Even though Flash cannot replay or save all steps, it can undo and redo all steps.

Examining the History Panel

The History panel helps you automate and streamline the way you work in Flash. As you work in Flash, the History panel is tracking all your steps behind the scenes. With the History panel, you can do any of the following:

- ◆ Undo or redo steps to correct mistakes.

- ◆ Replay selected steps for new tasks to streamline repetitive work.

- ◆ Record steps for replay from the Commands menu to automate your work.

The History panel doesn't replace the Undo, Redo, and Repeat commands on the Edit menu, it simply tracks every step you perform in Flash. When you undo or redo one or more commands, the History panel displays the results; the Undo/Redo slider moves according to the commands you select.

You can open the History panel using the Window menu like any of the other panels in Flash. Each step you take in the active document during a work session (since you created or opened the document) appears on a separate line in the History panel. The first step you perform in work session appears at the top of the list and the last step appears at the bottom. If a red X appears in the icon for a step, it indicates Flash cannot save or replay the step. Unlike other panels in Flash, the History panel includes a slider on the left side you can use to undo/redo steps; the Undo/Redo slider initially points to the last step you performed. The bottom of the History panel includes buttons to replay selected steps, copy selected steps to the Clipboard, and create a command from selected steps. The Options button displays commands, such as Clear History, specific to the History panel.

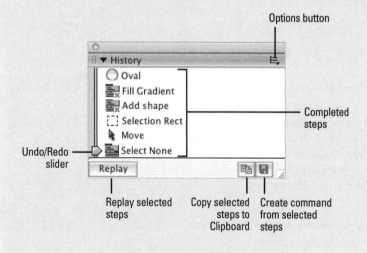

Options button

Completed steps

Undo/Redo slider

Replay selected steps

Copy selected steps to Clipboard

Create command from selected steps

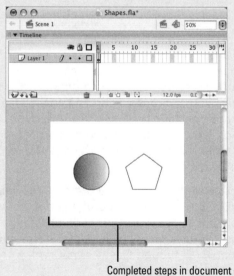

Completed steps in document

Using the History Panel

You can use the Window menu to open the History panel like any of the other panels in Flash; the History command appears on the Other Panels submenu. Each step you take in the active document during a work session appears on a separate line in the History panel. Steps you take in other Flash documents don't appear in other History panel lists. If you no longer need the steps in the History panel, you can erase the entire list. When you close a document, Flash clears the History panel.

Open and Close the History Panel

◆ To open the History pane, click the Window menu, point to Other Panels, and then click History.

TIMESAVER *Press ⌘+F10 (Mac) or Ctrl+F10 (Win) to open the History panel.*

◆ To close the panel, click the Close button, or click the Options button, and then click Close Panel.

Close button (Mac)   Close button (Win)

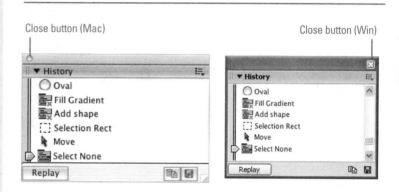

Clear the History Panel

1 Open or expand the History panel.

2 Click the Options button, and then click Clear History.

3 Click Yes to confirm the operation.

4 When you're done, click the Close button on the History panel.

Options button

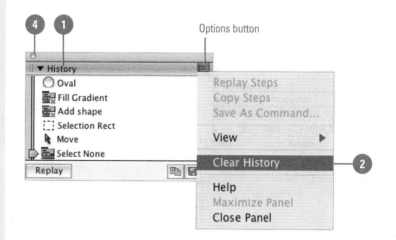

Undoing and Redoing Steps

You can undo or redo a single step or series of steps quickly with the History panel. The History panel contains the Undo/Redo slider which you can drag up to undo (restore previous steps) a series of steps, or drag down to redo (restore steps you've undone) a series of steps. You can also undo and redo previous steps one at a time using the Undo and Redo commands on the Edit menu. When you use these commands, the steps in the History panel change based on the command results. The History panel and the Undo command can undo steps up to a maximum number (from 2 to 9999) set in the General tab of the Preferences dialog box.

Undo Steps with the History Panel

① Open or expand the History panel.

② Drag the Undo/Redo slider up until the slider points to the last step you want to keep.

TIMESAVER *Position the pointer in the gray area to the left of a step, and then click the gray area to make the slider point to the step.*

Flash undos and grays out each selected step, starting from the bottom.

③ When you're done, click the Close button on the History panel.

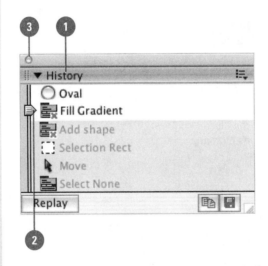

Did You Know?

You can undo steps using the Undo command. Click the Edit menu, and then click Undo, or press ⌘+Z (Mac) or Ctrl+Z (Win).

See Also

See "Examining the History Panel" on page 436 for information on different elements in the History panel.

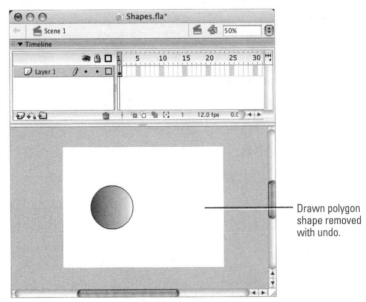

Drawn polygon shape removed with undo.

Redo Steps with the History Panel

1. Open or expand the History panel.

2. Drag the Undo/Redo slider down until the slider points to the last step you want to redo.

   Flash redoes and removes the gray highlighting for each selected step.

3. When you're done, click the Close button on the History panel.

Did You Know?

You can redo steps using the Redo command. Click the Edit menu, and then click Redo, or press ⌘+Y (Mac) or Ctrl+Y (Win).

You can change the number of undo levels for the Undo command. Click the Flash (Professional) (Mac) or Edit (Win) menu, click Preferences, click the General tab, enter a number (from 2 to 9999) in the Undo Level box, and then click OK.

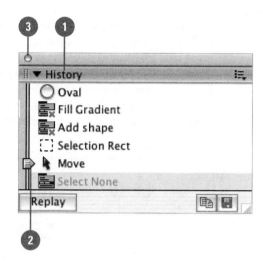

For Your Information

Saving Documents After Using Undo

When you delete an object in a document, and then undo the step using the Undo command or the History panel, the file size of the document doesn't change. The document still includes the size of the object you just deleted to preserve the possibility you might want to undo the step and restore the deleted item. If you know that you don't want the steps in the History panel, you can use the Save And Compact command on the File menu to clear the History panel, reduce the file size, and save the document. If you want to save the document and keep the steps in the History panel for the current session, use the Save command on the File menu.

Replaying Steps

You can replay steps from the History panel to the same object or to a different object in the document. You can replay steps only in the order in which you performed them; you can't rearrange the order of the steps in the History panel. If a red X appears in the icon for a step, it indicates Flash cannot save or replay the step. The Repeat command on the Edit menu also allows you to apply your previous step to another object. For example, if you fill a shape with a color or pattern, you can fill another shape with the same color or pattern by selecting the other shape and using the Repeat command.

Replay Steps to the Same Object or Another Object

1 Open or expand the History panel.

2 Select the steps you want:

- **One step.** Click a step.

- **Adjacent steps.** Drag from one step to another or click the first step, hold down the Shift key, and then click the last step.

- **Nonadjacent steps.** Hold down the ⌘ (Mac) or Ctrl (Win) key, and then click steps.

3 Select the same object used in the History steps or another object.

4 Click Replay in the History panel.

The steps are replayed in order, and a new step called Replay Steps appears in the History panel.

5 When you're done, click the Close button on the History panel.

See Also

See "Copying Steps Between Documents" on page 444 for information on replaying steps in a different document.

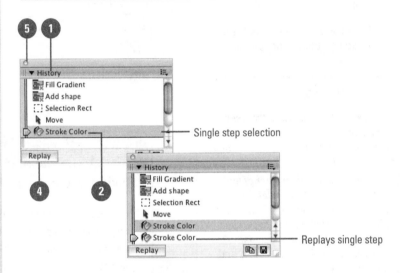

Single step selection

Replays single step

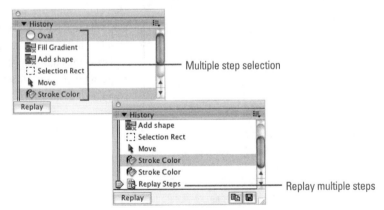

Multiple step selection

Replay multiple steps

Repeat the Previous Step on Another Object

1. Select an object, and then perform a command.

2. Select another object to which you want to perform the same previous command.

3. Click the Edit menu, and then click Repeat.

The command is performed on the selected object.

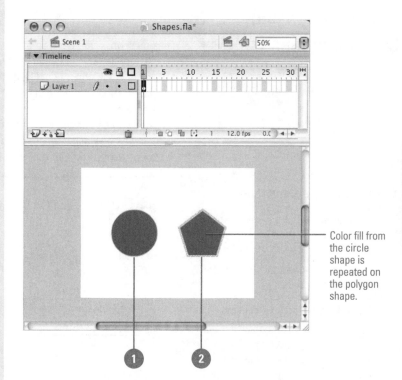

Color fill from the circle shape is repeated on the polygon shape.

For Your Information

Changing the View in the History Panel

The Options menu in the History panel allows you to change the way you view steps. You can view steps in the History panel with scripting arguments or JavaScript commands. Even if you are not a programmer, you can get a better idea about the functionality of each step by looking at the scripting argument or JavaScript commands. If you want to view scripting arguments or JavaScript commands in the History panel as you need it without having to change the view each time, you can view the information as a tooltip. To change the view, click the Options button in the History panel, point to View, and then click a view option: Default (steps only), Arguments In Panel, JavaScript In Panel, Arguments In Tooltip, or JavaScript In Tooltip.

Saving Steps and Using Commands

The History panel records the steps you take in the order in which you performed them in Flash. If you perform the same set of steps several times while you work on a document, you can save the steps in the History panel as a command on the Commands menu, which you can reuse again and again. Flash stores the commands you save for future use (even if you close the document). Some steps, including selecting a frame or modifying a document size, can't be saved as commands, but they can be undone and redone. If a red X appears in the icon for a step, it indicates Flash cannot save or replay the step. After you save steps as a command, you can run, rename, or delete commands.

Save Steps as a Command

1. Open or expand the History panel.

2. Select the steps you want to save.

3. Click the Save As Command button in the History panel.

4. Enter a name for the command.

5. Click OK.

   The command is available on the Commands menu and saved as a JavaScript file with the extension .jsfl in the Commands folder, which is located in Macromedia\ Flash MX 2004\First Run\.

6. When you're done, click the Close button on the History panel.

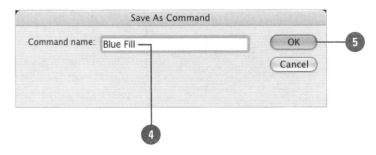

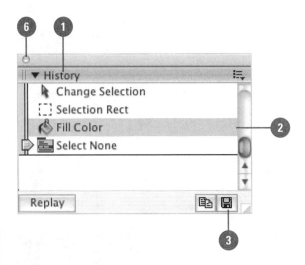

Did You Know?

You can delete a name from the Command menu. Click the Commands menu, click Manage Saved Commands, select the command you want to remove, click Delete, click Yes, and then click OK.

Run a Command

① Click the Commands menu.

② Click a command name from the list.

> ### Did You Know?
>
> **You can run JavaScript or Flash JavaScript commands.** Click the Commands menu, click Run Command, navigate to the script file, and then click Open.

Commands

Manage Saved Commands...
Get More Commands...
Run Command...

Blue Fill

Edit the Names of Commands

① Click the Commands menu, and then click Manage Saved Commands.

② Select a command to rename.

③ Click Rename.

④ Enter a new name for the command.

⑤ Click OK.

⑥ Click OK.

> ### Did You Know?
>
> **You can download commands from the Web.** The Flash Exchange Web site contains commands developed by other users you can download (some for a fee) and use in your documents. Click the Commands menu, and then click Get More Commands to quickly access the Macromedia Web site.

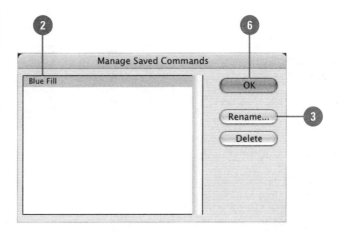

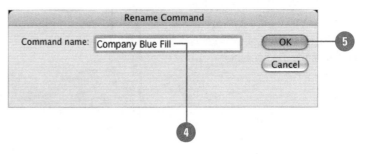

20

Copying Steps Between Documents

Each document only tracks its own set of steps in the History panel. When you close a document, Flash clears the History panel. If you want to use a set of steps in another document, you need to copy them from one History panel and paste them to another document. You can use the Copy Steps button on the History panel or the same command on the Options menu to complete the task. When you paste steps into another document, Flash replays the steps and the History panel shows the steps as only one step called Paste Steps (Mac) or Paste (Win).

Copy Steps Between Documents

1. Open a document containing the steps you want to copy.

2. Open or expand the History panel.

3. Select the steps in the History panel you want to copy.

4. Click the Copy Steps button in the History panel.

5. Open the document into which you want to paste the steps.

6. Select the objects to which you want to apply the steps.

7. Click the Edit menu, and then click Paste In Center.

   The steps play in the document as Flash pastes the steps into the History panel of the document. The steps appear in the History panel as a single step called Paste Steps (Mac) or Paste (Win).

8. When you're done, click the Close button on the History panel.

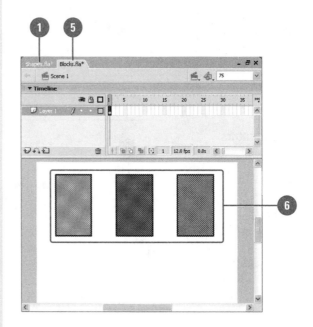

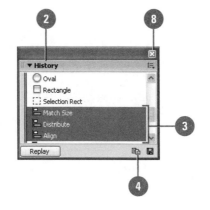

Steps pasted into the History panel of another document.

Publishing a Movie

Introduction

When you design a Flash movie you're actually working with two documents: A source document (.fla), and a publish document (.swf). The source document is the working document that the Flash application uses to edit the movie data. The published document is the compressed player document that, once created, can be inserted into an HTML document, burned onto a CD, or played directly from your hard drive.

You can publish a Flash document in one step, by clicking the File menu, and then clicking Publish. However, before publishing, it's a good idea to first check the publish settings by clicking the File menu, and then clicking Publish Settings. Using the Publish Settings dialog box, you can easily change the way your file is published. For example, the default settings for publishing a Flash document are to publish using the latest Flash plug-in, and to create an HTML container document to hold and play the published movie. Additional options include the ability to generate a JPEG, GIF, or PNG image of a selected frame in the Flash source document; even create a self-running player document for Macintosh or Windows. Publishing is not only necessary to create a Flash movie; it can be used to test the movie using different settings.

Once the correct publish settings are found, you can export the settings into a separate file, and then use them on new Flash documents. This not only makes the publishing process fast, it gives you consistency between documents.

Publishing Considerations

Publishing a Flash movie is the last step in a long journey from inception to the final product. Along the publishing road you'll encounter detours, stoplights; even get lost once in awhile. However, if you've had the foresight to plan your project, then the journey becomes one more of pleasure than pain.

Planning a project requires knowledge of where the final published document is headed. For example, you might be designing a Flash movie, where the intended audience is the World Wide Web, or it could be a project where the final destination is a CD. It could be an interactive form, or an animated cartoon. It's even possible that your goals for this project involve more than one destination.

Called Multi-purposing, Flash will help you design a project that is small enough to run efficiently, as well as a higher-quality version, intended to run directly off hard drive. It really doesn't matter where the project is headed, because Flash's advanced publishing options will effortlessly guide you through the process.

However, before you ever open Flash, before you create your first graphic, or write your first piece of text, always remember to plan the project. In other words, begin the project with the end in mind. That's not new, but it bears remembering. If you plan for the end of a project, you will create a road map that will accurately guide you to your final destination.

When you are ready to publish a Flash movie, you can use Flash publishing setting and tools in this chapter to make the job easier. You can also use the **Macromedia Flash deployment kit** to post Flash Player (.swf) files to your Web site and control the experience of visitors who do not have the Flash Player installed in their browser. Although not new to Flash the new MX version standardizes the method used for detection of the plug-in on the client-side, and reduces the amount of code that must be written to implement the detection option. If you're interested in working with the Flash Development Kit, simply point your browser to *http://www.macromedia.com/devnet/devices/development_kits.html*. Since Flash is always developing new ways for us to design great Flash documents, this site is constantly changing to reflect the latest technologies.

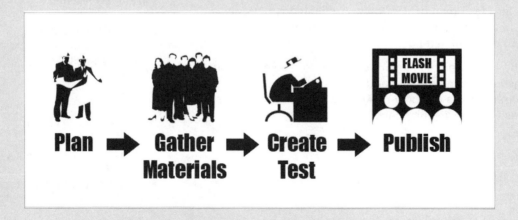

Plan ➡ Gather Materials ➡ Create Test ➡ Publish

Modifying Publish Settings

Once you've determined how your project will be published, it's time to let Flash assist you with all the details of getting your project from conception to an output file suited to your needs. Flash's publishing settings go far beyond converting a Flash source file (.fla) into a published movie (.swf); they give you the ability to adjust the output to a specific version of the Flash player, incorporate new Flash MX 2004 compression features, and even save screen shots of the source file's frames in several different formats. And, if a Flash movie is not what you're after, you can even save a Flash source file as a QuickTime movie. To utilize this feature, you may need to download the latest version of the QuickTime player; point your browser to *www.quicktime.com*. It's free and works equally well within the Windows, or the Macintosh environments.

Modify Publish Settings

1. Open a Flash source document.

   Generic publish settings are initially linked to a specific Flash file.

2. Click the File menu, and then click Publish Settings.

3. Select or clear the option check boxes to enable or disable the Publish Settings.

4. Enter a name for the individual options in the File name input box.

5. Click the Use Default Names button to revert the names to default.

   The default name refers to the name of the source document.

6. Click OK to save the changes.

   IMPORTANT *When you publish a Flash movie, the changes only effect the published .swf document, never the .fla source document. If you delete or misplace the .fla source document, you will never be able to re-edit, or republish the movie.*

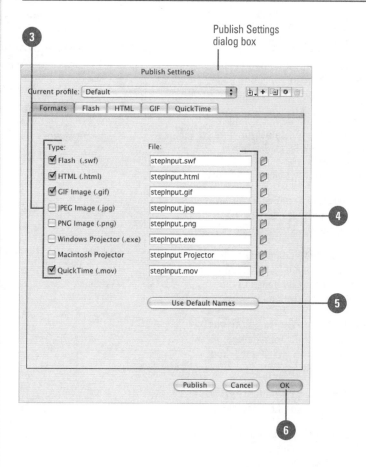

Publish Settings dialog box

Specifying Flash Options

A Flash document is like a fingerprint; no two Flash movies are the same. So it stands to reason that different Flash documents would require different publish settings. Flash gives you the ability to conform a Flash document using specific output settings. Everything from the version of the Flash plug-in, to the compression of embedded JPEG images.

Specify Flash Options

1. Click the File menu, and then click Publish Settings.

2. Select the Flash check box, and then click the Flash tab.

3. Click the Version popup, and then select the version of the player to publish the Flash document.

4. Click the Load Order popup, and then select to load the document Bottom up or Top down.

5. Click the ActionScript Version popup, and then select the version to publish the Flash document.

6. Select from the following options:

   ◆ **Generate Size Report.** Creates a frame-by-frame size report for the active document.

   ◆ **Protect From Import.** Prevents the published Flash document from being reopened in the Flash application.

   ◆ **Omit Trace Actions.** Prevents trace actions from being carried over to the published document.

   ◆ **Debugging Permitted.** Permits debugging of the Flash movie.

   ◆ **Compress Movie.** Compresses the Flash movie (available only for Flash documents played within the Flash 7 player).

   ◆ **Optimize For Flash Player 6r65.** Optimizes the Flash document for the Flash 6r65 player.

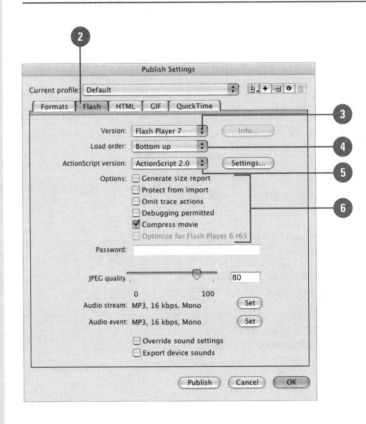

7 Enter a password for the Flash document.

This option is available if Protect From Import or Debugging Permitted are selected in step 6.

8 Drag the slider to increase or decrease the amount of compression applied to the image.

The lower the value, the more information is removed from the image.

9 Click Set to modify the Audio Stream settings for the active Flash document.

10 Click Set to modify the Audio Event settings for the active Flash document.

11 Select the Override Sound Settings check box to override any sound settings applied to the individual sound files within the active Flash document.

12 Click OK to save the settings.

See Also

See "Publishing Flash Documents Containing Audio" on page 284 for more information on choosing compression settings for Audio Streams and Audio Events.

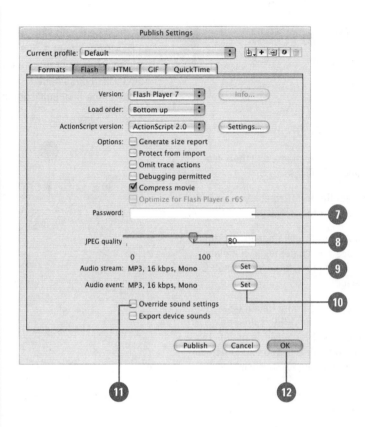

21

For Your Information

Improvements in Flash Player 7

The Flash Player 7 boasts boosts the performance of Flash movies up to 10 times. Other enhancements have been made to areas such as graphics display, video playback, XML parsing and back-end server connectivity. In addition, the player utilizes better client-end memory management. The player also includes built-in update notification so users can remain up-to-date with the latest version. The player also provides stricter security; SWF files with nonsecure protocols (HTTP) cannot access content loaded using secure protocols (HTTPS). Flash Player 7 also supports Unicode text encoding for SWF files, which allows you to use multi-language text when you create documents and others to view multi-language text in Flash Player 7, regardless of the language running on the viewer's computer operating system.

Specifying HTML Options

The most common ways to display a Flash movie is on the Internet, using an HTML document as the movie container. Flash publish settings give you the ability to create an HTML document specifically tailored to the active Flash document; including options to control the playback and quality of the final published document.

Specify HTML Options

 Click the File menu, and then click Publish Settings.

② Select the HTML check box, and then click the HTML tab.

③ Click the Template popup, and then select a Flash container template (including templates for PocketPC devices).

④ Enter a Width and Height (in pixels) for the JPEG image, or select the Match Movie option, to create a JPEG image that matches the size of the Flash movie.

⑤ Select from the following Playback options:

- ◆ **Paused At Start.** Select this option to pause the Flash movie, when loaded.

- ◆ **Loop.** Select this option to cause the Flash movie to loop, when loaded.

- ◆ **Display Menu.** Select this option to have the HTML document display a control menu for the Flash document.

- ◆ **Device Font.** Select this option to use device fonts in the Flash document.

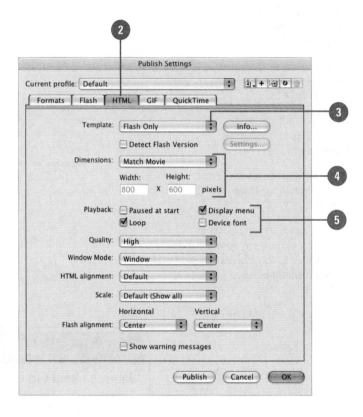

6 Click the Quality popup to select a quality level for the document.

7 Click the Window Mode popup to select a mode for opening the Flash document.

8 Click the HTML Alignment popup to select the alignment of the HTML page.

9 Click the Scale popup to select how to scale the Flash document, when loaded into the HTML page.

10 Click the Horizontal and Vertical popups to select how the Flash document is aligned with in the HTML page.

11 Click OK to save the HTML settings.

Did You Know?

The HTML tab in the Publish dialog box lets you create an HTML container document to hold the Flash movie. However, if you use Macromedia's flagship Web layout program, Dreamweaver, you can skip the HTML publish option and move the .swf document directly into Dreamweaver.

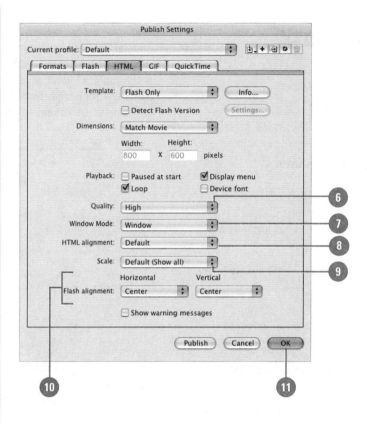

21

For Your Information

Using Version Detection

Version Detection checks what version of the Flash Player is running on your viewer's computer. If the Flash Player is missing or the version number is not high enough to display the movie, you can have Flash display a message, link to Macromedia's Web site to download the correct version, display an alternative image file, or display a different site. To detect a viewer's Flash Player version, click the File menu, click Publish Settings, click the Flash tab, click the Version popup, click Flash version 4 or higher, click the HTML tab, select the Detect Flash Version check box, click Settings, and then specify file names (.html) for Detection (detects Flash Player version), Content (displays the .swf file), and Alternate (displays a warning and link to download the Flash Player). To let Flash create its standard Detection and Alternate files, click the Generate Default option, or click Use Defaults. To use your own alternate file, click the Use Existing option, and then click Browse to select the file.

Specifying GIF Options

When you publish a Flash document, you're not limited to just the creation of the Flash movie, you can instruct Flash to create a GIF image of the Flash movie, based on the currently selected frame. The GIF file format (Graphics Interchange Format) is used primarily for clipart, text, and line art, or for images that contain areas of solid color. Once the image is created, you can open and use it in any application that supports the GIF file format.

Specify GIF Options

1. Select a specific frame on the Timeline.

2. Click the File menu, and then click Publish Settings.

3. Select the GIF check box, and then click the GIF tab.

4. Enter a Width and Height (in pixels) for the JPEG image, or select the Match Movie check box, to create a JPEG image that matches the size of the Flash movie.

5. Select from the following Playback options:

   ◆ **Static.** Prevents the GIF animation from playing.

   ◆ **Animated.** Animates the GIF document.

   ◆ **Loop Continuously.** Forces the animation into a continuous loop.

   ◆ **Repeat.** Enter a value representing the number of times the file loops.

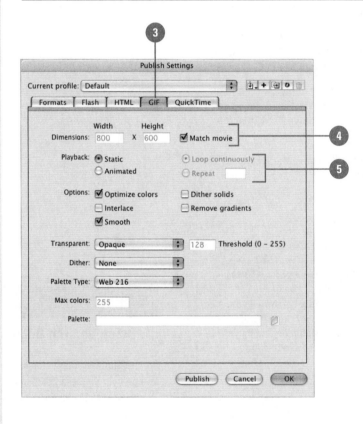

6 Select from the following Options:

◆ **Optimize Colors.** Creates an optimized (smaller) set of colors for the active document.

◆ **Interlace.** Creates an interlaced image where the file, when displayed on a Web page, loads in three passes.

◆ **Smooth.** Uses a color dithering scheme to create visually smoother color transitions.

◆ **Dither Solids.** Dithers (mixes) solid colors if they fall outside of the viewable color gamut.

◆ **Remove Gradients.** Removes gradients from the active image.

7 Click the Transparent popup, and then click Opaque, Transparent, or Alpha.

The Alpha transparency mask generates transparent areas within the GIF image.

8 Click the Dither popup, and then click None, Ordered, or Diffusion.

9 Click the Palette Type popup, and then click Web 216, Adaptive, Web Snap Adaptive, or Custom.

10 Enter a number for the Maximum Colors.

This is available for Adaptive and Web Snap Adaptive. Flash lets you select how many colors are available for the image's color table.

11 Click to select a color table for the Custom Palette Type.

12 Click OK to save the GIF settings.

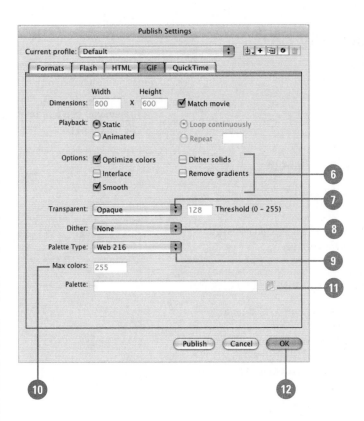

Palette Type Options

Option	Use
Web 216	Creates an image with only Web Safe colors.
Adaptive	Creates an image where the color table (CLUT) adapts to the image colors.
Web Snap Adaptive	Creates a color table that adheres closely to the Web Safe Color palette.
Custom	Creates a customized color palette.

Specifying PNG Options

When you publish a Flash document you're not limited to just the creation of the Flash movie. You can instruct Flash to create a PNG image of the Flash movie, based on the currently selected frame. The PNG file format (Portable Network Graphic), is a hybrid format designed to save both clip art, photographic images, text, and line art. Once the image is created, you can open and use it in any application that supports the PNG file format.

Specify PNG Options

1. Select a specific Frame on the Timeline.

2. Click the File menu, and then click Publish Settings.

3. Select the PNG check box, and then click the PNG tab.

4. Enter a Width and Height (in pixels) for the PNG image, or select the Match Movie check box to create a PNG image that matches the size of the Flash movie.

5. Click the Bit Depth popup, and then select 8-bit, 24-bit, or 24-bit With Alpha.

6. Select from the following Options:

   ◆ **Optimize Colors.** Creates an optimized (smaller) set of colors for the active document.

   ◆ **Interlace.** Creates an interlaced image where the file, when displayed on a Web page, loads in three passes.

   ◆ **Smooth.** Uses a color dithering scheme to create visually smoother color transitions.

   ◆ **Dither Solids.** Dithers (mixes) solid colors, if the colors fall outside of the viewable color gamut.

   ◆ **Remove Gradients.** Remove any gradients from the active image.

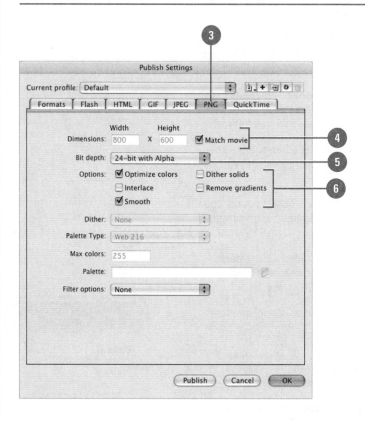

Bit Depth Choices	
Option	**Selection**
8-bit	Maximum of 256 colors
24-bit	Maximum of 16.7 million colors
24-bit with Alpha	Maximum of 16.7 colors and supports the alpha transparency

7 Click the Dither popup, and then click None, Ordered, or Diffusion to dither (mix) colors that fall outside the viewable color gamut.

8 Click the Palette Type popup, and then click Web 216, Adaptive, Web Snap Adaptive, or Custom, to select a specific palette type.

9 Enter a number for the Maximum Colors.

This is available for Adaptive and Web Snap Adaptive. Flash lets you select how many colors are available for the image's color table.

10 Click to select a color table for the Custom Palette Type.

11 Click the Filter Options popup, and then select from the available filter options to control the filtering of the colors in the active image.

12 Click OK to save the PNG settings.

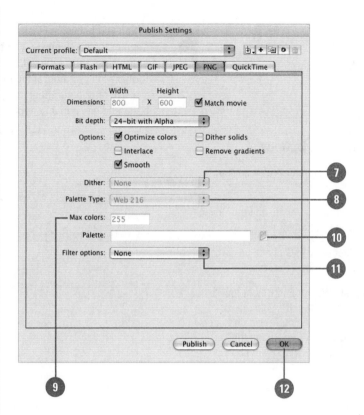

Specifying JPEG Options

When you publish a Flash document, you're not limited to just the creation of the Flash movie, you can instruct Flash to create a JPEG image of the Flash movie, based on the currently selected frame. The JPEG file format (Joint Photographic Experts Group), is used primarily to reduce the size of photographic images. Once the image is created, you can open and use it in any application that supports the JPEG file format.

Specify JPEG Options

1. Select a specific frame on the Timeline.

2. Click the File menu, and then click Publish Settings.

3. Select the JPEG check box, and then click the JPEG tab.

4. Enter a Width and Height (in pixels) for the JPEG image, or select the Match Movie check box to create a JPEG image that matches the size of the Flash movie.

5. Drag the Quality slider to increase or decrease the amount of compression applied to the image.

   The lower the value, the more information is removed from the image.

6. Select the Progressive check box to create a progressive JPEG image. The file, when displayed on a Web page, loads in three passes.

7. Click OK to save the JPEG settings.

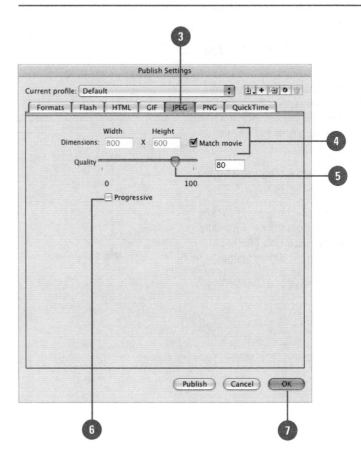

Creating a Windows or Macintosh Projector

The Flash publish settings gives you the ability to create a self-contained player document for the Macintosh or Windows operating system. When you publish a document using the projector options, Flash creates a Flash movie according to your setting, and embeds the player application into the file. Creating a projector document increases the size of the final document by almost 1MB, so this option would not be used to create Internet documents, but for movies destined for playing on a hard drive, or burned onto a CD. When you publish using the Projector options, there are no additional options.

Create a Windows or Macintosh Projector

1. Click the File menu, and then click Publish Settings.

2. Select the Windows Projector (.exe), and/or Macintosh Projector check boxes.

3. Click Publish.

   Flash generates the Macintosh or Windows Projectors documents, and saves them in the same location as the original source document.

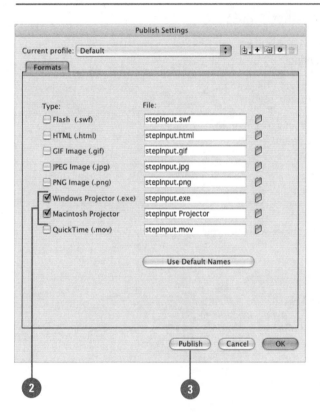

21

Creating a Publishing Profile ▶

Flash lets you generate profiles for often used publish settings within a Flash source file. For example, you're creating a multi-purpose Flash document and you need specific settings to create a fast-loading Internet version, as well as a version designed to run on a CD. You could create a publishing profile to fit both needs, and save them with the source document. The benefits of this are obvious: Not only can you quickly publish a Flash document using different profiles; you're assured the settings will be accurate every time. Fast and accurate are two words which describe Flash publishing.

Create a Publishing Profile

1. Click the File menu, and then click Publish Settings.

2. Click the Current Profile popup to select the profile.

3. Make the necessary changes in the Publish Settings dialog box.

4. Click OK.

5. Click the Create New Profile button.

6. Enter a unique name in the Profile Name box.

7. Click OK.

IMPORTANT *When you save a Flash profile, it's only available to that specific document.*

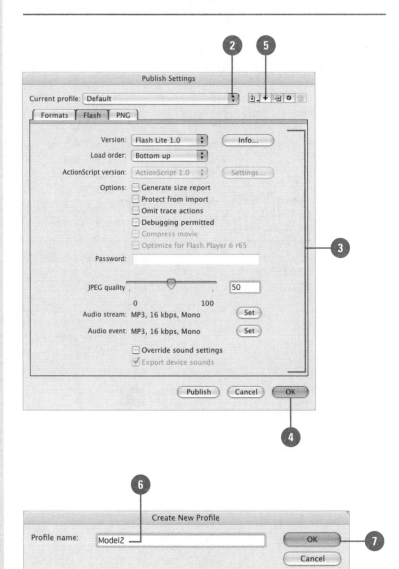

Editing Profile Properties

Once you create a unique profile settings file, it's available for use with the click of the Current Profile popup in the Publish Settings dialog box. Unfortunately, not everything is perfect the first time you do it, and it's possible that after you create a profile, you discover a mistake in the settings. The good news is that you don't have to begin again. All you have to do is edit the profile.

Edit Profile Properties

1. Click the File menu, and then click Publish Settings.

2. Click the Current Profile popup, and then select the profile you want to change.

3. Make the necessary changes in the Publish Settings dialog box.

4. Click OK.

5. Select the File menu, and then click Save.

    Flash profiles are saved when you save the Flash source document.

    IMPORTANT *Profile properties are recorded as you change them, and then saved when you save the file. If you change your mind after modifying the profile, your choices include manually changing the profile back to its original settings, or closing the file without saving. However, if you've also made changes to the Flash document, closing without saving will also cause you to lose those changes.*

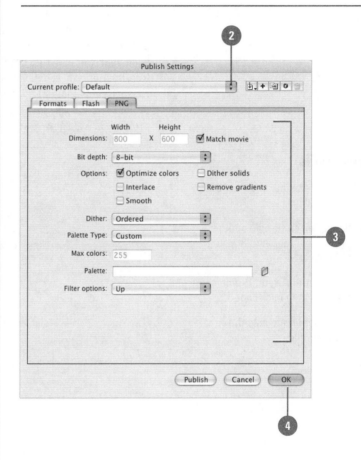

21

Exporting and Importing a Profile

Saving Flash profiles are a great way to cut down on repetitive publish settings. However, the disadvantage is the user-defined settings only relate to the original source document. If you open a new file, you're starting from scratch. It would be great to be able to create a series of setting files, and then use them over and over again on new Flash document. Flash understood this need, and gave Flash users the ability to create settings files, and then export them as a separate file. Then, if you need to use the settings in a new Flash document, all you have to do is import the settings file. Exporting Dreamweaver profiles gives you the ability to use the profile on multiple Flash projects. In addition, you can send copies of exported profiles to other Flash users, so they can benefit from your efforts. When you export a Flash profile, you have the ability to reuse it, via the Import option. It's a good idea to save (export) all of your profiles into a single location. That way, when you go to import a specific profile, you will know exactly where to point your finder.

Export a Profile

1. Click the File menu, and then click Publish Settings.

2. Click the Current Profile popup, and then select the profile you want to export.

3. Click the Import/Export Profile button, and then click Export.

4. Select a location to hold the exported profile.

5. Click Save.

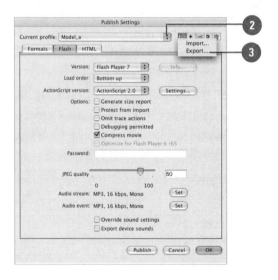

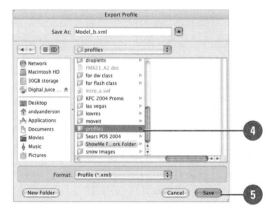

Import a Profile

1. Click the File menu, and then click Publish Settings.

2. Click the Current Profile popup, and then select the profile you want to import.

3. Click the Import/Export Profile button, and then click Import.

4. Select the location of the profile.

5. Select the file name of the exported profile.

6. Click Open.

IMPORTANT *Once a profile is imported into a Flash document, it becomes a copy of the original item. You can use it in the active document, or make some minor adjustments, and export it out as a new profile.*

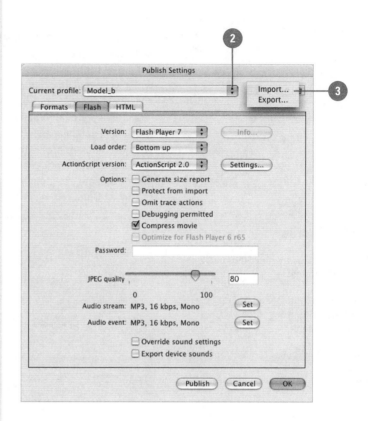

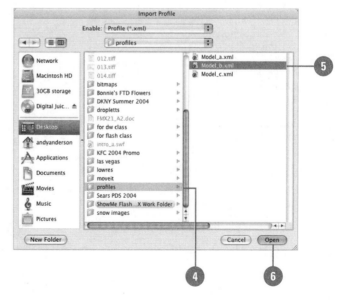

Duplicating a Profile

When you work with profiles, you're creating a timesaving file that lets you use the same settings over and over again. Not only does Flash make the creation of a profile easy; it will let you create a duplicate of the file. In truth, a duplicate file would not serve much of a purpose: Why would you want an exact copy of something that already exists? Actually, creating a duplicate can be a very smart thing to do. For example, say you create a profile for a specific job that involved several changes to the default settings, and you name it: Output_A. Then, two weeks later you need another profile that's almost exactly the same as Output_A, with one or two minor changes. Rather than start from scratch, you create a duplicate of Output_A, make the minor changes, and Export it using the name: Output_B. It's fast, easy, and means you're working smart.

Duplicate a Profile

1. Click the File menu, and then click Publish Settings.

2. Click the Current Profile popup, and then select the profile you want to duplicate.

3. Click the Duplicate Profile button.

4. Give the duplicate a new name.

5. Click OK.

See Also

See "Exporting and Importing a Profile" on page 460 for more information on how to export a Flash publishing profile.

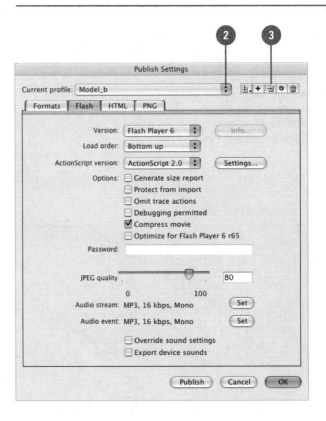

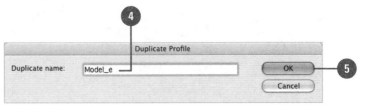

Testing a Movie

Testing a Flash movie is an important part of the design process. For example, as you work, you should periodically stop, and test the movie. It's also a good idea to periodically save your document. In fact, you should always save the Flash document before testing. That way, if there happen to be any problems, it's an easy matter of restoring the file, from the last-saved version. To preview your Flash SWF file with the publishing format and settings you've selected, you can use the Publish Preview command. This command exports the file and opens the preview within the default browser.

Test a Movie

1. Click the File menu, point to Publish Preview, and then select from the following options:

   ◆ **Default (HTML) F12**. Select this option to display the Flash document within an HTML document.

   ◆ **Flash**. Select this option to create and play a Flash .swf file.

   ◆ **GIF**. Select this option to create a GIF version of the currently selected frame in the Timeline.

   ◆ **JPEG**. Select this option to create a JPEG version of the currently selected frame in the Timeline.

   ◆ **PNG**. Select this option to create a PNG version of the currently selected frame in the Timeline.

   ◆ **Projector**. Select this option to display the Flash document in a self-contained projector file.

   ◆ **QuickTime**. Select this option to open QuickTime, and play the Flash movie as a QuickTime file.

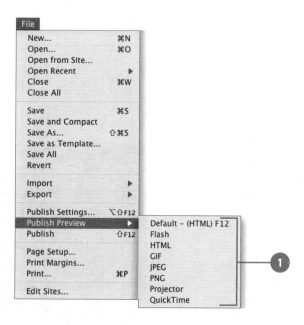

Using the Bandwidth Profiler

To view the performance of a Flash document using a graph, use the Bandwidth Profiler. The Bandwidth Profiler displays how much data is sent for each frame in the active Flash document, according to the modem speed you specify. The Bandwidth Profiler has two windows. The left window shows information about the active document, and the current download settings, and the right window displays information about each frame in the document. In addition, the Bandwidth Profiler lets you view how the page loads, based on a specific bandwidth. For example, you could specify to load the Flash document using a modem speed of 28.8Kbps. To maintain an accurate download test, the Bandwidth Profiler compensates for added compression support applied to .swf files, which reduces the file size and improves streaming performance.

Use the Bandwidth Profiler

1. Click the Control menu, and then click Test Movie.

2. Click the View menu, and then click Bandwidth Profiler.

3. Click the View menu, point to Download Settings, and then select from the available bandwidth options, or click Customize, and then create a user-defined setting.

4. Click the View menu, and then click Simulate Download.

   This tests the load of the Flash movie against the current settings.

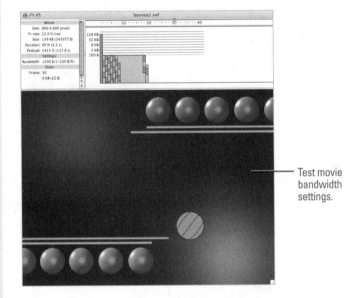

Test movie bandwidth settings.

For Your Information

Timing Rule

A timing rule used in Web design is called the 10-second rule. If documents load too slowly, there's a good chance that your visitors will not wait for the document to load, and will move on to other pages. The Bandwidth profiler gives you a real taste of what your visitors are going to experience when they download your Flash movies.

Printing from the Flash Player

In your browser, you can press Control+click (Mac) or right-click (Win) a Flash movie in a Flash Player to display a contextual, or shortcut, menu. The menu contains Flash Player related commands, such as Print. You can give viewers the option to print some, or all of your movie. Be default, the Print command prints every frame in the movie unless you restrict printing to specific frames by labeling them as printable in the Flash document before you publish it. You label frames as printable by typing #p in the Label box of the Frame Property Inspector.

Label Frames as Printable and Print from the Flash Player

1. Open a document.

2. Select the frames or keyframes in the Timeline you want to label as printable.

3. Type **#p** in the Label box in the Property Inspector.

4. Repeat steps 2 and 3 for each keyframe you want to label as printable.

5. Publish your movie using the Publish command on the File menu, and then view it in your browser using the Flash Player.

6. Press Control+click (Mac) or right-click (Win) anywhere in the movie window, and then click Print.

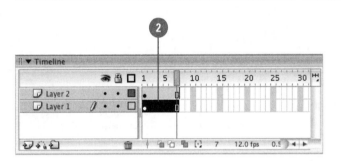

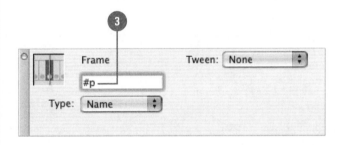

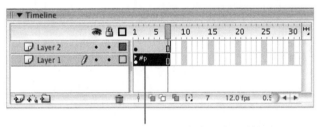

#p appears in the selected frames.

Did You Know?

You can disable printing from the Flash Player. Open the Flash document, select a frame in the Timeline, open the Frame Property Inspector, and then type **!#p** in the Label box.

You can disable the contextual menu in the Flash Player. Click the File menu, click Publish Setting, click the HTML tab, clear the Display Menu check box, and then click OK.

21

Exporting a Movie to Different Formats

Flash can export an entire movie or frame to several different formats that are not included in the Publish Settings dialog box. These formats include Adobe Illustrator, EPS, and DXF; PICT and Quick Time (for Mac only), Enhanced Metafile (EMF), Windows Metafile (WMF), Windows AVI, and WAV (for Windows only). When you export a movie or frame, some file formats require you to select additional format specific options to complete the operation.

Export a Movie or Frame to Different Formats

① Open a document.

② Select a frame you want to export in the Timeline.

③ Click the File menu, point to Export, and then click Export Image to print a frame, or Export Movie.

TIMESAVER *Press Option+ Shift+⊙⌘+S (Mac) or Ctrl+Alt+ Shift+S (Win) to export a movie.*

④ Navigate to the location where you want to save the file.

⑤ Enter a name in the Save As (Mac) or File Name (Win) box.

⑥ Click the Format popup (Mac) or the Save As Type list arrow (Win), and then select a file format.

⑦ Click Save.

Some file formats require you to select additional format specific options to complete the operation.

⑧ If a dialog box appears, select the options you want, and then click OK.

When you export a movie, Flash creates a separate file for each frame of the movie and numbers them in sequential order.

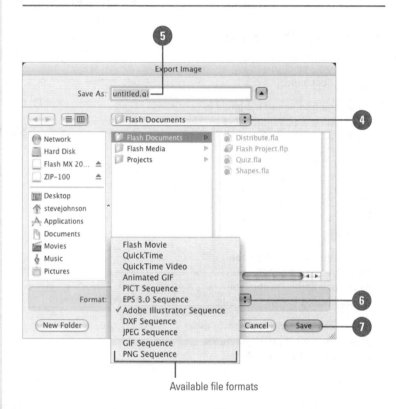

Available file formats

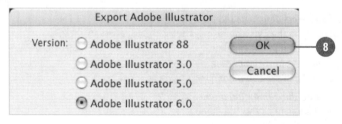

Using Flash MX Professional 2004 Features

22

Introduction

In the area of the Web, where new programs are released every month, few received such acclaim as the release of the MX version of Flash. Macromedia topped that with the recent release of Flash MX 2004, and Flash MX Professional 2004. Flash MX Professional 2004 was created with the advanced Web designer in mind. The Professional version of Flash includes all the features of Flash MX 2004, including several powerful new tools. It provides project management tools that allow for the optimization of the workflow between the members of a Web team. In addition, a Screen-based visual development environment makes designing Flash applications simpler. Add to that, the ability to export Flash movies directly into the FLV (Flash Video File) format, advanced video features, enhanced application binding components, and improved sound management, and you have a program suited for the most demanding of Flash designers.

Flash MX Professional 2004 lets you create two different types of screens within the active document: slide screens and form screens. A slide presentation, uses the slide screen, and a Flash form application uses the form screen as the default screen type. If you're creating a Flash document with a combination of slides and form screens, you have the ability to mix both screen types within a single Flash document. When you work with screens, you're creating complex applications without the use of multiple frames and layers on the main Timeline. As a matter of fact, screen applications can be created without ever viewing the main Timeline. When you create a slide or form screen document, Flash opens the document with the main Timeline collapsed, and the addition of slides of form components is accomplished using a control dialog box, located to the left of the document window.

What You'll Do

Create a Slide Presentation

Create a Form Screen

Create and Manage a Project

Test a Project

Use Version Source Control

Check Files In and Out

Export Directly to the FLV Format

Map MIDI Device Sounds

Use Advanced Component Enhancements

Creating a Slide Presentation

The Slide Screen feature allows you to create a Flash document using sequential content, for example, a slide show. The default behavior of a screen lets the visitor navigate between screens using the arrow keys. This is accomplished by automatically attaching a key object to the visitor's keyboard. To increase functionality, sequential screens can actually overlay each another so that the previous screen remains visible when the next slide is viewed.

Create a Slide Presentation

1. Click the File menu, and then click New.

2. Click the General tab.

3. Click Flash Slide Presentation.

4. Click OK.

5. Create, or select a backdrop for the slide show, and then place it on the presentation main page (optional).

6. Select Slide 1.

7. Drag an image from the Library onto the Slide 1 Stage, or click the File menu, and then click Import to select an image from an external source.

Did You Know?

Graphics aren't the only items that can be placed on a slide. You can display video clips, Flash movie clips, even audio on a slide. It's totally up to you. The animation, video, or audio files will begin to play when the visitor clicks to access the slide.

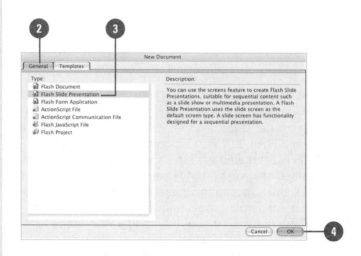

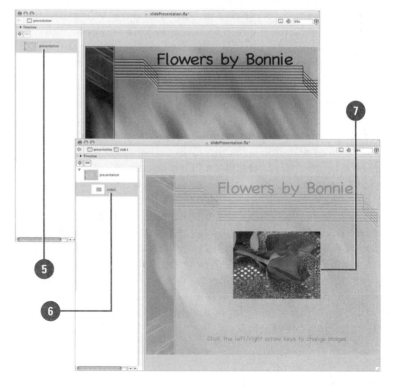

8 Click the Insert Screen button (+).

9 Select Slide 2, and then add another image.

10 Click the Insert Screen button (+), and then repeat step 5 to add as many slides as required.

11 Select a slide, and then click the Delete Screen button (-) to remove the slide from the set.

12 Click and drag a slide up or down to reorder the slide with the stack.

13 Click the Control menu, and then click Test movie.

14 Use the left and right arrow keys to maneuver between slides.

> **IMPORTANT** *If you right-click on a slide, you can choose to insert a nested screen. Nested screens are always visible, but appeared grayed out when viewed.*

22

Creating a Form Screen

Flash MX Professional 2004 lets you create form screens for documents, such as: online registration forms or even e-commerce forms. Form screens are actually containers that you add structure and organization to a form-based application. A form screen has functionality designed for a nonlinear, form-based application, with multiple options available in one visual space. Use form screens when you want to manage the visibility of individual screens yourself. For example, you could use forms to create an interactive search engine, or an interactive data collection form.

Create a Form Screen

1. Click the File menu, and then click New.

2. Click the General tab.

3. Click Flash Form Application.

4. Click OK.

   This creates a default application with two nested form screens.

5. Add a backdrop to the application form by creating it directly in Flash, or by using a graphic image (optional).

6. Select form1.

7. Add the required UI components to form1.

   IMPORTANT *The application form is the parent of the other forms within the application. Anything you put on that form will also appear on any of its child forms.*

See Also

See Chapter 17 "Adding Display Components" on page 371 for more information on adding interactive components to a Flash document.

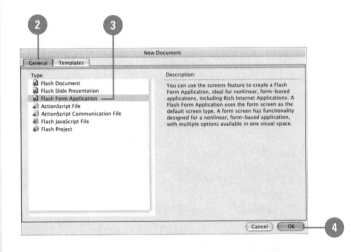

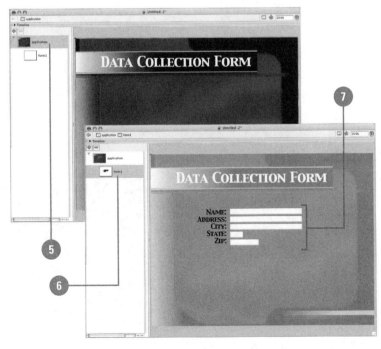

8. Click the Insert Screen button (+).

9. Add component buttons to the second screen, and then use the Component Inspector panel to link the buttons to the form.

10. Click the Control menu, and then click Test movie.

See Also

See Chapter 19 "Adding and Modifying Data Components" on page 413 for more information on binding components.

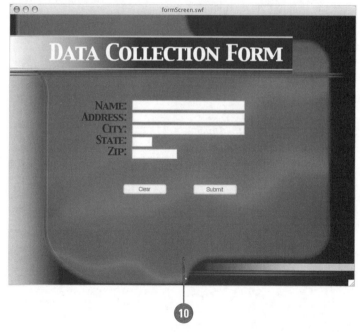

22

Creating and Managing a Project

In Flash MX Professional 2004, you can manage multiple document files within a Flash Project. A Flash Projects lets you group multiple and related files together to help you keep track of complex applications. In addition, Flash lets you apply version-control to ensure that the correct file versions are used during editing, and to prevent accidental overwriting. A Flash Project is essentially a collection of any Flash or other file types; including previous Flash .swf and .fla files. A Flash Project is an XML file with a file extension of .flp. The XML file contains references to the entire group of associated document files contained within the Flash Project. When you open an existing project, the Project panel gives you instant access to all the various parts of the project. The Flash Project panel is used to create and manage projects. The Project panel displays the contents of a Flash Project using a collapsible tree structure. Flash limits you to opening or creating one project at a time. In addition, any changes made to the project are automatically saved to the .flp file, it's not necessary to perform a Save operation.

Create and Manage a Project

1. Click the Window menu, and then click Projects.

2. Click the Create a New Project link.

3. Name the new project, and then choose a location to save the project .flp file.

4. Click Save.

IMPORTANT *Click the Open button in the Project panel, to open an existing project (you will be prompted to locate the project file name in the File Find dialog box).*

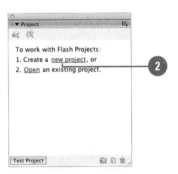

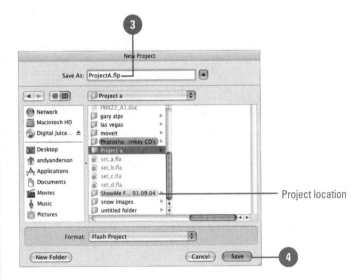

Project location

5. Select the New Project folder, located in the Project panel.

6. Click the Add Folder button to add a nested folder to the project.

7. Type the folder name, and then click OK.

8. Click the Add File button to add files to the project.

9. Click the Trashcan button to delete a selected project asset.

Did You Know?

You can manage projects using the Project panel. Managing projects from this panel does more than help you organize your Flash movies, HTML document, and objects into one definable place. It organizes you. Staying organized gives you more time to work, and be creative, and since most studies suggest that organizing a project can cut production time by 20 percent, you will save time.

Folder name

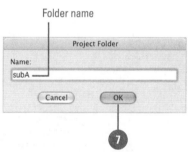

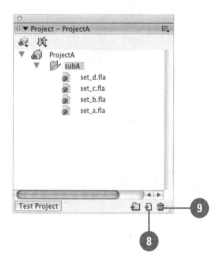

22

Testing a Project

A project is a collection of files that constitute a complex project. For example, you can create a Flash project that contains 5 Flash documents, with interactive buttons on the pages to call the other pages. If all of the .fla files are located within the same project, it's an easy matter to test the entire project. You must first select one of the files as the main file, and then simply click the Test button. Flash will automatically publish all of the Flash documents in the project, display the main file, and then allows you to test its operation. It's that simple.

Test a Project

1. Click the Window menu, and then click Projects.

2. If the project you want to test is not open, click the Open link in the Project panel, and then select the appropriate file.

3. Click Open.

   IMPORTANT *Since testing a project involves moving from Flash movie to Flash movie, your published documents will have to have interactive buttons linked to all the other pages within the project, or the test will not work.*

See Also

See Chapter 4, "Working with Groups, Symbols, and Instances" on page 123 for more information on adding button objects to a Flash movie.

Project file to open

4. Right-click your mouse on one of the .fla or .html files in the project.

5. Click Make Default Document from the available options.

6. Click the Test Project button.

See Also

See Chapter 16, "Debugging a Movie" on page 357 for more information on how to perform debugging operations on a running Flash movie.

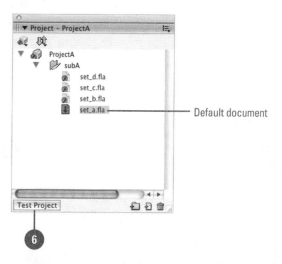

Default document

6

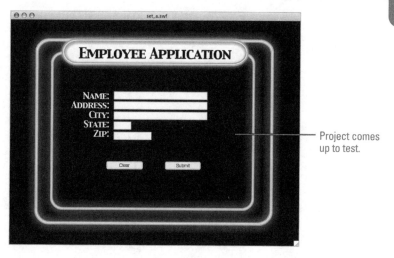

Project comes up to test.

22

Using Version Source Control

Flash lets you create complex documents using combinations of media and files to produce just about anything your imagination can dream. In many cases, a complex project is produced by more than one Flash author. When that happens, you might encounter problems when two authors check out, and edit the same file. Version control in Flash MX Professional 2004 lets you ensure that multiple authors working on the same project file are always using the latest version of a file, and that one author will never overwrite the work of another author. In order to use version-control, you must first define a site for the project.

Use Version Source Control

1 Create a Project, or open an existing Project.

2 Click the File menu, and then click Edit Sites.

3 Click New.

4 Enter the Site Name, the Local Root path, E-mail address, and the Check Out Name of the author.

5 Click the Connection popup, and then select whether the author will be using a Local/Network or FTP (File Transfer Protocol).

6 If an FTP connection will be used, enter the FTP Host, FTP Directory, Login Name, and Login Password for the FTP site.

7 Click OK.

8 Click Done.

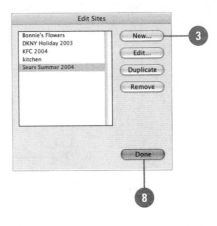

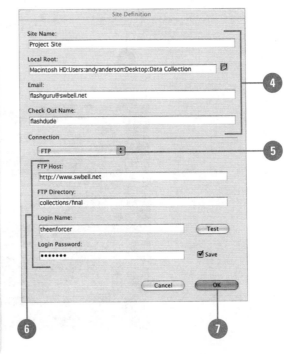

⑨ Right-click your mouse on the project, and then click Settings from the context-sensitive menu.

⑩ Click the Site popup, and then select the new Site Definition, created in steps 3 and 4.

⑪ Click OK.

⑫ Right-click your mouse on the project, and then click Check In.

⑬ Flash will check in all files within the current project into the site.

IMPORTANT *If the Flash designers working on the current project live in different areas, you will need to set up a sharing server using sharing technologies such as WebDav. It's important to set up the shared server using the proper protocols, to prevent the possibility of hackers entering the server through the shared connection. Contact your IP department or service provider for more information on setting up a shared server.*

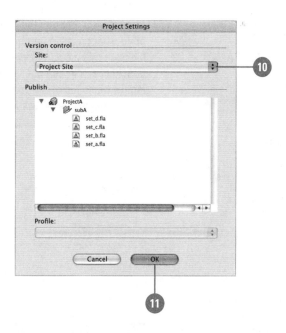

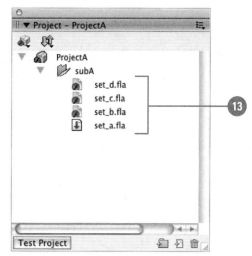

22

Checking Files In and Out

Once you've created and defined the site in the Project panel, the files become accessible for checking out or checking back in again. Once a file is checked out, it is no longer available to other authors until you check it back in again. This prevents the problems with two authors editing the same file at the same time. In this case, the last author to save the file would overwrite the other author's work.

Check Files In and Out

1. Click the Window menu, and then click Project.

2. Click the Open link.

3. Select the project that you want to work on.

4. Click Open.

5. Right-click your mouse on a file in the Project tree structure, and then click Check Out from the context-sensitive menu.

6. The icon next to the file name in the tree structure indicates the file is checked out.

7. Right-click on the checked out file, and then click Check In from the context-sensitive menu.

8. The icon is removed, giving other authors access to the file.

Project panel

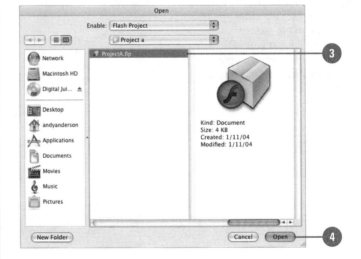

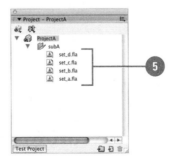

Exporting Directly to the FLV Format

The FLV or Flash Video file format allows you to import or export a static video stream including encoded audio. For example, you could use the FLV format to save video for use with communications applications, such as video conferencing. When an FLV clip is exported with streaming audio, the audio is compressed using the Streaming Audio settings in the Publish Settings dialog box, and the files are compressed using the built-in Sorensen codec. FVL files can be used with Flash's new media components to create streaming video files directly in a Flash movie.

Export Directly to the FLV Format

1. Select a video clip in the Library panel.

2. Click the Libraries Options button, and then click Properties.

3. Click Export.

4. Enter a name for the exported file.

5. Select a location where it will be saved.

6. Click Save.

7. Click OK.

   The Embedded Video Properties dialog box closes.

22

Mapping MIDI Device Sounds

Every day the world is getting smaller, and mobile devices are getting smaller, and smarter. Using Flash MX Professional 2004, you can include event sounds when creating documents for playback on mobile devices. Flash does not support sound file formats used for mobile devices (such as MIDI and others); when authoring for mobile devices, you must temporarily place a proxy sound in a supported format such as .mp3, .wav, or .aif in the Flash document. The proxy sound in the document is then mapped to an external mobile device sound, such as a MIDI file. During the document publishing process, the proxy sound is replaced with the linked external sound. The .swf file generated contains the external sound and uses it for playback on a mobile device.

Map MIDI Device Sounds

① Click the File menu, click Import, and then import one or more sounds into the Flash Library.

② Press Control+click (Mac) or right-click (Win) the sound you want to work with, and then select Properties.

③ Enter a path to the location where the mobile device sound is located.

④ Click OK.

⑤ Add a button instance to the Stage.

   IMPORTANT *You can use a pre-made Flash button. Click the Window menu, point to Other Panels, point to Common Libraries, and then click Buttons.*

⑥ Open the button in the Library, and then add the linked sound to the Hit frame of the button.

⑦ Click the File menu, and then click Publish Settings.

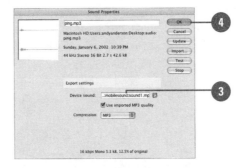

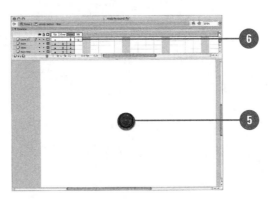

8. Click the Flash tab.

9. Click the Version popup, and then click Flash Lite 1.0. The Export device sounds option is automatically selected.

10. Click OK.

The .swf file now contains the linked mobile device sound.

11. Click the Control menu, and then click Test Movie.

12. Click the Control menu, and then click Disable Keyboard Shortcuts.

13. Press Tab to select the button, and then press Enter or Return to play the sound.

The mobile device sound has been modified to emulate the Flash .swf file sound.

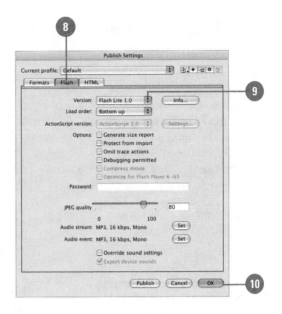

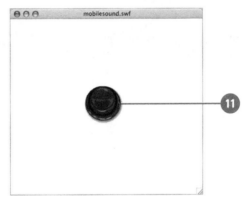

22

Using Advanced Component Enhancements

Components enable the separation of coding and design, and allow Flash authors to reuse and share code. Components allow coders to create functionality that designers can use in applications. Developers can encapsulate frequently used functionality into components, and designers can customize the look and behavior of components by changing parameters in the Property Inspector or the Component Inspector panel. The advanced components available only in Flash MX Professional 2004 are:

◆ **Accordion.** A set of vertical overlapping views with buttons along the top that allow users to switch views with the click of a button.

◆ **Alert.** A window that presents the user with a question, and buttons to capture their response.

◆ **DataGrid.** Allows users to display and manipulate multiple columns of data.

◆ **DateChooser.** Allows users to select a date or dates from a calendar.

◆ **DateField.** A view only text field with a calendar icon. A click anywhere inside the component displays a DateChooser component.

◆ **Menu.** Allows users to select one command from a list such as: a standard desktop application pull-down menu.

◆ **MenuBar.** A horizontal ruler bar containing clickable buttons that allows a user to navigate between pages.

◆ **Tree.** Create a tree-like structure to the defined data, and allows a user to manipulate through the hierarchical information with a click of the mouse.

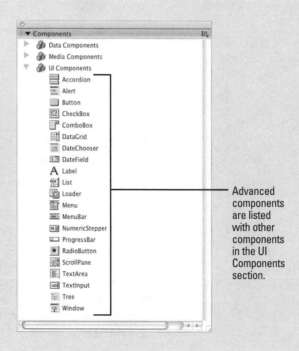

Advanced components are listed with other components in the UI Components section.

New! Features

Macromedia Flash MX 2004

Each new release of Flash brings with it new features, improvements, and added sophistication. To start, Macromedia have split the Flash development environment into two products: Flash MX 2004 and Flash MX Professional 2004. The standard edition is aimed at Web and multimedia designers and the Professional edition is for the application developer. They are essentially the same application with some added functionality in the Professional edition that can be enabled when purchased.

- **Start Page (p. 4)** When Flash MX 2004 is launched a Start page appears that allows you to access recently used files, create new files, retrieve up-to-date help information and access the Macromedia Web site.

- **Templates (p. 13, 468-471)** Flash now includes a set of templates for creating a variety of projects such as Web advertising banners and pop-ups, slide and video presentations, and projects destined for broadcast. These pre-built, pre-formatted files designed to conform to known standards are a great starting point.

- **Document Tab (p. 18)** Tabs for each open document appear at the top of the Document window so you can quickly switch between open documents (Windows only).

- **Help Panel (p. 24-25)** This context-sensitive panel includes the complete documentation for Flash as well as tutorials and an ActionScript language guide. You can also keep the Help up-to-date with the Macromedia site.

- **Customize Tool Panel (p. 48-49)** Customize the Tool Panel by rearranging or adding new tools. You can create your own tools using the JSFL language or install tools created by other users.

- **Polystar Tool (p. 80)** Flash now includes is a Polystar tool to create polygons and polystars with up to 32 sides.

- **Snap Align Objects (p. 94-95)** Snap Align objects with precision while dragging with a new dashed line that appears when drag is triggered.

- **Vertical and Horizontal Text (p. 158-159)** Vertical or horizontal orientation of text is now featured. You can now easily implement scrollable text with vertical or horizontal scroll bars. You can even embed a JPEG or SWF into a text field in an HTML fashion. Text will automatically wrap around the embedded object.

- **Small Text Display (p. 164)** In the case of small fonts or fonts used in cell phone or PDA displays, easily turn off the anti-aliasing for a specific font in the Property Inspector.

- **Globalization and Unicode (p. 168)** Flash now supports multi-language authoring using any character set.

- **Languages and the Strings Panel (p. 169)** The increasing need for localization of Flash content has created this new built-in method for tracking strings in a project. The Strings panel makes it possible to track all localized text string data, saving versions in multiple languages in an XML document. Each version can be selected and exported separately.

- **Cascading Style Sheets (CSS) (p. 171)** Flash now supports Cascading Style Sheets helping to bridge the visual gap between HTML and Flash content. Specify font style, size, and color and share these settings with Dreamweaver MX; easily add rollover effects to dynamic text fields.

- **Spell Checker (p. 172-173)** The spell checked searches the text a document for spelling errors. The spell checker includes a personal dictionary to recognize unique words in your documents.

- **Find and Replace (p. 174)** The Find and Replace command locates and replaces text, a font, a color, a symbol, a sound file, a video file, or an imported bitmap file.

- **File Import (p. 178-179)** Flash MX 2004 can now import Adobe Illustrator 10 and Adobe PDF files bridging the gap between these industry standard formats and Flash. MP3 ID3 tags are preserved and can now be read on import.

- **Video Import Wizard (p. 288-289)** The Video Import Wizard streamlines the importing of video files into the Flash environment. Store settings such as cropping, scaling, and color correction to be used again. You can now target a specific data rate and stream the native Flash video format (FLV) over http. Flash will maintain the level of quality you set. The new robust Flash 7 Player can handle higher frame sizes and frame rates.

- **Timeline Effects (p. 305-320)** You can now easily apply built-in transition and animation effects, such as Blur, Copy to Grid, Distribute Duplicate, Drop shadow, Expand, Explode, Transform, and Transition to objects on the Stage.

- **Built-in Behaviors (p. 321-332)** Simple interactivity and navigational controls can now be quickly implemented through the Behaviors panel without writing any scripting code. Included are event handlers, video and sound controls and many more that can be downloaded from the Macromedia Web site. Flash MX Professional 2004 includes enhanced behaviors.

- **ActionScript 2 (AS2) (p. 333)** This change to ActionScript was designed with the programmer in mind. It is fully compliant with the European Computer Manufacturers Association programming model and will appeal to the java programmer. This will be editable only in the Professional version but is supportable by both versions. For the standard edition, ActionScript 1 is still used with the addition of several new classes with some new methods and properties. Additionally, the "Normal" mode has been removed.

◆ **Accessible Authoring and Components (p. 372)** There is now a set of tools for creating accessible applications. Through the Accessibility panel, text headings can be substituted for buttons and other interactive elements, such as tab ordering and tab focus management, which can be read by screen readers and other assistive technologies, such as closed-caption programs. Accessibility support also provides keyboard shortcuts for navigating and for using interface controls without using a mouse.

◆ **Built-in Components (p. 374-375, 382-383, 386-389, 392-393, 396-405, 408-412)** Application interfaces can be built with a complete set of built-in UI components, such as buttons, menus, and scroll bars. Create your own components with the V2 Component Architecture. Flash MX Professional 2004 includes enhanced components.

◆ **History Panel and Commands (p. 435-444)** The History panel allows you to automate repetitive tasks. Record all of the steps taken to complete a task and save it as a Command macro that can be reused.

◆ **Publish Settings (p. 447-451)** Easily create, save and reuse Publish Settings, set Publish locations (including staging servers). There is an HTML template that enables Flash version detection and Size Reports now include ActionScript and compression ratios.

◆ **Flash Deployment Kit (p. 446)** The new Flash MX Deployment Kit removes the need to write additional JavaScript for HTML pages where Flash content is embedded. It also standardizes the method for plug-in detection.

◆ **Flash Player 7 (p. 449)** The Flash Player 7 boasts a 2-10x boost in runtime performance for many tasks. Other enhancements have been made to such areas as graphics display, video playback, XML parsing and backend server connectivity, as well as better memory usage. The player also includes built-in update notification so users can remain up-to-date with the latest version. The player also provides stricter security; SWF files with nonsecure protocols (HTTP) cannot access content loaded using secure protocols (HTTPS). The Flash Player 7 now supports Microsoft Active Accessibility (MSAA) which enhances the rich media experience for visually disabled people.

◆ **Flash Player Detection (p. 451)** Flash Player Detection allows you to publish SWF files with related files that detect if a viewer has a specified version of the Flash Player on their computer and to use alternate files if they don't have the specified version.

◆ **Publish Profiles (p. 458-462)** Easily create profiles to save your publish settings, which you can export and use with other Flash projects.

◆ **Extensibility Architecture and Third-Party Extensions** Take advantage of the extended functionality created by third party developers to extend the authoring environment. The Flash JavaScript application programming interface (JSAPI) allows anyone to create extensions or plug-ins for Flash to implement new behaviors, Timeline effects and animation.

Flash MX Professional 2004

Flash MX 2004 has been split into two products: Flash MX 2004 and Flash MX Professional 2004. The Professional version contains all of the features and functionality of the regular version with additional ones for creating more sophisticated data-driven Internet applications and improvements for more efficient delivery of video content over the Web. There is new support for streamlining the creation of content for other devices such as mobile phones and PDAs by providing a cross-platform development environment. In addition there have been several enhancements for implementing video into Flash with an improved encoder, enhanced playback, and new media components. With the addition of these new features Flash MX Professional 2004 is now a robust and comprehensive Web application development environment.

♦ **External ActionScript File Editing (p. 338)**   Implement external ActionScript files and utilize an external script editing environment in conjunction with Flash MX Professional.

♦ **Exporting and Importing Flash Video (p. 302-304, 479)**   With Flash MX Professional 2004 you can now export to the FLV (Flash Video Format) from a variety of professional video editing and compositing applications including Apple Final Cut Pro, Avid Media Composer, Xpress DV, Discreet Cleaner, and Anystream Agility with compression options not available in Flash such as variable bit rate. Import these files into Flash without any further compression. Add playback controls and interactivity, and create your own skins for a video playback interface. Media components for controllers, displays, and playback will connect to video on a Web server or stream from a Macromedia Flash Communications Server.

♦ **Data Connector Components (p. 414-419, 421-423)**   The heart of Flash MX Professional 2004 is in the Data Connectivity functionality included making it a so-called Rich Internet Application (RIA). You can develop data-driven applications with little scripting using pre-built components set up to connect to a variety of external data sources such as Web services or XML. These components can be integrated with an application server or ColdFusion using Macromedia Flash Remoting Integration. Component functionality can be implemented by drag and drop or controlled solely through ActionScript. Component properties can be connected to the data received in an XML file, Web service call, or record set by using binding tabs keeping them in sync.

Utilizing the Connector and Resolver components will ensure that data updates and transfers are as efficient as possible. Data Source Shadowing monitors any changes made to a dataset. When a database is updated the best performance is achieved through Delta Packets, which will update only the records or fields that have been changed. Because the data components only read data and are independent of the visual layer the user sees, they can adapt to changes in the data without having to be re-coded to accommodate.

◆ **Create Slides (p. 468-469)**   Using the new Slide properties and Transition behavior functionality to easily create sophisticated presentations and mock-ups for user interfaces. These new templates help organize content and create transitions, sequencing them with interactive elements without having to code.

◆ **Forms and Advanced Components (p. 470-471)**   The key features for application development in the Professional version include a forms-based development environment. This environment is familiar to developers who are accustomed to using Microsoft Visual Basic and other similar tools. It is now integrated with the Flash Timeline and can be used in conjunction with or in place of it making it ideal for the developer interested in implementing Flash content without having to acquire new skills or face the learning curve required to create in the traditional Flash environment. Sophisticated applications are quickly assembled with the new ECMA-compliant ActionScript 2.0. Components that were introduced in Flash MX have been expanded and made more sophisticated. Inclusion in Flash MX Professional are new components including an improved list box, data grid, calendar, menu, and accordion tabbed panes. Each Flash user interface component contains parameters that specify the appearance and behavior of each Component instance. This allows for much more versatility and ease in creating sophisticated visual interfaces.

◆ **Project Panel (p. 472-475)**   The Project panel allows you to mange files, assets, code and components in one convenient place. Files are managed in a collapsible tree control and nested folders. Additionally, project files can be split into several files that share libraries so that a team of people can work simultaneously on various files contained in the project. A file check in/ check out system (similar to that employed in Dreamweaver MX) prevents files from being overwritten.

◆ **Source Code Control (p. 476-477)**   Project files can now be synchronized with the source control system API of your choice, including Microsoft Visual SourceSafe, or file-level locking that can be used locally, networked or via ftp.

◆ **Device Deployment (p. 481)**   Flash content deployment is expanding from the Web to other mediums. The last couple of years have seen an explosion in the manufacturing and use of cell phones, PDAs, and consumer electronic devices. Because of the versatility of Flash MX and the relatively small file sizes it is the perfect environment for creating content destined for these devices. Flash MX Professional 2004 comes equipped with a template library of cell phone and PDA interfaces which can be developed for and then previewed in Flash Player emulators. Troubleshoot compatibility issues and performance conflicts before deploying to the target device. New profiles for licensees of the Macromedia Flash Player can be added as they become available. Additionally MIDI ring tones and sounds can be implemented while authoring.

Keyboard Shortcuts

If a command on a menu includes a keyboard reference, known as a keyboard shortcut, to the right of the command name, you can perform the action by pressing and holding the first key, and then pressing the second key to perform the command quickly. In some cases, a keyboard shortcut uses three keys. Simply press and hold the first two keys, and then press the third key. Keyboard shortcuts provide an alternative to using the mouse and make it easy to perform repetitive commands.

Keyboard Shortcuts		
Operation/Tool	**Windows**	**Macintosh**
Arrow tool (select in Toolbox)	V	V
Arrow tool (temporary access)	Ctrl	⌘
Brush tool (select in Toolbox)	B	B
Constrain (ovals to circles, rectangles to squares, lines and rotation to 45-degree angles)	Shift+drag	Shift+drag
Convert corner point to curve point (Subselection tool)	Alt+drag	Option+drag
Create new corner point (Arrow tool)	Alt+drag a line	Option+drag a line
Drag a copy of selected element	Alt+drag	Option+drag
Drag a copy of selected keyframe unit in Timeline	Alt+drag	Option+drag
Dropper tool (select in Toolbox)	I	I
End open path (Pen tool)	Ctrl+click	⌘+click
Eraser tool (select in Toolbox)	E	E
Fill Transform tool (select in Toolbox)	F	F
Free Transform tool (select in Toolbox)	Q	Q
Hand tool (select in Toolbox)	H	H
Hand tool (temporary access)	Spacebar	Spacebar
Select the Stage	Ctrl+Alt+Home	⌘+Option+Home
Select object on the Stage (with Stage selected)	Tab	Tab

Keyboard Shortcuts *(continued)*

Operation/Tool	Windows	Macintosh
Show/Hide all but one layer	Alt+click active layer's eye column	Option+click active layer's eye column
Ink bottle tool (select in Toolbox)	S	S
Lasso tool (select in Toolbox)	L	L
Line tool (select in Toolbox)	N	N
Lock/unlock all but one layer	Alt+click active layer's lock column	Option+click active layer's lock column
Magnifier tool (select in Toolbox)	M,Z	M,Z
Magnifier zoom-in tool (temporary access)	Ctrl+Spacebar	⌘+Spacebar
Magnifier zoom-out tool (temporary access)	Ctrl+Shift+Spacebar	⌘+Shift+Spacebar
Move keyframe unit in Timeline	Click+and+drag	Click+and+drag
Nudge selected element down 10 pixels	Shift+Down arrow	Shift+Down arrow

Command	Menu	Windows	Macintosh
100% (View)	View > Magnification	Ctrl+1	⌘+1
400% (View)	View > Magnification	Ctrl+4	⌘+4
800% (View)	View > Magnification	Ctrl+8	⌘+8
Accessibility Panel (Show/Hide)	Window > Other Panels	Alt+F2	Option+F2
Actions Panel (Show/Hide)	Window > Dev. Panels	F9	F9
Add Shape Hint	Modify > Shape	Ctrl+Shift+H	⌘+Shift+H
Align (Objects) Bottom	Modify > Align	Ctrl+Alt+6	⌘+Option+6
Align (Objects) Left	Modify > Align	Ctrl+Alt+1	⌘+Option+1
Align (Objects) Right	Modify > Align	Ctrl+Alt+3	⌘+Option+3
Align (Objects) to Stage (toggle)	Modify > Align	Ctrl+Alt+8	⌘+Option+8
Align (Objects) Top	Modify > Align	Ctrl+Alt+4	⌘+Option+4
Align (Text) Center	Text > Align	Ctrl+Shift+C	⌘+Shift+C
Align (Text) Left	Text > Align	Ctrl+Shift+L	⌘+Shift+L
Align (Text) Right	Text > Align	Ctrl+Shift+R	⌘+Shift+R
Align Panel (Show/Hide)	Window > Design Panels	Ctrl+K	⌘+K
Anti-alias Text	View > Preview Mode	Ctrl+Alt+Shift+T	⌘+Shift+Option+T
Anti-alias	View > Preview Mode	Ctrl+Alt+Shift+A	⌘+Shift+Option+A
Auto Format	Actions Panel Options	Ctrl+Shift+F	⌘+Shift+F
Bandwidth Profiler (Show/Hide)	View (Test Movie mode)	Ctrl+B	⌘+B

Keyboard Shortcuts (continued)

Command	Menu	Windows	Macintosh
Behavior Panel (Show/Hide)	Window > Dev. Panels	Shift+F3	Shift+F3
Bold (Text)	Text > Style	Ctrl+Shift+B	⌘+Shift+B
Break Apart	Modify	Ctrl+B	⌘+B
Bring (Selected Item) to Front	Modify > Arrange	Ctrl+Shift+Up	⌘+Shift+Up
Bring (Selected Item) Forward	Modify > Arrange	Ctrl+Up	⌘+Up
Center Horizontal (Objects)	Modify > Align	Ctrl+Alt+5	⌘+Option+5
Center Vertical (Objects)	Modify > Align	Ctrl+Alt+2	⌘+Option+2
Check Syntax	Actions Panel Options	Ctrl+T	⌘+T
Clear Frames	Edit > Timeline	Alt+Backspace	Option+Delete
Clear (Stage)	Edit	Backspace or Delete	Delete or Clear
Clear Keyframe	Modify > Timeline	Shift+F6	Shift+F6
Close (File)	File	Ctrl+W	⌘+W
Color Mixer Panel (Show/Hide)	Window > Design Panels	Shift+F9	Shift+F9
Color Swatches Panel (Show/Hide)	Window > Design Panels	Ctrl+F9	⌘+F9
Component Inspector Panel (Show/Hide)	Window > Dev. Panels	Alt+F7	Option+F7
Components Panel (Show/Hide)	Window > Dev. Panels	Ctrl+F7	⌘+F7
Continue	Control (Test Movie mode)	F10	F10
Convert to Blank Keyframes	Modify > Timeline	F7	F7
Convert to Keyframes	Modify > Timeline	F6	F6
Convert to Symbol	Modify	F8	F8
Copy (Selection)	Edit	Ctrl+C	⌘+C
Copy Frames	Edit > Timeline	Ctrl+Alt+C	⌘+Option+C
Cut (Selection)	Edit	Ctrl+X	⌘+X
Cut Frames	Edit > Timeline	Ctrl+Alt+X	⌘+Option+X
Debug Movie	Control	Ctrl+Shift+Enter	⌘+Shift+Return
Debugger Panel (Show/Hide)	Window > Dev. Panels	Shift+F4	Shift+F4
Decrease (Tracking)	Text > Tracking	Ctrl+Alt+Left	⌘+Option+Left
Default (Publishing)	File > Publish Preview	F12	F12
Deselect All	Edit	Ctrl+Shift+A	⌘+Shift+A
Distribute Heights	Modify > Align	Ctrl+Alt+9	⌘+Option+9
Distribute to Layers	Modify > Timeline	Ctrl+Shift+D	⌘+Shift+D

Command	Menu	Windows	Macintosh
Distribute Widths	Modify > Align	Ctrl+Alt+7	⌘+Option+7
Document Properties	Modify	Ctrl+J	⌘+J
Duplicate (Selection)	Edit	Ctrl+D	⌘+D
Edit Grid	View > Grid	Ctrl+Alt+G	⌘+Option+G
Edit Guides	View > Guides	Ctrl+Alt+Shift+G	⌘+Shift+Option+G
Edit Symbols	Edit	Ctrl+E	⌘+E
Enable Simple Buttons	Control	Ctrl+Alt+B	⌘+Option+B
Export Script	Actions Panel Options	Ctrl+Shift+X	⌘+Shift+X
Export Movie	File > Export	Ctrl+Alt+Shift+S	⌘+Shift+Option+S
Fast (View)	View > Preview Mode	Ctrl+Alt+Shift+F	⌘+Shift+Option+F
Find and Replace	Edit	Ctrl+F	⌘+F
Find Next	Edit	F3	F3
First (Scene)	View > Go to	Home	Home
Frame (Add)	Insert > Timeline	F5	F5
Frame-by-Frame Graph (Show)	View (Test Movie mode)	Ctrl+F	⌘+F
Go to Line	Actions Panel Options	Ctrl+G	⌘+, [comma]
Grid (Show/Hide)	View > Grid	Ctrl+'	⌘+'
Group (Selected Items)	Modify	Ctrl+G	⌘+G
Guides (Show/Hide)	View > Guides	Ctrl+;	⌘+;
Help	Help	F1	F1
Hide Edges (Show/Hide Selection Highlight)	View	Ctrl+H	⌘+Shift+E
Hide Panels	Window	F4	F4
History Panel (Show/Hide)	Window > Other Panels	Ctrl+F10	⌘+F10
Import to Stage	File > Import	Ctrl+R	⌘+R
Import Script	Actions Panel Options	Ctrl+Shift+I	⌘+Shift+I
Increase (Tracking)	Text > Tracking	Ctrl+Alt+Right	⌘+Option+Right
Info Panel (Show/Hide)	Window > Design Panels	Ctrl+I	⌘+I
Italic (Text)	Text > Style	Ctrl+Shift+I	⌘+Shift+I
Justify (Text)	Text > Align	Ctrl+Shift+J	⌘+Shift+J
Last (Scene)	View > Go to	End	End
Library Panel (Show/Hide)	Window	Ctrl+L, F11	⌘+L, F11

Command	Menu	Windows	Macintosh
List Objects	Debug (Test Movie mode)	Ctrl+L	⌘+L
List Variables	Debug (Test Movie mode)	Ctrl+Alt+V	⌘+Option+V
Lock (Group)	Modify > Arrange	Ctrl+Alt+L	⌘+Option+L
Lock Guides	View > Guide	Ctrl+Shift+;	Shift+Option+;
Make Same Height	Modify > Align	Ctrl+Shift+Alt+9	⌘+Option+Shift+9
Make Same Width	Modify > Align	Ctrl+Shift+Alt+7	⌘+Option+Shift+7
Movie Explorer Panel (Show/Hide)	Window > Other Panels	Alt+F3	Option+F3
New (File)	File	Ctrl+N	⌘+N
New Symbol	Insert	Ctrl+F8	⌘+F8
New Window	Window	Ctrl+Alt+K	⌘+Option+K
Next (Scene)	View > Go to	Page Down	Page Down
Open (File)	File	Ctrl+O	⌘+O
Open External Library	File	Ctrl+Shift+O	⌘+Shift+O
Optimize (Curves)	Modify > Shape	Ctrl+Alt+Shift+C	⌘+Shift+Option+C
Outlines (View As)	View > Preview Mode	Ctrl+Alt+Shift+O	⌘+Shift+Option+O
Output Panel (Show/Hide)	Window > Dev. Panels	F2	F2
Panels (Show/Hide, plus Toolbar)	Window	F4	F4
Paste (Clipboard Contents)	Edit	Ctrl+V	⌘+V
Paste Frames	Edit > Timeline	Ctrl+Alt+V	⌘+Option+V
Paste In Place	Edit	Ctrl+Shift+V	⌘+Shift+V
Plain (Text)	Text > Style	Ctrl+Shift+P	⌘+Shift+P
Play (Movie)	Control	Enter	Return
Previous (Scene)	View > Go to	Page Up	Page Up
Print	File	Ctrl+P	⌘+P
Project Panel (Show/Hide)	Window	Shift+F8	Shift+F8
Properties Panel (Show/Hide)	Window	Ctrl+F3	⌘+F3
Publish	File	Shift+F12	Shift+F12
Publish Preview	File > Publish Preview	F12	F12
Publish Settings	File	Ctrl+Shift+F12	Option+Shift+F12
Quit (Exit)	File	Ctrl+Q	⌘+Q
Redo	Edit	Ctrl+Y	⌘+Y
Remove All Breakpoints	Control (Test Movie mode)	Ctrl+Shift+A	⌘+Shift+A

Command	Menu	Windows	Macintosh
Remove Breakpoint	Control (Test Movie mode)	Ctrl+Shift+B	⌘+Shift+B
Remove Frames	Edit > Timeline	Shift+F5	Shift+F5
Remove Transform	Modify > Transform	Ctrl+Shift+Z	⌘+Shift+Z
Replace	Actions Panel Options	Ctrl+H	⌘+Shift+H
Reset (Tracking)	Text > Tracking	Ctrl+Alt+Up	⌘+Option+Up
Rewind	Control	Ctrl+Alt+R	⌘+Option+R
Rotate 90 CCW	Modify > Transform	Ctrl+Shift+7	⌘+Shift+7
Rotate 90 CW	Modify > Transform	Ctrl+Shift+9	⌘+Shift+9
Rulers (Show/Hide)	View	Ctrl+Alt+Shift+R	⌘+Shift+Option+R
Save As	File	Ctrl+Shift+S	⌘+Shift+S
Save	File	Ctrl+S	⌘+S
Scene Panel (Show/Hide)	Window > Design Panel	Shift+F12	Shift+F12
Select All	Edit	Ctrl+A	⌘+A
Select All Frames	Edit > Timeline	Ctrl+Alt+A	⌘+Option+A
Send (selected item) to back	Modify > Arrange	Ctrl+Shift+Down	⌘+Shift+Down
Send (selected item) backward	Modify > Arrange	Ctrl+Down	⌘+Down
Shape Hints (Show/Hide)	View	Ctrl+Alt+H	⌘+Option+H
Show All	View > Magnification	Ctrl+3	⌘+3
Show Code Hint	Actions Panel Options	Ctrl+Spacebar	Control+Spacebar
Show Frame	View > Magnification	Ctrl+2	⌘+2
Show Grid	View > Grid	Ctrl+' (apostrophe)	⌘+Shift+' (apostrophe)
Show Guides	View > Guides	Ctrl+;	⌘+;
Simulate Download	View (Test Movie mode)	Ctrl+Enter	⌘+Return
Snap to Grid	View > Snapping	Ctrl+Shift+' (apostrophe)	⌘+Shift+' (apostrophe)
Snap to Guides	View > Snapping	Ctrl+Shift+;	⌘+Shift+;
Snap to Objects	View > Snapping	Ctrl+Shift+/ (slash)	⌘+Shift+/ (slash)
Step Backward	Control	, (comma)	, (comma)
Step Forward	Control	. (period)	. (period)
Step In	Control (Test Movie mode)	F6	F6
Step Out	Control (Test Movie mode)	F8	F8
Step Over	Control (Test Movie mode)	F7	F7

Keyboard Shortcuts *(continued)*

Command	Menu	Windows	Macintosh
Stop Debugging	Control (Test Movie mode)	F11	F11
Streaming Graph (Show/Hide)	View (Test Movie mode)	Ctrl+G	⌘+G
Strings Panel (Show/Hide)	Window > Other Panels	Ctrl+F11	⌘+F11
Test Movie	Control	Ctrl+Enter	⌘+Return
Test Scene	Control	Ctrl+Alt+Enter	⌘+Option+Return
Test Project	Control	Ctrl+Alt+P	⌘+Option+P
Timeline (Show/Hide)	Window	Ctrl+Alt+T	⌘+Option+T
Tools Panel (Show/Hide)	Window	Ctrl+F2	⌘+F2
Transform Panel (Show/Hide)	Window > Design Panels	Ctrl+T	⌘+T
Undo	Edit	Ctrl+Z	⌘+Z
Ungroup	Modify	Ctrl+Shift+G	⌘+Shift+G
Unlock All	Modify > Arrange	Ctrl+Alt+Shift+L	⌘+Shift+Option+L
View Line Numbers	Actions Panel Options	Ctrl+Shift+L	⌘+Shift+L
Web Services Panel (Show/Hide)	Window > Design Panel	Ctrl+Shift+F10	⌘+Shift+F10
Work Area (View)	View	Ctrl+Shift+W	⌘+Shift+W
Zoom In	View	Ctrl+= (equals sign)	⌘+= (equals sign)
Zoom Out	View	Ctrl+- (minus sign)	⌘+- (minus)

Troubleshooting

Index